Praise for *More Agile Te*

"I love this book. It will help to ~~...~~ .... ~~. .. ...~~ .. ..~~ ~~ gooa tning, since anyone who reads this will want to have one on their team."

—*Liz Keogh, agile coach, Lunivore Limited*

"This book will change your thinking and move your focus from *tests* to *testing*. Yes, it is not about the result, but about the activity!"

—*Kenji Hiranabe, cofounder of Astah and CEO, Change Vision, Inc.*

"To my mind, agile development is about learning—that one word captures the true spirit of what agile is all about. When I had the chance to read through their new book, I could only say, 'Wow! Janet and Lisa have done themselves proud.' This is not a book about testing; this is a book about learning. Their clear explanations are accompanied by great true stories and an impressive list of books, articles, and other resources. Those of us who like learning, who love to dig for more information, can rejoice! I know you're always looking for something interesting and useful; I can guarantee that you will find it here!"

—*Linda Rising, coauthor of* Fearless Change: Patterns for Introducing New Ideas

"Janet and Lisa's first book, *Agile Testing*, drew some general principles that are still important today but left me wondering, 'how?' In this second book, they adapt those principles to today's development landscape—with mobile, DevOps, and cloud-based applications delivered in increasingly compressed release cycles. Readers get specific testing tools for the mind along with new practices and commentary to accelerate learning. Read it today."

—*Matt Heusser, Managing Principal, Excelon Development*

"An excellent guide for your team's agile journey, full of resources to help you with every kind of testing challenge you might meet along the way. Janet and Lisa share a wealth of experience with personal stories about how they helped agile teams figure out how to get value from testing. I really like how the book is filled with techniques explained by leading industry practitioners who've pioneered them in their own organizations."

—*Rachel Davies, agile coach, unruly and coauthor of* Agile Coaching

"Let me net this out for you: agile quality and testing is hard to get right. It's nuanced, context-based, and not for the faint of heart. In order to effectively balance it, you need hard-earned, pragmatic, real-world advice. This book has it—not only from Janet and Lisa, but also from forty additional expert agile practitioners. Get it and learn how to effectively drive quality into your agile products and across your entire organization."

—*Bob Galen, Principal Consultant, R Galen Consulting Group, and Author of* Agile Reflections *and* Scrum Product Ownership

MORE AGILE TESTING

Selenium Web Driver

Java

J Meter

JIRA

SQL

Continuous delivery

Cloud test services

Rest / Soap web services

MORE AGILE TESTING

LEARNING JOURNEYS FOR THE WHOLE TEAM

Janet Gregory
Lisa Crispin

Addison-Wesley

Upper Saddle River, NJ • Boston • Indianapolis • San Francisco
New York • Toronto • Montreal • London • Munich • Paris • Madrid
Capetown • Sydney • Tokyo • Singapore • Mexico City

For information about buying this title in bulk quantities, or for special sales opportunities (which may include electronic versions; custom cover designs; and content particular to your business, training goals, marketing focus, or branding interests), please contact our corporate sales department at corpsales@pearsoned.com or (800) 382-3419.

For government sales inquiries, please contact governmentsales@pearsoned.com.

For questions about sales outside the United States, please contact international@pearsoned.com.

Visit us on the Web: informit.com/aw

Library of Congress Cataloging-in-Publication Data
Gregory, Janet, 1953–
  More agile testing : learning journeys for the whole team / Janet Gregory, Lisa Crispin.
     pages   cm
  Includes bibliographical references and index.
  ISBN 978-0-321-96705-3 (pbk. : alk. paper)
  1. Computer software—Testing. 2. Agile software development. I. Crispin, Lisa. II. Title.
  QA76.76.T48G74 2015
  005.1—dc23

                                                     2014027150

ISBN-13: 978-0-321-96705-3
ISBN-10: 0-321-96705-4
Text printed in the United States on recycled paper at RR Donnelley in Crawfordsville, Indiana.
First printing, October 2014

To my grandchildren, Lauren, Brayden, and Joe, who kept
me laughing and playing throughout this past year.

—Janet

To my family, those still here and those sadly gone, and my dear friends
who are part of my chosen family.

—Lisa

CONTENTS

Foreword

By Elisabeth Hendrickson

Just ten years ago, agile was still considered radical. Fringe. Weird. The standard approach to delivering software involved phases: analyze, then design, then code, then test. Integration and testing happened only at the end of the cycle. The full development cycle took months or years.

If you have never worked in an organization with long cycles and discrete phases, the idea may seem a little weird now, but it was the standard a decade ago.

Back when phases were the norm and agile was still new, the agile community was mostly programmer-centric. Janet and Lisa and a few others from quality and testing were there. However, many in the agile community felt that QA had become irrelevant. They were wrong, of course. QA changed, reshaped to fit the new context, but it did not go away.

It took people like Janet and Lisa to show how QA could be integrated into agile teams instead of bypassed. Their first book together, *Agile Testing*, carefully explained the whole-team approach to quality. They covered the cultural changes needed to fully integrate testing with development. They explained how to overcome barriers. It's a fantastic book, and I highly recommend it.

However, questions remained. How could the practices be adapted to various contexts? How do you start? What should testers learn in order to be more effective?

This book picks up where *Agile Testing* left off and answers those questions and more.

Even if that were all this book did, it would be an excellent sequel.

It's more than that, though. Within these pages you will find a theme—one that Janet and Lisa have woven so deftly throughout the text you might not even realize it as you are reading. So I am going to call your attention to it: this is a book about adapting.

Reflect-and-adapt is the one simple trick that can enable your organization to find its way to agile. Experiment, try something different, distill lessons learned, repeat. The next thing you know, your organization will be nimble and flexible, able to shift with market demands and deliver incrementally.

This book teaches you about adapting even as it is teaching you about agile testing.

Part II, "Learning for Better Testing," isn't just about how you learn as an individual but also about building a learning culture. Part VII, "What Is Your Context?," isn't just about variations in agile tailored to different situations; it's also a field guide to various types of adaptations.

The world is changing so very quickly. Just a decade ago agile was weird; now it is mainstream. Just five years ago, tablets like iPads weren't even on the market; now they're everywhere. Practices, tools, technology, and markets are all changing so fast it's hard to keep up. It's not enough to learn one way of doing things; you need to know how to discover new ways. You need to adapt.

This book is a fantastic resource for agile testing. It will also help you learn to adapt and be comfortable with change.

I hope you enjoy it as much as I did.

FOREWORD

By Johanna Rothman

What do testers do? They provide information about the product under test, to expose risks for the team.

That's exactly what Janet Gregory and Lisa Crispin have done in their new book, *More Agile Testing: Learning Journeys for the Whole Team*. Do you have risks in your agility? There are plenty of ideas to help you understand the value of sustainable pace, creating a learning organization, and your role in testing.

Not sure how to test for a given product, on a single team, or in a program? There's an answer for that, too.

How do you work with people in the next cube, down the hall, and across the world? Janet and Lisa have been there and done that. Their focus on roles and not titles is particularly helpful.

There are plenty of images in this book, so you won't have to wonder, "What do they mean?" They show you, not just tell you.

More Agile Testing: Learning Journeys for the Whole Team is much more than a book about testing. It's a book about how to use testing to help your entire team, and by extension, your organization, and transition to agile in a healthy way.

Isn't that what providing information about the organization under test, exposing risks in the organization, is all about?

If you are a tester or a test manager, you need to read this book. If you integrate testing into your organization, you need to read this book. How else will you know what the testers could be doing?

PREFACE

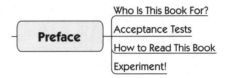

This book carries on where our first book, *Agile Testing: A Practical Guide for Testers and Agile Teams*, left off. We avoid repeating what we covered in our first book but give enough context so it stands alone if you have not read *Agile Testing*. We refer to the first book as *Agile Testing* when we think it might be helpful for the reader to explore basic concepts in more detail.

WHO IS THIS BOOK FOR?

We assume that you, the reader, are not a beginner in the world of agile testing, that you have some agile and testing experience and now you're looking for help in the areas beyond where *Agile Testing* goes. If you feel that you would like an introduction to agile development that includes some basics of testing in agile before you read this book, *The Agile Samurai* (Rasmussen, 2010) is an excellent place to start.

This book is aimed at anyone who is interested in testing activities on an agile team. In our experience, this includes not only testers and test managers, but programmers, product owners, business analysts, DevOps practitioners, line managers—pretty much everyone.

ACCEPTANCE TESTS

In addition to sharing what we've learned over the past several years, we wanted to make this book as useful to our readers as the first one. We wanted to know what readers of the first book still needed to know after reading it, so we asked practitioners from the *Agile Testing* mailing list to send us their "acceptance tests" for this second book. We distilled those responses to this list of acceptance tests for *More Agile Testing* and did our best to satisfy these as we wrote the book.

You'll note that we've used a style used in behavior-driven development (BDD), which we'll talk more about in Chapter 11, "Getting Examples":

Given <precondition>,

When <trigger, action>,

Then <the expected result>.

- Given that I am an agile tester or manager, when I hire new testers with no agile experience, then I'll learn how to bring them up to speed and avoid throwing them into the deep end without a life jacket.
- Given that I am a team member on an agile team, when I finish this book, then I expect to know how to fit exploratory testing in with automated tests and to get a picture of the overall test coverage, without resorting to heavyweight tools.
- Given that I am an experienced agile test manager, when I finish this book, then I will understand how to approach agile testing techniques with multiple teams to allow my successful agile organization to grow.
- Given that I am an experienced agile test manager, when I finish reading this book, then I should have ideas about how to coordinate test automation activities across iterations and teams, with ideas on how to improve.
- Given that I am an experienced agile manager, when I've read this book, then I will understand how other teams have adapted agile testing practices to suit their own context and will have ideas about how to apply them to mine.
- Given that I am an agile team member who is interested in testing, when I finish this book, then I expect to have examples of what tests should and should not look like and how I can design tests effectively.

- Given that I am an experienced agile tester, when I find an interesting topic in this book about which I'd like to learn more, then I can easily find references to web resources or other books.
- Given that I am an experienced agile coach or manager who is reading the book, when I see a concept that would help my team, then I have enough information to be able to devise a strategy to get the team to try an experiment.
- Given that I am an agile team member who is concerned about testing and keeping the customers informed, when I have read this book, then I'll understand good ways to communicate with customer team members about testing activities.
- Given that I am an experienced agile test manager, when I have read this book, then I will know how mainstream adoption of agile is being done, and I will understand the working context of testers from other organizations when they apply for jobs on my team. (*Note:* This acceptance test is not part of this release, but we think some of the examples and stories in the book will help to achieve it.)

HOW TO READ THIS BOOK

Though we've organized this book in a way that we feel flows best, you don't have to start with Chapter 1 and keep going. As with *Agile Testing*, you can begin with whatever topics are most useful to you. We try to cover each topic in detail only once, but because so many of these concepts, practices, and principles are interrelated, you'll find that we refer to some ideas in more than one chapter.

Part I: Introduction

Read this part to understand where testing started in agile teams and how it has evolved to become the cornerstone of agile development and continuous delivery of products. Part of successful agile development is an organization's ability to learn what's most critical for long-range success with agile testing.

- Chapter 1, "How Agile Testing Has Evolved"
- Chapter 2, "The Importance of Organizational Culture"

Part II: Learning for Better Testing

Both technology and the craft of testing are continually evolving, and lines between different disciplines are becoming more blurred. Even experienced practitioners have to keep growing their skills. This part includes examples of what testers and other disciplines such as business analysis and coding need to know to meet more difficult testing challenges. We explain the benefits of generalizing specialists and list some of the intangible thinking skills and specific technical testing skills that help testers and teams improve. Different aspects of what and how to learn are covered in the following chapters:

- Chapter 3, "Roles and Competencies"
- Chapter 4, "Thinking Skills for Testing"
- Chapter 5, "Technical Awareness"
- Chapter 6, "How to Learn"

Part III: Planning—So You Don't Forget the Big Picture

Planning "just enough" is a balancing act. While we need to work in small increments, we have to keep an eye on the larger feature set and the entire system. This part covers different aspects of test planning, from the release level down to the task level. It also explores different models such as the agile testing quadrants and some of the adaptations people have suggested.

- Chapter 7, "Levels of Precision for Planning"
- Chapter 8, "Using Models to Help Plan"

Part IV: Testing Business Value

If, like so many agile teams, you deliver robust code in a timely manner, only to find it isn't what the customers wanted after all, the information in this part will help. We cover tools and practices, particularly those from the agile business analysis profession, to help you test ideas and assumptions early and ensure that everyone knows what to deliver. We address other overlapping disciplines and expanding mindsets. This is a big area, so there are several chapters:

- Chapter 9, "Are We Building the Right Thing?"
- Chapter 10, "The Expanding Tester's Mindset: Is This *My* Job?"
- Chapter 11, "Getting Examples"

Part V: Investigative Testing

The programmers have delivered some code to test. Where do you start? If you or your team lacks experience with exploratory testing, you'll find some help here. We outline several exploratory testing techniques such as using personas and tours to help generate test charter ideas, as well as managing charters with session-based test management and thread-based test management.

Along with all those different ways to do exploratory testing, we look at other ways to verify that delivered code meets a wide range of business and user needs. This part covers ways to mitigate risks and generate useful information in several different types of testing that present challenges to agile teams. The investigative testing chapters are

- Chapter 12, "Exploratory Testing"
- Chapter 13, "Other Types of Testing"

Part VI: Test Automation

We see more and more teams finding ways to succeed with test automation. However, for many teams, automated tests produce sporadic failures that are expensive to investigate. The time (cost) spent on each failure may be more than the test is worth. There are plenty of pitfalls in automating tests. In this part we give examples of ways to make technical debt in testing visible. We look at different ways to use the agile testing pyramid effectively to help you think about how to plan your automation. We've introduced a few alternative pyramid models to approach automation from different perspectives. You'll learn ways to design automated tests for optimum reliability and ease of maintenance. This part also includes examples of scaling test automation in a large enterprise company.

The chapters in Part VI are

- Chapter 14, "Technical Debt in Testing"
- Chapter 15, "Pyramids of Automation"
- Chapter 16, "Test Automation Design Patterns and Approaches"
- Chapter 17, "Selecting Test Automation Solutions"

Part VII: What Is Your Context?

Your approach to agile testing will naturally depend on your context. Do you work with large enterprise systems? Maybe you're newly tasked with testing mobile apps or embedded software. Perhaps your team is challenged with finding good ways to test data that helps businesses make decisions. Have you wondered how agile can work in testing regulated software? Finally, we look at the synergies between testing and the DevOps movement. The chapters in this part cover a variety of areas, so we have included a number of stories from people who are currently working in those situations. Some of these chapters may not apply to your working environment today, but tomorrow—who knows?

- Chapter 18, "Agile Testing in the Enterprise"
- Chapter 19, "Agile Testing on Distributed Teams"
- Chapter 20, "Agile Testing for Mobile and Embedded Systems"
- Chapter 21, "Agile Testing in Regulated Environments"
- Chapter 22, "Agile Testing for Data Warehouses and Business Intelligence Systems"
- Chapter 23, "Testing and DevOps"

Part VIII: Agile Testing in Practice

We wrap up the book with a look at how teams can visualize quality and testing, and a summary of agile testing practices that will give your team confidence as you make release decisions. Creating a shared vision for your team is critical to success, and we share a model to help bring testing activities to the whole team. If you're feeling a bit overwhelmed right now and aren't sure where to start, read these chapters first:

- Chapter 24, "Visualize Your Testing"
- Chapter 25, "Putting It All Together"

The book also includes two appendixes: Appendix A, "Page Objects in Practice: Examples," and Appendix B, "Provocation Starters."

Other Elements

Since teams use such a wide variety of agile practices and approaches, we've tried to keep our terminology as generic as possible. To make sure we have a common language with you, we've included a glossary of the terms we use.

You'll find icons in the margins throughout the book where we'd like to draw your attention to a specific practice. You'll find all six icons in Chapter 1, "How Agile Testing Has Evolved," and Chapter 25, "Putting It All Together." An example of the icon for learning can be seen next to following paragraph.

We hope you'll want to learn more about some of the practices, techniques, and tools that we cover. Please check the bibliography for references to books, websites, articles, and blogs. We've sorted it by part so you can find more information easily when you're reading. Sources that are mentioned directly in the book are listed alphabetically in the reference list for easy lookup.

The mind map overview from *Agile Testing* is included on the book website, www.agiletester.com, so that you can get a feel for what was covered there if you haven't already read it.

EXPERIMENT!

Linda Rising encouraged us years ago to try small experiments, evaluate the results, and keep iterating to chip away at problems and achieve goals. If you read something in this book that sounds as if it might be useful for you or your team, give it a try for an iteration or two. Use your retrospectives to see if it's helping, and tweak as necessary. If it doesn't work, you learned something, and you can try something different.

We hope you will find many experiments to try in these pages.

ACKNOWLEDGMENTS

This book has been a group effort. Please learn about all the wonderful practitioners who shared their stories as sidebars in "About the Contributors." Many are success stories, some describe lessons learned the hard way, but we know all will benefit you, the reader.

We're extremely grateful to Jennifer Sinclair for her wonderful illustrations. She came up with such creative ideas to help us get across some important concepts.

We referenced the ideas of so many other people who have taken ideas from *Agile Testing*, adapted them to meet their needs, and were willing to share with the world—thank you.

Our tireless reviewers helped us shape the book and cover the right topics. We're especially grateful to Mike Talks, Bernice Niel Ruhland, and Sherry Heinze, who slogged through every chapter, in some cases multiple times. Thanks to Augusto Evangelisti, Gojko Adzic, Adam Knight, Steve Rogalsky, Aldo Rall, Sharon Robson, James Lyndsay, JeanAnn Harrison, Ken Rubin, Geoff Meyer, Adam Yuret, and Mike Cohn for their valuable feedback. Each of our story contributors also helped review the chapters that included their stories.

Special thanks to our technical reviewers, whose feedback on our final draft was immensely helpful: Tom Poppendieck, Liz Keogh, Markus Gärtner, and George Dinwiddie.

Thank you, Christopher Guzikowski, for making this book possible in the first place, and Olivia Basegio, for answering a thousand questions and keeping us organized. We are grateful to our developmental editor, Chris Zahn, Kesel Wilson our production editor, and to Barbara Wood for doing the final copy edit. It was wonderful working with the Addison-Wesley crew again.

Thanks to a new English grad, Bea Paiko, who did a preliminary copy edit that helped us write a bit more cleanly. Thank you, Mike Cohn, for letting us be part of a great group of agile authors. Thanks to Ellen Gottesdiener and Mary Gorman for sharing some of their book-writing process tips with us; those helped us organize the book more easily.

We are both fortunate to have worked alongside so many amazing people over the years who taught us so much about delivering valuable software. They are too numerous to name here, but we refer to some in the text and the bibliography. We're lucky to be part of a generous global software community.

Finally, a thank-you to our wonderful, supportive family and friends.

Janet's personal thanks:
Thank you to my husband, Jack, for all the contracts reviewed, suppers prepared, and errands run, and for letting me work long into the evenings. I know I pretty much ignored you again for as long as it took to write this book. Your encouragement kept me going.

Lisa, we complement each other in our writing styles, and I think that is what makes us a great team. Thank you for providing a great place for reviewing our first draft and a chance to meet your donkeys.

And finally, I want to acknowledge the power of wireless capability and the Internet. While writing this book, I traveled north to Helsinki, Finland, and camped in Grande Prairie, Canada. I was south to Johannesburg in South Africa and camped in Botswana and Zimbabwe, writing between watching lions and elephants. As well I was in Australia, although I did not test wireless in the outback there. I even was as high as 3,000 meters (~10,000 feet) in Peru. There were only a few places where I could not connect at all. This writing was truly a distributed team effort.

Lisa's personal thanks:

Thanks to my husband, Bob Downing, without whose support I could never write or present anything. He never guessed that one day he'd be out mucking a donkey pen while I slaved over a keyboard. He has kept me and all our pets well fed and well loved. You're still the bee's knees, my dear!

Thank you, Janet, for keeping us on track and doing so much of the heavy lifting to get us organized, writing, and coming up with so many great visuals. Working with you is always a privilege, a learning experience, and a lot of fun. And I also thank Janet's husband, Jack, for his help with the fine print and for enabling Janet to share all this fun and hard work with me!

If readers learn a fraction of what I've learned while writing this book, I'll consider it a success!

About the Authors

Janet Gregory is an agile testing coach and process consultant with DragonFire Inc. She is coauthor with Lisa Crispin of *Agile Testing: A Practical Guide for Testers and Agile Teams* (Addison-Wesley, 2009) and *More Agile Testing: Learning Journeys for the Whole Team* (Addison-Wesley, 2015). She is also a contributor to *97 Things Every Programmer Should Know*. Janet specializes in showing agile teams how testers can add value in areas beyond critiquing the product, for example, guiding development with business-facing tests. Janet works with teams to transition to agile development and teaches agile testing courses and tutorials worldwide. She contributes articles to publications such as *Better Software, Software Test & Performance Magazine*, and *Agile Journal* and enjoys sharing her experiences at conferences and user group meetings around the world. For more about Janet's work and her blog, visit www.janetgregory.ca. You can also follow her on Twitter: @janetgregoryca.

Lisa Crispin is the coauthor with Janet Gregory of *Agile Testing: A Practical Guide for Testers and Agile Teams* (Addison-Wesley, 2009) and *More Agile Testing: Learning Journeys for the Whole Team* (Addison-Wesley, 2015); she is also coauthor with Tip House of *Extreme Testing* (Addison-Wesley, 2002), and a contributor to *Experiences of Test Automation* by Dorothy Graham and Mark Fewster (Addison-Wesley, 2011) and *Beautiful Testing* (O'Reilly, 2009). Lisa was honored by her peers who voted her the Most Influential Agile Testing Professional Person at Agile Testing Days 2012. Lisa enjoys working as a tester with an awesome agile team. She shares her experiences via writing, presenting, teaching, and participating in agile testing communities around the world. For more about Lisa's work, visit www.lisacrispin.com, and follow @lisacrispin on Twitter.

About the Contributors

Gojko Adzic is a strategic software delivery consultant who works with ambitious teams to improve the quality of their software products and processes. He specializes in agile and lean quality improvement, in particular agile testing, specification by example, and behavior-driven development. Gojko is the author of *Specification by Example* (Adzic, 2011), winner of the 2012 Jolt award; *Impact Mapping* (Adzic, 2012); *Bridging the Communication Gap* (Adzic, 2009); an award-winning blog; and other testing- and agile-related books. In 2011, he was voted by peers as the most influential agile testing professional.

Matt Barcomb is passionate about cultivating sustainably adaptive organizations, enjoys being out-of-doors, loves puns, and thrives on guiding companies toward more rewarding and productive self-organizing cultures. Matt has done this in his roles as a product development executive, organizational design consultant, agile coach, development team manager, and programmer. He believes that evolving companies to customer-focused humanistic systems is the biggest challenge facing businesses today. As such, he has dedicated an inordinate amount of his time and energy to finding ways of helping organizations become better places to work.

Susan Bligh has been in the IT industry for seventeen years and has an enthusiasm for business process and operational excellence through the use of technology. She is currently a lead business analyst at an oil and gas company in Calgary, Alberta, Canada. Susan has led business analyst efforts for large-scale projects affecting many disciplines and across broad geographies. She has previously worked in software development, training, and client management, as well as database administration.

She has a degree in computer science with a minor in management from the University of Calgary.

Paul Carvalho is dedicated to helping software development teams deliver high levels of quality with confidence. He inspires collaborative, agile, test-infected teams with a holistic approach to quality. Paul has devoted over twenty years to learning and applying testing approaches, models, methods, techniques, and tools to enlighten decision makers. He passes on that knowledge to individuals and organizations through coaching, consulting, training, writing, and speaking internationally. Paul is passionate about understanding human ecosystems for delivering great products that satisfy and delight customers, which he finds to be a natural fit with the agile community. Connect with him through STAQS.com.

Augusto Evangelisti is a software development professional, blogger, and foosball player with a great interest in people, software quality, and agile and lean practices. He enjoys cooking, eating, learning, and helping agile teams exceed customer expectations while having fun.

David Evans is an experienced agile consultant, coach, and trainer with over twenty-five years of IT experience. A thought leader in the field of agile quality, he has provided training and consultancy for clients in the UK, United States, Ireland, Sweden, Germany, France, Australia, Israel, South Africa, and Singapore. A regular speaker at events and conferences across Europe, David was voted Best Keynote Speaker at Agile Testing Days 2013. He has also had several papers published in international IT journals. He currently lives and works in the UK, where he is a partner, along with Gojko Adzic, in Neuri Consulting LLP. He can be reached at david.evans@neuri.co.uk on email and @DavidEvans66 on Twitter.

Kareem Fazal is a platform software senior development engineer in the Dell Enterprise Solutions Group. He has seven-plus years of experience in the firmware industry working on automation and product development. He joined Dell in 2010 as test lead and then transitioned into the firmware development organization to lead automation strategies and product development.

Benjamin Frempong, a senior test engineer in the Dell Enterprise Solutions Group, has over ten years of experience leading hardware and software QA programs in Dell's Client and Enterprise organizations. He is currently focused on helping teams implement efficient and sustainable test automation strategies.

Chris George has been a software tester and question asker since 1996, working for a variety of UK companies making tools for database development, data reporting, and digital content broadcasting. During that time he has explored, investigated, innovated, invented, planned, automated, stressed, reported, loaded, coded, and estimated on both traditional (waterfall) and agile software teams. He also presents at software conferences on testing topics and writes a blog, www.mostly-testing.co.uk.

Mary Gorman, a leader in business analysis and requirements, is vice president of quality and delivery at EBG Consulting. Mary coaches product teams, facilitates discovery workshops, and trains stakeholders in collaborative practices essential for defining high-value products. She speaks and writes for the agile, business analysis, and project management communities. A Certified Business Analysis Professional, Mary helped develop the IIBA's *A Guide to the Business Analysis Body of Knowledge* and certification exam. She also served on the task force that created PMI's Professional in Business Analysis role delineation. Mary is coauthor of *Discover to Deliver* (Gottesdiener and Gorman, 2012).

Ellen Gottesdiener, founder and principal of EBG Consulting, helps people discover and deliver the right software products at the right time. Ellen is an internationally recognized leader in agile product and project management practices, product envisioning and roadmapping, business analysis and requirements, retrospectives, and collaboration. As an expert facilitator, coach, and trainer, Ellen works with clients around the world and speaks frequently at a diverse range of industry conferences. She is coauthor of *Discover to Deliver* (Gottesdiener and Gorman, 2012) and author of two other acclaimed books: *Requirements by Collaboration* (Gottesdiener, 2002) and *The Software Requirements Memory Jogger* (Gottesdiener, 2005).

Jon Hagar is an independent consultant working in software product integrity, verification, and validation testing at Grand Software Testing. Jon publishes regularly, including a book on mobile/embedded software testing: *Software Test Attacks to Break Mobile and Embedded Devices* (Hagar, 2013). His interests include agile, mobile, embedded, QA, skill building, and lifelong learning.

Parimala Hariprasad spent her youth studying people and philosophy. By the time she got to work, she was able to use those learnings to create awesome testers. She has worked as a tester for over ten years for domains such as customer relationship management, security, e-commerce, and health care. Her specialty is coaching and creating great teams—teams that ultimately fired her because she wasn't needed anymore. She has experienced the transition from web to mobile and emphasizes the need for design thinking in testing. She frequently rants on her blog, Curious Tester (http://curioustester.blogspot.com). She tweets at @CuriousTester and can be found on LinkedIn at http://in.linkedin.com/in/parimalahariprasad.

JeanAnn Harrison has been in the software testing and quality assurance field for over fifteen years, including seven years working within a regulatory environment and eight years performing mobile software testing. Her niche is system integration testing with a focus on multi-tiered system environments involving client/server, web application, and stand-alone software applications. JeanAnn is a regular speaker at many software testing conferences and other events and is a Weekend Testing Americas facilitator. She is always looking to gain inspiration from fellow testers throughout the software testing community and continues to combine her practical experiences with interacting on software quality and testing forums, attending training classes, and remaining active on social media sites.

Mike Heinrich has been working as a tester for over a decade, working in logistics, banking, telecommunications, travel, and utilities. Throughout his career, Mike has focused on data and integration testing. His passion for data and delivering customer value has afforded him the opportunity to present to a number of North American organizations on agile data warehousing and data testing. In his free time, Mike enjoys traveling the world, playing volleyball, and coaching basketball.

Sherry Heinze is a test strategist, tester, QA analyst, and trainer with a broad background in analysis, design, testing, training, implementation, documentation, and user support. For the last 17 years, Sherry has focused on testing from analysis and design forward, sometimes on cross-functional teams, sometimes with teams of testers, sometimes alone. Sherry has extensive experience working in various methodologies with both users and technical staff to identify and test requirements, design, create, test, implement, and support systems.

Matthew Heusser has spent his adult life developing, testing, and managing software projects. Along the way Matt served as a contributing editor for *Software Test & Quality Assurance* magazine, organized the Agile Alliance Sponsored Workshop on Technical Debt, and served on the board of directors for the Association for Software Testing. Perhaps best known for his writing, Matt was the lead editor for *How to Reduce the Cost of Software Testing* (Heusser, 2011) and is currently serving as managing editor for Stickyminds.com. As the managing consultant at Excelon Development, Matt manages key accounts for the company while also doing consulting and writing. You can read more about Matt at the Excelon website, www.xndev.com, or follow him on Twitter: @ heusser.

Michael Hüttermann, a Java champion, is a freelance delivery engineer and expert for DevOps, continuous delivery, and source control management/application life cycle management. He is the author of *Agile ALM* (Hüttermann, 2011a) and *DevOps for Developers* (Hüttermann, 2012). For more information see http://huettermann.net.

Griffin Jones, an agile tester, trainer, and coach, provides consulting on context-driven software testing and regulatory compliance to companies in regulated and unregulated industries. Recently, he was the director of quality and regulatory compliance at iCardiac Technologies, which provides core lab services for the pharmaceutical industry to evaluate the cardiac safety of potential new drugs. Griffin was responsible for all matters relating to quality and FDA regulatory compliance, including presenting the verification and validation (testing) results to external regulatory auditors. He is a host of the Workshop on Regulated Software Testing (WREST) and a member of ASQ, AST, ISST, and RAPS.

Stephan Kämper studied physics, wrote his diploma thesis about holography, and then joined the oceanography group at the University of Bremen. In 2001 he started in software development by joining the test team for an object-oriented database system. He never left software testing and specialized in automated software tests and agile methods. He worked on topics as diverse as precision navigation systems, payment platforms, health care systems, telecommunication, and social networks. Working in these different fields helped him recognize common patterns, which he found useful in software testing. His languages are (in alphabetical order) English, German, and Ruby. Follow him on Twitter at @S_2K, and see his website: www.seasidetesting.com.

Trish Khoo has worked in test engineering and test management for companies such as Google, Campaign Monitor, and Microsoft. She maintains a blog at www.trishkhoo.com and a podcast at testcast.net, enjoys speaking at conferences, and writes articles for technical publications. When she's not doing all of that, she's busy traveling the world, sketching robots, or maybe just sleeping until noon. Trish earned a bachelor's degree in information technology from the University of Queensland, where she graduated with honors.

Adam Knight has been testing data storage and analysis software for ten years, with seven of those spent working in an agile team. Adam is an enthusiastic exponent of exploratory testing approaches backed by discerning use of automation. He is a great believer in creating multi-skilled teams based on rich and unique individual skill sets. At his current employer, RainStor, Adam has overseen the testing and technical support of a large-scale data storage system from its initial release through successful adoption in some of the largest telecommunication and financial services companies in the world. He writes at www.a-sisyphean-task.com.

Cory Maksymchuk is a software developer who is passionate about agile processes and lean software development. He has spent most of the last 12 years working in the Java stack as part of large software development initiatives. His true passion in life is finding elegant solutions to difficult problems, and he truly gets excited about seeing great ideas come to life.

Drew McKinney is a user experience designer with Pivotal Tracker and Pivotal Labs. Before Pivotal, Drew ran Bloomingsoft, a mobile design and development consultancy. In the past Drew has worked with companies such as Disney Animation Studios, Audi USA, Cook Medical, and Deloitte Consulting. He is an active member of the design community and has spoken about design at numerous Indiana and Colorado technology events.

Geoff Meyer, a test architect in the Dell Enterprise Solutions Group, has over twenty-eight years of software industry experience as a developer, manager, business analyst, and test architect. Since 2010, a secondary focus of Geoff's has been fostering the agile-based software development and test practices of more than eight hundred development, test, and user experience engineers across four global design centers. Geoff is an active member and contributor to the Agile Austin community.

Jeff "Cheezy" Morgan, chief technology officer and a cofounder of LeanDog, has been teaching classes and coaching teams on agile and lean techniques since early 2004. Most of his work has focused on the engineering practices used by developers and testers. For the past few years he has experienced great success and recognition for his work focused on helping teams adopt acceptance-test-driven development using Cucumber. He has authored several popular Ruby gems used by software testers and is the author of the book *Cucumber & Cheese—A Testers Workshop* (Morgan, 2013).

Claire Moss became the first discrete mathematics business graduate from the Georgia Institute of Technology in 2003 and immediately jumped into software testing. She has been following this calling ever since, working with agile product teams as a testing teacher, unit and integration test adviser, exploratory tester, and test automator. Although she'll always go back to scrapbooking, her dominant hobby in recent years has been writing, speaking, and nerding about testing. Claire has always had a passion for writing, and she continues to use her evil powers for good on the job and on her blog at http://aclairefication.com.

Aldo Rall started off in testing as a junior programmer at the start of the Y2K bubble. Since then, working in South Africa and the UK, he gained practical experience in testing across a plethora of titles, assignments, and projects. His greatest passion lies in the "people" dimension and how that translates into successful products, teams, and testers. Through this background, he enjoys opportunities to develop, grow, and mature testing, testers, and teams.

Sharon Robson is the software testing practice lead for Software Education. A passionate tester and a natural-born trainer, Sharon delivers and develops courses at all levels of software testing from introductory to advanced. Sharon also focuses on agile and spends a significant amount of her time working with teams (training, coaching, and mentoring) to assist them in their transitions. Sharon is currently researching and writing about agile test approaches in various business domains. She presents at both local and international conferences and contributes to the testing and agile community via blogs, tweets, conference involvement, and mentoring.

Steve Rogalsky, recognizing that software development culture, management, and process can be frustrating and inhibiting, has invested significantly in finding ways to overcome and counteract those effects. He's found that valuing simplicity, respect for people, continuous improvement, and short feedback loops are powerful tools for addressing these shortcomings. Since software development doesn't own those frustrations, he's also been translating what he's learned into other areas of the organization, family life, community groups, and coaching. He speaks regularly at conferences in Canada and the United States, has been featured on InfoQ, cofounded the Winnipeg Agile User Group, and works at Protegra. You can read more about what he's learned at http://WinnipegAgilist.Blogspot.com.

Bernice Niel Ruhland, with over twenty years of professional experience encompassing a variety of technical disciplines, currently serves as the director of quality management programs for ValueCentric LLC. Applying her proficiencies in software programming, testing, assessment, and implementation, Bernice leads the company's software testing department. As the driving force behind ValueCentric's company-wide quality programs, she draws upon practices in the context-driven and agile theories and methodologies to guide foundational efforts. When not working, she maintains a successful blog, www.TheTestersEdge.com, a collection of her observations related to a variety of technical topics including software testing, leadership, and career development.

Huib Schoots is a tester, consultant, and people lover. He shares his passion for testing through coaching, training, and giving presentations on a variety of test subjects. Curious and passionate, he is an agile and context-driven tester who attempts to read everything ever published on software testing. He's also a member of TestNet, AST, and ISST; a black belt in the Miagi-Do School of Software Testing; and coauthor of a book about the future of software testing. Huib maintains a blog on www.magnificant.com and tweets as @huibschoots.

Paul Shannon and **Chris O'Dell** joined the 7digital team in 2010 and 2011 respectively, both starting in the team responsible for the 7digital API. They worked on improving the quality of the testing in the API, and Chris now leads that team, concentrating on improving the platform for continuous delivery, resilience, and scaling. Paul works across all teams in the 7digital technology team that are geared toward continuous improvement and quality-driven software development practices. The team follows a test-first approach with a highly collaborative and visible workflow, and all absolutely love technology and testing.

Jennifer Sinclair has been an artist, art instructor, and educator since 1995. During that time, she has lived in Canada, Japan, and the United States and has worked to improve art exploration for children and adults of all ages and abilities. She has designed and illustrated images for the Alberta Teachers' Association Early Childhood Education Council and the Alberta Education Council in Canada. She is currently working on developing art lessons that integrate easily into the core subjects of elementary education. As a homemaker, freelance artist, and volunteer art instructor, she is passionate about continuing to develop her skills and knowledge and share them with as many people as possible. You can reach her at jvaagesinclair@live.com.

Toby Sinclair joined the software testing business as a university graduate in 2007 and hasn't looked back. He has worked for various software testing consultancies in the UK and is currently working with J. P. Morgan to advance its testing capabilities to support the transition to agile. Toby is an active member of the testing community and can be found on Twitter: @TobyTheTester.

Tony Sweets is a 20-year veteran of the software industry, currently working as an information technology architect. For the past 13 years he has been working on Java enterprise web applications in the financial sector. Tony possesses a wide range of skills but likes to work mostly on Java applications and the tools that make the development process better. Tony holds a bachelor's degree in computer science from the University of Wyoming.

Mike Talks was 26 when he first gave IT "a go" as a career. Before that, he'd been a teacher, research scientist, and data analyst, and his parents worried he'd never "get a proper job." Although originally a programmer, it was in testing where he flourished. He originally worked on long, requirements-rich military waterfall projects in the UK, but since moving to New Zealand he's found himself increasingly working on projects with companies such as Assurity, Kiwibank, and Datacom, where timely delivery is a key factor.

Eveliina Vuolli acts currently as operational development manager in Nokia Solutions and Networks. She has been working with the network management system R&D development team for 15 years, acting in different kinds of roles in the global, multinational organization: integration and verification process owner, project manager and trainer in various areas, and also coach. In addition, she has been involved in the agile transformation in her own product area.

Pete Walen has been in software development for over twenty-five years. He has worked in a variety of roles including developer, business analyst, and project manager. He is an independent consulting contractor who works with test teams over extended periods, coaching them and working to improve their testing techniques and practices. Pete describes himself as a "Software Anthropologist and Tester," which encompasses the examination of how software and people relate and interact. He has worked in a variety of shops using a variety of development methodologies and has adopted an attitude of "do what makes sense" for the organization and the project.

Mary Walshe helps teams deliver successful solutions to business problems and plays a major role in striving for a kaizen culture in these teams. Mary was the driving force behind the introduction of acceptance-test-driven development in her department. She has been working in the industry for four years, and currently she works on a team in Paddy Power as an agile tester. Her team is using kanban to help them measure their experiments and in order to continually improve. In her spare time Mary runs adventure races, mountain bikes, and just recently found a new love for skiing.

Christin Wiedemann, after finishing her Ph.D. in physics at Stockholm University in 2007, began working as a software developer. Christin soon discovered that she found testing to be more challenging and creative, and she joined the testing company AddQ Consulting. There, she worked as a tester, test lead, and trainer, giving courses on agile testing, test design, and exploratory testing. In late 2011, Christin moved to Vancouver, Canada, joining Professional Quality Assurance. In her roles as tester, test lead, trainer, and speaker, Christin uses her scientific background and pedagogic abilities to continually develop her own skills and those of others.

Lynn Winterboer, with a proven background in a variety of data projects and agile practices, teaches and coaches data warehouse/business intelligence teams on how to effectively apply agile principles and practices to their work. For more than fifteen years, Lynn has served in numerous roles within the analytics, business intelligence, and data warehousing space. She very well understands the unique set of challenges faced by teams in this area that want to benefit from the incremental style of agile development; Lynn leverages her experience and training to help deliver practical solutions for her clients and students. Lynn can be reached at www.LynnWinterboer.com.

Cirilo Wortel is an independent tester and trainer from the Netherlands. In 2006 Cirilo first got involved in agile software development. He has worked with several enterprise companies, coaching and helping to implement test automation during their agile adoption. Cirilo cohosted, with Janet Gregory, a master class in agile testing for several years in the Netherlands. He has contributed back to the community by founding the Federation of Agile Testers, the largest agile testing user group in the Netherlands, and is a frequent speaker at international conferences. With several colleagues at Xebia, Cirilo developed Xebium, an automation tool for web applications.

Alexei Zheglov is dedicated to discovering and practicing new methods of managing and leading the improvement of modern, complex, knowledge-intensive work. He came to this after a long software engineering career, during which he learned to see and to solve many problems in software delivery. Alexei presents his findings frequently at conferences in Canada and abroad. He is recognized as a Kanban Coaching Professional and an Accredited Kanban Trainer. Alexei lives in Waterloo, Ontario, Canada. His blog can be found at http://connected-knowledge.com.

Part I

INTRODUCTION

In this first part, we go through a brief history of how agile testing has changed since we first worked on agile teams. We introduce some of the new concepts and go into more detail about the importance of a learning organizational culture.

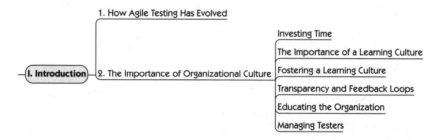

- **Chapter 1,** "How Agile Testing Has Evolved"
- **Chapter 2**, "The Importance of Organizational Culture"

Chapter 1

How Agile Testing Has Evolved

Each of us started our "agile" career as the lone tester on an Extreme Programming (XP) team. At the time, none of the publications about XP even mentioned having testers on the team. There were two roles: programmer and customer. Customers would specify all the acceptance tests, programmers would automate them, and presto, you're done. When we went to XP conferences, we were usually the only people attending who self-identified as testers, although we knew that testers had a lot of value to add. We experimented, we discussed testing with the XP pioneers, and we traded ideas with each other and with other members of our respective teams.

Driving development with examples

Agile development evolved, and agile testing evolved along with it. Teams started developing test libraries and frameworks for test automation above the unit level. By the time we wrote *Agile Testing*, many agile practitioners acknowledged the contributions of experienced testers such as Elisabeth Hendrickson and Michael Bolton. Practitioners such as Brian Marick and Joshua Kerievsky had pioneered the idea of using examples and story tests to guide development.

Ward Cunningham created Fit (Framework for Integrated Test), a tool to help define those examples, and Dan North introduced behavior-driven development (BDD) (North, 2006), which paved the way for popular new tools. Agile teams had begun to understand the value of exploratory testing. Testing on agile teams had gone beyond the functional to embrace many types of testing, as illustrated by Brian Marick's agile testing matrix (Marick, 2003), which we adapted into the agile testing quadrants (we also refer to them as the Quadrants).

Of course, there were still challenges that hindered agile testing success. We testers envied all the aids for unit testing that were built into the programmers' integrated development environments (IDEs). We wanted that same ease for testers specifying tests. We found huge benefits in applying the "Power of Three," or "Three Amigos," as George Dinwiddie calls it (Dinwiddie, 2010), where a customer, programmer, and tester collaborate anytime there are questions about how a feature should behave. However, we still found it difficult to capture many dimensions of customer requirements such as design, usability, data, and other quality attributes. These are some of the challenges we address in this book.

Practitioners in several disciplines have been filling in gaps in the practice of agile testing. We're fortunate to be able to share other practitioners' stories about how they have succeeded with agile testing in different contexts.

One key idea has become part of our everyday thinking: testing in agile teams is an activity, not a phase. We learned this concept from Elisabeth Hendrickson (Hendrickson, 2006) and apply it throughout the book to emphasize that testing is something that all disciplines need to consider while developing software.

Continual
learning

As we've continually learned more and better techniques for testing in agile, we've discovered how generalizing specialists with both depth and breadth in their skill sets help teams tackle difficult testing challenges. Practitioners have created practices and patterns that help team members in different disciplines collaborate and learn "just enough" of the specialties from each other.

Practitioners such as the members of the Agile Alliance Functional Test Tools (AA-FTT) group have led the way to better tooling for testing. Today, writing test code is on a par with writing production code. We've learned better ways to identify which frameworks, test libraries, and drivers are a good fit for a specific team's needs.

Business analysts have brought their specialized skills at discovering customer requirements into agile development. Testing and business analysis share complementary skills that help teams deliver the right business value. Similarly, user experience (UX) experts have shown us good, simple ways to get customer input as new features are designed. DevOps practitioners have blended development, operations, and testing skills to advance quality in new dimensions such as delivery and deployment and to help shorten release cycles to reduce risk and the impact to customers.

Exploratory testing

We continue to meet many more agile teams that understand the value of exploratory testing than we saw a few years ago. Although our first book covers exploratory testing, it's clear that teams can take advantage of its power in many more ways. We're fortunate that people who practice exploratory testing in an agile context are sharing their expertise.

We've seen new, creative approaches to test planning and collaboration. Teams today find more ways to visualize quality. The Quadrants and the test automation pyramid have been adapted and extended to represent more dimensions.

Context sensitivity

More teams today are faced with testing mobile apps and embedded software, on an ever-expanding range of devices and platforms. Large and complex data sets with new technology to store, manage, analyze, search, and visualize the data define a new category: Big Data. Testing has to keep up.

Feature testing

Agile development arose for use in small, colocated teams. Now we see that large organizations, some of which started as small agile companies, as well as distributed teams, are using an agile approach to development. In organizations with enterprise-wide software solutions, testing runs into different obstacles, such as heavyweight organizational constraints. At the same time, organizations are finding new ways to develop minimum viable products (MVPs), using iterative releases with fast feedback loops and validated learning.

While some companies may have been testing in production back in 2008 when we wrote our first book, we didn't start hearing about that technique until later—unless you count releasing without testing and hoping for the best! Today, releasing updates to a small percentage of production users while monitoring log files for errors, and other techniques of getting fast feedback from production users, can be a valid and necessary strategy in the appropriate context.

Keeping
it real

All these changes and innovations prompted us to share what we and other practitioners have learned. Agile is about continually improving, and many of you may now be several years into an agile adoption, changing your process as you learn. The testing-related problems you face now are likely much different from what they were during your initial transition to agile. We hope the experiences shared in this book will give you some ideas for experiments to try as you visualize quality for your product and then inspect and adapt your process.

SUMMARY

As agile software development evolves, we continually inspect and adapt agile testing to keep pace. In this chapter, we looked at some ways agile testing has been changing.

- We've recognized that testing is an activity that is crucial to product success and is of interest to every member of the product team from stakeholders right through to operations and support.
- Agile teams increasingly recognize the ways practitioners from other disciplines such as business analysis, user experience design, and DevOps have expanded our ability to build in the quality our customers desire.
- Tooling for agile testing continues to make great strides forward, enabling agile teams to implement the infrastructure needed to support learning and quick feedback.
- Agile teams are learning the value of exploratory testing and other practices that help us provide essential information to customers and developer teams.
- Agile testing has to keep up with fast-changing technology and new contexts for agile development. We'll explore these ideas throughout this book.

Chapter 2

THE IMPORTANCE OF ORGANIZATIONAL CULTURE

We've noticed a common theme in organizations that are transitioning to agile methods. Development teams are able to adopt agile values, principles, and practices. However, the business side of the company may be slow to understand the benefits of agile and may often take longer to adjust to the change. For a successful transition to agile, it is important that both development and business be in sync and understand each other's reality.

When you work in a company whose leaders understand that focusing on quality is one of the best ways to deliver business value to customers frequently, your team—and company—are likely to succeed. Frequency and consistency of delivery improve over time. Conversely, if a company's focus is on speed first, often quality is sacrificed. Technical debt in the form of fragile, hard-to-change code and slower feedback cycles decreases the team's ability to deliver consistently.

If teams feel pressured to meet unrealistic deadlines with a defined scope, they're no longer in control of their own workload. As the deadline looms close, developers feel they have fewer options and make choices to fit the deadline rather than satisfy the customer (Rogalsky, 2012). They're likely to start cutting corners and make decisions

Figure 2-1   Too many features for the infrastructure

without thinking of potential ripple effects, and they may fall into a death spiral of ever-growing technical debt.

Teams need to be able to articulate the dangers of an unsustainable pace so that company leaders are aware of the risks and the consequences. Sometimes a team needs to slow down to address technical debt, or maybe to learn new concepts or apply new ideas. Janet uses a picture (Figure 2-1) in her presentations to show how adding more and more features without considering the infrastructure can actually be detrimental. The picture shows four superpowered cars sitting in a lineup on a road—going nowhere because the traffic is so heavy. Why add more features when the ones you have don't work as intended? When you build up too much technical debt, your team suffers a similar state of gridlock.

INVESTING TIME

Creativity is required to give customers useful software solutions, and people need time to think and use their ingenuity. We also must keep learning new technical skills and tools in order to conduct small experiments that might help address their problems.

In an article titled "Slow Ideas" (Gawande, 2013) Atul Gawande explored why some innovations, such as surgical anesthesia, catch on quickly, while others, such as antiseptics, take many years or may never get traction. His observation was that change can occur only with learning, practice, and a personal touch. In the programs he studied, people learned best when they performed the new activity themselves and described it in their own words, with guidance from a trainer. It may seem cheaper or faster to have a trainer demonstrate the activity or have people watch a video, but the hands-on approach produces real, sustainable change.

In the software profession (as in many others), people seem to forget that it takes time to learn and practice a new skill. They also often neglect to have that trainer alongside to guide the learners.

Spend Time on the Right Thing

David Evans, *an agile quality coach, shares a metaphor he uses to explain the idea of spending time on the right thing.*

I sometimes get management resistance to my suggestions to invest time in collaboratively writing acceptance tests before implementing each story. The usual argument is that if the team spends more time on acceptance tests, it will slow down the rate of development. I concede that yes, in a very limited sense, it will slow down, but only in the same way that stopping for passengers slows down the public bus. Trying to optimize the speed of the bus is missing the point, since it has nothing to do with the purpose or success of public transport. Imagine a bus driver suggesting that he could improve his performance metrics if he didn't stop for elderly passengers, as they seem to be the slowest to board. In fact, if he didn't pick up any passengers at all, he'd be much faster and wouldn't have to stop at all those bus stops on his winding route. Instead, he could get on the expressway and be back in the depot in no time at all!

This is the same mistaken logic that says that working on tests will slow down development. In *Test-Driven Development: By Example*, Kent Beck has a nice statement (Beck, 2002): "Code that isn't tested doesn't work—this seems to be the safe assumption." If spending time creating acceptance tests before coding slows anything down, it is only slowing the rate at which we are creating code that doesn't work.

Manufacturing companies that embrace lean values have taught us that respecting individuals' ability to contribute ideas as well as working continually to improve translate into innovative products that customers love. When organizations give teams time and support to learn and experiment, those teams can do their best work. In Part II, "Learning for Better Testing," we will explore some of the practices we think merit an investment in learning.

Gojko Adzic (Adzic, 2013) has noted that great results happen when

- People know **why** they are doing their work
- Organizations focus on delivering **outcomes and impacts** rather than features
- Teams decide what to do next based on **immediate and direct feedback** from the use of their work
- Everyone **cares**

Some companies have tried to create slack and give employees time to learn by building in slack time to work on personal projects, either as a percentage of work time or dedicated "hack" weeks or days. Lisa has worked on teams that use this practice, and they experienced good results in keeping technical debt low and throughput consistent. However, it's important to understand the principles behind utilization and capacity. Otherwise, teams might face trying to squeeze even more work in between hard deadlines.

Capacity Utilization

Alexei Zheglov, *a consultant in lean and kanban for knowledge-work organizations, explained the theory behind capacity utilization and how to escape the pitfalls of 20% time. We've included a portion of his sidebar here; the complete one can be found on the book's website.*

The main reason for 20% time is to keep the average capacity utilization at 80% rather than at 100% to build in slack time. We can think of a software development organization as a system that turns feature requests into developed features. We can then model its behavior using queuing theory.

Theory

If requests arrive faster than the system can service them, they queue up. When arrivals are slower, the queue size decreases. Because the arrival and service processes are random, the queue size changes randomly with time (Figure 2-2).

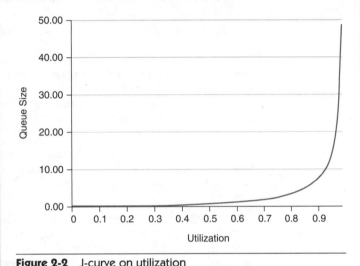

Figure 2-2   J-curve on utilization

The average queue size remains low while utilization is up to 0.8, then rises sharply and goes to infinity. We can understand this intuitively by thinking about our computer's CPU: when its utilization is low, it responds instantly to our inputs, but when a background task pushes its utilization close to 100%, the computer becomes frustratingly slow to respond to every click.

Practice

It is essentially the slack that keeps the system responsive. Several practical conclusions about what not to do are

- Cost accounting (engineers' time costs X, but the company may not be able to afford it). The economic benefit comes from reducing the cost of delay.
- Setting up a proposal system for people to submit projects to do in their "20% time."
- Tracking the 20% time by filling out time sheets.

- Using innovation as a motivator for the 20% time. While new products have come out of 20% projects, they were not the point. If your company cannot innovate during its core hours, that's a problem!
- Relying on the 20% time to encourage creativity. Saying you'll unleash your creativity with 20% time begs the question of why you're not creative enough already during your core hours.
- Allocating the 20% time to a Friday every week.

Those Are All Don'ts; Where Are the Dos?

OK, what about doing it right? Let's answer with the best question we've heard while discussing this subject with practitioners: "If 20% of your capacity is mandated to be filled with non-queue items, then you've just shrunk your capacity to 80%, and 80% is your new 100%. Right?"

Yes, "80 is the new 100" highlights the main problem with the attempts to mandate the 20% time without understanding the theory. You want to escape the utilization trap, not to stay in the trap and allocate time differently.

Utilization depends on two processes: arrival process (demand) and service process (capability). You can't really choose your utilization. It is what it is because the processes are what they are. You can, however, work on the processes by improving your company's software delivery capability and shaping the demand. As you make progress, slack will emerge.

The bibliography for Part I, "Introduction," includes resources where you can learn more about managing capability and throughput. One of the most important things to remember is that overutilization impacts flow, and unsustainable pace actually reduces throughput.

THE IMPORTANCE OF A LEARNING CULTURE

If you can "fail fast" enough so that the failure isn't too costly, you can learn from those mistakes to improve. You can also use fast feedback loops to refine your trials to change something that worked "OK" into something that works great. If your organization's culture is such that mistakes aren't tolerated, innovation is unlikely. Doing the same process, even if it's not working, feels safe, so there is no reason to change.

Lisa's Story

I've been fortunate to spend most of my career on teams that worked at a sustainable pace and valued continual improvement. When I've encountered environments where questions and experiments are discouraged, it feels like I've slammed into a brick wall. On one team I worked with for a short time, a ScrumMaster told me that I was an "impediment to the team" because I kept raising issues at standup. He was under pressure from management to get the team to deliver. He didn't want to be slowed down by someone pointing out that there had been no test environment for three weeks. There were lots of great people on the team, but they weren't allowed to do their best work. My attempts to be a change agent in this organization failed, so, as they say, I changed my organization.

In her talk on the power of retrospectives (Rising, 2009), Linda Rising pointed out that often, when confronted with practices such as pair programming or retrospectives, some managers have this reaction: "We don't have time for thinking." If we believe we can improve, we will—perhaps not all at once, or overnight, but we can find better ways to work, one baby step at a time.

FOSTERING A LEARNING CULTURE

Get your team together to see what skills might be missing and what people are interested in learning. Let them manage their workload so they can build in time for experiments, reading, training courses, and practicing new skills. Team members should feel empowered to research a new technique or try out a new tool. For example, they could be allowed to devote some time daily or weekly to work on anything they like, whether it's learning facilitation skills or finding a new solution for automating regression tests. Hack weeks where team members work on experimental projects or learn a new technology are an increasingly popular approach. Team members share what they've learned, helping to foster a learning culture.

Gojko Adzic told us that he has had success working with management and asking them if they expect the teams to improve their process over time, or if they think the process is already the best it can be. Having established that the process could indeed be improved, he works with them to develop a budget, not necessarily in terms of money, but instead in time. For example, team members should spend 10% of their time actively improving their process. Every team needs to decide how to use it, but as part of the negotiation, management can withdraw this budget for a short period of time when needed. If the budget is constantly withdrawn, it's a warning sign that another serious conversation is required.

One way an organization can encourage a learning culture is by setting up communities of practice (some organizations call these guilds) and allowing these groups to take time to discuss and share ideas during work time. Over and over, we have heard about these communities discussing books or sharing their work with other like-minded individuals.

Quality Guilds

Augusto Evangelisti, *a test engineer at Paddy Power, shares how the testers in his workplace created a quality guild.*

In my current place of work, we have a quality guild composed of 20% testers, 20% kanban facilitators, and 60% developers. Do we need somebody to tell us what to do, what problems we need to address, and what innovation we should work on? Believe me, no. We started with five people, and after a couple of months we had 20 people with incredible ideas for improving quality and making our life better. We meet every two weeks and always have a list of items to talk about.

I tried the same exercise as a manager, and I ended up with five testers who had to be there, sitting and waiting for me to tell them what to do. It is very different when the people are empowered to make their own lives better.

We're fans of Lean Coffee sessions, which encourage participants to bring up new ideas or concerns and talk openly about them. Conducting a Lean Coffee–style session that is open to everyone in an organization may lead to clearing up misunderstandings. Check the Lean Coffee links in the bibliography for Part I to get started.

Something as simple as pairing with another team member, remote or colocated, can be a learning or training opportunity, especially if you are trying to learn a new skill that someone else has already mastered.

Changing an established culture is difficult. If agile is new for your team, help team members adapt by taking small steps. Help them adopt new habits, and make sure each team member feels valued and safe.

Learn to Adapt to Change

Bernice Niel Ruhland, *a director of quality management, shares her experiences of adopting a daily standup meeting.*

Many teams call themselves "agile" but are not following the principles behind the Agile Manifesto charter. They are "agile" in spirit, but not necessarily in practices common to self-managed teams. Understand the practices and adopt what works for your team. Start with something small and let your ideas evolve naturally. Failures can lead to new information to understand where and how to apply different approaches and techniques.

For example, if you want to start a daily standup meeting, schedule 15 minutes at the same time and at the same location every day. Start with the questions typically used by agile teams: What did you do yesterday; what will you do today; and are there any obstacles in your way? Evaluate how those questions are working—perhaps for your project different questions are necessary.

Short standup meetings are a great way to keep everyone moving in the right direction and to promote face-to-face communication. Stay focused on the positive output of the daily meeting instead of defending the format. Facilitate the meetings to keep them short, so that participants know their time is valued, and modify the format if needed.

In Chapter 6, "How to Learn," we'll look at more ways teams can learn and practice the skills they need to succeed with testing in agile teams.

TRANSPARENCY AND FEEDBACK LOOPS

Short feedback loops are an important aspect not only of testing but also of the complete agile software delivery cycle. Transparency in decision making is needed for long-term success in providing high-quality software.

If you're a line manager in a software organization, or aspire to be, learn good ways of building feedback loops and transparency into your team culture. Read books oriented toward agile development, such as *Management 3.0* by Jurgen Appelo (Appelo, 2011). Articles and blog posts by leaders in agile organization culture, such as Johanna Rothman and Esther Derby, are excellent sources for ideas. See the bibliography for Part I for more resources.

When our work is transparent to the organization, the need for control is reduced. Visibility into what the development teams are doing helps build trust with the business stakeholders and company executives. Trust is built over time with patience and practice and consistency (see Figure 2-3).

Mastering agile values and principles requires a huge cultural shift for the organization. To quote Johanna Rothman, "Agile is for people who want to and can manage the cultural change that it requires" (Rothman, 2012a). Our real goal isn't implementing agile; it's delivering products our customers want. Spotify, a digital music service, is often cited as a company that successfully adopted an agile culture and has grown and adapted and made the whole process transparent. Henrik Kniberg has shared Spotify's experiences in an animated video that is worth watching (Kniberg and Spotify Labs, 2013).

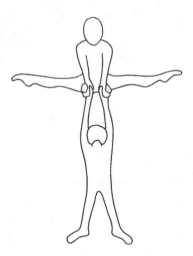

Figure 2-3   Trust takes practice and patience and consistency.

Celebrating successes—both big and small—is important. Make people aware of others' successes so that they want to be part of a culture that celebrates people's and teams' achievements.

EDUCATING THE ORGANIZATION

For a company culture to change, the top executives must be on board with changing it. This means they must understand what the change means for them.

Before you try to educate your company's executives, educate yourself about their roles and responsibilities. For example, the company CFO projects financial performance and tries to predict the return on potential investments. That person knows a lot about all aspects of the business and is likely keen to understand how software projects are progressing and what might cause delays.

Find ways to quantify and articulate the advantages of the changes you want, as well as the cost of ongoing problems such as accumulating technical debt. Show executives how the problems impact the business's bottom line.

When business leaders work with the development teams to set goals that are business driven, the teams gain an understanding of what is important. They then can make suggestions for prioritization and cutting unnecessary scope. We talk more about the idea of impact mapping to help with this in Chapter 9, "Are We Building the Right Thing?"

Stakeholders can prioritize outcomes, so the team can deliver valuable increments within the necessary time frame and use fast feedback loops to keep improving the product and giving visible feedback about the progress of projects and development.

Build trust by delivering value regularly, even if it's a small amount. As Bob Martin warns (Martin, 2011), don't say, "I'll try" when given unrealistic deadlines. Instead, help managers understand what your team can realistically deliver, quantify the cost of any shortcuts you might have to take, and help them cut scope so that they get their top-priority features.

In our experience, business executives are uncomfortable with the uncertainty that is inherent in software development. As software developers, we may be able to reliably predict delivery dates for features that are simple or that we've done before and understand well. However, stakeholders tend to want shiny new capabilities that the competition doesn't have. If the business wants something that's unpredictable, explain the complexities to them. Consider an approach such as Real Options (Matts and Maassen, 2007). Chris Matts has adapted this idea from the financial world in which options are kept open until the last responsible moment when a decision is required. Paying to extend options builds in time to learn about alternative solutions, which allows teams to make better choices. For example, we can choose technology that makes changes easier, or agree on a range of dates instead of one deadline (Keogh, 2012b).

The Cynefin framework, developed by Dave Snowden, provides a way to evaluate whether a new feature will be straightforward to deliver or has unknowns that need to be explored before a solution can emerge. See the links in the bibliography for Part I for more information about ways to "embrace uncertainty" (Keogh, 2013b).

Whether or not you use a defined approach or framework for managing risk and uncertainty, teams can help company decision makers understand why we often can't reliably predict progress, and how testing can help keep them informed.

Janet's Story

One organization I worked with found a very creative way of getting executives to understand some of the teams' issues very quickly. There were multiple teams, all working on the same product, so they had crosscutting concerns. All the daily standups were held at either 9:15 or 9:30 a.m. At 10:00 a.m., they held a Scrum-of-Scrums in a conference room where all the ScrumMasters talked about those crosscutting concerns. At 10:15, one ScrumMaster stayed behind, and any executive who had a vested interest in the product came into that room. They discussed any new issues and then reviewed outstanding issues that were assigned and dated and listed on a whiteboard. If an issue had been resolved, it was wiped off. Any new issues that had to be dealt with outside the 15 allotted minutes were added, assigned, and dated.

The book *Fearless Change* (Manns and Rising, 2005) explains good ways to introduce new ideas. For guidance while meeting with executives, check out the pattern "Whisper in the General's Ear" (pp. 248–49).

Whenever you interact with people who are not part of the delivery team, take the opportunity to educate them about how you are working. Ask them what they might need to know to do their jobs, and be willing to articulate what you might need from them.

Managing Testers

In *Agile Testing*, we talked quite a bit about test managers and what their new role could be. However, we still get a lot of questions about it and see frequent conversations about this topic on different forums. There is no one right answer—so much depends on your context. For example, if you have a small organization with only a couple of teams, you may not require a separate line manager at all.

We know of teams where all members report to a delivery or development manager, and it works very well if the manager has a good appreciation of what testers do. Augusto Evangelisti's story of guilds earlier in this chapter illustrates this approach. In his company, senior testers mentor new hires, and they all work on improving their system. Currently they have six teams, and Augusto feels strongly that as they grow, their culture will enable them to maintain this way of working.

Some organizations may need a secondary reporting structure, or someone specifically to help the learning between teams. Adam Knight shared his experience of this with us. For him, the role of a test manager extends beyond the scope of the day-to-day work of the agile team. Much of his work involves looking outside of the iteration activities and more at the cultural and strategic needs of the testing operation. He thinks it is necessary to have someone representing testing at the same level as the development director, to ensure a balanced approach that considers each discipline equally. Often in larger organizations, the disciplines are more specialized, so this may make sense. Adam also works to ensure that the organization has the appropriate balance of skills across the testing operation and that the testers in the agile teams are working collaboratively and not duplicating effort.

A test manager can also be a type of coach for the communities of practice within an organization. The test manager is not there to prescribe but can facilitate learning sessions where interested parties can discuss new ideas. As we said, there is no one right way. Understand your context and what you need, so you can practice agility and get the most benefit for your organization.

Reach out to the global software development and testing communities for help in making cultural changes that support building quality in, delivering value frequently, and working at a sustainable pace. We will mention some helpful online communities in Chapter 6, "How to Learn."

Summary

This chapter was about the importance of changing and adapting organizational culture. We stressed some ideas that need nurturing at a team and organizational level:

- Focus on quality, which leads to long-term sustainable pace and consistency of delivery in software development.
- Build slack into your workload by improving software delivery capability and managing scope, so your company can respond to opportunities.
- Nurture a learning culture where teams identify impediments to quality and have time to try small experiments to improve testing practices and processes.
- Educate stakeholders about how good practices pay back for the business.
- Make your process visible to help build trust between executives and delivery teams.
- Remember to celebrate successes, big and small.

Part II

LEARNING FOR BETTER TESTING

As the years go by, we encounter more and more teams where people in all roles, not only the testers, engage in testing activities. At the same time, we've found that as testers, we need to broaden and deepen our range of skills in order to help our teams deliver the value our customers require.

In Part II, we'll explore team roles and competencies related to testing and quality, along with the types of skills needed to create high-quality software, from both a "thinking" perspective and a "technical" perspective. The last chapter in this part emphasizes the importance of learning for individuals and teams.

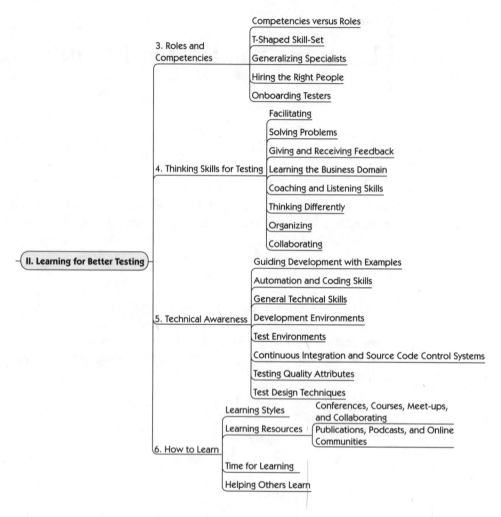

- ▪ **Chapter 3,** "Roles and Competencies"
- ▪ **Chapter 4,** "Thinking Skills for Testing"
- ▪ **Chapter 5,** "Technical Awareness"
- ▪ **Chapter 6,** "How to Learn"

Chapter 3

ROLES AND COMPETENCIES

The range of testing challenges that any team may encounter seems to widen on a daily basis. Your team may work on a web-based product and suddenly, your company decides it also needs an app that works on mobile devices. Teams adopt new technologies, development practices, tools, and frameworks while, at the same time, customer priorities shift. It follows that testing activities will have to change, too.

One of the ways teams handle these changes without constantly being in chaos is by managing what and how they learn.

Self-Managed Teams

Bernice Niel Ruhland, *a director of quality management, shares her thoughts about self-managed teams.*

We often hear about the benefits and success of self-managed teams. For some people the change can be liberating, whereas others might find it challenging. Providing a team with a project and letting them determine how to manage the work tasks can be daunting. I have encountered self-managed teams that cannot move forward without an assigned leader. Some people look to be assigned tasks; others do not feel comfortable telling other people what to do; and sometimes one or two people end up with the bulk of the work.

This does not mean these teams cannot make the transition to being self-managed; they just need help. I find it helpful to hold an initial team meeting to discuss the project, answer questions, and help the team set ground rules, with a manager, coach, or facilitator present. As a facilitator, I can work with them to define milestones but allow them to determine how they will work together. If you're in a lead or managerial role, try to delegate most of the responsibility to the team. If they are struggling with self-organizing, have a coach periodically attend a meeting to help guide when needed. However, as soon as it is reasonable, turn the meeting back over to the team.

Sessions where each team member discusses his or her skills and potential contribution to the project have also proven useful for my teams. Often people have hidden skills of which their peers are not aware. As an example, a tester may have experience with a programming language that could be used to automate some repetitive work. Progress the conversation past technical skills to include skills such as time management, conflict resolution, and relationships internal and external to the team that might be beneficial. If helpful, create a skills matrix to get the team started. Over time, shift the focus from documented skills to building relationships within the team.

Building trust between team members is even more important for a self-managed team. Some teams share common interests and create personal relationships. There are many different types of team-building activities; just be sure to use techniques that the team respects.

During retrospectives, ask what works to reinforce good behavior and discuss what team members find challenging to help make changes. Be sure to celebrate the successes and help to facilitate change when needed.

COMPETENCIES VERSUS ROLES

We've seen a positive move toward emphasizing competencies in a team rather than roles or titles. As teams make that change, we see fewer "It's not my job" excuses and more "How can I help?" conversations. Team members will continue to have core competencies in some areas more than others, but they may not identify as strongly with a particular role. For example, saying, "I am a tester" really means, "I perform mainly testing activities because that is my primary passion and strength. I can provide leadership and guidance to others, and I may also help in other areas."

Are Titles Important?

*One day at a conference, **Pete Walen**, from Michigan, USA, was giving out his business card, so Janet happily accepted it. However, his title caught her attention, so she asked him about it. Here's his response.*

My business card has three different things on it, other than my name and contact information.

The obvious item is "Software Tester." That is what I do, in one form or another. I test software and work with people who also test software and help them do a better job of testing.

"Software Anthropologist" was added after much consideration. It was finally added at CAST (Conference of the Association for Software Testing) in 2011. Michael Bolton gave a talk on software development, and testing in particular, as a social science. This triggered consideration in my mind and set other things in motion. Crucial among them were questions around interaction among and between software applications and how people interact with the same software. In evaluating how software behaves, these interactions are important and form an integral part of what makes testing, testing.

This brings us to the third and most important item, "Question Asker." It seems quality assurance, QA, is a term that often gets mixed up with testing and has for as long as I have been in software development. This has irked me for some time. In 2009 I found myself in a conversation with Michael Bolton, Fiona Charles, Lynn McKee, Nancy Kelln, and a few others. In the course of the conversation, the idea of "testers asking questions that lead to information on how the software behaves or is expected to behave" kept floating in and out. Asking questions leads us to information about the software, how we interact with it, and, ultimately, more questions—at least, more questions until all the questions of interest to us and the stakeholders have been asked and answered.

Which brings us back to "Software Tester."

We like the term *question asker*, which can also be useful in planning sessions. See Part IV, "Testing Business Value," for more on this subject.

Teams in which Lisa has worked have blurred the lines between roles. Some programmers are experienced testers. Sometimes it's a tester who comes up with a simple solution to a tricky code design problem. In addition, individuals with a wide range of competencies fill more than one role. For example, Lisa's current team has coders who also do system administration and have operations duties.

In the past few years, terms such as DevOps have gained wider use, indicating the interdependence of software development with infrastructure and operations. Although the terms may be newly popular, doing work normally done by someone in a specialized role has been a hallmark of agile teams. (We will explore the mutually beneficial collaboration between DevOps and testers in Chapter 23, "Testing and DevOps.")

Forget Developers in Test; We Need Testers in Development

Trish Khoo, *a test engineer originally from Australia, shares her experiences of what happens when the whole team thinks about testing.*

Last year I started working on a small team with developers who really value testing and treat it as an integral part of the development cycle. I'll never forget one of our first planning meetings when we were discussing a feature that we were about to build and a developer frowned and said, "Yeah, but how are we going to test it?" As a result, they changed the whole design.

I think I just about fainted with shock, having never heard that in my career. The key part of this was that it wasn't the team asking me, the tester, how *I* was going to test it. It was a question asked of the whole team: "How are we as a team going to test it? How can we build this so that we have confidence that it will work as we build it?"

As we built features, the developers would always write tests—everything from unit tests to browser-level tests—and have another developer do some manual testing before it was passed to me for testing in a fully integrated environment. By the time it was handed to me this way, I rarely found bugs that were due to carelessness. Most of the bugs I found were due to user scenarios or system scenarios that hadn't been thought of earlier.

So you might think, as a tester, did I really have much to do on a team like this? My most valuable asset in this process was still the way I thought about the product from a testing standpoint, from a user standpoint. What I found was that my testing expertise became less valuable at the end of the cycle and much more valuable at the start.

The more effort I put into testing the product conceptually at the start of the process, the less effort I had to put into manually testing the product at the end because fewer bugs would emerge as a result.

I just want to break that last bit out into a big fancy-font quote here because I think it's quite important. ***The more effort I put into testing the product conceptually at the start of the process, the less effort I had to put into manually testing the product at the end.***

But the key part of this was that I knew that the development team was testing the product effectively by thinking about testing, writing tests, and manually testing as the product was being developed. I could trust that if we had thought of a scenario during planning, it would be effectively developed and tested with automated regression tests in place by the end of the process.

I've had a lot of discussions this year around the role of the tester. Let's put that aside for now and start thinking about the role of a software developer. A software developer needs to be able to build a product with confidence that it does what it's expected to do. Knowing how to do that at a basic level should be critical to the role of a good software developer. For that reason, we need more testing in software development. And it needs to be done by the people who are building the product.

Having a testing specialist on the team is a valuable asset, but the responsibility for testing shouldn't be restricted to a single person. You might also have a database specialist on your team, but it doesn't mean that he or she is the only person working with databases. The same goes for testing. The specialist can help with the really difficult testing problems, knowing that the rest of the team is capable of dealing with the simple testing problems.

Then it's shorter feedback loops, greater confidence, and faster quality releases for all. Who doesn't love that?

We explored the interaction between customer and developer teams in *Agile Testing*. Since then, many agile teams have incorporated specialists with different competencies. For example, it's more common now to find business analysts on an agile team, as well as testers who are doing a lot of business analysis activities. Boundaries between roles continue to blur. At the same time, creating a cross-functional team doesn't mean dispensing with specialties. It's been our experience that teams often feel blocked because a particular skill set is missing from their team.

Sometimes the solution is simple: hire someone with those skills, or find ways to train existing team members.

Lisa's Story

At my last job, my team became frustrated because we'd start a new iteration with several stories that were not well defined by the business experts at the parent company. As a result, we were constantly going to the product owner for clarification of requirements, or to show him what we had developed, only to be told it was wrong.

We testers suggested hiring a business analyst (BA) who could work with the product owner to help the customers better articulate what they needed. Our product owner was unfamiliar with the new parent company, and although he met with the stakeholders, he didn't know the right questions to ask to get to the heart of the features they wanted. A skilled BA would know how to collaborate with the customers and ask the right questions.

Unfortunately, the manager wasn't willing to hire a BA, so we formed a business analysis community of practice. Testers, the product owner, the ScrumMaster, the development manager, and interested programmers got together and identified ways to build our analysis skills. We read books and articles, attended conference workshops, and participated in webinars to gain competency in business analysis. We met at regular intervals to share information and documented it on the team wiki.

It might have been better to hire an expert, but our efforts paid off. The product owner learned techniques to use when meeting with stakeholders from the parent company, so he understood the desired features better. We still sometimes lacked context for what business problems the customers were trying to solve, but we no longer spent so much time going back and forth to the product owner for information on the stories we were developing.

T-SHAPED SKILL SET

In *Agile Testing*, we described ten principles for agile testers, which emphasized attitude and mindset over specific technical skills. As a quick review, they are:

- Provide continuous feedback.
- Deliver value to the customer.
- Enable face-to-face communication.
- Have courage.
- Keep it simple.
- Practice continuous improvement.

- Respond to change.
- Self-organize.
- Focus on people.
- Enjoy.

However, we still hear the question, "Do testers on agile teams need to be programmers?"

Our answer is that testers need T-shaped skills (see Figure 3-1), a term first defined by David Guest (Guest, 1991). To work effectively on any given team, we need both broad and deep skill sets. Broad knowledge in areas other than our own specialty enables us to collaborate across disciplines with experts in other roles. Deep knowledge and extensive practice in a single field ensure that we bring something essential to the team. Rob Lambert has a nice blog post on this subject (Lambert, 2012).

The top of testers' "T" typically includes technical skills such as a basic understanding of their system's architecture, knowledge of general programming concepts and design principles, ability to do basic database queries, and competence with such tools as integrated development environments (IDEs) and continuous integration (CI) dashboards.

Team members in other roles need basic testing concepts among other skills in their T-bar. Shallow domain knowledge may be adequate in

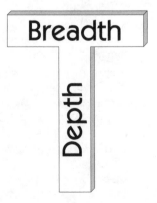

Figure 3-1   T-shaped skill set

some situations. In others, the ability to deliver business value requires that some team members, perhaps testers or business analysts, need to know the business in depth. Get the whole team together to talk about T-shaped skills and how to fill in any gaps. And don't forget those ten principles for agile testers. Attitude really is everything.

Square-Shaped Team

Adam Knight, *a director of QA and support in the UK, shares his story about his experience with T-shaped team members to make a square-shaped team.*

My team and I have been working on testing a Big Data storage system for seven years. The system is a large-scale data storage system combined with a SQL query engine that runs on various operating systems, primarily Linux. One of the major problems that I have encountered in testing a product of this nature is the range of relevant skills that are required to perform all of the tasks necessary to test the system. The testers in our company needed the ability not only to test the product from the perspective of the various stakeholders, but also to build and maintain the various testing environments and architectures that were needed. Some of the skills that we required were

- Operating system knowledge in Linux/UNIX to create and maintain test environments and monitor those environments to assess the impact of the software upon them

- Virtualization and cloud knowledge to expand the testing into environments that could support the multiple machine clustered environments

- Scripting knowledge to continuously develop and maintain the numerous harnesses required to test the product via the server command-line tools

- Programming knowledge to develop and maintain the harnesses required for functional and scalability testing of the client API interfaces where these differed from our core product programming languages of C and C++

- SQL and database knowledge to understand the implementation domain and test the extensive SQL engine with a range of realistic queries

- Exploratory testing skills to identify and exercise the range of states and combination of operations that can affect the data storage layer

It became apparent very quickly that we were unlikely to find such a wealth of skills in one individual. Instead, I took the approach of trying to populate the team with a number of testers who, in combination, possessed the range of skills that would allow the team to address the multiple challenges that it was facing. Each individual would need to have a general set of abilities to understand the product and the general testing approach.

As we brought on new team members, we made sure that each one possessed a deep set of abilities, which included the priority skills the team had identified. These abilities were complementary to those of the other team members and to those of the team as a whole.

When I first read about the concept of the "T-shaped" individual, it resonated with what we were doing. The idea of a broad set of general skills combined with a deep core of specialist abilities was exactly the shape of individual that we had tried to recruit. So, for example, I was already very fortunate to work with one tester who possessed solid database and SQL language knowledge combined with domain knowledge from a previous role as a database administrator (DBA).

We employed one individual with strong scripting skills to maintain the core harness, backed up with excellent exploratory testing abilities. Another had great operating system abilities to create test environments, virtual clusters, and Hadoop and cloud testing, combined with knowledge of soak and performance testing. Figure 3-2 shows how each tester has different depth of skills with the same breadth.

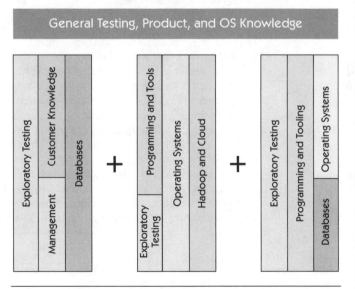

Figure 3-2   Three testers with different strengths

I felt that the T-shaped concept was missing one of the core reasons for our taking the approach that we did. The concept of the T-shaped individual is limited to exactly that: an individual. What I felt was the true power of the T-shaped tester was when those individuals combined their abilities into a team in the manner that we had done, a concept I labeled the "square-shaped team," as shown in Figure 3-3.

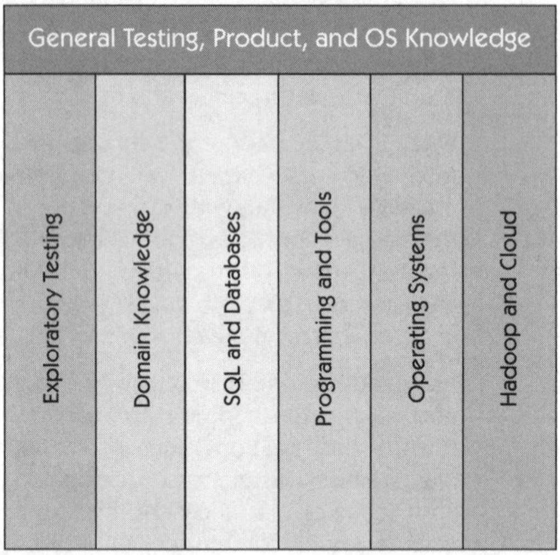

Figure 3-3   Square-shaped team

Each tester we've hired has brought unique skills to the team. Some of these skills we knew were a priority when we were in the process of hiring; others were less apparent at the time but still valid. For example, one tester we hired was less of an obvious choice, having a consulting background working on implementation projects. This meant, however, that his abilities in reporting and requirements analysis made him an excellent addition for understanding stakeholder concerns and defining acceptance criteria accordingly. I've also used his exceptional test reporting as an exemplar to the rest of the team. If we had looked at such an individual in isolation, he or she may not have been considered for a testing role on the product. By taking a holistic approach to building the team, we could integrate new members well, and all would benefit from the unique perspective that each one had.

Like Adam, we think it is important to look at the team skills as well as the individual. Together the whole team can solve most anything. Don't be afraid to look around you and use the knowledge that other people bring to the table.

GENERALIZING SPECIALISTS

Agile development attracts generalizing specialists. This term has been used to mean individuals with a deep level of knowledge in at least one domain and an understanding of at least one other. Hmm, sounds a lot like T-shaped skills. Sometimes the term is used to describe a person who is good at everything, but that is not what we mean. We run the risk of diluting our strengths, and instead of doing a few things well, we do many things with mediocrity. However, in order to collaborate well with team members in other roles, we need to know some basics of their specialty.

Becoming a Generalizing Specialist

> **Matt Barcomb**, *an organizational design specialist, shares his ideas about how a generalizing specialist evolves.*

It's one thing to know what a generalizing specialist is, but how do you actually go about becoming one? Most people spend a lot of time becoming very good at their specialty but don't understand how to generalize effectively without simply becoming a specialist in another area.

What a Generalizing Specialist Isn't

I've been to a number of places in the past few years where management glommed onto the term too excitedly. The enticing but misguided belief was that programmers, testers, designers, analysts, technical writers, release engineers, and just about everyone else (except the managers) would all eventually know how to do each other's work and could be swapped, interchangeably, for any other person on the team. Imagine how simple the resource-balancing spreadsheets and project plans would become!

That situation is not a team of generalizing specialists; it would be a team of generalizing generalists. It is also pure fiction, as it would be impossible for all the people involved in releasing enterprise software to know every other person's function with the depth that would be needed to deliver effectively.

So What Is a Generalizing Specialist?

Being a generalist on a cross-functional team means being able to effectively appreciate, communicate with, and collaborate with other team members and roles with different specialties. It does not mean the person can do the same work as different specialists with equal skill or enthusiasm.

For example, a programmer with a deep knowledge of code craft is not interchangeable with a tester and vice versa. However, both might be able to collaborate, as a pair, on either person's tasks. Ideally the difference is obvious and the example could just as easily be applied to any other role on the team, such as tester, designer, analyst, operations, technical writer, or even manager!

How to Become a Generalizing Specialist

There are many approaches to becoming a generalizing specialist. There is no one right way to learn, and ultimately becoming a generalizing specialist is all about learning!

I approach becoming T-shaped as a skill acquisition problem. There are many models for skill acquisition, but for the purpose of becoming a generalizing specialist I use three categories: (1) Basic, (2) Advanced, and (3) Meta, combined with an associated amount of "stuff to learn." The amount of stuff to learn varies based on the category; Basic has a small amount, Advanced has the most significant amount, and finally Meta has a lower amount, but more than Basic.

This might look like the model shown in Figure 3-4.

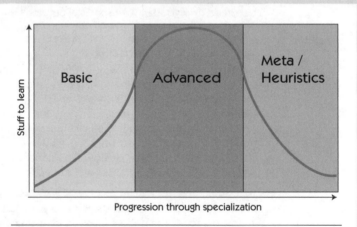

Figure 3-4   Model for becoming a generalizing specialist

This model actually shows how to become a specialist. However, it also offers hints for how to become a generalist. According to the model, every beginner has to learn the basics of a skill or specialty (like testing or programming). This is equally true for generalists or aspiring specialists.

So, the first step to becoming a generalist is that you have to learn the basics of the specialty. For a tester on a cross-functional team, this might mean the technical awareness that Lisa and Janet refer to in Chapter 5, "Technical Awareness." For example, testers might learn more about the deployment pipeline or target environments; they might learn about how to query a database, or about the syntax, structures, and tools the programmers use for developing the product.

The specialist then spends years (sometime the majority of a career) learning the advanced subject matter of his or her specialty and even longer to derive the Meta knowledge about the specialty. Obviously, having everyone on a cross-functional team spend so much time to learn a specialty is not the most effective way to become a generalizing specialist. So the question is, How can an individual continue to grow as a generalist but skip over the years required to progress through Advanced and into Meta?

The answer to the question lies in understanding the nature of the derived Meta skills. Meta knowledge of a specialty is that intuitive, tacit knowledge one develops after years of applying advanced knowledge from a specialty in many different situations—almost a sixth sense within a domain. A specialist might describe something as "just not feeling right" or the "shape" or "smell" of something like the code, design, or architecture of a product. The point is that there is something the specialist is sensing, some sign to look for.

Such signs can be taught to non-specialists as heuristics or rules of thumb and is the next way a generalist can grow. A generalist can pair with a specialist and offer valuable help with signal detection of potential problems. The heuristic may not always be right, but that's OK; that's how rules of thumb work. So, while knowing how to correctly apply Meta knowledge in a given situation can take years to develop, generalists can be taught the heuristic signals to look for.

Some examples of this for a tester generalizing toward programming might be the rules of clean code (Martin, 2009), the principle of DRY (don't repeat yourself), length or counts of classes, variables, function arguments, or too many if-statements in a method. The generalist would not need to know how to fix these things, and sometimes there may be good reasons that a rule is being broken. The value-add is helping the specialist with signal detection, not problem correction.

> The reason this is valuable is because individuals tend to engage at a lower level or in a more focused and analytical way when executing a task or implementing something. Applying Meta knowledge or looking for heuristics requires a higher-level view or a more abstract way of thinking about the task at hand. It is difficult for a single person to perform a task in both an analytical and an abstract fashion simultaneously.
>
> So, when generalists learn the basics and, more importantly, the heuristics of a specialty, they are able to more effectively communicate with those specialists. This is a very important first step in having an effective cross-functional team. Moving from communication toward true collaboration is key for a more mature cross-functional team.

The concept of generalizing specialists applies to all roles on the team, not only testers. When programmers learn testing basics, they can communicate more effectively with testers and learn better ways to prevent defects and build quality in as they develop the software. In our experience, pairing with a tester is the easiest way for programmers to build up their testing knowledge.

Lisa's teams benefited from documenting checklists and specialized testing information on the team wiki. While information on a wiki is no substitute for face-to-face conversation, it can serve as a memory jogger.

In Chapter 6, "How to Learn," we will explore ways that testers can learn the basics of other specialties such as programming and database design so that they can communicate more easily with teammates in other roles.

HIRING THE RIGHT PEOPLE

Lisa was influenced early in her agile career by Alistair Cockburn's paper "Characterizing People as Non-Linear, First-Order Components in Software Development" (Cockburn, 1999). After studying dozens of software projects over 20 years, he found that the common success factor in software development was that "a few good people stepped in at key moments." Having good people made projects successful, not the programming language, tools, or methodology used.

In our experience, it's critical to get people with the right attitude for the team. Take the time you need to find testers who are a good fit. If you hire people who express curiosity, want to learn, and aren't shy about going out of their comfort zone, they can be trained for your specific needs. Although colocation has great advantages over distributed teams, consider enlarging your geographical search. Testers working remotely can be effective if the team is disciplined about using good communication practices and takes advantage of today's technology.

Hiring Geeks That Fit by Johanna Rothman (Rothman, 2012b) offers more help on finding and hiring testers with cultural fit and the abilities your team needs. Each individual brings his or her strengths and unique perspective, and it's important to look at all aspects of the value each individual contributes. Diversity within a team is essential to get different perspectives. Sometimes the person who isn't a good fit at the beginning, but is passionate about delivering a quality product for the customer, may still play a valuable role.

ONBOARDING TESTERS

Even experienced agile testers need help finding their place on a new team. We find it helpful to set expectations. What can that person expect to know by the end of the first day? The first week? The first month? Put this information on a wiki page or some other easily accessible and maintainable location.

Help the new hire get to know members of both the development and customer teams. Provide a list of "who knows what," and introduce the new person to each of those people. Schedule time for the new person to sit with business experts and find out what they do in their jobs. Take steps to ensure that the new tester has plenty of time to learn and doesn't feel pressure to "produce" right away. Help the new hire feel safe about asking for help and posing questions at any time.

In our experience, pairing is the best way to bring new people up to speed. Pair the new tester up with other testers, with programmers, with BAs, with DevOps, with business experts. It's helpful to assign a buddy or mentor as the first line of support for the new hire; the two can act as a default pair. There's a bonus to pairing with the new person who provides a fresh set of eyes.

I was pairing with a highly experienced tester who was new to our financial services domain. One of our test results came out a few pennies different from the expected result. I'd seen this many times over the years and wrote it off to a rounding difference. But the discrepancy bugged our new tester. He went over to talk to one of the programmers about it.

It turned out to be an actual bug that we had all been ignoring for years. Tests were written, the problem was fixed, and we no longer saw the discrepancies. Pennies add up, so I feel bad thinking that some of our customers may have been slightly shortchanged! Nothing beats a fresh set of eyes. Lesson learned: don't discount anything a new tester observes!

Be creative as you plan training for your team's new tester. Set up a session with someone who can explain the system architecture. Schedule time for a programmer or system administrator to walk the new tester through the CI process. Provide training on the automated test suites and the living documentation that these provide. One-to-one discussions add tremendous value to the regular practice of reading all the documentation because the new employee has an opportunity to ask questions. New team members may get overwhelmed with the complexity of trying to learn everything at once. Try breaking the training into smaller chunks. Perhaps after a session of training, give them a charter to explore that area. There's more on charters and exploratory testing in Chapter 12, "Exploratory Testing."

Mike Talks told us that he tries to spend 15 to 30 minutes every day for the first two weeks catching up with new employees. After that, he drops it to weekly, and then monthly. It will be many months before they're up to speed, so don't try to rush the process. Everyone benefits from a thoughtful approach to bringing along a new tester.

SUMMARY

Teams that succeed in creating high-quality software include people in a variety of roles and with a wide range of competencies. Look for ways to get the ones you need on your team.

- Teams whose members have a variety of T-shaped skill sets succeed with testing in fast-changing environments.
- All team members need broad agile testing basics, allowing them to collaborate well for improving quality, but each one may contribute a different deep, specialized skill.
- Testers communicate better with programmers, business analysts, product owners, managers, DevOps practitioners, and other team members when they know the basic concepts of those other specialties.
- Hire team members who are passionate about quality and learning, whose T-shaped skills complement each other's.
- Set realistic expectations for new hires, and build in visibility and feedback.

Chapter 4

THINKING SKILLS FOR TESTING

4. Thinking Skills for Testing
- Facilitating
- Solving Problems
- Giving and Receiving Feedback
- Learning the Business Domain
- Coaching and Listening Skills
- Thinking Differently
- Organizing
- Collaborating

The *Oxford English Dictionary* defines soft skills this way: "personal attributes that enable someone to interact effectively and harmoniously with other people." "Soft" seems to imply that these skills are easier to learn or less important than "hard" skills such as technical competencies. There's a lot of debate over the best term to describe these abilities. Some like to call them people skills. We prefer the term *thinking skills*, because in addition to our relationships with people, these skills apply to other areas such as problem solving, understanding the business domain, using the right thinking style for a given testing activity, and organizing our time.

Thinking skills are not tangible in the sense that we can say, "I've learned that; I can practice it perfectly now." Abilities such as communication, collaboration, facilitation, problem solving, and prioritization can be the most difficult to master, yet they are the most crucial for success in agile testing.

In many organizations, when testers are part of a separate team, they tend to talk only to other testers, possibly to programmers, but rarely to anyone on the customer team. On agile teams, however, testers and other team members work closely with business stakeholders and product owners and managers to elicit requirements and uncover hidden assumptions. Programmers, analysts, and team members in other roles also contribute to eliciting requirements, helping to address the impact of technical issues and dependencies. This is why concepts such as systems thinking—how we got here, and what changes impact other parts of the system—are so critical.

Testers and other team members engaged in testing and quality-focused activities can apply interpersonal and leadership skills to help the development and customer teams improve their software product and process.

FACILITATING

Activities such as specification workshops (Adzic, 2009) work best when someone skilled in facilitating helps to guide the discussion. A facilitator (see Figure 4-1) who isn't engaged in capturing the requirements would be ideal, but any team member who has key thinking skills, such as how to get people in different roles to work together and stay focused on a common objective, can step up if needed. Specification workshop facilitators help stakeholders set business goals and help both the development and customer team members collaboratively define the scope that will achieve those goals.

Similar skills help you facilitate informal brainstorming sessions, ensuring that each participant feels free to express ideas without being

Figure 4-1   Facilitation helps teams gain common understanding.

criticized. Working on acquiring these skills helps you find creative ways for your team to solve problems. See the bibliography for Part II, "Learning for Better Testing," for more recommended books to help you hone your facilitation skills for gathering requirements and collaborating effectively.

Solving Problems

When we talk about nontechnical skills, we don't mean they are easy to master. For example, many of us continually work to improve our problem-solving skills; some university computer science or IT programs may teach skills like this, but often they aren't in the curriculum. People generally need to acquire them on the job.

Janet's Story	I remember when I first wrote my exam for the ASQ Certified Quality Manager, I failed the written part, which was how to address two specific problems. I believe I failed because I didn't remember how to apply my problem-solving skills. I first learned those skills when I took Physics 101 at the University of Alberta, but I didn't apply them on a regular basis. When I failed my exam, I sat back, figured out the root cause, and went back to basics by reviewing how to solve a problem. In physics, that started with drawing a picture. I rewrote my exam following the principles of problem solving and passed. I then presented what worked for me to the next group of people who wanted to write the exam, which reinforced what I had learned.

Problem solving is one of those transferable skills that can be applied to test design, debugging, coaching, or teaching. Perhaps the most useful thinking skill is to know how to help your team address its problems, rather than going in and fixing the symptoms. Courses such as Problem Solving Leadership (PSL) (Derby et al., 2014) are a good way to learn how your team can reframe problems, resolve conflicts, and communicate more effectively. You don't have to be in a management position to provide leadership for your team and help them improve their problem-solving effectiveness.

Tools that help us visualize our thinking, such as mind mapping, impact mapping (see Chapter 9, "Are We Building the Right Thing?"), and root-cause analysis tools, are good additions to a toolkit for testing. The "5 Whys" (Wikipedia, 2014a) use an iterative question-asking technique to explore root causes of a problem. Fishbone or Ishikawa diagrams (Wikipedia, 2014h) can be used for defect prevention and for identifying risks and potential pitfalls. After generating ideas in a brainstorming session, use techniques such as affinity diagrams or impact maps (see Figure 4-2) to organize the insights and potential experiments. Try different thinking tools to help elicit requirements and examples from customers. Drawing on a physical or virtual whiteboard enhances communication and creativity. Try it the next time your team gets together to identify impediments and experiments to chip away at them.

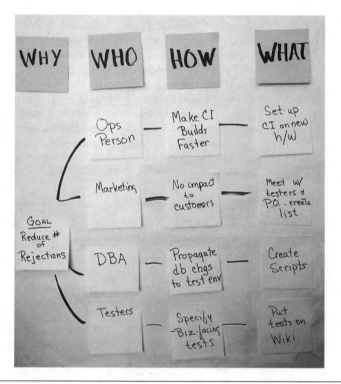

Figure 4-2   Sample impact map

GIVING AND RECEIVING FEEDBACK

Giving and receiving feedback is almost an art form. Ideally, the giver's intention is to aid in the receiver's learning and to grow the relationship between them. We learned from Ellen Gottesdiener that feedback may actually say more about the giver than the receiver. The person giving feedback is basing it on his or her perceptions, and it is shaped by the person's emotions at the time of giving. Since we tend to give feedback about what matters to us, not what matters most to the other person, it is easy to miss context. Our tone, the words we choose, and our nonverbal communication may obscure our message.

Bear this in mind when you feel the urge to deliver your observations to another person. Think about how you'd want to receive the same feedback. Knowing how to keep the focus on the work, not on the person, is essential. Bug reporting is one way to provide feedback, but usually not the most effective. It takes time and practice to learn how to engage colleagues in a positive exchange when talking about negative issues. For example, "I read this to say . . . could it be changed to be more meaningful?" comes across better than, "You must change this. . . ."

Jurgen Appelo's "Feedback Wrap" workout (Appelo, 2013) describes ways to give constructive feedback that helps build trust within the team. As Jurgen notes, giving feedback gets harder to do as so many teams have less face time with coworkers, due to distributed teams, remote working, and flexible hours. He points out that written feedback, done in an honest and friendly way, allows you to think more carefully and present observations and feelings in a more balanced way. It can be done fast and frequently. Experiment with different ways to provide timely feedback to team members, and keep inspecting and adapting your feedback process.

Empathy is essential for providing good feedback. Think about how you would want to receive unwelcome information. Toastmasters International, a nonprofit organization for public speaking, teaches skills for giving speech evaluations, and these are transferable to providing feedback on software teams. Giving feedback and providing information are part of testing, and there are many opportunities to practice. In collaboration with stakeholders, identify ways to measure how successful a new feature might be. Make testing visible and transparent. If your customers always know the team's current status and trust that they'll be told of any risks or issues, they'll be more receptive to any news (good or bad) you have to deliver. Testers learn constructive ways to provide feedback, such as showing defects to programmers, without causing offense or hurt feelings. This sensitivity applies anytime you're delivering feedback.

We've talked a lot about giving feedback. What about receiving it? Strive to understand what the message being delivered is about before you jump to conclusions. Thank the people who give you feedback for their honest input. Ask questions to clarify. Too often we, as receivers, take in the emotion and the delivery rather than the message. Receivers may also have previous experiences that could cause them to hear something different from what was actually said. Listen to learn. See the bibliography for Part II for recommended readings to learn good feedback techniques.

LEARNING THE BUSINESS DOMAIN

Domain knowledge is an example of a skill that may be either part of your broad set of skills or part of your specialty—deep and thorough. Teams with both a broad and deep understanding of the business can better help stakeholders prioritize features, simplify solutions, or even offer alternatives outside of new software to solve a problem.

Lisa's Story

Learning firsthand how customers use a software product helps us do a better job of delivering the right value to them. On my current team, testers handle customer support via email, with help from the programmers. We also monitor our product's community forum. We've had to practice our patience and tact so we can ask good questions, listen to the responses, and build a rapport with users so they feel free to share their feedback. We learn firsthand how our customers use our product and get valuable feedback on what features would provide the most value for them. We use our judgment to decide when an issue or feature request needs to be escalated. We often encounter scenarios that provide useful test cases or test charters for us to use while testing new features.

I've had a lot of experience working in customer support for a software product company. Understanding the product from the users' perspective has proven valuable for helping to build in the quality they desire.

Knowing how the business operates allows you to explore the software in the same ways real end users will use it. Not only does this prevent bugs from going out to production, but testers and other team members with domain knowledge can also give business experts ideas for new features.

Learning the Domain with Help from the Call Center

Mike Talks, *a software tester from New Zealand, shares an experience he had collaborating with call center staff and learning more about how they used their product.*

A few years ago, I worked for a very delivery-focused but diverse team at a bank. What was superb about this situation was that I had access to everyone who was connected to the product.

What turned out to be really useful was having access to the call center staff. They gave me a practical introduction to how they used the product day to day. Some features and behavior I found a little surprising, but it led to me getting to know how the system actually worked. I learned to demonstrate that knowledge to marketing managers, business analysts, and product owners.

It was great to be colocated so these kinds of relationships could be built up. The relationship with the call center was really something important. I'd sometimes show them behavior on upcoming builds, but likewise they'd show me any "oddness" in production. It seems call center staff have a different mentality from testers, in that if something goes wrong, they don't want to touch it again.

It was a really rewarding team because I felt we were all contributing toward a goal, with no barriers to communication.

COACHING AND LISTENING SKILLS

A team member with good coaching skills is better able to help less experienced team members. Since everyone on an agile team engages in testing activities, it's much more valuable to guide others in solving their own testing and quality issues than to just give them the answers.

Telling stories from your own experience is a powerful way to demonstrate how something can be done. It depersonalizes criticism and allows people to remember how you handled a specific problem; they can learn to adapt your solution to their context. Think about how you have handled certain situations and how you can apply that experience to your current context. Storytelling doesn't come naturally to many people; it takes practice. See the Part II bibliography for references on coaching.

Observing and listening (see Figure 4-3) are critical communication and collaboration skills. Is someone complaining? Maybe it's a legitimate complaint. Does a teammate have an idea but feels too shy to speak up? Give her a comfortable opportunity to share with you over coffee. Knowing when and how to listen helps the team grow and improve. As

Figure 4-3 Listening—seeking to understand

Naomi Karten has pointed out (Karten, 2009), listening is a sometimes-overlooked component of being a good collaborator.

THINKING DIFFERENTLY

We've discussed several thinking skills that we find helpful as we engage in testing activities. Be conscious of the style of thinking you adopt for each situation. The next story explains some thinking tools and styles.

Thinking for Testing

Sharon Robson, *a software testing practice lead from Australia, shared her experiences with ways people tasked with testing can maximize their time by applying basic thinking skills.*

Thinking is a skill that can be learned and improved. As with any skill, practice and exposure to new techniques and approaches can hone an innate or organic talent. By learning about and practicing new ways of thinking, basic skills can be sharpened and new skill levels exposed. We all think, but thinking constructively, with purpose and the goal of achieving the desired outcomes, is an ever-evolving skill set.

There are many different ways of thinking, such as critical thinking (examining the accuracy of a statement), analytical thinking (decomposing the subject into component parts and considering them and their relationships), and creative thinking (synthesizing new knowledge from existing data). Testers need to recognize the skill needed in each situation and pick and choose the tools that will assist them in gaining the desired outcome.

There are many different thinking tools that are available too, such as Socratic questioning (Wikipedia, 2014k), functional decomposition, prioritization, compare and contrast, Ishikawa diagrams for the more critical or analytical approaches, as well as the creative thinking approaches such as brainstorming, mind mapping, elaboration, and relationship mapping.

In *Pragmatic Thinking and Learning* (Hunt, 2008), Andy Hunt discusses the concept of L-Mode (linear and slow) and R-Mode (nonlinear, fast, "rich" mode) and how to employ these modes when needed. Tools such as working to define SMART (specific, measurable, achievable, relevant, and time-boxed) goals help people realize what mode they need to be in and then employ other tools to move to the right mode to maximize effective thinking. One of Hunt's most powerful tools is called the "beginner's mind"—keep asking, "What if . . . ?" a lot! Hunt also advocates taking time to see and understand clearly what is happening. He cleverly articulates that information is raw data. Knowledge imparts meaning to the information, and context allows true understanding. As testers, we should focus on gathering true understanding and not stop at information or knowledge. Much of a person's perception is based on prediction, and prediction is based on context and past experience. From the viewpoint of a tester, this is very powerful as our perceptions could be clouded and not reflect reality. Testers need to use their thinking skills to move beyond pure perception into evidence-based results.

The key is to recognize the type of thinking required and make the effort to go to the right thinking mode to meet the needs of the situation. There are a variety of works on thinking that cover these various thinking modes. Daniel Kahneman (Kahneman, 2011), in *Thinking, Fast and Slow*, discusses System 1 (intuitive, fast) and System 2 (systematic, slow) and talks about aspects that are important to testers, such as recognizing cognitive bias or the use of heuristics as a risk, and then methods that can be used to move from System 1 to System 2 to quantify and establish evidence of the information provided by System 1.

Edward de Bono (de Bono, 1998), in *Thinking for Action*, discusses the tools that can be used to enhance how testers look at and consider the information presented to them. Techniques such as OPV (other people's views) and Logic Bubbles (assuming everyone is very intelligent and that they think and act logically from their perspectives) can allow testers to identify when and where defects may occur. Professor de Bono also uses the "hypothesize and then prove it" approach—make a guess, then find the evidence to prove or disprove the guess. He focuses a lot on the mindset for testing in the types of information-gathering tools he introduces—checking (yes/no answers) versus exploring (asking open questions).

Elisabeth Hendrickson (Hendrickson, 2013) uses some fabulous tools for structured and focused thinking in *Explore It!*. She discusses using diagrams and maps to consider the solution from different aspects, and the heuristics of "always/never," "inverting the result," and "nouns and verbs" to focus the testing mind on the correct things. These tools are very useful in changing the way we think, which we often have to do.

Dan Ariely (Ariely, 2008) discusses the decisions we make and how as humans we tend toward the default position. As testers it is important that we recognize the default position and check our tendencies and those of the people using our solutions to be swayed (fairly or unfairly) by the options they are presented with. This can manifest in many ways, even cognitive bias (we agree with findings/evidence that supports our position and can fail to see things that refute our position).

Depending on what they are doing, testers may need to recognize their mode and make an effort (using tools) to move to a new mode.

See the bibliography for Part II for references to learn more about the ideas Sharon mentions.

ORGANIZING

Time is always a constraint, so if we're going to accomplish essential testing activities, good organizational skills are vital. Knowing how to plan and manage your time well, using approaches such as risk-based testing, can help you focus on the right tasks. With so many demands on time, including meetings, email, instant messages, planning, and tracking activities, it can be hard to do actual testing. It's too easy to end up thrashing, repeating the same tests over and over. Knowing how to organize your time also helps ensure that you have time to learn any other skills your project may require.

Janet's Story

In Chapter 3, "Roles and Competencies," we talked about competencies and strengths. I'll share a personal story about one of my strengths and how we incorporated it into the process of writing the book. We have deadlines that we agreed to with the publisher. Using my organizational skills, I created the release plan and kept it visible so Lisa and I could talk about risks and plan accordingly. I created the shared spreadsheet to keep track of who gave us stories and when they were updated. These simple tools helped to keep us on track; organization is essential in almost everything we do.

Of course, I have weaknesses, too. For example, wordsmithing is not my strength, so often when I have an idea, I convey it the best way I can and then have Lisa work her magic.

COLLABORATING

Be sensitive to the downsides of task switching as you plan each day. And if you're feeling overwhelmed, don't be afraid to ask for help. Agile testing needs to be a collaborative effort.

An Effective Collaboration Process

We've discussed a wide range of thinking and interpersonal skills in this chapter. **Sharon Robson** *pulls many of these together to show how they can help teams collaborate for more effective testing.*

One of the key goals of an agile team (ideally any team) is to collaborate on the work they are doing. Collaboration adds to the quality of the outputs and the buy-in of the team working together. However, collaboration is hard! To collaborate well, team members need to understand why they are collaborating and then plan how they will collaborate effectively and efficiently.

The Collaboration Process

All these steps need to be done as a team for each collaboration session. Each session should be focused on one goal and ideally not exceed one hour. Some sessions will need more process definition than others.

1. Define the goal of the session—ensure that there is a clear and specific outcome, for example, to define the XYZ stories, to elaborate story 57, to coordinate our work for the day. Once the goal is clearly understood and agreed, document it simply and move on to the next step.

2. Define the language to be used. Each session will use specific words that have contextual meaning; within the context of the session the meaning must be clearly understood by all collaborators. Any unclear, ambiguous, or confusing words should have definitions or assumptions made about them to enable the team to discuss step 3.

3. Define the process to achieve the goal (e.g., brainstorming, chartering, discussion, diagramming) based on the goal of the session. What activities need to be completed to achieve the goal? These are usually in the form of a discovery or investigation stage (brainstorming), then an analysis stage (grouping, discussing).

> These lead to an understanding or evaluation stage (diagramming or mapping), followed by a conclusion or decision stage.
>
> **4.** Set the time boxes for the process stages. Once all the stages have been set out, allocate times to each of them that fit within the overall time box. *Note:* Allow time for rework!
>
> **5.** Follow the process, adding to or tweaking the process, assumptions, and language as you go. Keep focusing on the goal! Keep asking yourself if the current activity is driving toward the goal.
>
> **6.** Assess the goal. Has it been met? If yes, conclude the session; if no, change something.
>
> **7.** Repeat steps 2 through 6 as necessary until the goal has been met.

The collaborative sessions Sharon describes require competent facilitation. Even if your team has an experienced facilitator, understanding meeting dynamics and learning facilitation skills will help everyone on the team get more value from meetings and collaboration sessions.

SUMMARY

Thinking skills play a big part in all aspects of software testing. Some of the most important ones to practice include

- Facilitating
- Problem solving
- Giving and receiving feedback
- Learning the business domain
- Coaching and listening skills
- Thinking differently, and applying different styles of thinking to different testing activities
- Organizing
- Collaborating, using a step-by-step process

Chapter 5

TECHNICAL AWARENESS

Thinking skills help the whole team work well together to ensure that all necessary testing activities are planned and executed. Technical testing skills help bridge the gap between what the business needs and how the delivery team supplies it. We've used the term *technical awareness* to cover the ideas of technical skills needed for testing and communicating with other members of the development team. The first time Janet heard the term *technical awareness* was at a local testing workshop where Lynn McKee used it during one of the discussions. It seemed to capture the intent without getting hung up on existing terms. We believe that testing is in itself a specialist technical skill, so we've decided to devote this chapter to many types of technical skills that will be useful in your agile testing toolkit.

GUIDING DEVELOPMENT WITH EXAMPLES

We have conversations with customers about examples of desired and undesired behavior for each new feature and story. These examples can be turned into automated business-facing tests that guide development. Some well-known approaches for this are specification by example (SBE), acceptance-test-driven development (ATDD), and behavior-driven development (BDD). If you're not yet familiar with these, check the bibliography for Part II, "Learning for Better Testing," for some good places to start learning. *ATDD by Example* by Markus Gärtner (Gärtner, 2012), *Specification by Example* by Gojko Adzic (Adzic, 2011), and *The Cucumber Book* by Matt Wynne and Aslak Hellesøy (Wynne and Hellesøy, 2012) are good introductions. Capturing appropriate examples and turning them into automated tests requires a certain amount of technical awareness to be able to collaborate with your programmers. We'll talk in more detail about this practice in Part IV, "Testing Business Value."

AUTOMATION AND CODING SKILLS

When testers collaborate with programmers, system administrators, database experts, and people in other technical roles, they can help each other design effective tests at all levels and automate day-to-day tasks such as deploying code to test environments. This collaboration is easier when testers have some technical knowledge and all development team members have some testing skills.

If testers learn to use the same integrated development environment (IDE) as the coders, pairing to look at code becomes easier, and the language used to discuss the application becomes a shared language.

Tests may be specified in a natural style, using a domain-specific language (DSL), or by using keywords or data to guide the tests. However, there is underlying code that executes the tests and produces the results. Someone has to write that, and test automation code is, well, code. If you, as a tester, do not know how to code, it is important to be able to understand what the code does.

When a team guides development with business examples and practices test-driven development (TDD), the tests help create good code. They provide living documentation of how the production code behaves and ensure that it keeps behaving that way. If the code needs changing later, the tests make doing so safer and faster. Therefore, we should treat test code with the same care and respect as production code—they are equally valuable.

Applying good design practices helps keep automation cost-effective. For example, we strive to keep each automated test focused on a single clear purpose and extract duplication into macros and modules. Our goal is to make it easy to diagnose test failures and change the tests in only one place when the code changes. You can find more detail about that in Chapter 16, "Test Automation Design Patterns and Approaches."

Learning how to write pseudo code can help you design automated tests. Gain a basic understanding of object-oriented principles like SOLID (Single responsibility, Open/closed, Liskov substitution, Interface segregation, Dependency inversion) (see Wikipedia, 2014m).

If you know how to read the code and understand your team's coding standards, you may be able to pair with programmers to write tests, review code, and perhaps help with debugging problems. At the very least, you'll be able to have meaningful conversations with the programmers on your team to learn which areas of the code are most fragile and where to focus testing efforts. This is also an opportunity to improve your coding and scripting skills. As a side benefit, you might uncover defects while you're pairing.

If you don't have programming experience, practice some basics on your own. Check the bibliography for Part II for helpful books on learning to code, such as *Everyday Scripting with Ruby* by Brian Marick (Marick, 2007). There are also online courses, tutorials, and screencasts.

Coding skills are also useful to help set up data and scenarios for exploratory testing charters. Even if you lack programming skills, knowing what could be automated will help you collaborate with programmers on your team to do time-saving automation and free testers up for activities where they contribute the most value.

Learn your software product's architecture, at least at a high level. Ask teammates to identify the risky areas. Lisa's team represents more fragile areas of the architecture with dotted lines in diagrams. This visibility helps you to focus on different types of testing effectively and consider test automation strategies together with your team. Systems design knowledge can help you test efficiently. For example, if you know that a search function used throughout the application is encapsulated in one part of the code, you may be able to test it thoroughly via an API and need only cursory checks in other parts of the application.

Understanding the system interfaces lets you recognize their possible weaknesses. There is more than the user interface (UI); watch for others such as logging and monitoring for operations, messaging, or communication protocols.

Figure 5-1 shows an example of the type of architecture diagram that provides a good starting point for understanding the components of a system and how they relate to each other. This one shows the architecture for an API that Lisa's team developed. It helped the team visualize how the software would generate user documentation and request validation data as well as execute commands to add, change, or delete data resources.

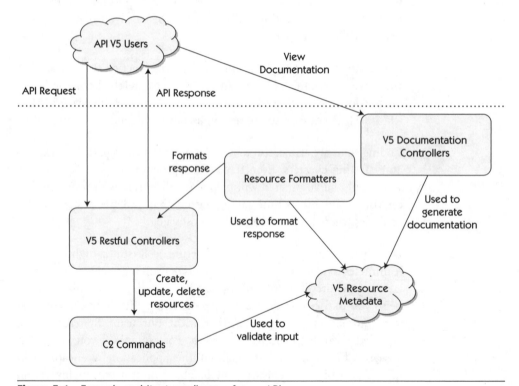

Figure 5-1   Example architecture diagram for an API

GENERAL TECHNICAL SKILLS

Every team and organization we work with has different needs and different contexts. The technical skills that are necessary to test effectively vary from team to team. However, there are some basic technical skills that will serve you well in any environment.

Knowing how to monitor processes, memory, and CPU, read log files, and interpret profiling statistics can help you identify potential resource misuse or leaks. Also watch for and understand important performance characteristics that might otherwise go unnoticed until your product gets into production. Using monitoring and logging is another area where a tester and programmer or DevOps practitioner can pair to really dig into elusive problems. The ability to view or tail a log file while testing is a necessity with most software products. Being comfortable on a command line with basic UNIX shell commands is useful for a wide range of activities, such as maintaining test environments, monitoring log files, and testing APIs.

Most testing requires at least some database knowledge. Checking data is only one aspect of testing. We also need to verify relational integrity and constraints. Basic SQL or other query language skills are a must for testing any application that uses a relational database for persisting data. Pairing a database expert with a tester is an excellent way to verify quality attributes of the database, while transferring skills. We will address testing data and databases more in Chapter 22, "Agile Testing for Data Warehouses and Business Intelligence Systems."

DEVELOPMENT ENVIRONMENTS

The ability to update, build, and deploy your team's latest code to your local machine provides more flexibility in testing and debugging issues. If you're helping to automate tests, you'll probably want to check out the latest code, write the tests, run them locally, and check in the new tests. Of course, this depends on your context. For example, Adam Knight told us that his team pulls the build from the continuous integration (CI) system artifacts and executes multiple test runs in parallel so the testers have a massive automation effort with no involvement in building the code.

Another benefit of being able to see the latest code is that we can often save time by doing some of the "fixes" ourselves. When Lisa sees a spelling mistake in a help page, she can fix it herself, run the automated tests, and check in the fix. Whatever checks and balances are in place for your programmers apply to testers as well. No matter what your role, if you are touching code, you need to follow coding standards and practices and ensure that appropriate testing is done.

In order to do this type of work, testers need to get up to speed on the source code control tool that their team uses and, ideally, the IDE. This is something that is easily done with tester/programmer pairing. When Lisa pairs with a teammate to work on code, she makes notes of techniques she might need later and keeps them on the team wiki for future reference and to share with other testers.

TEST ENVIRONMENTS

Many agile teams struggle with creating and maintaining useful test environments. Some teams configure their CI builds to automatically deploy build artifacts to test environments when test suites pass. In other teams, testers deploy the artifacts they want to test when they are ready. Sadly, some teams still don't have a CI process, and some don't even have adequate test environments. Without a dependable build process, it is hard to give fast feedback to the team on stories delivered. Without adequate test environments, it is hard to supply correct information on the state of the code.

A standard practice we've seen work in many teams is to have several test environments for different purposes. Programmers generally use a local sandbox that they maintain themselves for testing purposes. Each tester may also have her own local test environment. Ideally, a team has at least one test environment that mimics the production system for realistic exploratory testing. Teams also need a staging environment that's a copy or at least a good representation of production where they can test each release, including any data migrations. A common practice is to copy a snapshot of production data, with any sensitive data scrubbed, into the staging environment, so you're testing with realistic data.

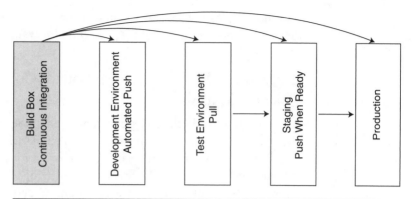

Figure 5-2   Simple build pipeline

There can be many more test environments, such as one specialized to measure load and performance, or one to run the automated test suites. Figure 5-2 represents the simplest form of a build pipeline, but these can be complex. In Chapter 23, "Testing and DevOps," a contributor shares how he managed his test environments.

Teams that have multiple code bases or branch their code from the master (main development trunk) source code control version generally need additional test environments. Lisa's team has test servers that are used to test architectural or code design spikes, or special projects that aren't yet part of the production code. These are also useful when upgrading to a new version of the programming language or development framework.

Testers should learn about all the different test environments and know when to ask for different configurations or additional servers. In our experience, testing is most effective when testers know what code and data should be on a given test environment and have the skills to ensure that it is there. Janet worked with a team that listed all the test environments on a large whiteboard. It showed exactly what version of the build was on which environment and when it had been deployed. A quick visual check ensured that the team knew what they were testing. Lisa's team documents the various test and staging environments, including the purpose of each one, in a spreadsheet on the team wiki.

CONTINUOUS INTEGRATION AND SOURCE CODE CONTROL SYSTEMS

As teams grow, so do the complexity and the number of CI builds and test suites. Teams start encountering the dilemma where the unit tests pass, but the tests for a particular browser, or an integration test suite, fail. We need to question, "Is this code worthy of testing in any environment?" It is important to have a common understanding of what it means to the team to get all the tests passing—getting to green—again.

Take time to understand your team's CI configurations. For example, if your CI process deploys automatically to a test environment, make sure you know which test suites must pass before the build can deploy. Testers need to learn what the different CI jobs are and how the success or failure of each relates to testing. If you're testing the business logic on the server side, it may not matter that a particular browser test suite failed. But if you're testing client-side logic, you may prefer to wait for all regression tests on all browsers to pass.

Understand what the risk is for your system. Know which programmers to talk to if a particular test suite is failing. Sometimes the tests that are failing don't affect the particular feature you want to test, so it may be possible to manually deploy the code and continue testing.

Having multiple development teams complicates the CI process. What we've seen most often is that individual teams have their own CI process for their code, and most testing can be done in the team's own test environment. Their code is also tested as part of a company-wide CI process. Regression failures in other teams' code could affect your ability to test the larger system. If there isn't already a process to identify the source of failures in a company-wide CI and some means to get the responsible team to fix the problem, try to get the right people together to put one in place to determine how to solve the issue.

Branching complicates CI issues. If your team always stays on the master (sometimes called main or trunk), life is simple. But let's say your

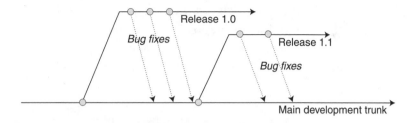

Figure 5-3   A possible branching strategy

team is doing a big refactor on master, while a bug fix needs to go out on the production branch. You need to be sure to check out the right thing and/or deploy the correct build to the appropriate test environment for verification. This is another area where collaborating with programmers and possibly DevOps is essential. In the diagram shown in Figure 5-3, the bug fixes are either merged into the main development trunk or double-punched (both updated with the same fix).

A Simple Branching Strategy

Augusto Evangelisti, *an agile testing enthusiast from Ireland, shares his story about how his organization handles branching in the simplest way possible.*

We have resolved the issue around branching and merging quite drastically by removing branching altogether and doing pure continuous integration, with everyone coding directly on trunk. We are lucky that we have only two or three teams pushing at any one time, as well as a very advanced and fast CI system that makes it very smooth. We have recently introduced feature toggling because we are doing continuous delivery and sometimes our customers are not ready to use a new user story. We test it in our internal environments, but we toggle it in production through Spring configuration.

We use Git, a distributed source code management tool, and each developer's box is a "branch" as such until he or she checks in the code.

Ideally, we could all work on the master of our source code, and many organizations are able to succeed with that strategy. However, as organizations grow or perhaps have more complicated systems, other strategies evolve.

A More Complex Branching Strategy

Adam Knight, *a director of QA and support from the UK, shares his team's branching experiences, which are completely different from Augusto's and are much more complex.*

Because we are a database product company with a traditional delivery model of supported software releases, branching and merging are unfortunate facts of life. As our customers implement our product on-site as part of major installations, we need to maintain branches of previous releases that are still in production on customer sites around the world.

We use Subversion and keep the tests along with the code. At the point of each release, we branch the tests along with the code onto a release branch for that version. Should any major fixes be required, we apply these to the trunk code and test. We then push both the fix and the new tests back to any relevant release branches and issue update releases as required.

One of the main challenges that we face is trying to keep these release branches "linear," as often different customers require different fixes and don't necessarily want to risk having other fixes in their update releases. So far I've managed to win this game, as I believe that having separate individual patches exposes a huge amount of risk given the exponential number of untested combinations in which those patches could be applied. I have had to explain to some customers who have questioned this approach the vast difference in risk between a patch and a full version of the software that has been through all of our automated testing prior to being released.

Another situation where branches may be created is if we are involved in a proof of concept (POC) where the requirements of the POC demand additional work to be done on the code base to achieve them. In this situation we branch the code and add a high-priority prototyping story to the iteration to try to achieve the specified targets (usually around query performance or concurrency for a specific data set). Once these items are complete, we create stories for subsequent iterations for each feature that we want to bring into the main trunk.

> Those stories involve reworking the features to make them release quality and to fully integrate them with the rest of the product with appropriate testing. The major risk with this approach is that there is a perception of a higher level of completion of those prototype items than is actually present and consequently an unrealistic expectation around how quickly they can be converted into releasable code.
>
> As I said, the need to maintain multiple branches is not a desirable situation but a fact of life given our context and delivery model.

As Adam notes, testers and their development teams also must manage tests and test code within the context of the team's source code control system. Automated tests should be versioned with the code that they test. If you aren't already familiar with your team's source code control system, pair with a programmer, system administrator, or DevOps person to learn how to use it and how your team's code is organized.

Testing Quality Attributes

Agile Testing explained how to use the agile testing quadrants (Figure 5-4) to help ensure that the team plans and executes the types of

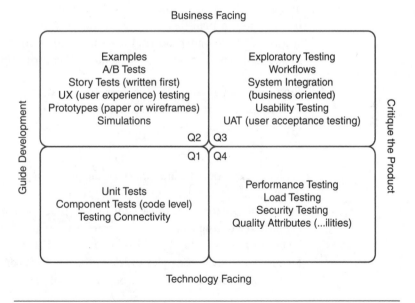

Figure 5-4   Agile testing quadrants

testing that they need. Chapter 8, "Using Models to Help Plan," goes into detail on planning for all four quadrants, but in this chapter we'll cover some of the technical abilities you may want to enhance.

The tests in Quadrant 4 (technology-facing tests that critique the product) are sometimes ignored or underestimated since they are often where testing skills are the weakest. This quadrant contains important quality attributes or constraints that are frequently not specified in the stories. An example of an unstated constraint is that "performance on all web pages must respond in less than three seconds." If your team uses analytical tools to measure performance, you will want to learn how to run them and interpret the results.

Organizations may lack people with the skills for some specialty areas. For example, maybe your team has no security testing specialists. Your team can learn some basic security testing techniques to help give your company some degree of safety. Learning about SQL injection and cross-site scripting will cover some of the basic areas of vulnerability. Janet had a recent experience with a website that wanted payment and asked for full credit card details. She noticed it was not an HTTPS site so did a bit of testing. The site didn't even hide the details in the page, and a simple "view source" after submitting showed all the details she had entered in plain text. However, there's a lot more to ensuring the security of a software product. Educating your company about the value of a security audit may be the most valuable contribution you can make.

Find out what is important to your organization and become technically aware in that area. Perhaps it is enough to know that you can recommend they hire an expert.

We place exploratory testing in Quadrant 3 (business-facing tests that critique the product), and we have devoted Chapter 12, "Exploratory Testing," to the subject. However, we wanted to call it out here because it is a skill set that you must continue to practice and grow. Teaching exploratory testing skills to programmers on your team can help them be better coders. In her book *Explore It!* (Hendrickson, 2013), Elisabeth Hendrickson gives examples of how programmers can use exploratory testing at a code level as well. Sometimes, thinking about the ripple effects of small pieces of code will help them avoid breaking other parts of the application with new code or changes to existing code. Pairing with testers helps coders gain testing awareness.

TEST DESIGN TECHNIQUES

When you are deciding what and how to test, it is important to have a toolbox full of techniques, such as the use of state transition diagrams or decision tables. We've included recommended books and courses on test design and domain testing in the bibliography for Part II.

SUMMARY

"T-shaped" team members need technical awareness in a variety of areas to effectively plan and execute testing activities. There's a wide variety of basic knowledge that will help team members in all roles collaborate more effectively for testing. Testers bring in-depth testing skills to the party but need to communicate effectively with programmers, system administrators, and other technical roles. At the same time, team members in other roles who engage in testing activities should also practice these skills. These include

- Guiding development with examples
- Technical awareness of architecture and code design
- Automation and coding skills
- Maintaining test environments
- Understanding source code control and continuous integration
- Testing quality attributes, guided by the agile testing quadrants
- Test design techniques

Chapter 6

HOW TO LEARN

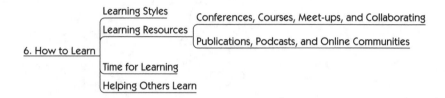

In Chapter 3, "Roles and Competencies," we explained the importance of becoming a generalizing specialist who is able to collaborate with team members who have other specialties while contributing one's own deep expertise. In Chapter 4, "Thinking Skills for Testing," and Chapter 5, "Technical Awareness," we explored a variety of skills that help software teams do a better job of testing and delivering a high-quality, high-value product. Growing all these different skills broadens our perspective and lets us approach our work more creatively. In this chapter, we'll look at ways to learn these diverse skills. There are plenty of educational resources around, but first, think about your learning style and your team culture, both of which affect your success at acquiring new abilities.

LEARNING STYLES

Each of us has preferred ways of learning. Some of us learn best by listening—we're auditory learners. Some of us like to see pictures—we have a visual preference. Many of us learn by doing—some people call that kinesthetic learning. Many times we need to absorb information in more than one way. For example, Janet is an auditory learner, but she needs to practice skills to internalize them. However, when she tries to get a concept across to others, she needs to draw it to help explain it. Different avenues of learning apply to everyone but to different degrees.

Figure 6-1   How do you learn?

What is your preferred style? Understand yours so you can get the best out of each learning experience.

Emotions affect the way we take in information. All of us have blind spots that may prevent us from learning, triggers that cause us to shut down so that we don't hear the message anymore. To learn and question, we need a safe environment. If you're helping other team members learn a new skill, keep in mind that people may have emotional reactions to what you are saying or how you are saying it. They may not be taking in the message if they don't like the delivery format. Figure 6-1 shows the many styles people have—what works for one person may not work for another.

As you're learning, whether it's a training class, online tutorial, or one-on-one session, reflect on what emotional "hot buttons" you have. When you feel yourself blocking out information because of the way it's presented, try to focus on the value you can get from the instructor or material. Keep this in mind when collaborating with developer teammates and business experts, and take in all the information that will enhance testing. Look for your own blind spots that may prevent you from learning, and observe to recognize them in others (Gregory, 2010).

Figure 6-2　Helpers

David Hussman and Jean Tabaka facilitated a workshop called "Zen, the Beginner's Mind," designed to open minds to new ideas (Levison, 2008), at Agile 2008. Janet participated and learned that when we approach issues with closed minds and start every sentence with, "But that won't work because . . ." or, "That didn't work when we tried it in . . ." we close our minds to opportunities. Maybe it was just a small, solvable problem that made it fail before. That doesn't mean the fundamental idea was flawed. Or perhaps you weren't ready to hear it. Sometimes we don't have the basic information that will enable us to grasp a concept. Open your mind to the wonder of learning; reading books in philosophy or other studies can show you different ways to look at a problem.

Look beyond the software testing and development profession for learning opportunities. Instructors, coaches, or mentors in other fields may fit your learning style and bring a different perspective. The right helper can show us ways to reach for new ideas (see Figure 6-2).

Janet's Story

When Lisa and I started developing and teaching our agile testing course, I started to read about teaching strategies. I picked up a few tips from the books and applied them. I also watched other instructors and tried to find the style that suited me. However, one of the people I turned to the most for mentoring was my sister, Carol Vaage. She was a grade-one teacher with her master's degree in early childhood learning, and she opened my eyes to new ways to approach teaching and working with my classes.

For example, she introduced ways of using open-ended questions to get her classes to start thinking about a topic. I've included a few here, but the list is much longer and is included in Appendix B, "Provocation Starters."

- Let's figure out how that could be . . .
- What would happen next?
- Why would that be?
- Why do you think that happened?
- Did you notice?

If we think about how children learn and give ourselves permission to explore our natural curiosity about the world, think how far we could go.

Carol also has some amazing stories and pictures of how far children can go to learn, which we've included in the bibliography for Part II, "Learning for Better Testing."

You can learn from people you admire even without a formal mentoring relationship. Most people are happy to help, so have the courage to ask questions.

LEARNING RESOURCES

Seek out places to sharpen your skills. You may find good resources online, in your local community, or farther afield. Let's look at some examples of good learning opportunities. See the Part II bibliography section "Courses, Conferences, Online Communities, Podcasts" for links to the activities mentioned in this section.

Conferences, Courses, Meet-ups, and Collaborating

A good conference can provide a variety of takeaways, ranging from specific techniques you can try right away, to groundbreaking new ideas or technologies you can continue to research. Most importantly, you'll meet practitioners and thought leaders with whom you can form a lasting network, a constant source of inspiration and ideas.

Consider different types of conferences. Testing conferences are an obvious choice for testers, but consider others, such as those that help you work on specific skills such as scripting languages. If your employer can't afford to send you to a conference and you can't afford to pay your own way, consider proposing a paper or session to a testing or software development conference. This may earn you a free or discounted conference registration. And remember, teaching a skill to someone else is the best way to learn it yourself. Find out if the conferences need volunteers, or if you qualify for grants or discounts. If you can't travel to attend a conference, consider virtual conferences, which are becoming more popular, or sign up for webinars.

Conferences aren't only for learning specific testing and technical skills. Many software conferences have sessions and tracks on collaboration, organizational culture, learning, coaching, working with customers, and mentoring. Janet has even attended sessions by Portia Tung on the "Power of Play." Figure 6-3 shows people learning and playing together.

The most important learning at conferences often takes place at break times and in the hallways and dining areas, as you meet new people who become part of your network.

Figure 6-3 Collaborative learning and play

Most metropolitan areas have testing and development user groups and meet-ups, which convene regularly. These can be a great resource for free training and information, as well as a place to meet people who have tried different tools and techniques. Make the most of these networking opportunities.

If you want to improve your teaching and coaching skills, consider a coaching retreat such as Agile Coach Camp. Agile games gatherings such as Play4Agile are a great place to get ideas for participatory learning and building trust in teams. Portia Tung (Tung, 2011) says that play breaks down barriers between people and opens the mind to enable learning.

There are workshops and courses designed to help you learn leadership and relationship skills, such as Problem Solving Leadership (Derby et al., 2014) and those offered by the Satir Global Network (Satir Global Network).

To get better at almost anything, we need to practice. Musicians, athletes, and video game players all spend time practicing. At code retreats (Haines et al.), programmers practice repeatedly writing code that they'll throw away. Lisa finds that code retreats are a great learning experience even if you're not much of a coder. She learned lessons about problem solving and practicing one's craft. There are good ways to practice testing skills, too; for example, attend a testing dojo, or organize your own.

Groups such as Weekend Testing give you the opportunity to practice testing techniques in real time with testers around your continent or around the world. If you have a spare hour and want to practice a specific skill, get someone to pair with you. Lisa recently reached out to her Twitter contacts, and several volunteered to pair with her virtually to practice Ruby Koans. Your own teammates may be ready and willing to help you practice.

You may be able to find courses offered in subjects that interest you. Many of these are on a specific topic such as user interface (UI) test automation. Some organizations bring instructors in to teach the whole team at once so everyone has a common understanding of the subject.

Online courses, screencasts, webinars, and tutorials offer convenient learning opportunities for all aspects of testing and agile development, as well as the nontechnical thinking skills. Some online training is free or inexpensive, though more sophisticated courses, or those that include time online with the instructor, can cost more. You can usually work through them at your own pace.

Janet's Story

I recently took a course on personal kanban through www.udemy.com. I could take my time with it and work through the course anywhere I traveled and at my own pace; both aspects were really important to me. I used what I learned to help me focus on tasks that were highest priority and not get sidetracked on tasks that were less important at the current time.

If there's a specific skill you want to acquire, look for online videos from conference sessions, user group meetings, and training courses.

Publications, Podcasts, and Online Communities

Information about all aspects of software testing is available both in book form and on the Internet. We're fortunate to have many good books available about all aspects of software testing. You'll find references to books, articles, and blog posts throughout this book, and the bibliography for Part II has a complete list.

Podcasts are a convenient way to learn. You can listen to interviews with experts, training sessions on specific topics, conference keynotes, webinars, and panel discussions.

Podcasts Changed My Life

Steve Rogalsky, *an agilist at Protegra, shares his story about podcast learning.*

My wife likes to tell the story of when I came home from work and announced, "Podcasts have changed my life." Her natural response was: "What? Podcasts? Not me, not our children, but podcasts?" I persisted with my original assertion. "Yes, podcasts. They've changed my life."

Up until that time I had been largely relying on the organizations I worked for to do the hard work of identifying what I needed to learn next and how. When a friend commented several years ago that he listened to podcasts on the way to work, I decided to give it a try. After only a few episodes I was hooked. I looked forward to my time in the car when I could explore what other people were discovering about software development, testing, management, and other topics. On many occasions I would hear a new term, tool, or acronym in a meeting, download a related podcast before leaving work, and return the next day knowledgeable enough to apply the information at work.

I had discovered a way of learning that I enjoyed, that fit into my existing schedule, and that made my job more enjoyable. Through podcasts I was introduced to many new people and ideas that have made my work experience more successful and rewarding. Yes—by giving me a vehicle to own my personal learning, podcasts changed my life.

Look to the global testing and software development community for more people with whom you can exchange ideas and experiences. For example, the Agile Testing mailing list is a good place to ask if others have had the same problem you're facing and how they solved it. Online communities such as Software Testing Club are a great place to learn by participating in forum discussions and by blogging your own experiences. Mailing lists and social networks such as Twitter can introduce you to articles and blog posts on topics that interest you.

Open-source projects can be a good place to practice your skills, especially if you want some coding experience. You can refine other skills as you contribute to open-source projects, such as testing, writing help documentation, and providing training courses. (See the Part II bibliography section "Courses, Conferences, Online Communities, Podcasts" for links to the activities mentioned in this section.)

If testers are integrated into software delivery teams in your company, a testing community of practice (CoP) is a good place to learn and share experiences with others who are interested in testing. Lunch-and-learn sessions and book groups within an organization are other effective learning mechanisms. For example, several teams have read our previous book together, reading a different chapter each week. They spend a lunchtime or meeting discussing what they have read and how it applies

Figure 6-4 Pairing—a great way to learn

to their situation (Ruhland, 2013a). An added bonus of leading your team's journal club effort is honing your own facilitation skills!

Pair with your fellow team members (see Figure 6-4). Pair with people outside your development team. The marketing and sales people know a lot about your customers, as do your user experience (UX) designers. People in other departments such as human resources (HR) or accounting would provide a great fresh set of eyes on your product. There's a lot you can learn from your own coworkers, and a lot you can teach them.

Lisa's Story

I was part of a team that decided we would pair on every coding and testing task. When I paired with a programmer to automate UI acceptance tests that would guide coding, I noticed how naturally the programmer found duplication in the test code and immediately extracted it out into our library of macros. I sharpened my automated test design skills considerably as a result.

Iteration demos are another useful learning opportunity. Try rotating the duty of demonstrating what the team delivered. It's a great way to practice your presentation and facilitation skills.

TIME FOR LEARNING

Learning takes time. If you are constantly running just to keep up, you won't have time to learn and try new ideas. In Chapter 2, "The Importance of Organizational Culture," we talked about the significance of

Figure 6-5   Make time for learning.

nurturing a learning culture so that team members feel they can take time to research, to experiment with new techniques, or just to think (see Figure 6-5).

Bernice Niel Ruhland suggests scheduling time for reading or other learning activities when you have the most energy. For example, if you're a morning person, try getting up a little earlier. Bernice allocates some lunchtimes and Sunday afternoons to reading.

Update Constantly

Mike Talks, *a software tester from New Zealand, explains how learning is a constant challenge that all of us should be up for.*

Most people's working life will span at least 40 years. When you look at the field of software development and work out how much change happened within that time, it's obvious that the skills of graduates today will feel obsolete come their retirement. Just looking back 10 or 20 years; it's like stepping into another world. Smartphones, tablets, broadband Internet—things we've already begun to take for granted—these are all recent developments.

When I started out 15 years ago as a programmer, I was told that FOR-TRAN and C would be the only languages I would need—and these have since been superseded by Java, C++, and C#.

What this means is that software professionals cannot just coast through their careers with their current skill set. New developments will mean new learning. Holding onto the mantra "We've always done it this way" is not good enough. One way to stay relevant is to find ways to continually learn and take on new ideas.

What I would really like to go on record as saying is that learning is itself an agile process. Don't look at learning as a "big bang" process: you know nothing, read a book, and two days later you're an expert. Learning, like features, is something you do in iterations, adding a bit more knowledge at a time, and then building on it the next iteration. It's not a race to the finish, and there is always something more to learn. Often the people who seem to pick up knowledge more slowly are the ones who are actually learning it on a much deeper level.

In my book *The Software Minefield* (Talks, 2012), "Closing Thoughts" talks about channels of learning and is really like my experience report on learning.

If your team meets the "Agile Acid Test" (Hendrickson, 2010) and delivers software frequently at a sustainable pace, you should have some free time outside of work for professional growth. Just as musicians practice their instruments outside of performances, we all need to hone our skills outside of work. If you love what you do, this is a joy, not a burden. As Steve Rogalsky says, learning more will increase your passion and your joy.

HELPING OTHERS LEARN

All team members, including testers, can use their coaching and leadership skills to help their teammates learn.

Gaining Confidence

Aldo Rall, *a test manager in South Africa, tells us how he helped new team members gain confidence.*

New testers on our team were too afraid to participate in the normal collaborative mechanisms of working in agile teams. They also had some cultural disadvantages that made them reticent to question or challenge the team's current thinking or process.

The organization was also not very well educated about what testing entailed. I implemented a lot of ongoing education for the clients, the business analysts, the programmers, and the project manager to open their minds to different ways of doing things and raise awareness of alternative approaches to development.

As a result of our training efforts, the testers started acting as a community of practice. Testers shared problems with each other and debated best solutions for their respective projects within this community of practice.

Loads more exploratory testing occurred. The testers were no longer afraid to speak their minds to their project teams. The testers were accepted as valued, contributing, cooperating, and collaborating team members. The programmers took advice from testers about releases into production seriously. Production incidents went down to a trickle. What is more, the testers developed a very important attribute: they had confidence in their ability to do testing.

Getting people over their fear of the unknown is a giant step toward empowering them to take control of their own professional development. As Aldo says, training and support for learning also help people reach out and collaborate with other team members.

Learning is often an important side effect of trying a series of small experiments to solve a problem that's holding up the team. What you learn may be more valuable than overcoming the original obstacle!

Surprise Learning

Claire Moss, *a tester in the United States, shares her story of how she led her team through a series of small experiments to solve a problem. It generated unexpected opportunities for the team to improve communication and learn to collectively own testing activities.*

As the tester on a cross-functional Scrum team, I knew about defects. Being a visual thinker, I put sticky notes on a small whiteboard by my desk. Since I'd never used a board like this before, I tried a few different categories to better prepare for talking to my product team members about testing results. Although other people could see the board, I always thought of it as keeping things straight in my own head. Figure 6-6 shows my initial attempt.

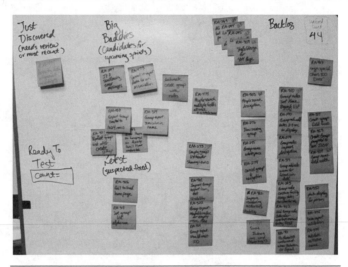

Figure 6-6 Initial bug board

One day, I walked into the office and found that my teammates had rearranged my sticky notes, engaging with my board. I was fascinated that they found my personal record keeping interesting and useful. By prioritizing my defect backlog, my product owner team revealed their desire for more information about testing. I seized the opportunity to use this big visible chart as a means to the end of better shared understanding.

I paid careful attention to the changes my colleagues made and did some research to see how other agile teams were using big visible charts. Thus began my series of experiments.

The most common question about defects seemed to be, "How bad is it?" so I tried rearranging the bugs based on severity (i.e., impact on the user). Since my developers scrupulously resolved the worst problems quickly, we ended up with large buckets of low-impact problems. Although our communication definitely improved, we still needed to represent the business's judgment about priority. Not all bugs of a given severity are equally detrimental in the eyes of the business.

To satisfy this need, I tried another way of looking at the problem. Although I wanted to provide deeper information about the sources of bugs, initially I reported the user-facing symptoms. By co-opting the site map I'd made for test planning, I showed the bigger picture of where bugs were surfacing. The team could literally take a step back to see clusters of problems that might indicate a need for UX redesign or code refactoring. See Figure 6-7 for an example. That worked for a while as well.

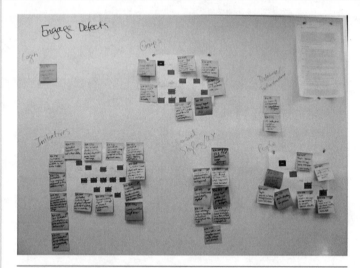

Figure 6-7   Bug board—clustered

All this time our team members were learning to talk more comfortably about each other's work. Each of us became more T-shaped, broadening our understanding of areas outside our specialization. We realized that the disconnection between the bug backlog and the user story backlog was a problem we had created for ourselves. So we removed the impediment.

We began pulling bugs into sprint backlogs based on priority, which included analysis of user impact.

We pulled related bugs into our stories to give us more context in which to execute the user stories we had planned. We disposed of the bugs during a story, either fixing them or delaying them as we deemed appropriate. Having this deliberate decision in place helped us to focus on the whole product backlog so that we no longer needed or valued a separate bug board.

Representing all the team's development work as a single backlog was a step in the right direction. We adapted our big visible charts after conversations about the value they provided. However, all of these iterations focused on understanding defect reporting, which had been the most visible part of the testing activities. Our team was well on the way to a whole-team testing approach, but we still needed to delve deeper, beyond defects. Our big visible charts helped us to find the path and opened up team communication to encourage collective ownership of testing.

If you see someone you can help, take the initiative. Make a big visible chart as Claire did, start a testing community of practice, or perhaps a testing journal or book club. Sometimes, a new idea is as simple as seeing, and seizing, an opportunity.

SUMMARY

There's a lot to consider as you grow the T-shaped skills needed to succeed with testing. Widen your search to include less obvious opportunities, perhaps outside of the software development field.

- Know your preferred learning style and use it as a basis to optimize learning opportunities.
- There is a wide variety of venues for learning. Try more than one and see which ones work for you.
- Build in time for learning.
- Try experiments to engage everyone on the team; work with business stakeholders and help them learn what they need to know.
- Keep in touch with the larger testing communities in local and Internet user groups, and then try the new ideas you get.
- Spend time practicing your skills.
- Take control of your own professional development.

Part III

PLANNING—SO YOU DON'T FORGET THE BIG PICTURE

It amazes us how many times we still hear, "But we don't need to plan now because we are doing agile." We agree that in agile development, we don't do big, up-front planning all in one phase. But planning is important, and it is part of agile. We plan as we need to—just in time. Lean thinking refers to the idea of the last responsible moment, so that you don't waste your time on details you don't need yet.

We divided this part into two chapters. In Chapter 7, we deal with the idea of levels of precision for planning: understanding what is needed at the level you are currently planning. In Chapter 8, we talk about how different models can help us plan our testing. We cover the agile testing quadrants, not in the detail that we did in *Agile Testing*, but to reiterate the concepts behind them. We introduce two variations on the Quadrants that express some of the changes in thinking over the last few years. We look at some of the other models that can help with planning, including the test automation pyramid.

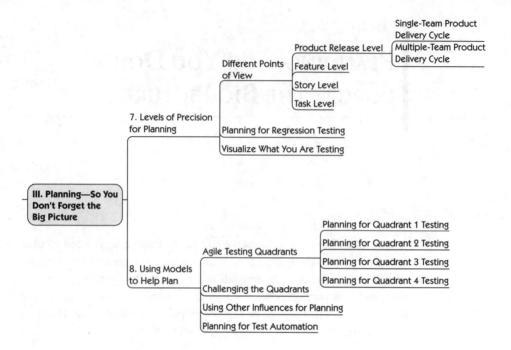

- **Chapter 7**, "Levels of Precision for Planning"
- **Chapter 8**, "Using Models to Help Plan"

Chapter 7

LEVELS OF PRECISION
FOR PLANNING

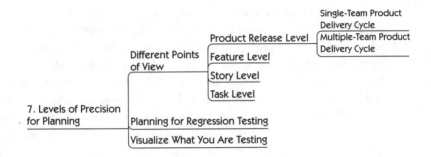

A frequent misperception about agile development is that it requires no planning, because the Agile Manifesto says agile practitioners value responding to change over following a plan. In reality, a good agile team tends to plan more than phased and gated project teams. It's done in smaller chunks, with enough for what is needed, and it uses fast feedback to learn and adapt. Test planning is the same—small chunks and short feedback loops. As you plan testing, focus on what you need to know now.

DIFFERENT POINTS OF VIEW

In small, colocated teams, planning for testing can be simple. The team considers the types of testing they need to do, perhaps using a model like the agile testing quadrants (see Chapter 8, "Using Models to Help Plan") to help identify what testing needs to occur or what their automation requirements might be. Team members can vocalize their testing needs in planning sessions or represent them visually, perhaps on a whiteboard.

In large organizations where multiple teams work on the same product, test planning can get complicated. Regardless of company or project size, the basic principles apply.

In agile projects, we don't know all the details about each feature at the beginning of a delivery cycle. Some may be straightforward and predictable because we've done similar features before. Others may be more complicated, or they may be so new and unknown that it's difficult to come up with examples of desired behavior. Our approach must be different from one that assumes the requirements are known up front and where planning is based on that information. Using agile principles of simplicity and iterative development, we look at levels of planning (or levels of precision of detail) and ask what information the team and stakeholders need to know at each level. Different organizations will have different contexts, so you need to know what is important to your team and your organization. We discuss this approach in the context of time-boxed iterations, but the concepts can be applied to flow-based methods such as kanban. Teams using a flow-based process may release after each story is completed, or they may accumulate the stories until a feature is complete and then release to production.

Figure 7-1 shows four levels of detail that we have to consider when planning, while at the same time keeping the whole product (the system) in mind. We use the following terms for these different levels of precision or points of view for test planning:

- **Product release:** One or more teams working on a single product, releasing at specific intervals or on defined dates. A product release may have one or many features.
- **Feature:** Some business capability or piece of functionality that is useful to the business; it could be part of a larger feature set. A feature usually has many stories, and the entire feature may require multiple iterations to complete. A feature delivery team is the cross-functional team working on one or more features for a product stream. It may be the only team or perhaps one of many teams working toward a larger product release.
- **Story (may be referred to as a "user story"):** A small, testable chunk of functionality that generally can be finished ("done")

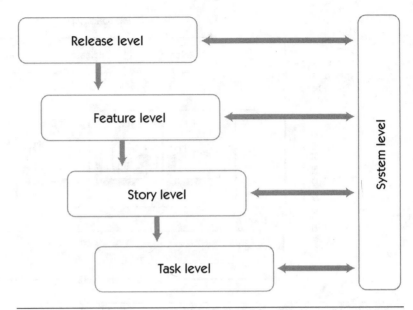

Figure 7-1   Levels of detail (precision) for planning

within one to three days. It may or may not be releasable to production on its own. A story has many tasks.

- **Task:** A piece of work that's part of a story, taking less than one
  day to complete.

For consistency of terms, let's assume we have a three-month (quarterly)
product release with two-week iterations for each team. There are multiple features that each team completes in the release cycle. Figure 7-2
shows this setup.

Let's explore how you may adapt your test planning to each level, as well
as discuss what documentation and/or artifacts might be expected at
each of the four levels. At each level, we consider a different level of risk.

Product Release Level

At the product release level, teams should have a good idea of the product vision, perhaps by using impact mapping as discussed in Chapter 9,

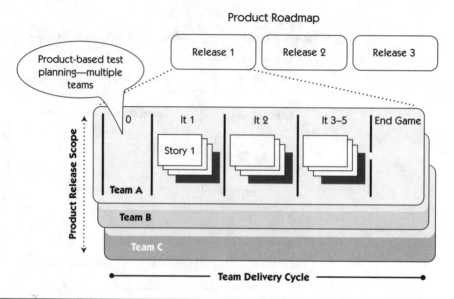

Figure 7-2   Levels of precision of planning for the product level

"Are We Building the Right Thing?" The high-level test approach should cover what is important to this product delivery cycle. The time when you are planning what will be in the release is the best time to identify the need for new test tools or environments.

This is also a good time to think about what additional testing will need to be done during the end game—the time before releasing a product to production. These activities may involve more groups outside your delivery team, such as operations, customer support, training, and marketing. For example, you may need to do final user acceptance testing (UAT) or test integration with an external system that couldn't be done in the delivery team's test environment. See pages 456–57 in *Agile Testing* and links in the bibliography for Part III for more information.

If the release includes new technology or features that are not yet well understood, the team might plan to do some spikes, small experiments to learn more about a possible problem or design solution. It may be appropriate to wait to learn from the spikes before trying to plan, even at a high level.

Single-Team Product Delivery Cycle

When your team is the only team responsible for delivering the release to your customers, your team is responsible for the completion of all testing activities. You may still need to use outside help such as performance experts, but your team is accountable. If yours is the only team working on a product, you can jump to the next section on feature-level test planning.

Multiple-Team Product Delivery Cycle

Having multiple teams work on the same product adds complexity, and an overall test approach should take into account dependencies between teams or between features. At this high level, there should be a few people who understand the big picture and how this release integrates into the system as a whole.

Janet finds that starting with a high-level context diagram (see Figure 18-2 for an example) helps visualize the risks and provides a starting point for thinking about dependencies outside the product teams or between features. By continually looking at the big picture, we can aim to find possible integration issues early and not only at the end of the delivery cycle. This will reduce the risk.

Consider the return on investment for tests such as interoperability, browser compatibility, or testing across different mobile devices. For example, individual teams may not be able to handle performance and load testing in their existing test environments. Consider the types of testing that might require a specialized test team, such as system integration. Chapter 18, "Agile Testing in the Enterprise," presents ideas on how to handle testing in large agile organizations.

If it's deemed useful to have a product release test plan written before you start your delivery cycle, we recommend keeping it as simple and clear as you can. It should not duplicate information in your organizational Test Strategy or Test Approach document (see Crispin and Gregory, 2009, p. 87). That document contains information that is common to all testing done for your product. For your current product release test planning, address only what is different for this particular release at a high level. Consider who the audience is and what is important for them to know. The less fluff there is, the more likely they will see the pertinent information about the potential risks in the new release.

At the product release level, test planning should include identifying testing risks and assumptions for the current release. It should highlight testing issues for possible cross-team dependencies as well as product integration issues.

Feature Level

As features representing some business-value capability are broken up into stories, we need to make sure they are testable so that the team gets into a cadence of coding and testing each individual story until the complete feature is "done." Remember, a feature usually has many stories, and each delivery team concentrates on a particular feature. There may be multiple teams working in parallel, and there may be dependencies between the teams. Figure 7-3 shows how to think about dependencies between teams.

 Each delivery team works with its product owner to determine how much work it might get completed during the delivery cycle. Often, a team release-planning session is held so teams can size the features and stories in their team product backlog. Testers help during this planning session by asking clarifying questions that may help the team determine the size of the feature or story. The team should consider impacts to the system as a whole.

Testers can also help when they apply an exploratory mindset to what performance or security concerns there might be, or whether a feature or story will affect other functionality. As with release-level planning, teams may defer test planning until after any necessary spike solutions or experiments are done and more is known about complex features.

Capture feature-level testing risks and assumptions that need to be monitored on a whiteboard, wiki, or other medium that is visible to both the delivery team and customers. Experiment with using diagrams, mind maps, bullet points, a matrix, or another lightweight format understandable to all. Watch how the teams use this information, and discuss it in retrospectives if you find there are communication gaps. Look for the best fit for your situation.

Sometimes clients or managers insist on a formal test document outlining what your team is going to test in this delivery cycle. Before you

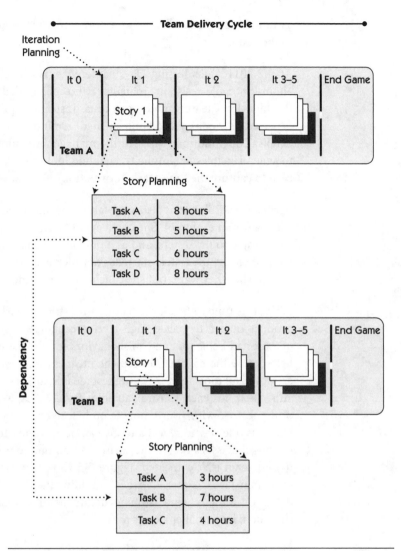

Figure 7-3 Levels of precision of planning at the team level

create a formal deliverable, think about who will use it and why they want it. Keep it as simple as possible—preferably less than one page. Since the functionality is not set yet, avoid getting into details of scope unless there is a risk involved that needs to be communicated to others. If a document is not needed, simply record the testing risks and assumptions that need to be monitored on a whiteboard that is visible to the team.

At the 2011 Agile Testing Days conference, Huib Schoots told a story about an agile-resistant manager who demanded a document of the high-level feature and story tests. Instead of providing what was expected (a document), Huib created a mind map to capture those details. The mind map satisfied the manager and allowed Huib to keep to agile principles of simplicity, enabling him to stick to a one-page test plan to capture the important information.

Bernice Niel Ruhland is also a big fan of the one-page test plan (see Figure 7-4 for an example). She challenges herself to keep it to one page as an example to the testers, and as a practice manager, she created a basic template to get the testers started. They pick what they need and are free to add what they want, but she coaches them to find the right balance.

When it is time to break the feature into stories, work with your team's product owner to create high-level acceptance tests, using examples of expected behaviors and misbehaviors for the feature. Doing so will help define the scope and keep the business value visible. Mind maps are powerful tools for generating test ideas at any level, and we find creating them for each feature valuable. Try creating a testing mind map of the feature with your whole team before breaking it down into stories. It is one way to reveal and give an opportunity to explore some of the possible issues before they arise. Use an online mind-mapping tool if your team isn't colocated. Figure 7-5 shows an example of a testing mind map. See Chapter 9, "Are We Building the Right Thing?," for more details on ways to help customers define the most valuable features and slice them into smaller stories for development.

Planning testing activities for large features containing multiple stories that cross iterations can be complicated. Janet has found that teams benefit from creating a "Test the feature" story for these. The tasks in this story are mostly about testing activities, such as "Explore the feature," "Perform load testing," or "Automate the workflow." Lisa's team writes exploratory testing charters as stories in their online project-tracking tool. At the appropriate time, any team member or pair can perform these charters, or the feature-testing stories. This type of story ensures

Test Plan for Fitness Application Feature
Adding BMI Calculator

Test Scope

- A BMI (body Mass Index) Calculator is being added to the fitness Application to calculate an individual's body fat. Data entered by the user is stored in the cloud and is shared across calculators with the ability for the user to change the data within each calculator. Initial testing will be performed using an iPhone, iPad mini, and a Nexus tablet.

Testing Approach

- The BMI calculator functionality will be tested based upon identifying the appropriate combinations and boundaries based upon the BMI requirements. Exploratory testing will be performed based upon how the users typically use the Fitness Application and anticipated usage of the new calculator. For this release, testing is limited to functionality, integration, exploratory, and regression. Device specific testing such as low-battery or other device conditions is not part of this testing.

Risks

- Look and feel across devices may not be consistent. Additional devices may need to be tested beyond the initial sample.

Regression

- Calculators using height and/or weight will be tested to ensure that shared fields across the calculators reflect the correct information and calculations are correct.

Features to Test

- BMI calculator (Functional testing)
- BMI Graph (Functional testing)
- Progress Report of Current Results Across Calculators (Integration testing)
- BMR Calculator & Body Fat Calculator (Regression testing)
- Cross-device testing based upon the usability of the screens

Features Not to Test

- Waist to Hip Ratio Calculator
- Weight Goal Tracker and Report
- Food Tracking Plan
- Settings Options

Data Validation

- Based upon US and Metric Scale using height and weight
- Identify combinations and boundaries (underweight, normal, overweight, and obese; and age range) to identify test data
- For other calculators using height and/or weight, identify previous tests to compare results when performing regression testing. Identify tests to perform across calculators to ensure the Progress Report of Current Results reflect the correct information

General Considerations

- Features not identified as part of the testing scope should have smoke tests performed before integration and exploratory testing begins.

Figure 7-4   Example lightweight test plan

that the feature testing is not forgotten. If your organization has an integration team doing post-development testing, they should be involved in defining these testing stories and tasks.

You may also want to think about developing personas and tours for extra exploratory testing ideas and coverage for each feature or for the end game. Chapter 12, "Exploratory Testing," goes into more detail about these techniques.

Story Level

Once we are working at the story level, we start getting into more detail. At this level of precision, it doesn't really matter whether you are using time-boxed iterations or flow-based methods. For each story, we need high-level acceptance tests: an example of expected behavior and at least one example of misbehavior that defines the scope of the story. Chapter 11, "Getting Examples," gives more detail on this subject. Our just-in-time planning for the story level happens during story readiness sessions (sometimes called preplanning or backlog refinement).

Our tests for the story evolve from these sessions, as well as other conversations, and then can be expanded during the iteration. Start writing test ideas and variations during story readiness sessions, continue during iteration planning, and then use all the tools in your toolbox to define other tests that will prove that the story works as expected. Remember to write down exploratory test ideas through all of this, so the exploratory testing charters will be ready as code is completed. You're likely to think of additional tests as you explore later.

Task Level

Programmers practice test-driven development (TDD), writing one test at a time before they code. This is a form of design, of planning what they are going to build at a detailed level.

When thinking about testing activities at the task level, do less planning and more doing and adapting. For example, if your task is to create test data, you might find yourself having to change where you get the data.

Some teams choose to estimate tasks in actual hours during their iteration planning. We find that this can be helpful for teams that are new to agile. The goal isn't to see how accurately you can estimate, but to learn where your time goes.

In *Agile Testing*, Chapter 17, we talked about several ways to create testing tasks, but we have found that creating separate task cards (virtual ones, if you're using an online tracking tool) for independent testing tasks seems to work the best. When a testing task takes significantly longer than anticipated, call attention to it during daily standups to ask for help or to see if it will affect the rest of the story. The team and the product owner should determine the best solution for finishing testing activities.

PLANNING FOR REGRESSION TESTING

Regression testing is about checking to make sure the system does what it did yesterday. Automated regression tests running in a continuous integration system deliver fast feedback to the team. As the team test-drives stories and features at the unit and business-facing levels, many (if not most) of the tests will be added to the regression suites. Your team needs to plan how to keep the suites up-to-date by determining what tests will be updated as you change or add functionality. When you remove functionality, you also must remember to delete the corresponding tests.

Regression tests need to be organized by system functionality so that you can locate tests easily to change, update, or delete them, or use them to demonstrate to someone how the system behaves. Many agile teams use an online tracking tool to maintain their stories, and some attach tests to the stories. This works when testing within an iteration but is not maintainable over the long run. Many teams find this out the hard way when they try to locate tests six months after the story is "done." Whether your tests are manual or automated, they should be migrated from a story-based grouping to an organization based on product functionality or business area.

Some teams add the story tests to the regression suite as soon as they complete a story; some wait until the feature is complete. Some teams add their tests at the end of every iteration, deciding which ones provide enough valuable coverage to keep. Unit-level tests created as part of TDD are added automatically as they are checked into version control along with the code that they support. Your team should experiment with different ways of building and maintaining regression suites, evaluating their return on investment at regular intervals.

VISUALIZE WHAT YOU ARE TESTING

We find that visual aids help keep the whole team aware of what testing activities need to happen and track what still needs to be done. As mentioned earlier in this chapter, one effective way to visualize while brainstorming testing is mind mapping.

Start by putting your central theme or problem in the main "node," and as you think of related topics, draw new nodes in an appropriate hierarchy. There's no right or wrong way; just capture the ideas without criticizing them. Both whiteboards and online mind-mapping tools let you easily move nodes around as you go, and many online tools have a task completion marker to mark progress. Color coding is an effective way to show relationships. You might end up with a mind map such as the one in Figure 7-5.

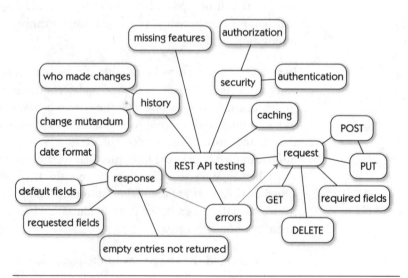

Figure 7-5   Mind map of testing ideas

A colocated team can keep the testing mind map up in the team area, have conversations around it, and update it, checking off the completed testing activities. Distributed teams can use an online mind-mapping tool, though it will take more practice and discipline to develop the habit and keep it virtually visible. A testing mind map keeps testing status front and center and reminds the whole team what testing remains to be done.

Another effective way to capture high-level test ideas at the release level is a test matrix. Collaborative techniques such as mind mapping can be used to generate test ideas for a release-level testing matrix, as shown in Figure 7-6. Visuals such as these provide a different viewpoint into planned testing activities. The rows are features, and the columns are test conditions/capabilities. In the example in Figure 7-6, the pattern shows progress: white means not tested; checkered ▦ (or green, if in color) means good to go; dots ▨ (yellow, if in color) means some testing done but may need more; striped ▧ (red, if in color) means broken; gray means not applicable, doesn't need testing.

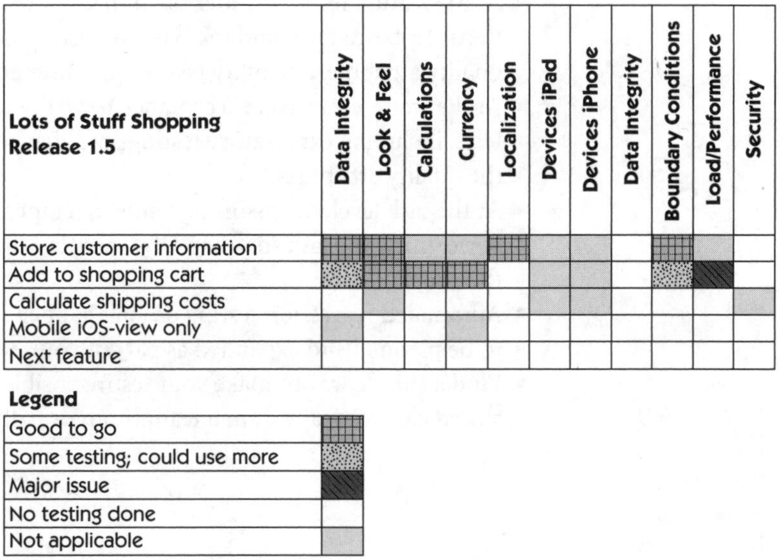

Lots of Stuff Shopping Release 1.5	Data Integrity	Look & Feel	Calculations	Currency	Localization	Devices iPad	Devices iPhone	Data Integrity	Boundary Conditions	Load/Performance	Security
Store customer information	▦	▦	░	░	▦			░	▦		
Add to shopping cart	▨	▦	▦	▦		░	░	░	▨	▧	
Calculate shipping costs			░			░		░			
Mobile iOS-view only	░			░							
Next feature											

Legend

Good to go	▦
Some testing; could use more	▨
Major issue	▧
No testing done	
Not applicable	░

Figure 7-6   Release-level test matrix

However you visualize your planned testing, try to keep it simple so that it can keep pace with your team. Use big visible charts or their virtual substitutes so all team members and stakeholders can see completed and planned testing at a glance. And make it valuable to your team or management; after all, you really want to be testing and not documenting.

SUMMARY

In this chapter, we talked about understanding what level of detail is needed for test planning as well as the importance of visualization.

- At the product release level, think about system impacts and what testing needs to be done during the end game, including, but not limited to, final UAT, load, and performance testing.
- If you are part of multiple teams working at the product release level, also consider high-level dependencies between components and teams, and what the integration system testing might include.
- For your delivery team planning at the release level, think about feature or story dependencies, risks, assumptions, and test environments.
- At the feature level, consider the impacts that affect this feature, the acceptance tests, and the types of testing needed, including quality attributes, usability testing, and user acceptance testing.
- At the story level, create acceptance tests, the remaining story tests, including exploratory testing, and maybe testing some of the quality attributes.
- At the task level, the planning tends to happen while you are performing the task such as TDD—writing the test first, then the code.
- Automated regression testing doesn't happen by chance. It needs to be planned and expanded as part of your everyday work.
- Find a simple way to make your testing visible, whether it is stored electronically or in a team room or hallway.

Chapter 8

USING MODELS TO HELP PLAN

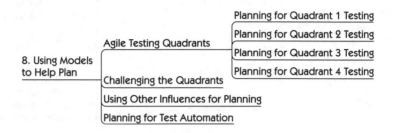

As agile development becomes increasingly mainstream, there are established techniques that experienced practitioners use to help plan testing activities in agile projects, although less experienced teams sometimes misunderstand or misuse these useful approaches. Also, the advances in test tools and frameworks have somewhat altered the original models that applied back in the early 2000s. Models help us view testing from different perspectives. Let's look at some foundations of agile test planning and how they are evolving.

AGILE TESTING QUADRANTS

The agile testing quadrants (the Quadrants) are based on a matrix Brian Marick developed in 2003 to describe types of tests used in Extreme Programming (XP) projects (Marick, 2003). We've found the Quadrants to be quite handy over the years as we plan at different levels of precision. Some people have misunderstood the purpose of the Quadrants. For example, they may see them as sequential activities instead of a taxonomy of testing types. Other people disagree about which testing activities belong in which quadrant and avoid using the Quadrants altogether. We'd like to clear up these misconceptions.

Figure 8-1 is the picture we currently use to explain this model. You'll notice we've changed some of the wording since we presented it in *Agile*

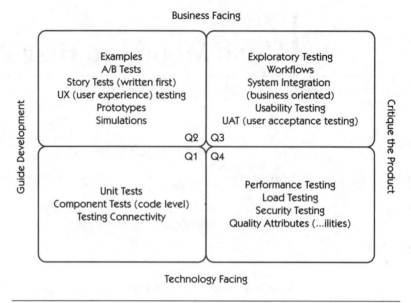

Figure 8-1   Agile testing quadrants

Testing. For example, we now say "guide development" instead of "support development." We hope this makes it clearer.

It's important to understand the purpose behind the Quadrants and the terminology used to convey their concepts. The quadrant numbering system does *not* imply any order. You don't work through the quadrants from 1 to 4, in a sequential manner. It's an arbitrary numbering system so that when we talk about the Quadrants, we can say "Q1" instead of "technology-facing tests that guide development." The quadrants are

- **Q1:** technology-facing tests that guide development
- **Q2:** business-facing tests that guide development
- **Q3:** business-facing tests that critique (evaluate) the product
- **Q4:** technology-facing tests that critique (evaluate) the product

The left side of the quadrant matrix is about preventing defects before and during coding. The right side is about finding defects and discovering missing features, but with the understanding that we want to find them as fast as possible. The top half is about exposing tests to the business, and the bottom half is about tests that are more internal to the team but equally important to the success of the software product. "Facing" simply refers to the language of the tests—for example, performance tests satisfy a business need, but the business would not be able to read the tests; they are concerned with the results.

Most agile teams would start with specifying Q2 tests, because those are where you get the examples that turn into specifications and tests that guide coding. In his 2003 blog posts about the matrix, Brian called Q2 and Q1 tests "checked examples." He had originally called them "guiding" or "coaching" examples and credits Ward Cunningham for the adjective "checked." Team members would construct an example of what the code needs to do, check that it doesn't do it yet, make the code do it, and check that the example is now true (Marick, 2003). We include prototypes and simulations in Q2 because they are small experiments to help us understand an idea or concept.

In some cases it makes more sense to start testing for a new feature using tests from a different quadrant. Lisa has worked on projects where her team used performance tests for a spike for determination of the architecture, because that was the most important quality attribute for the feature. Those tests fall into Q4. If your customers are uncertain about their requirements, you might even do an investigation story and start with exploratory testing (Q3). Consider where the highest risk might be and where testing can add the most value.

Most teams concurrently use testing techniques from all of the quadrants, working in small increments. Write a test (or check) for a small chunk of a story, write the code, and once the test is passing, perhaps automate more tests for it. Once the tests (automated checks) are passing, use exploratory testing to see what was missed. Perform security or load testing, and then add the next small chunk and go through the whole process again.

Michael Hüttermann adds "outside-in, barrier-free, collaborative" to the middle of the quadrants (see Figure 8-2). He uses behavior-driven development (BDD) as an example of barrier-free testing. These tests are written in a natural, ubiquitous "given_when_then" language that's accessible to customers as well as developers and invites conversation

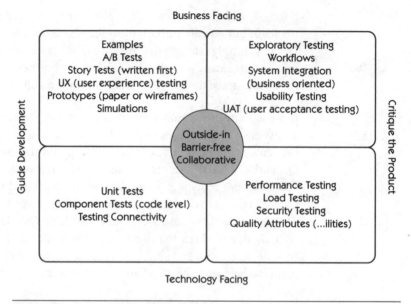

Figure 8-2 Agile testing quadrants (with Michael Hüttermann's adaptation)

between the business and the delivery team. This format can be used for both Q1 and Q2 checking. See Michael's *Agile Record* article (Hüttermann, 2011b) or his book *Agile ALM* (Hüttermann, 2011a) for more ideas on how to augment the Quadrants.

The Quadrants are merely a taxonomy or model to help teams plan their testing and make sure they have all the resources they need to accomplish it. There are no hard-and-fast rules about what goes in which quadrant. Adapt the Quadrants model to show what tests your team needs to consider. Make the testing visible so that your team thinks about testing first as you do your release, feature, and story planning. This visibility exposes the types of tests that are currently being done and the number of people involved. Use it to provoke discussions about testing and which areas you may want to spend more time on.

When discussing the Quadrants, you may realize there are necessary tests your team hasn't considered or that you lack certain skills or resources to be able to do all the necessary testing. For example, a team that Lisa worked on realized that they were so focused on turning business-facing examples into Q2 tests that guide development that they were completely ignoring the need to do performance and security testing. They added in user stories to research what training and tools they would need and then budgeted time to do those Q4 tests.

Planning for Quadrant 1 Testing

Back in the early 1990s, Lisa worked on a waterfall team whose programmers were required to write unit test plans. Unit test plans were definitely overkill, but thinking about the unit tests early and automating all of them were a big part of the reason that critical bugs were never called in to the support center. Agile teams don't plan Q1 tests separately. In test-driven development (TDD), also called test-driven design, testing is an inseparable part of coding. A programmer pair might sit and discuss some of the tests they want to write, but the details evolve as the code evolves. These unit tests guide development but also support the team in the sense that a programmer runs them prior to checking in his or her code, and they are run in the CI on every single check-in of code.

There are other types of technical testing that may be considered as guiding development. They might not be obvious, but they can be critical to keeping the process working. For example, let's say you can't do your testing because there is a problem with connectivity. Create a test script that can be run before your smoke test to make sure that there are no technical issues. Another test programmers might write is one to check the default configuration. Many times these issues aren't known until you start deploying and testing.

Planning for Quadrant 2 Testing

Q2 tests help with planning at the feature or story level. Part IV, "Testing Business Value," will explore guiding development with more detailed business-facing tests. These tests or checked examples are derived from collaboration and conversations about what is important to the feature or story. Having the right people in a room to answer questions and give specific examples helps us plan the tests we need. Think about the levels of precision discussed in the preceding chapter; the questions and the examples get more precise as we get into details about the stories. The process of eliciting examples and creating tests from them fosters collaboration across roles and may identify defects in the form of hidden assumptions or misunderstandings before any code is written.

Show everyone, even the business owners, what you plan to test; see if you're standing on anything sacred, or if they're worried you're missing something that has value to them.

Creating Q2 tests doesn't stop when coding begins. Lisa's teams have found it works well to start with happy path tests. As coding gets under way and the happy path tests start passing, testers and programmers flesh out the tests to encompass boundary conditions, negative tests, edge cases, and more complicated scenarios.

Planning for Quadrant 3 Testing

Testing has always been central to agile development, and guiding development with customer-facing Q2 tests caught on early with agile teams. As agile teams have matured, they've also embraced Q3 testing, exploratory testing in particular. More teams are hiring expert exploratory testing practitioners, and testers on agile teams are spending time expanding their exploratory skills.

Planning for Q3 tests can be a challenge. We can start defining test charters before there is completed code to explore. As Elisabeth Hendrickson explains in her book *Explore It!* (Hendrickson, 2013), charters let us define where to explore, what resources to bring with us, and what information we hope to find. To be effective, some exploratory testing might require completion of multiple small user stories, or waiting until the feature is complete. You may also need to budget time to create the user personas that you might need for testing, although these may already have been created in story-mapping or other feature-planning exercises. Defining exploratory testing charters is not always easy, but it is a great way to share testing ideas with the team and to be able to track what testing was completed. We will give examples of such charters in Chapter 12, "Exploratory Testing," where we discuss different exploratory testing techniques.

One strategy to build in time for exploratory testing is writing stories to explore different areas of a feature or different personas. Another strategy, which Janet prefers, is having a task for exploratory testing for each story, as well as one or more for testing the feature. If your team uses a definition of "done," conducting adequate exploratory testing might be part of that. You can size individual stories with the assumption that you'll spend a significant amount of time doing exploratory testing. Be aware that unless time is specifically allocated during task creation, exploratory testing often gets ignored.

Q3 also includes user acceptance testing (UAT). Planning for UAT needs to happen during release planning or as soon as possible. Include your customers in the planning to decide the best way to proceed. Can they come into the office to test each new feature? Perhaps they are in a different country and you need to arrange computer sharing. Work to get the most frequent and fastest feedback possible from all of your stakeholders.

Planning for Quadrant 4 Testing

Quadrant 4 tests may be the easiest to overlook in planning, and many teams tend to focus on tests to guide development. Quadrant 3 activities such as UAT and exploratory testing may be easier to visualize and are often more familiar to most testers than Quadrant 4 tests. For example, more teams need to support their application globally, so testing in the internationalization and localization space has become important. Agile teams have struggled with how to do this; we include some ideas in Chapter 13, "Other Types of Testing."

Some teams talk about quality attributes with acceptance criteria on each story of a feature. We prefer to use the word *constraints*. In *Discover to Deliver* (Gottesdiener and Gorman, 2012), Ellen Gottesdiener and Mary Gorman recommend using Tom and Kai Gilb's Planguage (their planning language; see the bibliography for Part III, "Planning—So You Don't Forget the Big Picture," for links) to talk about these constraints in a very definite way (Gilb, 2013).

If your product has a constraint such as "Every screen must respond in less than three seconds," that criterion doesn't need to be repeated for every single story. Find a mechanism to remind your team when you are discussing the story that this constraint needs to be built in and must be tested. Liz Keogh describes a technique to write tests about how capabilities such as system performance can be monitored (Keogh, 2014a). Organizations usually know which operating systems or browsers they are supporting at the beginning of a release, so add them as constraints and include them in your testing estimations. These types of quality attributes are often good candidates for testing at a feature level, but if it makes sense to test them at the story level, do so there; think, "Test early." Chapter 13, "Other Types of Testing," will cover a few different testing types that you may have been struggling with.

CHALLENGING THE QUADRANTS

Over the years, many people have challenged the validity of the Quadrants or adjusted them slightly to be more meaningful to them. We decided to share a couple of these stories because we think it is valuable to continuously challenge what we "know" to be true. That is how we learn and evolve to improve and meet changing demands.

Gojko's Challenge to the Quadrants

Gojko Adzic, *an author and strategic software delivery consultant, challenges the validity of the Quadrants in the current software delivery era.*

The agile testing quadrants model is probably the one thing that everyone remembers about the original *Agile Testing* book. It was an incredibly useful thinking tool for the software delivery world then—2008. It helped me facilitate many useful discussions on the big picture missing from typical programmers' view of quality, and it helped many testers figure out what to focus on. The world now, as of 2014, looks significantly different. There has been a surge in the popularity of continuous delivery, DevOps, Big Data analytics, lean startup delivery, and exploratory testing. The Quadrants model is due for a serious update.

One of the problems with the original Quadrants model is that it was easily misunderstood as a sequence of test types—especially that there is some kind of division between things before and things after development.

This problem is even worse now than in 2008. With the surge in popularity of continuous delivery, the dividing line is getting more blurred and is disappearing. With shorter iterations and continuous delivery, it's generally difficult to draw the line between activities that support the team and those that critique the product. Why would performance tests not be aimed at supporting the team? Why are functional tests not critiquing the product? Why is UAT separate from functional testing? I always found the horizontal dimension of the Quadrants difficult to justify, because critiquing the product can support the team quite effectively if it is done in a timely way. For example, specification by example helps teams to completely merge functional tests and UAT into something that is continuously checked during development. Many teams I worked with recently run performance tests during development, primarily not to mess things up with frequent changes. These are just two examples where things on the right side of the Quadrants are now used more to support the team than anything else. With lean startup methods, products get a lot of critiquing even before a single line of production code is written.

Dividing tests into those that support development and those that evaluate the product does not really help to facilitate useful discussions anymore, so we need a different model—in particular, one that helps to address the eternal issue of so-called nonfunctional requirements, which for many people actually means, "It's going to be a difficult discussion, so let's not have it." The old Quadrants model puts "ilities" into a largely forgotten quadrant of technical tests after development. But things like security, performance, scalability, and so on are not really technical; they imply quite a lot of business expectations, such as compliance, meeting service-levels agreements, handling expected peak loads, and so on. They are also not really nonfunctional, as they imply quite a lot of functionality such as encryption, caching, and work distribution. This of course is complicated by the fact that some expectations in those areas are not that easy to define or test for—especially the unknown unknowns. If we treat these as purely technical concerns, the business expectations are often not explicitly stated or verified. Instead of nonfunctional, these concerns are often dysfunctional. And although many "ilities" are difficult to prove before the software is actually in contact with its real users, the emergence of A/B split testing techniques over the last five years has made it relatively easy, cheap, and low risk to verify those things in production.

Another aspect of testing not really captured well by the first book's Quadrants is the surge in popularity and importance of exploratory testing. In the old model, exploratory testing is something that happens from the business perspective in order to evaluate the product (often misunderstood as after development). In many contexts, well documented in Elisabeth Hendrickson's book on exploratory testing (Hendrickson, 2013) and James Whittaker's book *How Google Tests Software* (Whittaker et al., 2012), exploratory testing can be incredibly useful for the technical perspective as well and, more importantly, is something that should be done during development.

The third aspect that is not captured well by the early Quadrants is the possibility to quantify and measure software changes through usage analytics in production. The surge in popularity of Big Data analytics, especially combined with lean startup and continuous delivery models, enables teams to test relatively cheaply things that were very expensive to test ten years ago—for example, true performance impacts. When the original *Agile Testing* book came out, serious performance testing often meant having a complete hardware copy of the production system. These days, many teams de-risk those issues with smaller, less risky continuous changes, whose impact is measured directly on a subset of the production environment. Many teams also look at their production log trends to spot unexpected and previously unknown problems quickly.

We need to change the model (Figure 8-3) to facilitate all those discussions, and I think that the current horizontal division isn't helping anymore. The context-driven testing community argues very forcefully that looking for expected results isn't really testing; instead, they call that checking. Without getting into an argument about what is or isn't testing, I found the division to be quite useful for many recent discussions with clients. Perhaps that is a more useful second axis for the model: the difference between looking for expected outcomes and analyzing unknowns, aspects without a definite yes/no answer, where results require skillful analytic interpretation. Most of the innovation these days seems to happen in the second part anyway. Checking for expected results, from both a technical and business perspective, is now pretty much a solved problem.

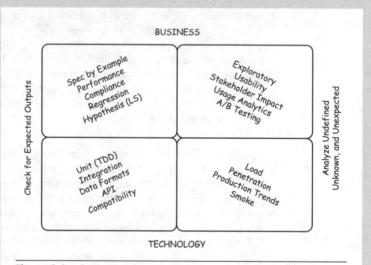

Figure 8-3   Gojko Adzic's version of the agile testing quadrants

Thinking about checking expected outcomes versus analyzing outcomes that weren't predefined helps to explain several important issues facing software delivery teams today:

Security concerns could be split easily into functional tests for compliance such as encryption, data protection, authentication, and so on (essentially all checking for predefined expected results), and penetration/investigations (not predefined). This will help to engage the delivery team and business sponsors in a more useful discussion about describing the functional part of security up front.

Performance concerns could be divided into running business scenarios to prove agreed-upon service levels and capacity, continuous delivery style (predefined), and load tests (where will it break?). This will help to engage the delivery team and business in defining performance expectations and prevent people from treating performance as a purely technical concern. By avoiding the support the team/evaluate the product divisions, we allow a discussion of executing performance tests in different environments and at different times.

Exploration would become much more visible and could be clearly divided between technical and business-oriented exploratory tests. This can support a discussion of technical exploratory tests that developers should perform or that testers can execute by reusing existing automation frameworks. It can also support an overall discussion of what should go into business-oriented exploratory tests.

Build-measure-learn product tests would fit into the model nicely, and the model would facilitate a meaningful discussion of how those tests require a defined hypothesis and how that is different from just pushing things out to see what happens through usage analytics.

We can facilitate a conversation on how to spot unknown problems by monitoring production logs as a way of continuously testing technical concerns that are difficult to check and expensive to automate before deployment, but still useful to support the team. By moving the discussion away from supporting development or evaluating the product toward checking expectations or inspecting the unknown, we would also have a nice way of differentiating those tests from business-oriented production usage analytics.

Most importantly, by using a different horizontal axis, we can raise awareness about a whole category of things that don't fit into typical test plans or test reports but are still incredibly valuable. The early Quadrants were useful because they raised awareness about a whole category of things in the upper-left corner that most teams weren't really thinking of but are now taken as common sense. The 2010s Quadrants need to help us raise awareness about some more important issues for today.

	✔ **CONFIRM**	🎩 **INVESTIGATE**
BUSINESS	BUSINESS-FACING EXPECTATIONS	RISKS TO EXTERNAL QUALITY ATTRIBUTES
TECHNOLOGY	TECHNOLOGY-FACING EXPECTATIONS	RISKS TO INTERNAL QUALITY ATTRIBUTES

Figure 8-4   Elisabeth Hendrickson's version of the agile testing quadrants

Elisabeth Hendrickson also presented an alternative to the existing Quadrants in her talk about "The Thinking Tester" (Hendrickson, 2012). It is similar to Gojko's version but has a different look. You can see in Figure 8-4 that she relabeled the vertical columns to "confirm" and "investigate," while the horizontal rows still represent business and technology.

The top left quadrant represents the expectations of the business, which could be in the form of executable (automated) specifications. Others might be represented by paper prototypes or wireframes. At the top right are tests that help investigate risks concerning the external quality of the product. It is very much like the original quadrant's idea of exploratory testing, scenarios, or usability testing. Like Gojko's model, the bottom right quadrant highlights the risks of the internal working of the system.

Both of these alternative models provide value. We think there is room for multiple variations to accommodate a spectrum of needs. For example, organizations that are able to adopt continuous delivery are able to think in this space, but many organizations are years from accomplishing that. Check the bibliography for Part III for links to additional testing quadrant models. Use them to help make sure your team covers all the different types of tests you need in order to deliver the right value for your customers.

USING OTHER INFLUENCES FOR PLANNING

There are many useful models and ideas for helping us in our test planning, and we shouldn't throw them away. As Tim Ottinger and Jeff Langr have said (Ottinger and Langr, 2009b), a mnemonic for thinking about what are called nonfunctional requirements is still useful. The FURPS model (see Figure 8-5) was developed at Hewlett-Packard and was first publicly elaborated by Grady and Caswell (Wikipedia, 2014f); it is now widely used in the software industry. The + was later added to the model after various campaigns at HP to extend the acronym to emphasize various attributes.

James Whittaker developed a methodology he calls the Attribute Component Capability (ACC) matrix (Whittaker, 2011) to help define what to test based on risk. ACC consists of three different parts that define the system under test: Attributes, Components, and Capabilities. He defines these as:

- **Attributes** (adjectives of the system) are qualities and characteristics that promote the product and distinguish it from the competition; examples are "Fast," "Secure," "Stable," and "Elegant."
- **Components** (nouns of the system) are building blocks that together constitute the system in question. Some examples of

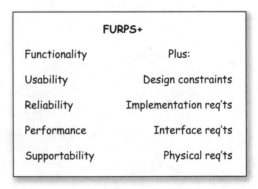

Figure 8-5   FURPS+ flash card (Ottinger and Langr, 2011)

Components are "Firmware," "Printing," and "File System" for an operating system project, or "Database," "Cart," and "Product Browser" for an online shopping site.

- **Capabilitie**s (verbs of the system) describe the abilities of a particular Component to satisfy the Attributes of the system. An example Capability for a shopping site could be "Processes monetary transactions using HTTPS." You can see that this could be a Capability of the "Cart" component when trying to meet the "Secure" Attribute. The most important aspect of Capabilities is that they are testable.

Creating a high-level matrix using this model can be a simple way to visualize your system. Figure 8-6 shows an example of what such a matrix might look like. Gojko Adzic agrees that exposing system characteristics and providing more visibility is definitely a good idea (Adzic, 2010a), though he cautions that while we can learn from other fields, we should be careful about using them as a metaphor for software development.

Use heuristics such as Elisabeth Hendrickson's "Test Heuristics Cheat Sheet" (Hendrickson, 2011) or tried-and-true techniques such as state diagrams or truth tables to think of new ideas for attributes. Combine these ideas with models like the Quadrants so that the conversations about the system constraints or usability can extract clear examples. Using all the tools in your toolbox can only help increase the quality of the product.

Components			Capabilities	Attributes		
Mobile App	Firmware	Printing		Fast	Secure	Stable
			Manage profile			
			Send messages			
			Update network			
INFLUENCE AREA				RISK / IMPORTANCE		

Figure 8-6   ACC example

PLANNING FOR TEST AUTOMATION

Since Mike Cohn came up with his test automation pyramid in 2003, many teams have found it a useful model to plan their test automation. To take advantage of fast feedback, we need to consider at what level our automation tests should be. When we look at the standard pyramid, Figure 8-7, we see three levels.

The lowest level is the base—the unit tests. When we consider testing, we should try to push the tests as low as they can go for the highest return on investment (ROI) and the quickest feedback.

However, when we have business logic where tests need to be visible to the business, we should use collaborative tools that create tests at the service layer (the API) to specify them in a way that documents system behavior. See Chapter 16, "Test Automation Design Patterns and Approaches," for

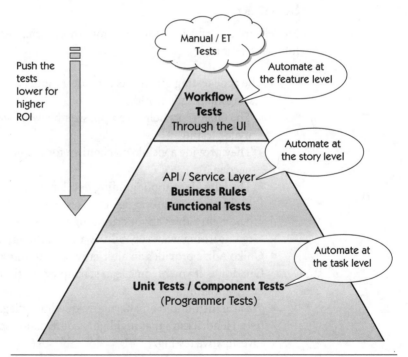

Figure 8-7 Automation pyramid

more details. It is at this layer that we can automate at the story level so that testing and automation can keep up with the coding.

The top layer of the pyramid consists of the workflow tests through the user interface (UI). If we have a high degree of confidence in the unit tests and the service-level or API-level tests, we can keep these slower, more brittle automated tests to a minimum. See Chapter 15, "Pyramids of Automation," for more detail on alternative pyramid models.

Practices such as guiding development with examples can help define what the best level for the test is. A team's cadence can be set by how well they plan and execute their automation and how well they understand the level of detail they need. Consider also how to make your automation test runs visible, whether displayed in the continuous integration environment or on a monitor that is in the open.

SUMMARY

Models are a useful tool for planning. In this chapter, we covered the following points:

- The agile testing quadrants provide a model for thinking about testing in an agile world.
  - The Quadrants help to emphasize the whole-team responsibility for testing.
  - They provide a visible mechanism for talking about the testing needed.
  - The left side is about guiding development, learning what to build, and preventing defects—testing early.
  - The right side is about critiquing the product, finding defects, and learning what capabilities are still missing.
- Gojko Adzic provides an alternative way to think about the Quadrants if you are in a lean startup or continuous delivery environment.
- We also introduced an alternative quadrant diagram from Elisabeth Hendrickson that highlights confirmatory checks versus investigative testing.

- There are already many tools in our agile testing toolbox, and we can combine them with other models such as the Quadrants to make our testing as effective as possible.
- FURPS and ACC are additional examples of models you can use to help plan based on risk and a variety of quality characteristics.
- The automation pyramid is a reminder to think about automation and to plan for it at the different levels.

Part IV

TESTING BUSINESS VALUE

In her book *Explore It!* (Hendrickson, 2013), Elisabeth Hendrickson describes two facets of a test strategy (pp. 5–6). Per Elisabeth, "checks" are tests that verify that "the implementation behaves as intended under supported configurations and conditions." She explains exploring as testing that involves scouting around the areas that the checks don't cover, "designing and executing tiny experiments in rapid succession using the results from the last experiment to inform the next." In Elisabeth's opinion, a comprehensive test strategy needs both checking and exploring.

The distinction between checking and exploring is interesting, but we're not sure that testing definition goes far enough. Testing is more than "just" testing software. It is about testing ideas, helping business experts identify the most valuable features to develop next, finding a common understanding for each feature, preventing defects, and testing for business value.

A whole-team approach to quality means incorporating testing activities from the time a feature is first conceptualized. In this part, we'll cover some tools and techniques that let us help customers focus on features to help achieve their most valuable business goals. Testers make important contributions during these activities, and we'll point out what testers can learn from other specialists to help customers articulate requirements and examples of desired system behavior. We'll also go into detail on guiding development with examples and good ways to obtain those examples.

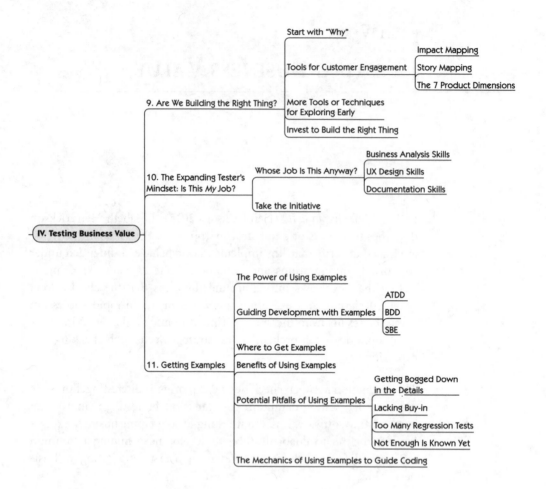

- ▪ **Chapter 9**, "Are We Building the Right Thing?"
- ▪ **Chapter 10**, "The Expanding Tester's Mindset: Is This *My* Job?"
- ▪ **Chapter 11**, "Getting Examples"

Chapter 9

ARE WE BUILDING THE RIGHT THING?

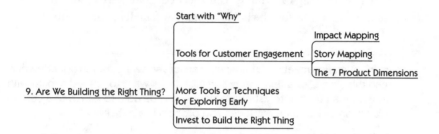

Most of us feel there is never enough time to test. But the truth is, testing the software is only one part of the equation. Unfortunately, we often waste time developing software that doesn't meet the customers' highest-priority needs or software they will never use, or we may simply deliver products whose cost exceeds their value to the company.

Many teams we've worked on have mastered development practices and learned how to deliver robust applications. Most of the reported bugs or deviations turned out to be missed or missing requirements. When teams experiment with better ways to ask their customers the right questions early, they understand the purpose of each feature more clearly and are better able to develop what the customers really need. Think about it as testing early or testing the business value. As with all testing activities, our whole delivery team should take responsibility for making sure we learn what our customers really need.

START WITH "WHY"

In our experience, one of the most important ways testers can help both their customer and delivery teams is by focusing on the purpose of each potential new feature or user story. When we start asking why the customers want the feature (the problem they are trying to solve), we're more likely to build the right thing. As we discuss the goals that the feature should meet and how we might measure success, we can get good examples of desirable system behavior. The developer and customer teams can sketch out a roadmap and set milestones to help us know when we're Feature Done.

A discussion about "why" often leads to the realization that the customer isn't asking for what is really needed. If we were to just build what the customer asks for, the business may suffer. Here's an example.

Lisa's Story

In an estimating meeting for financial services software, our product owner read this story: "As a third-party administrator, I want to upload a loan, with my own loan term, interest rate, amount, and be able to generate a corrective action to liquidate the funds and process the out check."

Without getting into a lot of details about what that means, I instantly recognized that the PO was giving us a "what" and was even telling us how to implement a new feature, without telling us why the business wanted it. Our application already had a full-featured loan system, so clearly something was odd. I asked, "What is the purpose of this story? What business problem is being solved?"

It turned out that third-party administrators used our system but had different rules around loans, and different terms and interest rates. They couldn't use our loan system as is. The PO was trying to find a cheap way of giving those users what they needed. He latched onto a feature we had developed shortly before, which involved uploading files to distribute funds.

Once we understood the reason for the story, we rewrote it. "As a third-party administrator with special loan rules, I want to be able to request, on behalf of a 401(k) participant, a loan that is not subject to the normal system validations, so that the participant can receive the loan funds and repay the loan."

The best way to implement the feature was to update our existing system to have special validations for loans whenever a third-party administrator requested a loan on behalf of a client. No new code was required to process the loan and disburse the funds.

Both functionality and return on investment are key components of the software's business value. Keep thinking about building the "right thing," and ask the necessary questions to keep product quality high. Use Real Options to help you optimize the process of deciding what solution to deliver. If your delivery team uses good practices so they can implement new features quickly, you can take more time to learn what option will be most valuable (Matts and Maassen, 2007).

Tools for Customer Engagement

There are many effective exercises to help stakeholders and delivery teams figure out the right things to build. We proposed some tools for eliciting examples and requirements in *Agile Testing* (pp. 153–64), including checklists, mind maps, spreadsheets, mock-ups, flow diagrams, and wikis.

Here, we suggest some additional practices that we've found valuable for understanding customer needs and use them to create tests that guide development. Experiment with them, and see which work best for your team to help build quality into your product.

Impact Mapping

In his book on impact mapping (Adzic, 2012), Gojko Adzic explains how delivery teams and business stakeholders can collaborate to quickly identify alternative paths to deliverables that provide the best value. By answering the questions "Why?" "Who?" "How?" and "What?" teams construct a roadmap that helps them quickly learn whether a particular approach will produce the desired results and be adaptable to the inevitable changes.

Impact mapping has been adapted from other brainstorming and planning tools, such as mind mapping and story mapping. It's a simple, structured way to focus the team on the purpose of what to build, and it helps to identify the most worthwhile features to build first. The focus shifts from "What are we going to do?" to "Why are we doing this, what is our goal, who can help us, and who is getting in our way?" This also helps determine whether a particular problem may be best solved outside of the software. For example, the solution might be better training for system users.

In our experience, business stakeholders tend to tell us *what* they want us to implement: "Create an interface just like X, but make it do Y instead." They may even think they're saving us time by reusing existing code. Once we understand the purpose, the team might be able to propose a simple technical implementation.

We'll work through an example to help you understand. Let's say we're a retail Internet site startup, and our business stakeholders want to encourage new customers as well as keep existing customers. They come to us with a feature:

> *Force customers to create an account when they check out, so we can save their billing, shipping, and payment information.*

We would like to understand better what the business wants. We bring our business experts together with the delivery team to create an impact map. First, we ask the business experts why they want this feature and learn that they want to retain customers. We work together to create a specific, measurable, actionable, realistic, and timely goal. In this case, the goal is to achieve a 90% customer retention rate within the next three months.

Next, we look at who can help us achieve or influence our ability to achieve that goal. These could be people who can help us, but we should also think about who might get in our way. There can be many other stakeholders (actors) besides our delivery team, such as the marketing department and the vendors who supply our products.

Once they are identified, we want to think about how these different actors help or hinder our ability to achieve our goal. Marketing could come up with a compelling loyalty program. Our user experience (UX) designers could make our site enjoyable to use. Our security experts could find ways to give our customers confidence that our site is secure. These "hows" are the impacts that different actors can have on the business goal.

After identifying impacts, we address what we and the actors we identified can accomplish to move the business toward the goal. These are the deliverables. In our example scenario, one deliverable could be coupons created by our marketing group to encourage repeat purchasing. Another deliverable could be a secure, easy-to-use interface where

Figure 9-1   Sample impact map

customers can save their payment information to make future buying easier. Figure 9-1 shows an example of information that might be on our impact map for this feature.

As we brainstorm these dimensions of who could influence our ability to reach our goal, how they could help or hinder, and what deliverables could move us toward the goal, we identify potential experiments we can try with quick feedback loops built in. An impact-mapping session is one way to focus on the next most valuable thing to deliver to the business. It helps identify the simplest way to solve business problems and avoid wasting time on features that turn out to be unwanted or too expensive.

This is a great time to start thinking about testing risks. Can a customer be prevented from repurchasing later? To whom do we need to talk to get test data? What other impacts might there be? Our domain expertise may help us think of ways to achieve the goal without developing new software features. Impact mapping is one way to think creatively about the testing you need to do and to prioritize the areas that deserve the most focus. As we think about testing, we look for ways to promote collaboration in the team and plan testing in a format that is easy to keep up-to-date.

The impact map itself might serve as a form of test plan, and as discussed in Chapter 7, "Levels of Precision for Planning," mind maps are excellent planning tools. The physical form of a deliverable isn't generally important. What matters is that we anticipate our testing needs and make sure we budget enough time and other resources for adequate testing. The alternative paths we can generate via impact mapping help ensure that we mitigate risks appropriately.

Story Mapping

Story mapping is a hands-on way to model a high-level feature and slice it into user stories in a two-dimensional fashion. Jeff Patton first wrote about it in a January 2005 *Better Software* article, "How You Slice It" (Patton, 2005). The process of creating and walking through a story map helps identify where to start with a new feature, visualizing the minimum viable product (MVP). The story map also helps the team stay focused on the right areas, track progress, and make course corrections as development proceeds. You can start the learning with an impact map, and when you have identified your features (the deliverables), you can get into more detail with the story map.

Get your development team and business stakeholders together for a workshop. Create personas to represent the various types of your users and their roles, and then think about how each persona would use your system or feature. What would they do first? What would they do next? Make a timeline of user activities using index cards (or sticky notes) on a wall, table, or floor. Then go back and look at each user activity in detail and create user tasks and details about those tasks. Write those on cards, too, and stack them vertically under the corresponding user activity.

Once the story map is in place, you can slice the stories into high-level user stories and plan which ones may go into each iteration and release. The highest-priority activities are at the top of the story map and can become your MVP. Some people call this a "walking skeleton" (Freeman and Pryce, 2009)—the least amount you can deliver that will add value for your customer. Walk through the story map with stakeholders and see if you can think of any other issues. You aren't going into details yet, but you're identifying slices of features that will deliver the most value.

The process of mapping stories helps customers and delivery teams identify the smallest possible release, determine what's in scope for that release, and prioritize stories accordingly. To learn more about story mapping, read Jeff Patton's book *User Story Mapping* (Patton, 2014). See the bibliography in Part IV, "Testing Business Value," for additional references.

Story Maps and Testing

Steve Rogalsky, *an agilist from Winnipeg, Canada, tells why he thinks testers should care about story mapping.*

So you're an agile tester and wonder why you should care about story maps. You may already be convinced that modeling your backlog in two dimensions is useful for helping the whole team visualize the big picture. However, story maps are also a valuable testing tool, providing two additional testing avenues. In the first case, the map itself offers the ability to test the validity of a solution. In the second, a story map improves a team's ability to identify story slices and then test them.

Testing What to Build

User story maps are a representation: they provide a means to visualize a system that might be built and are useful for testing the validity of that system before investing significant time and money. A story shared at a recent Agile Winnipeg event demonstrated this principle well. The company involved used story mapping to test an idea before building any software. The team had a project idea that they thought would serve their client well. After quickly building a story map around that idea, they presented the map to the client at the next customer conference. Although it soon became clear that the idea missed the mark, the customer was able to collaborate with the team on the spot to adjust the map until it represented what they actually wanted built. The map itself was the tool that allowed for the idea to be tested (and then adjusted) and moved the project forward.

Testing Application Slices

As Crispin and Gregory demonstrated in their first book, identifying thin slices and small chunks is important for testing agile projects. Story maps help identify those slices, but, perhaps more importantly, they help us understand how those thinly sliced stories might fit together to form a thin slice of the whole application. When undertaking an agile project, testers are required to make a vital shift in thinking: test only small pieces at a time. Despite this fundamental change, it is also important to ensure that the first few pieces fit together, enabling end-to-end testing as early as possible. The story map helps to identify and prioritize that first application slice. It may be based on a user scenario or just a string of stories that represent the smallest stories that allow left-to-right movement on the map.

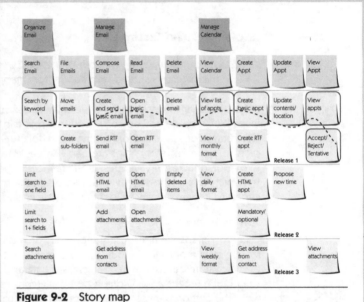

Figure 9-2   Story map

As the team identifies that first slice, using excellent testing skills is crucial. By looking at the map (see Figure 9-2), you can identify areas that will be difficult to test, areas where the test variations are still relatively unknown, or areas that represent higher risk. This activity can help identify stories that should be included in the first application slice.

When coding and testing begin, personas and user scenarios that were created can be revisited, helping to flesh out the map and application slices. Testing with a persona in mind helps ensure that the targeted customer will be satisfied with the solution. It may not be possible or wise to test if the application works well for everyone—but testing should evaluate whether the targeted personas can use the application easily and that the new functionality fits into, or adds to, their current processes without getting in the way.

> ### Story Maps—a Testing Tool after All
> At first glance, the story map doesn't appear to be an obvious asset for testing, but upon closer inspection, it proves its value in any testing toolbox. The map itself is a reliable way to test that the right system is being built before any code is written. The map also provides a visual aid for testing in horizontal application slices, allowing for early confirmation that a project is on the right track.

As Steve points out, although story mapping is essentially a requirements-gathering tool, it is also a great way to start testing before any code has ever been written. As you are looking for testing ideas, remember to consider the quality attributes that also need testing. Identify areas of uncertainty and risk, and look for simpler alternatives that might make testing easier.

The 7 Product Dimensions

Business analysts (BA) can teach us many practices to help us partner with customers to elicit the information necessary to create valuable products. Whether or not your team already includes BAs, the team should learn and experiment with analysis practices. Many business analysis techniques are already in a tester's toolbox and need only to be adapted slightly to be used effectively. For example, state diagrams and context diagrams are used not only for creating test variations, but also for determining what to build. If testers start applying these techniques during story readiness sessions, the switch to preventing defects—instead of concentrating on finding them after the software is coded—has started.

One analysis tool we've found especially useful is the 7 Product Dimensions (Gottesdiener and Gorman, 2012), which help identify product needs at all levels of planning. These dimensions include:

- **User:** Who values, benefits from, and/or uses the product? The user could be a person or another system that interacts with the product. Personas are one way to describe a typical (human) user.
- **Interface:** What mechanisms are needed to connect users with the product? How will the product send and receive data or

messages? Relationship maps, context diagrams, prototypes, and wireframes are ways to visualize the interfaces.

- **Action:** What are the product's capabilities? How are actions triggered, and in what sequence? How does the product respond? How do actions affect data? Process diagrams, story maps, and value stream maps visualize the actions' flow and sequence. Think about potential scenarios where a step is skipped or done in the wrong sequence.

- **Data:** What data does the product receive, from where, and how is the data validated and stored? What data do users need, in what context, and for how long is it valid? Data models are used to visualize data relationships; state diagrams show the transitions between data states.

- **Control:** What constraints does the product need to enforce, for example, policies, regulations, business rules? What's the risk of noncompliance? Decision tables and trees are useful for organizing sets of rules.

- **Environment:** Think about the physical properties of the product: Where will it be used? How will it be installed, configured, licensed, and operated? What about the development environment—what software, hardware, and standards will be used? A company may have multiple environments, so identify which apply for the product being planned.

- **Quality attribute:** What are the levels of service for operational qualities such as availability, recoverability, safety, usability, and so on? For development qualities, think about the definitions for attributes such as efficiency, modifiability, and testability. Think about how you are going to measure these attributes.

We've found it helpful to consider all seven dimensions during release, feature, and iteration planning. Often you'll realize a dimension has been overlooked, and additional stories or resources are required. For example, when focusing on the data dimension, you realize your application will receive data from a third party. Are the validation rules known? Is the third party participating in the testing? When should this testing start? How will invalid data be handled? Will the sender receive appropriate error messages? Is there a secure way for the third party to send the data, and is a "handshake" required when it is received? Do you have sample data from the third party for testing purposes? Do any regulations apply, and does any information need to be disclosed to users? Where will the data be persisted? Will the quantity of data affect system performance? These are examples of very powerful questions that are best asked early. Bring your tester mindset to the game!

Structured Conversations Using the 7 Product Dimensions

Mary Gorman and **Ellen Gottesdiener**, *authors of* Discover to Deliver *(Gottesdiener and Gorman, 2012), describe a client that was undergoing a large agile transformation and how the power of structured conversations helped to build the "right" thing.*

The organization needed to elevate its testing and analysis practices quickly. The leaders envisioned transforming the way they elicited, communicated, and tested agile requirements. With 40-plus testers and analysts, many of whom were new to the disciplines of quality and business analysis, the challenge was large.

Both the test manager and the business analysis manager made no bones about the fact that they had, at best, ad hoc practices. Even with basic agile training, using kanban to visualize the teams' work, writing stories, and employing a rough form of given_when_then for specifying requirements, the teams were still acting in a handover mode. This meant they were not having timely, just-in-time conversations about requirements at either the iteration (Now-View) or release (Pre-View) level. Teams were finding defects late that would have been avoidable with good analysis. They were somewhat demoralized because they struggled to deliver "done" stories within an iteration.

The leadership team needed the testers and analysts to play a leadership role by exemplifying to the developer and business communities how to effectively collaborate around agile requirements.

Mary Gorman guided all the testers and business analysts in learning and applying the Discover to Deliver framework. A critical project was the focus of a clinic that engaged the entire agile team in identifying high-value features and stories for the next release and iteration. The team collaboratively discovered options for all 7 Product Dimensions (see Figure 9-3).

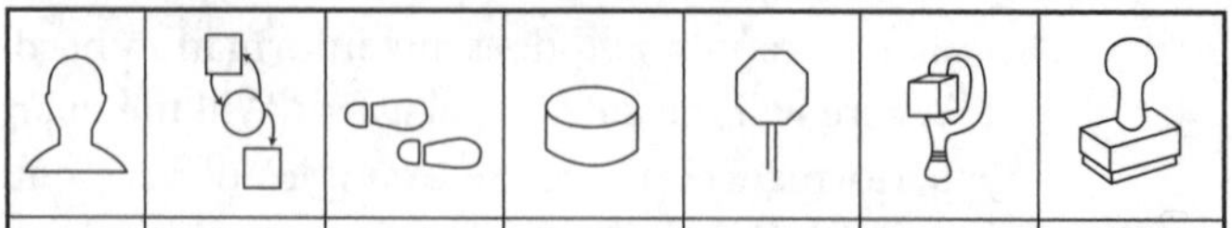

User	Interface	Action	Data	Control	Environment	Quality Attribute
Users interact with the product	The product connects to users, systems, and devices	The product provides capabilities for users	The product includes a repository of data and useful information	The product enforces constraints	The product conforms to physical properties and technology platforms	The product has certain properties that qualify its operation and development

Figure 9-3 The 7 Product Dimensions
Source: Ellen Gottesdiener and Mary Gorman. 2012. *Discover to Deliver: Agile Product Planning and Analysis.* Sudbury, MA: EBG Consulting. Used with permission.

The team used the Options Board to display and analyze their findings. (The Options Board hangs on a long wall with the 7 Product Dimension symbols placed across the top. Under each dimension the team lists options and sketches appropriate analysis models.) They employed the three-part structured conversation to guide their work:

- Explore options.
- Evaluate options within and across the 7 Dimensions and identify high-value candidate solutions.
- Confirm the solution by defining acceptance criteria. There were whole-group activities as well as cross-functional subgroup work.

At the end of the session, folks reflected and noted: "We reached a shared understanding of the stories; team is all actively engaged and contributing; our conversation had focus; we were able to flesh out a lot of really good details." One week later, the product owner and tech lead shared their insights.

Product Owner: "In the last day and a half I feel that our team has made better/more progress than we did all last week (iteration 1). As a result, our team is not becoming frustrated by lack of progress or understanding, but instead is encouraged by the progress being made, which in turn leads to a more positive working environment."

Tech Lead: "Just wanted to pass on to you some positive feedback from our team's discovery sessions this week. I think everyone felt we have been more successful this week. I took a quick survey as to why people thought that was. Some comments:

- "'We are not trying to get it perfect.'
- "'We are not so focused on just filling in the story card; rather the story card is a by-product of the discussion.'
- "'We are more focused on understanding the requirements, not trying to fit the story to an expected solution.'
- "'The 7 Product Dimensions approach is helping to focus the discussion.'"

Mary and Ellen recently followed up with the business analysis and test leaders. They shared:

- "Teams use the 7 Product Dimensions in all their requirements conversations. They hang the 7 Dimensions images near their kanban boards and use them to guide discovery and analysis. The results are more efficient and effective conversations and higher-quality requirements."
- "The key was making these requirements conversations a collaboration among all the stakeholders. Since analysis and the tester mindset are everyone's responsibility, this has made a big impact on the development and business owner communities."
- "They use a list of what they call 'probing questions' for each of the 7 Dimensions. The questions combine the 'Focus Questions for the Structured Conversation' provided in *Discover to Deliver: Agile Product Planning and Analysis* with testing heuristics."
- "The project teams are getting closer and closer to truly doing just-in-time and just-enough analysis."

The test and business analysis teams are serving as leaders in using the 7 Product Dimensions for test planning, specification, and deeper collaboration. The successes achieved to date in conducting timely, focused, and holistic structured requirements conversations have been critical in fueling the transformation project.

Experiment with practices from the agile business analysis experts, such as the 7 Product Dimensions and structured conversations, to help your team identify what features to build. Remember to ask questions and to aim for that shared understanding of what your team is building.

MORE TOOLS OR TECHNIQUES FOR EXPLORING EARLY

Eric Ries (Ries, 2010) talks about the mindset needed by companies that are innovating and trying new ideas. The ideas he recommends for lean startups can be used in many situations. Build-measure-learn (BML) is all about building small chunks, measuring, and learning by getting early feedback and validating ideas. Sounds like testing, doesn't it?

Testers can add value in these situations by asking questions and helping to determine what can be measured. Sometimes we can do simple things like review paper mock-ups that programmers or UX designers have created.

A/B testing is one technique that can be used to test a hypothesis. The idea is to develop two separate implementations and put both out for customers to actively use, and then to measure the results. Users are directed to different implementations. The company monitors statistics such as which customers click through or buy something and which leave right away. In this way, companies can decide which experience the customers like better based on actual evidence. One of our contributors has shared his story about A/B testing in Chapter 13, "Other Types of Testing."

As we mentioned in Chapter 7, "Levels of Precision for Planning," visualizing different options with tools such as mind maps is a powerful way to uncover hidden assumptions.

INVEST TO BUILD THE RIGHT THING

The future is unpredictable; we can only make our best educated guess. However, by asking good questions and visualizing possible answers, we can help our customers target the most valuable features to develop next. Start by learning the purpose of each proposed feature. Think ahead to what would happen when the feature is deployed to production. How will we know it's successful? How will we judge whether it provided the right value? How will we measure or monitor? Answering those questions early can help avoid spending time on the wrong things.

There are many aspects of quality, and we realize that techniques such as the 7 Product Dimensions just scratch the surface. We have to balance functionality with reliability, security, performance, and other attributes valued by our customers. We have to weigh the cost of delaying a release while we work to build a feature that's good enough against the need to delight our customers and make them want to buy our product.

Invest time to help customers identify the most valuable feature to build next, and deploy the minimum viable product. If you can avoid wasting time delivering the wrong thing, your team will have more time for critical testing activities.

In the next chapter, we'll go into more detail about synergies between testing and other skill sets that help us start each new product cycle with a focus on building the right thing.

SUMMARY

It's hard for customers to know what they want, and even harder for them to explain it to the delivery team. We can help them identify the most valuable features to build and help them articulate what features they want so that we have that shared understanding of what to build. In this chapter, we looked at the following concepts:

- Start with the "why," the purpose of the software we're developing.
- Try out some different tools for helping customers articulate what they want, including
  - Impact mapping
  - Story mapping
  - 7 Product Dimensions
  - Lean startup techniques
- Experiment with different tools that help your development and customer teams collaborate to build the right thing.
- The process needs cycles of modeling, hypothesis, experiments, discovery, and learning, just what a testing mindset provides.

Chapter 10

The Expanding Tester's Mindset: Is This *My* Job?

In the preceding chapter, we mentioned the overlap between business analysis and testing. Both business analysts and testers work with customers to understand their desires for each feature, but other roles get involved, too. For example, user experience (UX) design experts seek to understand both how people will use the product and the value the business hopes to derive from proposed new capabilities. Technical writers must understand how different users will use the system so they can document how it meets their business or technical needs. However, a team or organization might lack those specialized skills, so when the need arises, team members can learn and use some valuable practices and techniques from those other specialties.

Whose Job Is This Anyway?

As we mention in Chapter 3, "Roles and Competencies," agile development encourages generalizing specialists with T-shaped skills. Nevertheless, we often need team members with specialized training and experience in certain areas to understand business needs.

Business Analysis Skills

We've realized more and more, since writing *Agile Testing*, that BAs bring some important specialized skills to the agile team party. They facilitate structured conversations with the business experts. They remember to ask questions about all dimensions of the product. They understand the whole business domain, not just the parts that are automated with software. Business analysts historically help business experts communicate their needs to delivery teams. Bernice Niel Ruhland told us about her experiences managing both testers and business analysts. Often the same people did both roles. Having both skill sets on the team worked well because they were always thinking about testing and requirements together.

Like testing experts, BA experts know how to ask good questions and to start with the "whys." Many BAs know how to specify tests based on customer examples and likely have some tools in their toolkit that are beyond the experience of most testers. We need to think about the business problem first, and from a testing perspective, we may focus on the solution too early. That means that, as testers, we may need to think differently when trying out BA skills.

Putting on the BA Hat

> **Mike Talks**, *a tester from New Zealand (Kiwiland), tells us that when he first tried writing requirements, he focused on the solution rather than the business problem.*

Something I really encourage people to do is rally around the Kiwi ideal of "having a go" at something outside their comfort zone within their team. This goes back to the early days of New Zealand as a pioneering colony, where resources and skills were sparse, and generally a culture of generalizing specialists was encouraged. Sound familiar?

One project I was on needed some major up-front business analysis, and I'd tested enough business requirements in my life to think it would be easy. I went around, had my consultations with the business, and wrote everything up. Unfortunately what I documented didn't describe the issues very well and was far too detailed. I probably learned more in a month of doing the BA job than in years of being on the other end of business requirements. It also gave me much more empathy with people in the BA role.

Returning the favor, our project business analyst then helped me with testing and, like me, also trod the crooked path before coming out all right. That glimpse and empathy helped us work more closely together and understand how our jobs fed into each other's work. In my experience of giving the BA role a try, the hardest thing was learning to get the level of required detail right. Focus on the needs, and try not to shoehorn a design solution in—otherwise you're constraining your team's ability to meet those needs.

If your team has testers but not BAs, or vice versa, look for ways to acquire missing skills that might help your team do a better job of learning what to build. Lisa's team, unable to hire a BA, formed a BA community of practice, where team members met to share BA skills learned from books, articles, and conference sessions. They learned better ways to talk with business stakeholders and expanded their perspective to include more dimensions of quality. For the full story, check out Chapter 5, "Technical Awareness."

Considerations on Requirements and the Purpose of Testing

Pete Walen *shares his thoughts about the intertwining of defining requirements and testing.*

It is good to know what the requirements are, what tests exist, which tests are set up, and which ones have been run. However, little of that matters if we do not know the problem the project is intended to address. It is crucial to know the business purpose the system is intended to fulfill.

When you sit down and actually speak with business people in a conversation, you can learn things that may not otherwise be discussed. When your attitude is "Please help me to understand so I can help you better"—as a servant, not a superior—walls come tumbling down, and oftentimes a weird thing happens: people tend to share information freely.

When programmers, designers, or testers come in as the experts who know how to fix problems that business customers have, it can seem condescending. When we approach the problem as colleagues, we can find ways to inform our decisions.

What about Business Analysts?

A good business analyst can gain information and pass it on to the team. However, with each layer introduced in the information flow, the information passed along will be altered. Sometimes information may be lost; other times material may be added. The "clarification" may critically change part of the message. I find that when I get close to the people doing the work, I often learn stuff that is important to me as a tester that other people shrug off as unimportant.

If I can understand the customer's needs better, I can exercise the software more efficiently. If the tests I write and run do not explicitly exercise the requirements, are they really needed? Are they real, or my interpretation of something someone said?

Of course, important ideas will be identified in the documented requirements. There may be other things like, "Don't corrupt the database" or, "This needs to be reflected in the ziggidy-splat system" or, "This value should match what is on this other screen." Do these things make the users' list of expectations? Are the business needs reflected completely in the documented requirements? Only in these conversations do I find the answer.

My advice: exercise both the requirements and the stories. If you can't exercise both, exercise the stories, and then have folks from the business go through the results with you.

UX Design Skills

Companies such as Apple have proven the importance of product design. As Andy Budd has noted (Traynor, 2011), "delightful attractions" such as the swipe to unlock the iPhone "make people fall in love with a product." UX designers are integral, key members of agile software teams today.

Testers and UX designers collaborate productively from the early stages of feature design. Testers, especially those who have direct contact with end users or who use the product themselves, provide useful feedback on UI mock-ups, workflow, and other aspects of design. Good UX designers know how to get value from usability testing and are happy to partner with testers to do those activities. Some activities centered on usability that are common to both UX designers and testers are A/B testing, focus groups, and even paper prototyping.

Planning techniques such as impact mapping can help you better understand the business needs and wants. We don't know how the iPhone was designed, but we can imagine an example impact map for it:

- **Why (Goal):** Gain a market share of 70%
- **Who (People):** Prospective and existing iPhone users
- **How (Behaviors):** Easy phone unlock that users fall in love with
- **What (Activity/Feature):** Design swipe gesture to unlock

The team (including testers, of course) could then brainstorm other Behaviors and Activities that might meet the goal.

Lisa's Story

Our team had one UX designer who worked remotely and was spread much too thin in our team of around 20 developers. When we hired a second UX designer in our Denver office, new opportunities opened up for us testers.

Another tester on my team had the idea to set up a brainstorming meeting with all three testers and both designers. The topic was "visibility of design prior to production."

We've been trying some of the resulting action ideas, which included:

- Go over design features for stories together. Note subsequent changes (for example, due to implementation constraints) in story comments.
- Designers pair with testers for accepting stories that include implementing feature design.
- Designers involve testers more in testing interaction and flow design choices.

These experiments have helped reduce time wasted in reworking user interface (UI) design after coding starts. Acceptance testing goes more smoothly when we pair since the UX designers can spot implementation issues such as an incorrect font or color right away. Even when we don't pair, designers are available to answer questions immediately, so we are never blocked.

We testers helped the designers refine their usability testing script. Thanks to our designers' expertise and experience with usability testing, we received useful feedback from our product's users early in the development process. Testing our new UI design was easier with help from the designers. Once our new UI design was released in beta, customer feedback was overwhelmingly positive.

Even if you don't have specialists in things like UX design and usability testing on your team, you can learn enough to get valuable feedback from users. See Chapter 13, "Other Types of Testing," for examples of usability testing.

Documentation Skills

Many teams still have the need for user documentation, whether it is electronic or paper based. If you are on one of the fortunate teams that are able to work closely with technical writers, you probably already know how valuable they can be. In *Agile Testing* (pp. 208–9), we gave some examples based on our experiences. Technical writers are in a unique position to challenge ideas; when you have to articulate a concept, it sometimes doesn't translate as well as you think.

When you do not have a technical writer on your team but still are responsible for user documentation, consider adding the task "Create content" to each story. This task can be completed by anyone on the team. At the feature level, there can be a task to "Complete user documentation." By then, the user interface is stable, so if you need to take screen shots, you can. The content can then be assembled and edited by anyone on the team, or perhaps by the company technical writer.

Another idea is to pair with others on your team. For example, Lisa paired, not with a technical writer, but with the UX designers on her team when testing extensive online documentation for their API.

Take the Initiative

The joy of blurred roles on agile teams is that it makes our jobs more interesting! If you sense that your team and its customers are struggling to define a feature, put on another hat. What practices from a different profession can you try?

Lisa's Story

I worked for many years on a team producing financial services software. Our software managed all aspects of 401(k) retirement plans. The system was originally modeled so that only one person from each employer with a 401(k) plan could log in and administer that employer's plan. This "plan sponsor" did activities such as submitting payroll contributions, enrolling new employees in the plan, and approving distributions and loans from 401(k) accounts.

The "plan sponsor" term was used all over our website. At one point, we started a feature to allow multiple user accounts to do "plan sponsor" activities. However, by law, the actual plan sponsor is the employer. We had a number of small-group discussions about terminology. Everyone had a different opinion.

I finally scheduled a meeting with all the stakeholders to make a final decision on terminology. Is getting people together like this a tester's job? Why not? Our ScrumMaster happened to be out sick, and our product owner was always swamped. Development on the feature had started, and we were wasting time with indecision over verbiage.

In 15 minutes, the various business managers agreed on the term "plan administrator" for all the users from a given employer who would log in to do what used to be termed "plan sponsor" activities. There would still be just one plan sponsor per plan whose name would be used in all the legal documents.

Since the product owner was too busy to do it, I mocked up all the changes for the many pages on the site that, up to now, had said "Plan Sponsor" (see Figure 10-1). I posted them on the wiki so our remote programmer (who works in India) could see them and added a task card to the relevant story row on our board. By the next morning, our remote programmer had completed most of the changes, and another programmer completed the rest. I verified the changes, showed the customers, and updated an automated regression test.

Figure 10-1   Simple mock-up

Yes, it would have been preferable to get the terminology worked out prior to starting the story. After this and other similar experiences, we started pushing back on the business to have all the business rules and examples ready by the start of the iteration. If we lacked the necessary information, we postponed the story to the next iteration. We know questions and changes during development are inevitable. But whenever we can find ways to move forward and save time and improve quality, whoever has the initiative can lead the way!

Many of the skills that business analysts and UX designers practice are really what we call 'testing for business value.' Challenging ideas, and testing those ideas and assumptions, moves us closer to the features that our customers value. In the next chapter, we will talk about how to get examples to express a shared understanding. It is about developing the right "thing."

SUMMARY

Blurring the distinctions between roles can make our jobs so much more interesting. This chapter was about expanding your mindset and learning from others.

- Brainstorm with the team to identify what skills may be missing.
- Try creative experiments; add to your T-shaped skills to fill skill gaps. Wear a different specialty "hat" when needed.
- Business analysts' skills are synergistic with those of testers. If your team has both testers and BAs, they can work together for better software quality.
- Testers and UX designers can partner for activities such as usability testing, prototyping, and getting fast feedback from users. This helps the team save time and stay on track.
- All team members can put on a technical writer's hat if necessary and create content, think about how a concept might be translated into words, and perhaps even edit and test user and technical documentation.
- Learn practices from other professions, such as business analysis and UX design, to help build multiple dimensions of quality into software features.
- When you see a problem, take the initiative to get the right people together and discuss possible solutions.

Chapter 11

GETTING EXAMPLES

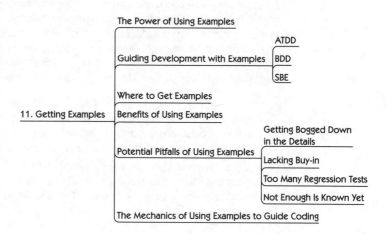

11. Getting Examples
- The Power of Using Examples
- Guiding Development with Examples
  - ATDD
  - BDD
  - SBE
- Where to Get Examples
- Benefits of Using Examples
- Potential Pitfalls of Using Examples
  - Getting Bogged Down in the Details
  - Lacking Buy-in
  - Too Many Regression Tests
  - Not Enough Is Known Yet
- The Mechanics of Using Examples to Guide Coding

In our experience, eliciting examples from customers is a powerful way to guide development with both the technology and business-facing tests. Examples form the heart of Quadrants 1 and 2, whether it's a paper prototype, a flow diagram drawn on the whiteboard, or a spreadsheet with inputs and expected outputs. In *Agile Testing*, we talked about examples in just about every chapter, and that's true in this book as well. One of our favorite questions we ask if we're not sure about what is under discussion is, "Can you give me an example of that?" We suggest you do the same.

THE POWER OF USING EXAMPLES

We first learned about example-driven development from Brian Marick back in 2003. As we explained in *Agile Testing* (pp. 378–80), we've depended on working with customers to get examples of desired and undesired system behavior so that we know the right things to build for our customers.

Examples in Real Life

The following story from **Sherry Heinze**, *a tester from Canada, shows how we can use examples in our everyday life.*

I was working at a client site that closed for four full days and two partial days over the holidays. Management sent out the holiday schedule in a table format. One manager who had both staff and contractors sent out a copy of the schedule with a note to help people book their time off correctly. *Note:* The company's regular schedule was 7.5 hours daily, Monday through Thursday, and 7 hours on Friday.

When entering time over the holidays, please look at the charts [see Figure 11-1] below. For office closures (other than Stat), please book your time to this Admin code, otherwise your time will be entered as Vacation or against standard billable codes.

If you are a contractor, please only enter time in the office and do not use the above Admin code. On days & times the office is closed, the time entered for contractors should be 0.

Date	If on Vacation			If Not on Vacation		
	Vacation	Stat Holiday	Admin	Regular Billing	Stat Holiday	Admin
Monday Dec 23 (Regular Office Hours)	7.5	0	0	7.5	0	0
Tuesday Dec 24 (Closed at 2:00)	4.5	0	3	4.5	0	3
Wednesday Dec 25 (Closed – Stat)	0	7.5	0	0	7.5	0
Thursday Dec 26 (Closed – Stat)	0	7.5	0	0	7.5	0
Friday Dec 27 (Closed)	0	0	7	0	0	7

Figure 11-1   Time chart

I looked at this chart and then asked some clarifying questions since I start work at 7:00 a.m. and am a contractor.

- Does this mean I can't bill for the 6 hours I normally would have on December 24?
- If not, should I leave at 11:30 to keep the 4.5 hours?
- Do you want all of us to come in at 9:00 on December 24?

> - Does this mean I can't work at home that day, as I usually do if the schools are closed?
> - What if I am an employee who works in a support group and must start earlier to answer the phones?
>
> What I found out was that the person who created this chart assumed that everyone else started work at 9:00 a.m. and worked only in the office.

Sherry's story shows us how an example as simple as a chart can give us a starting place to ask concrete questions, working toward a shared understanding of a feature's goal.

Functional test tools have matured over the last few years to help us capture examples and turn them into automated tests. This is a good thing, but it's possible to automate lots of tests and still fail to deliver what the customer really wants.

In his Agile Testing Days 2013 keynote, J. B. Rainsberger noted that many teams still do not take advantage of the simple idea of "talking in examples" (Rainsberger, 2013). His message echoes Liz Keogh's (Keogh, 2012a):

> **Having** conversations
>
> is more important than **capturing** conversations
>
> is more important than **automating** conversations

Likewise, many teams use a business-readable domain-specific language (DSL), often in a given_when_then format, to describe feature behavior without getting into implementation details. You can use this technique in automated test scripts, but it may have more value as an analytical tool. Collaborating with customers to create given_when_then-style examples helps define useful, appropriately sized stories that, when finished, will provide the desired feature. Automation becomes a useful side effect of using the tool.

If your team is not already working with stakeholders to get examples of desired and undesired system behavior, start experimenting with this approach. See if it helps you to understand more quickly what your customers want and to deliver the right things with less churn and wasted time. Janet has found this to be a useful rule of thumb: if you have more than one example of desired behavior, you might need more than one story.

We decided to focus a whole chapter in this book on getting examples because it is such a key practice and still hasn't caught on with many teams. Unfortunately, the name "example-driven development" never caught on either. The common names currently being used to describe the process are

- Acceptance-test-driven development (ATDD)
- Behavior-driven development (BDD)
- Specification by example (SBE)

In *Agile Testing* (pp. 99–101), we referred to these tests as business-facing or customer-facing tests that drive development in a similar fashion to test-driven development (TDD), but at the business level. They help define external quality by defining the features that customers want. In this book, we refer to the practice generically as "guiding development with examples." Feel free to exchange the term for whichever one you use on your team. We attempt to explain the differences here, but in reality they are all about starting with examples and conversations.

The choice of tool may determine which practice you adopt, so we advise that you know what you want before you choose a tool. For example, in workflow-type applications, describing the behavior may be applicable. If the application is calculation heavy, a spreadsheet or tabular test format with specific examples might be more appropriate. We give examples of both formats in Chapter 16, "Test Automation Design Patterns and Approaches."

Guiding Development with Examples

Don't get distracted by jargon or buzzwords. Whether you choose to call your process ATDD or BDD or SBE, the goal is the same—a common understanding to build the right thing the first time. All of them follow a flow similar to the one shown Figure 11-2 with slight variations in the

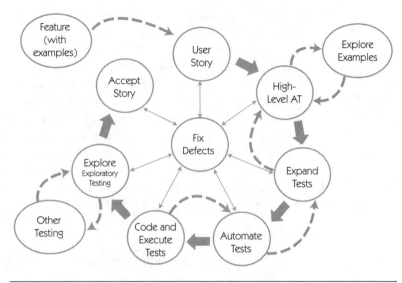

Figure 11-2   Guiding development with examples

naming. The most important thing is to remember to start with the end in mind.

ATDD

Jennitta Andrea has described ATDD as (Andrea, 2010)

> . . . the practice of expressing functional story requirements as concrete examples or expectations prior to story development. During story development, a collaborative workflow occurs in which: examples are written and then automated; granular automated unit tests are developed; and the system code is written and integrated with the rest of the running, tested software. The story is "done"—deemed ready for exploratory and other testing—when these scope-defining automated checks pass.

One problem with the label "acceptance-test-driven development" is that "acceptance test" is a vague term that means different things to different people. It can be confused with user acceptance testing (UAT), where an end user or outside vendor "accepts" the product. This acceptance may be tied to contractual payments.

We define acceptance tests as the tests that describe the business intent each story must deliver. Depending on how your team implements the practice, the acceptance tests may include only the high-level expected behavior and a couple of examples of misbehavior. However, they may also include a broad range of tests that encompass everything except TDD at the unit and component level. They may include quality attributes such as usability and performance, although we prefer to think of those as constraints that apply to all stories. Most people refer to functional tests when they talk about ATDD.

Delivering Value through Conversations at Paddy Power

Augusto Evangelisti, *a software development professional in Ireland, shares his experiences with conversations in his organization.*

I joined Paddy Power as a principal test engineer in 2012, and my task was clear from the very first day I met my boss. In fact, on that first day he said to me something along the lines of "Gus, you need to improve quality without negatively impacting throughput." Even though the remit was a challenging one, I had been in similar circumstances before, and I wasn't really scared (silly me).

I set about observing the teams so I could understand where improvements might be made. The teams were already composed of excellent developers who followed very good practices. They had very high unit test coverage, conducted code reviews, and pair programmed, and they had a really good continuous integration (CI) system.

They even did acceptance-test-driven development (ATDD). Now I was scared! I kept observing and started digging deeper to find what was missing. The first concrete suggestion I made was to embed the business analysts into the teams. They had been operating as a separate team up until that point. It was a small change that helped a little, but I was still at a loss as to what else might be going on.

A few more weeks went by, and slowly but surely I started to understand where the problem might lie and why we had quite a few incidents in UAT and even in production. The key was observing how people practiced acceptance-test-driven development. On the kanban board, there was a column called "Awaiting BA Sign-off," and after that, development began. Essentially the user stories were handed over from the business analysts (BA) to the developers through a formal sign-off, at which time the analysts moved on to begin work on the next set of user stories. There were no conversations. The developers would take the user stories and transform them into what they thought were the acceptance tests and corresponding code.

I was very lucky to find a great ally in Mary, another test engineer who shared the same desire to make things better. We worked together to size the problem, and we used an impact-mapping session to identify a possible solution. The approach we identified was to create and facilitate workshops on "real" ATDD with the development teams.

We tailored our ATDD approach to our specific context, using some of Elisabeth Hendrickson's ATDD approach and Gojko Adzic's specification by example. The key was emphasizing the importance of

Conversations over automation

We told the teams: ATDD is about people, communication, collaboration, and delivering business value.

We moved all the emphasis to this aspect and explained how the automated regression suite that is created during the process is no more than a natural outcome. The value is in collaboratively defining the user stories, sharing the understanding of the application, and delivering the business value to our customers.

To collaboratively define the user stories, we removed the "Awaiting BA Sign-off" column from the board and replaced it with a column called "Discuss," where the "3 Amigos" sit together, talk about the user story, and identify examples that will later become acceptance tests and, in turn, code and eventually business value. I thought this was a perfect example of

Customer collaboration over contract negotiation

The workshop approach really helped to trigger change in the team's behavior, and over a matter of weeks the development team members were implementing the new approach, with immediate and tangible impact.

After one year, the results have been amazing. The issues in UAT are practically nonexistent, and the same applies to production. The teams really understand the product they are building, and the business analysts, test engineers, and developers work as one strong, single unit. Last, but not least, we even improved throughput by removing the rework of issues as a result of poor quality. The misunderstandings that used to surface at the UAT stage are now identified and resolved before a line of code is written.

Ah, I almost forgot: we also have a lot of fun!

BDD

Behavior-driven development (BDD) uses natural language to capture customer examples in a domain-specific language. The goal is to have those important customer conversations and create given_when_then scenarios that express the behavior of a feature, including the expectations for a particular condition and action, in tests that everyone on the team understands.

Dan North's description of BDD (North, 2006) is a bit more complicated, but we interpret it as using the word *behavior* rather than *test*, and using the given_when_then guidelines to describe the precondition, trigger, and post-condition of what is expected—before coding starts. In a post to the Yahoo Agile Testing group in August 2010, Liz Keogh explained (Keogh, 2010):

> *BDD's focus is on the discovery of stuff we didn't know about, particularly around the contexts in which scenarios or examples take place. This is where using words like "should" and "behavior" comes in, rather than "test"—because for most people "test" presupposes that we know what the behavior ought to be. "Should" lets us ask, "Should it? Really? Is there a context which we're missing in which it behaves differently?"*

Originally a response to TDD, BDD has evolved into both analysis and automated testing at the acceptance level. Feature Injection is a business analysis process framework that focuses BDD and TDD on delivering business value (Matts and Adzic, 2011). Teams using Feature Injection start by defining and communicating business value, create a list of features to drive delivery of that business value, and then expand the scope of those features, investigating high-level examples of customer use. We include examples of BDD-style tests later in this chapter.

SBE

As a result of the Agile Alliance Functional Test Tools group (AA-FTT) workshop at Agile 2010, Declan Whelan, Gojko Adzic, and a few others came up with a diagram (Figure 11-3) to try to get a common understanding around specification by example.

Look closely at the diagram. You may notice that there is not a single mention of testing. SBE starts with the goal in mind to derive the scope. This is where techniques such as impact mapping give us a great start by first identifying the right goals. To get to key examples that explain the context sufficiently, the team specifies collaboratively, perhaps in a specification workshop or similar activity. These key examples become our high-level acceptance tests. We refine those examples, extracting a minimal set to specify a business rule adequately; these become the story tests. At this point, we automate without changing the meaning, and those automated tests become the checks to give fast feedback on a regular basis. The result: executable specifications or living documentation that describes the functionality of the system at any point in time.

Gojko Adzic has explained how teams can use specification workshops to create examples, getting the right people to collaborate to get a good understanding of what to build (Adzic, 2009). See the bibliography for Part IV, "Testing Business Value," for more links to learn about SBE.

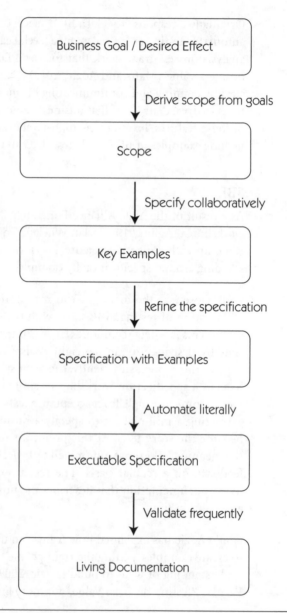

Figure 11-3   Specification by example (Adzic et al., 2010)

WHERE TO GET EXAMPLES

Whatever we call the process, we want to minimize rework and mis-understandings of what to build. In *Agile Testing* (pp. 378–80), we gave some simple ways to collaborate with customers to specify examples. We'll explore a few others here. The best way to get examples of how a particular feature or story should work is to sit with your customers and watch as they do their jobs. Try to imagine where the new feature will help or hinder them.

Informal brainstorming sessions where participants draw on white-boards (physical or virtual) usually work well. More formal specification workshops are another option; however, getting the right people to participate is key (Adzic, 2009).

Examples can be elicited as part of an impact-mapping session, and they naturally emerge in story-mapping workshops. See Chapter 9, "Are We Building the Right Thing?," for details on these practices. Whatever you use for the format of your meeting to obtain examples, set a time limit, and keep the meeting short and focused. People can stay fresh during an hour-long meeting, but if you need more time, schedule another session for a few days later. That gives everyone time to ruminate on what they want and come up with useful examples.

Support tickets and community forums can be sources of examples of what people need to do with your product. The frequency with which a particular feature is requested indicates what's most important to users.

Lisa's Story

We decided to upgrade our product's search engine. As this involved re-indexing everything in our database, it was a good opportunity to add some search functionality. We didn't have a lot of time to spend, but we could go for the "low-hanging fruit."

Our testing and customer support manager already had a good sense of what customers wanted. She looked through feature requests and complaints on our community forum as well as past customer support tickets and listed the most-requested search functionalities. Our delivery team was able to add a surprising number of them. It was a big win that really pleased our customers.

Ellen Gottesdiener and Mary Gorman use the template shown in Figure 11-4 to get examples in a given_when_then format (Gottesdiener and Gorman, 2012). It ties the story to the scenario, along with its data. It also makes the writer consider some of the dimensions we talked

Story	As a supervisor, I can search in the employee database so that I find a specific employee's information.
Scenario	Valid name search returns results.
Business rule	Search returns only employee names who report to the requesting supervisor.
Given	
Precondition(s), state	A supervisor exists with direct reports.
Fixed data	Supervisor: Kant Employee Last Name: Smith
When	
Action	Kant navigates to the employee name search page and enters the value "S."
Input data	Search criteria – "S"
Then	
Observable outcome: Message, output data	Kant sees a search result that includes Smith.
Post-condition(s), state	Smith is displayed in search result.

Figure 11-4   Given_when_then template (Gottesdiener and Gorman, 2012)

about in Chapter 9, "Are We Building the Right Thing?" Not all stories need a template like this, but it helps draw out the ideas in new areas of the code.

Use business rules, use cases, business expertise (customers, business analysts, domain experts, etc.), the expertise of the delivery team (programmers, testers, DBAs, etc.), along with any other supporting information you might have to get examples.

Make time to learn your business domain as much as is practical, so you can help stakeholders create and articulate useful examples. This knowledge enables you to zero in on the purpose of each feature and strip out unneeded functionality or simplify the approach.

BENEFITS OF USING EXAMPLES

We can get examples of desired system behavior from everyone with a stake in the solution. This is especially important for internal stakeholders such as those in the accounting and legal departments, who are often overlooked in the requirements-gathering process. Thinking in terms of concrete examples helps business experts articulate business rules and engages stakeholders more fully in the development process. If possible, sit down with a business expert, observe how they do their work, and create examples together.

Concrete examples make it much easier for the delivery team, including programmers, testers, operations, user experience designers, and database experts, to understand the needs of the different customers. Rather than having a philosophical discussion of what the best implementation might be, people draw on whiteboards and fill spreadsheets with example inputs and expected outputs to express business rules in terms everyone can understand. We bring all these examples together and turn them into tests to define system behavior, thereby reducing the uncertainty about what needs to be built.

A DSL is one way customers can express their examples in a way that they and the development team can use. A given_when_then style like the examples earlier in this chapter may suit your organization. If you're testing calculations and algorithms, you might prefer a tabular approach, such as a spreadsheet with defined inputs and expected outputs. Many test frameworks allow examples in a DSL format to be automated directly so they not only are readable by non-programmer team members but can also be executed as part of a continuous integration process.

Programmers can use the DSL examples to help with TDD as well, although TDD is as much about designing the code as creating the unit tests. The broad and deep understanding of the feature that examples provide helps programmers know what code to write.

Preventing Defects with Examples

> **Cory Maksymchuk**, *a programmer in Winnipeg, Canada, explains how test-first coding helps cover a range of example scenarios and prevents defects.*

I was once working on a section of a screen with a dynamically generated drop-down "select box." The contents of the select box would be different based on which user from which organization was viewing it. Although there were quite a few scenarios for what it should do, I had a good handle on them in my head and in the requirements document. At the time, we had quite a few developers and were low on analyst and tester availability, so I was working ahead of our test cases. I finished the code, complete with unit tests, sent it for code review, and committed it. A day later I received the test cases, of which there were 52. My work passed 14 of them and failed the other 38.

Had I only worked through a requirements document and my code made it to production, there would have been a defect log with a pile of work in it. By writing test cases first, we make sure all cases are covered before committing code. Without defects making it to production or even being seen by a business user, we increase confidence, eliminate months of rework and maintenance, and look like stars. After we recommitted to our test-first strategy, this project went live seven months later, on time and on budget. Four developers, two analysts, one tester, and a lead worked on it, and a year later we have received only one small defect report.

Test-first helps us cover all viable scenarios in a way that the users can read and understand. It allows us to understand what "done" means and to not waste our time writing code that is not covered by tests. Couple this with good coding style, thorough code reviews, and good coverage in unit and integration testing, and you are on your way to a no-defects world.

POTENTIAL PITFALLS OF USING EXAMPLES

As with any testing practice, there are risks to guiding development with examples. As your team learns to collaborate with customers to elicit examples and turn those examples into potentially executable tests, be aware of the ways this can go wrong.

Getting Bogged Down in the Details

Gathering any type of requirements before coding begins is a slippery slope toward a requirements phase. When you provide customers with an easy way to create examples, they may tend to get carried away. Detail-oriented business experts also may be overeager and provide every edge case they can think of. When programmers start working on the feature or story, they may be so overwhelmed with detail they can't see the main purpose of what they need to code.

Needing a large number of examples, or extremely complicated examples, may be a sign of a deeper problem, such as incorrect software design or inadequate models. If examples seem too complicated, there may be a flaw or some fundamental gap in the design or the domain model. The more complexity there is in a feature, the more conversation there needs to be to reduce the uncertainty.

Experiment with how much detail is appropriate for your team. If you're planning a feature similar to work your team has done before, you may not need to spend much time discussing examples. If your customers have prioritized a big, risky feature set, hold a time-boxed meeting a few weeks in advance of when development will start, with both development and customer teams, to start discussing examples. If you need more time, schedule another meeting.

In our experience, it works best to limit examples to a few happy path, sad path, and ugly path scenarios when working this far in advance. In story readiness meetings before the iteration, go through the stories again with the business experts to ensure a shared understanding of the feature. When coding begins on a story, it's time to get into the pickier details and make sure all viable cases are covered. Programmers can start by writing code to make the happy path tests pass, then move into the boundary conditions and negative and edge cases. In *Agile Testing*, we called this "working with steel threads"—work on the core, and then add complexity.

Chapters 8 and 18 of *Agile Testing* gave more information on the appropriate level of detail for examples throughout the incremental and iterative development process. Each situation is unique, so use retrospectives to see if tests based on examples are providing the right amount of information at different times in the coding and testing cycle.

Lacking Buy-in

Customers and delivery teams need to collaborate to get examples and use those to guide coding. This requires buy-in on all sides. Business stakeholders may feel they're too busy or that it's someone else's job to create requirements for features. We have to show them what's in it for them—what the benefits are.

Start by proposing an experiment. Explain the benefits of using examples, and suggest trying them for a new feature that's going to be developed soon. Schedule short meetings to create examples, and don't run over time. If you don't finish, schedule another meeting in a few days. Encourage customers to draw flow diagrams, mind maps, or other visuals as they think of examples. Use formats that are appropriate to the domain, such as spreadsheets for financial applications.

As you discuss more detailed examples, show business experts how you turn appropriate ones into executable tests in the agreed-upon DSL. Demo the resulting software early and often. Even seeing only the happy path behavior work will help customers feel their time is well invested.

Programmer buy-in can also be tricky. Programmers might feel they don't have time to bother with ATDD, especially if they're already doing TDD at the unit level. If the DSL used for acceptance-level examples is different from the format of their unit tests, it might mean too much task switching for their comfort level.

Testers might even need convincing if they are used to defining everything abstractly, such as, "Verify the name is valid," rather than using an example to say that, "Janet Gregory is an example of a valid name, but Janet#Gregory is not." Be prepared to iterate through different approaches to express and automate examples before finding the one that works for your team.

Too Many Regression Tests

Today's test frameworks make writing test cases in a DSL easy and fast. You can even use them for automated exploratory testing, especially at the API or service level, cranking through a wide variety of inputs and trying all the crazy edge cases. This is great, but beware of keeping all these executable tests in your automated regression suites. Automated regression tests provide a safety net, but they also need to give fast feedback, and we can't spend more time maintaining them than the value they deliver warrants. Once a test is passing, evaluate whether it adds enough value to include it in a regression suite. If it tests an edge case that, if it failed, would be low risk, you might prefer to leave it out or put it in a suite that runs only once per day or right before release. If unit tests cover the same area of the code fairly well, you may not need the higher-level test unless you need it for business visibility.

It's a trade-off between risk and cost. Over eight years, Lisa's previous team had two regression failures in production that required rolling back the release. They had created automated tests that would have caught both of the regressions, but the tests weren't in the suites that ran in the CI. They had made a conscious decision to leave them out, thinking they were edge cases that would never happen. On the one hand, this seems bad, but really, this was only two failures in eight years. That's offset by a lower test maintenance cost by having fewer automated regression tests. This is another area where lots of experimenting is needed to find the right balance.

Not Enough Is Known Yet

If your team starts on a new feature or capability that you've never done before, and nobody on the team has experience in that area, it may be too early to specify concrete examples. As Liz Keogh writes (Keogh, 2012a):

> *When you start writing tests, or having discussions, and the requirements begin changing underneath you because of what you discover as a result, that's complex. You can look back at what you end up with and understand that it's much better, but you can't come up with it to start*

with, nor can you define what "better" will look like and try to reach it. It emerges as you work.

When there are too many unknowns, or you don't even yet know what you don't know, it's more useful to spike solutions and get quick feedback to see if you're going in the right direction. Programmer-tester pairing to explore potential behavior may be useful at this time. The product ideas and technical implementations have to emerge.

THE MECHANICS OF USING EXAMPLES TO GUIDE CODING

Example-driven development, whether you use ATDD, BDD, or SBE, is a core practice for agile teams, and it takes work and practice to learn how to do it effectively. Please see the bibliography for Part IV for books and other resources that teach ATDD/BDD/SBE through examples.

SUMMARY

For years now, we've followed this motto coined by Brian Marick: "An example would be handy right about now." If you find yourself embroiled in an unending team discussion about how a particular feature should work, grab a marker and a whiteboard or flip chart (or the virtual equivalent) and start asking for concrete examples. You'll quickly make progress toward defining what that feature will look and act like once it's "done." Key points in this chapter are

- The power of using examples
- Overviews of the popular approaches to guiding development with business-facing examples:
  - Acceptance-test-driven development (ATDD)
  - Behavior-driven development (BDD)
  - Specification by example (SBE)
- Where and how to get examples from business experts
- Benefits of using examples
- Potential pitfalls of guiding coding with examples
- The mechanics of example-driven development

Part V

INVESTIGATIVE TESTING

In Part IV, "Testing Business Value," we looked at ways to help customers set goals that bring value to the business, expressed examples of how software will help achieve those goals, and turned those examples into tests that guide development. These activities give us confidence that we can build the right software for our business. However, we can't know for sure that the testing we do based on the initial ideas about how features should behave will actually ensure that all our customers' needs are met. We need to learn more about the features as we build them, working in a series of small experiments and building in short feedback loops to refine requirements.

As programmers commit new and updated code, we look at the product to see if it meets expectations based on the experience of the people testing it. We investigate the results of each experiment to inform the next. Exploratory testing is one way to investigate. Because agile teams deliver new code frequently, they may tend to focus on functional testing. However, there are many other kinds of tests that question the code and how the team interpreted the business needs. In Part V, we'll consider a variety of quality attributes that agile teams may need to investigate as code is completed.

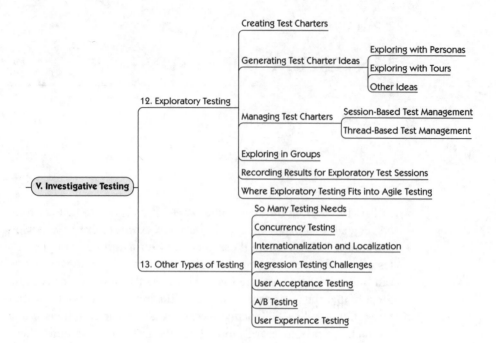

- **Chapter 12**, "Exploratory Testing"
- **Chapter 13**, "Other Types of Testing"

Chapter 12

Exploratory Testing

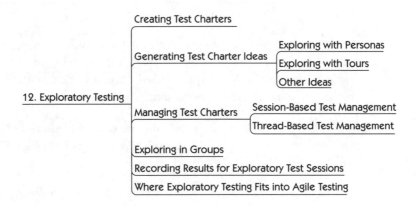

- 12. Exploratory Testing
  - Creating Test Charters
  - Generating Test Charter Ideas
    - Exploring with Personas
    - Exploring with Tours
    - Other Ideas
  - Managing Test Charters
    - Session-Based Test Management
    - Thread-Based Test Management
  - Exploring in Groups
  - Recording Results for Exploratory Test Sessions
  - Where Exploratory Testing Fits into Agile Testing

Exploratory testing combines test design with test execution and focuses on learning about the application under test. It requires a mixture of thinking processes: logical, calculating, and conscious, along with fast and instinctive. In Chapter 4, "Thinking Skills for Testing," we discussed how different styles of thinking are needed for different types of testing. Exploratory testing is one area that particularly benefits from applying different ways of thinking. In this chapter we will share how exploratory testing has developed and how you can practice it in your agile teams.

Exploratory testers must consider many aspects of the product, including its users, how the feature they're testing relates to the company's business goals, what ripple effects implementing the feature might have on other parts of the system, and what the competition is doing. In our experience, testers who are skilled at exploratory testing bring enormous value to their teams.

My current team hired its first full-time tester less than two years before I joined as the third tester. Working with testers was new to the company culture. The team developed everything test-first and did a great job of test automation at all levels. After we three testers had been working together with the team for more than a year, I was surprised and gratified when one of the programmers noted on a company forum that he thought that no amount of automated tests could replace skilled, dedicated testers who know how to do exploratory testing well.

Exploratory testers do not enter into a test session with predefined, expected results. Instead, they compare the behavior of the system against what they might expect, based on experience, heuristics, and perhaps oracles. The difference is subtle, but meaningful.

James Lyndsay explains the subtle difference between scripted testing and exploratory testing in his paper "Why Exploration Has a Place in Any Strategy" (Lyndsay, 2006). He notes:

> *An automated test won't tell you that the system's slow, unless you tell it to look in advance. It won't tell you that the window leaves a persistent shadow, that every other record in the database has been trashed, that even the false are returning true, unless it knows where to look, and what to look for. Sure, you may notice a problem as you dig through the reams of data you've asked it to gather, but then we're back to exploratory techniques again.*

In another paper, "Testing in an Agile Environment" (Lyndsay, 2007), James suggests that one of the roles that testers can play is the "bad customer." A bad customer goes off the happy path and may even try to break the system. Using your knowledge of potential issues, you can play the part of the "bad customer," whether that's someone who's malicious, in too much of a hurry, or simply incompetent. Here are some examples of actions you might try as this persona:

- Invalid parts of input—characters, values, combinations
- Time changes
- Unusual uses
- Too much—long strings, large numbers, many instances
- Stop halfway/jump in halfway
- Wrong assumptions

- Making lots of mistakes, compounding mistakes
- Using the same information for different entities
- Triggering error messages
- Going too fast

You may not consider yourself to be a skilled exploratory tester, but you may have tried typing in all the special characters on the keyboard or blowing out the buffer of an input field. You can use these instincts in a more mindful way. Elisabeth Hendrickson's "Test Heuristics Cheat Sheet" (Hendrickson, 2011) is a great place to start looking for ideas. Exploratory testing gives you the opportunity to use your ability to critique, assess, and challenge your understanding of the product in a purposeful manner, in order to provide critical information to your stakeholders. Later in this chapter we will suggest ways to give constructive feedback to stakeholders.

Exploratory testing and automation aren't mutually exclusive but rather work in conjunction. Automation handles the day-to-day repetitive regression testing (checking), which enables the exploratory testers to test all the things the team didn't think about before coding. As you explore, you may find additional tests that need more investigation or should be automated. You will likely use automation to set up exploratory scenarios, to monitor log files, or perhaps to explore scenarios that are not accessible through manual means. For complex new features where there are many "unknown unknowns," testers and programmers can explore together as they spike potential solutions to learn enough about the feature to start writing stories and tests to guide development.

There are multiple ways to explore. You may explore alone, or in pairs or groups. In this chapter, we'll discuss a few techniques that have worked well for us, and we've included stories from those who have had other experiences. We encourage you to experiment with these approaches as well, using lightweight strategies to manage them. The bibliography for Part V, "Investigative Testing," contains many books, articles, and other resources for learning more about this powerful testing approach. Make exploratory testing an important part of your toolkit when testing stories, features, and the system as a whole.

CREATING TEST CHARTERS

A test charter outlines a goal or mission for your exploratory session. There is no one right way to create a test charter, but we'll look at a few different methods. As always, it's best to experiment and find the one that works for you. You may find that one style works best for session-based test management (SBTM), while another works better for testing with thread-based test management (TBTM). Charters may range from happy path functional validation (although this is perhaps less valuable) to exploring failure modes, and performance and scalability.

Elisabeth Hendrickson's *Explore It!* (Hendrickson, 2013) has a section on creating good charters. It takes practice to find the right level of detail for your purposes. Too specific means that you don't have enough room to wander off the beaten path to make unexpected discoveries. Too vague or broad doesn't give enough focus and may cause you to waste time.

Experiment with how you word charters, as well as with the number of charters you create. Elisabeth notes that "a good charter is a prompt: it suggests sources of inspiration without dictating precise actions or outcomes" (Hendrickson, 2013, p. 16). One template Elisabeth has found that works well and gives enough guidance and focus is

> Explore . . . <target>
>
> With . . . <resources>
>
> To discover . . . <information>

It's better to have multiple charters, each of which is concise and focuses on a single area, for example:

> Explore editing profiles
>
> With real usernames
>
> To discover if there are instances where username constraints are not enforced

Another way to create a test charter is a mission statement and areas to be tested, for example:

Analyze the edit menu functionality of Product X

And report on areas of potential risk in Operating System Y

The simpler you keep a charter, the easier it is to stick to it. However, James Lyndsay reminds us that the broader you make a charter, the easier it is to consider distractions within the charter (Lyndsay, 2014). The breadth and specificity of the charter are tools to guide exploration. For example, a charter that says "Performance Test X" really gives no guidance.

Let's use an example of a web-based toy store to write a charter for the end game during a delivery cycle. *Note:* The feature would have been explored for the workflow as soon as it was completed.

Explore shopping for a new toy

With a real live user

To identify potential bottlenecks and unexpected disadvantages

Again, we're not suggesting that one way is better than another. On agile teams, we move at a fast pace, so we want to keep focused on the stories and features we're currently developing. At the same time, we have to keep the big picture in mind and make sure new code doesn't cause unintended effects elsewhere in the application.

About Sessions and Charters

Matt Heusser, *who writes and consults about testing and is based in the United States, shares his experiences with charters and session-based testing.*

A couple of years ago I was consulting for a large corporation that used an agile method. The business domain was incredibly complex, with legacy systems composed of many layers added by different people over decades. Each team contained everything needed to ship software, including support and operations, and each team determined its own work process independently. To try to share information, the company had a monthly "tester community of practice" meeting.

The "charters" the team adopted were one to three pages long in MS Word and were relatively prescriptive. It was an improvement from what they did before, but not what I think about when I say "test charter."

For me, a charter is a mission for testing. In an agile environment, where we assume regular functional testing as part of story work, a charter might address a risk we want to investigate or invest time to mitigate. Here are some examples:

- Test <feature> under <new browser version>
- Test <system subset> with tablets
- Test for failures with <third-party web services that are usually <up>
- Test multi-user and race conditions with <feature>
- Additional exploratory penetration testing for the new web front end as a system
- Customers see <X> but we are unable to reproduce the problem; can you troubleshoot?

Let's take another look at these charters. The examples are the intersection of a specific risk and a feature, but they don't have to be. I like my charters to be less than 200 characters long—most of the time, they fit into a tweet. That tweet is the title. If you have specific concerns or spend five minutes brainstorming, you might create a list of test ideas that become the "body" of the charter.

You can use charters in many ways. I've made heavy use of charters to help manage the release process with limited time. I tend to think of charters as small chunks of work, usually 30 to 60 minutes. Of course, if we identify a risk that can be investigated during the iteration, doing it earlier is better. When the charter makes sense to tie into a story, we can just put it in the story notes. When the charter addresses a crosscutting concern or is unrelated to current stories, I might suggest creating a new story.

By taking notes and debriefing a fellow team member on what we've done after the session, we have a chance to increase team knowledge about the system and test practices. This serves as a sort of mini retrospective for testing.

Start with the style of charter that seems most workable for your team. Trying different formats is a nice way to shake things up and help you see your software with a fresh perspective. You can think about the templates we've provided as training wheels until you find the one that works for you.

GENERATING TEST CHARTER IDEAS

There are a few techniques that can help generate test ideas that we'll share in this next section. It is not an exhaustive list, but we hope it will trigger some of your own ideas.

Exploring with Personas

Personas are a way of understanding your end users, and many companies create personas as part of their marketing strategy.

Jeff Patton (Patton, 2010) and David Hussman (Hussman, 2011) are among the many practitioners who create pragmatic personas to identify who actually uses a product. Personas are a good way to imagine different ways people will use an application. We explained how we use personas for usability testing in *Agile Testing* (pp. 202–4), but we think the concept can be taken beyond usability. If you currently don't have defined personas, conduct a quick workshop with your team to discover at least some of them to give you a start. We've mentioned James Lyndsay's "bad customer," and we've shared two personas (see Figures 12-1 and 12-2) that Mike Talks has used for testing login account functionality and security.

Concentrate as a user on the following chunks of functionality:

- Suspend your account.
- Deactivate the RSA token linked with an account.
- Delete your account.

Potentially this user will need help from the help desk.

The Security Worried User: This user has concerns about using the login service and wants to be protected from anything bad happening. After all, you hear such terrible things in the news about people's identities being stolen.

Figure 12-1 Security Worried User persona

Try to support the Help Desk admin with the following:

- Search user.
- Authenticate identity.
- Deactivate RSA token.
- Delete account.

Flows to follow:

- Create new account.
- Set account to be Help Desk User or Help Desk Admin.
- Delete account.
- Get reports of activity.

By its nature you will also be touching upon

- Monitoring activity
- Validation

Personas are a great way to look at your application from different angles.

The Help Desk Admin: The administrator can give permissions to other users to make them Help Desk Users or Help Desk Admins. The Help Desk Admin goes beyond the Help Desk User in what the person can support and change in people's accounts.

Figure 12-2   Help Desk Admin persona

Lisa's Story

My team experimented with creating a separate project for system testing a complete rewrite of our agile project-tracking product. A tester, a designer, and a marketing expert teamed up to identify various personas representing our users. Developer Denise and Product Paul were two representatives of our product's users. We wrote charters as user stories so we could track them in our online tracking tool. This was a good way to track the testing we felt was needed, but not a good way to capture the results of our exploratory testing sessions. See the section "Recording Results for Exploratory Test Sessions" later in this chapter on how we did that.

Persona: Paul is the project manager for Agile Toys. In his weekly iteration planning meetings (IPMs) with the team, he goes through stories in the upcoming iteration, answers questions, updates the stories with point estimates, and rearranges stories in the backlog according to priority. He typically uses his iPad in the IPM to make the changes. At his desk, he uses Chrome on a MacBook Air. Paul's main usage of the tracking tool is keeping the backlog organized and prioritized.

Charter: Explore as Paul, the project manager, in an IPM to discover any issues with concurrent updates to stories from different devices.

Scenarios:

* Pre-IPM backlog prioritizing
* Iteration planning meeting—updating stories

Each of us sets aside an hour a day for exploratory system testing for what we call "mini group hugs," where each tester chooses a persona and a browser and tests concurrent usage of the system. We recorded our test results on our team wiki.

Using this process, we've found important bugs that weren't found while doing exploratory testing on the individual user stories. For example, an exploratory testing session with a charter of updating stories as Paul would during an IPM turned up several new bugs related to concurrent usage.

If you use personas, make sure your whole team understands them and how they can help with testing. Make them visible, perhaps by pinning their pictures and profiles on the wall. It is a good way for the programmers to get a better understanding of the users, and it also helps raise awareness of the value of exploratory testing.

Exploring with Tours

Tours can be another useful tool to generate ideas for exploratory charters or to get familiar with a new product or capability. This technique uses a metaphor of tourism and can add useful variation to your explorations, uncovering issues you may not see otherwise. James Whittaker has described some unique exploratory testing tours (Whittaker, 2012).

For example, as a tourist, perhaps you want a strategy for seeing the most important sights in London. Who you are, or what your goal is, will determine your strategy. Whittaker suggests that visiting students would approach this situation much differently from a group of flight attendants who are there for a weekend. A similar approach can help you explore your software features. Check out Whittaker's defined tours, such as the Guidebook Tour (looking for bargains, shortcuts) or the Landmark Tour (hopping through an application's landmarks). In the

Landmark Tour, you would identify a set of software capabilities (the landmarks) and then visit those landmarks, perhaps randomizing the order. Changing the sequence of events may cause an unexpected error to occur. These are good places to start, but make them your own. For example, try combining personas with a tour to visit your most important landmarks.

Tours can be done at any time, but Janet has had great success defining tours for the end game, when you think your new release is ready to ship. Often this will give your team extra confidence that the most important features in your product work as expected. Be creative in how you document these touring sessions. Perhaps you can create a visual map to show where you've been. See the bibliography for Part V for links to explore some of the possibilities.

Markus Gärtner (Gärtner, 2014) recommends debriefing after completing each tour. As you debrief, you'll identify more charters, which will take you deeper into areas you briefly touched on in the tours.

Other Ideas

Some teams base their charters on their story acceptance criteria. For example, you may want to explore error handling, perceived response time, and complementary features.

If you have identified risks during story elaboration, you may create risk-based charters that will highlight likely problem areas or areas of uncertainty. A conversation with your programmer is an excellent source for identifying architectural risks and makes a great driver for test charters.

David Hussman (Hussman, 2013) suggests creating journeys to take the personas you've identified someplace interesting. Once you've learned more about the personas through story mapping, imagine where they might like to go. These journeys might also be a useful way to explore your system after it is built. For example, if we refer back to the story map in Chapter 9, "Are We Building the Right Thing?" (refer to Figure 9-2), one way to test it might be to describe a charter as a possible journey:

> **Journey:** Search by keyword, select an email, add sender to contacts, and reply.
>
> **Charter:**
>
> > Explore journey
> >
> > With different folders, different senders
> >
> > To discover if flow hangs together

In Chapter 13, "Other Types of Testing," we will look at some ways to use exploratory testing for several quality attributes beyond the scope of functional tests.

MANAGING TEST CHARTERS

By now you should have some great ideas for creating your exploratory test charters. The question now is, How do you keep them straight? There are a few different ways, and we've shared a couple of stories from exploratory testing practitioners about how they manage their charters.

Session-Based Test Management

Session-based test management (SBTM) is based on the idea of creating test charters or missions for a testing idea, exploring uninterrupted for a specific time period, recording the results, and following up with a debriefing session. We mentioned this technique in *Agile Testing* (p. 243) but will share a few other ideas we've gathered. For example, Bernice Niel Ruhland told us she uses SBTM to help train testers. The debrief session is a great way for her to provide immediate feedback to the new testers.

Managing Regression Tests with SBTM Charters

Matt Heusser *shares his experiences with SBTM and how he uses it to manage a manual regression suite.*

SBTM fits well in an agile development process. It radically improves the performance of the test process so that it can fit into tight time boxes in a way that stands up to scrutiny.

SBTM uses a cognitive, thinking, and investigative approach, which also makes it work well in an agile setting. Using SBTM, I've managed to compress regression testing to fit within an iteration for teams that have almost no test tooling and no customer-facing automated testing infrastructure. We do use automation to help, for example, when we generate test data and make build environments faster.

To make it work, the software has to be reasonably high quality before you get to the "final shakedown" test. Otherwise, the find/fix/retest loop kills you. Jon Bach's SBTM paper (Bach, 2000) gives more specifics, but here's one way to adapt the method in an agile context. Consider this exercise for a whole agile team:

1. Make a list of risks for the product in charters, 30 to 60 minutes apiece.
2. Put all the lists on a wall, whiteboard, or projected page.
3. Sort the list by risk. Dot vote if you'd like to determine priority.
4. Put the list on a kanban board.
5. Team members pull one charter at a time and test, reporting and fixing bugs as a whole team as they go.
6. At any time, anyone can change the order of the cards or add new cards.
7. When you run out of time, stop testing. Look at the known issues and the risks not tested, and ask yourself, "Are we ready to ship?" Conduct a Roman vote, thumbs up or down.

SBTM is a whole-team, people-centered approach to testing. It can help with designing a test strategy for a legacy application. If your application has complicated rendering code or business logic in the graphical user interface (GUI), consider using SBTM in combination with high-level GUI smoke tests, rather than trying to cover everything with automated GUI tests. This combination can provide better coverage at a lower cost and let your team make better use of their test time.

> Also consider SBTM when you see risks in platform or third-party com-patibility. For example, SBTM can help you catch failures, resulting in an upgrade to jQuery or a third-party open-source framework.
>
> SBTM is useful if you need to support a new platform. For example, if your team is unexpectedly faced with supporting mobile devices, the touchscreen platform poses usability and compatibility risks. You can manage these well through session-based testing.
>
> Complex business domains, high cost of failure, and other scenarios where early bug detection is critical are all motivating factors to use SBTM. By all means, tweak the process to improve the quality of the code before it gets to final test—but you can also add a layer of SBTM as a compensation mechanism. When the consequences of a mistake are high, you can reduce risk with SBTM.
>
> Exploratory testing provides a safety net. Managing exploratory testing through sessions provides one more layer of protection and includes a feedback mechanism to help the team learn to improve in its exploration.

Try SBTM with your team. As with any testing technique we mention, there's no one perfectly correct way to do it. Conduct a session, see how it works for you, inspect, and adapt. Check the Part V bibliography for resources to learn more, including James Lyndsay's "Adventures in Session-Based Testing" (Lyndsay, 2003).

Thread-Based Test Management

Thread-based test management (TBTM) is less rigid in terms of time-boxing a session than SBTM. It works on the idea of organizing tests around threads of activity, rather than test sessions or artifacts. A thread does not imply a commitment of a specific time box as SBTM does. Its flexibility may lead the tester in different directions. TBTM may work better in some situations with rapidly changing priorities or frequent interruptions.

Converting from Session-Based to Thread-Based

Christin Wiedemann, *a tester, trainer, and speaker from Vancouver, Canada, shares the challenges she faces with SBTM and how she adapted the process to TBTM with mind maps.*

Over the years, I have repeatedly found myself in environments that are too volatile for more rigid test approaches to work well, especially as deadlines draw nearer. One example is a small team of four developers and two testers, working on a product for an external client. We had adopted a hybrid test approach, mixing scripted manual test cases and exploratory testing, organized in sessions structured according to the principles of SBTM.

As we got closer to the launch date, the pace increased drastically. As a result of increased pace and the rapid changes, we abandoned the scripted tests and ran only exploratory test sessions. However, we would typically start a test activity but quickly get interrupted and not complete the task. Working in this manner caused a great amount of stress, since it felt as if we never finished anything and never made any progress. We also came to realize that in some cases we felt hemmed in by the actual session. Even if the conditions changed or something urgent came up, we still felt obliged to finish the session before we started a new activity. Something had to change, so we decided to give TBTM a try.

The first step was to make a mind map containing all test ideas as threads (see Figure 12-3). We grouped the test threads in different ways. Most groups represented function areas (e.g., installation), but other groups were formed based on the type of testing (e.g., stress testing). After a while we realized that we wanted a third type of group that corresponded to issues we encountered frequently—potential problem patterns or heuristics such as log files. Each group corresponded to a node in the mind map. In some cases, short notes were needed to explain the thread, and we simply added those notes to the mind map. We also prioritized the function areas based on risk and added this information to the mind map by labeling the different nodes with numbers. This simple, yet powerful, test plan took us less than an hour to draft.

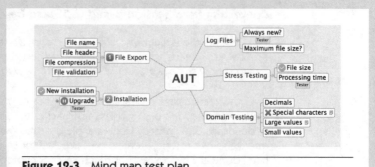

Figure 12-3   Mind map test plan

During the test period, we were constantly updating the mind map, and it always gave an accurate picture of the current status of testing (see Figure 12-4). As soon as someone started working on a thread, we would make a note in the mind map. Threads grew by the addition of short notes summarizing our testing and our observations, and we added new threads as we came up with new ideas. When we found defects, the corresponding thread was marked with a red cross, and the identification number from our defect-tracking system was added together with a short description (see Figure 12-5). Threads for which we felt sufficient testing for delivery had been done were checked off in green.

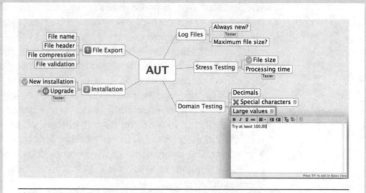

Figure 12-4   Test results with notes in a mind map

Initially our goal was to also write daily status reports containing a few short notes on what had been tested, but in reality we kept this up for only four days. With constant updates to the mind map, we really didn't feel a need for additional reporting. At the end of our test period, we used the latest version of the mind map as our test report, which was sent to the customer.

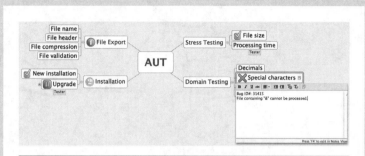

Figure 12-5   Defect logged in a mind map

What was the main difference between this project and previous projects I had worked on? The first thing that comes to mind is that this time we actually used the test plan to guide our work! In addition, the test report was continually read and reread, both to review our test results and to plan the testing on a subsequent project. Keeping the mind map up-to-date was much easier than updating any other kind of status document, which meant that it actually got updated. As it turned out, even the developers liked it—they preferred looking at the mind map over using our bug-tracking tool!

TBTM works very well under some circumstances, but I've found that mind maps are great tools regardless of the test approach. Nowadays I always use mind maps to plan testing. This not only allows me a higher degree of control without causing additional overhead, but it also makes it easier to initiate discussions and obtain feedback within the project team.

Christin's team grouped threads by functionality or type of testing, but threads can also be based around a feature or a story. They can be organized based on common resources—for example, small-scale functional data threads versus large-scale performance threads, or threads that focus on failure modes versus threads that focus on happy path workflow.

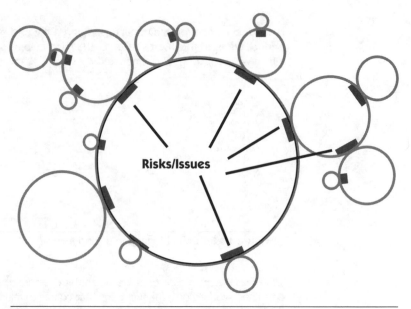

Figure 12-6   Fractal representation of TBTM

Adam Knight (Knight, 2011 and 2013) tackles his organization's large-scale data testing using thread-based testing, which allows testers to work on threads in parallel defined by test charters. Figure 12-6 is a representation of how he explains the benefits of an exploratory testing approach using threads to new testers in his company. They start with a feature area, idea, or risk in the center. As a flaw is discovered, they expand a new set of tests on that discovery. For most discoveries, this is done under the scope of the thread. If discoveries are made that are too large to be considered within the scope of the thread, a new thread is created to explore that area.

That mini exploration will result in a more targeted testing exploration around that feature area and can be represented as a circle off the original. In this way, the testing effort within each thread naturally focuses on the problem and risk areas as they are discovered.

Markus Gärtner (Gärtner, 2011) uses a slightly different tactic, which he calls Pomodoro Testing. He uses shorter sessions of 25 minutes and continues developing his testing mind map during the debriefings. You can find links to more about Adam Knight's experiences using TBTM and Markus's Pomodoro Testing in the bibliography for Part V.

EXPLORING IN GROUPS

Generally, teams think about exploring as an individual activity, or maybe an activity done by a pair. However, group exploring provides unique opportunities to discover issues or missing features in a new product or major update. We have facilitated exercises in shared exploration, and the results demonstrate the same thing—diversity creates different ideas.

Bernice Niel Ruhland (Ruhland, 2013b) uses this approach once in a while for more complex, riskier areas of a product, especially when time is working against the team. She had the testing team, programmers, and business analysts (BAs) participate in the testing. She recounts:

> We used an Excel spreadsheet to define the tests as we had specific test paths based upon coding risks to explore. In some cases critical bugs were fixed before we even finished the testing session. I received positive feedback from this approach. And of course how much or little documentation we provided changed based upon what we were testing and the testers' experience level with the functionality.

Lisa's Story

Spread the Testing Love: Group Hugs!

When our team is preparing a major new release, we sometimes organize "group hugs," where the whole team, or a subset of it, joins in for testing. Sometimes it's only testing team members, sometimes the entire product team, or something in between, but it's always useful. Some people refer to this type of activity as a "bug hunt," but we feel it's a positive activity that demonstrates our passion for building quality into our product; our focus isn't about finding bugs, but about consistency and confidence.

The iOS Group Hug

Recently we released some new features to our iOS app. We asked the team for volunteers for a group hug. Programmers, testers, and marketing folks joined in. We used a shared Google doc for the session, where we noted which device and version each participant was using, as well as already-known problems.

Our team is geographically distributed, so we used a videoconference meeting to communicate during the testing. People in each of our office locations gathered in one room, and remote people joined individually. We find it's helpful to be able to physically talk to each other. For example, if more than one person finds the same bug, we can avoid duplication in reporting it. Also, talking through what we've tried gives other team members ideas for interesting tests.

During the group hug, we found some new bugs, as well as some usability issues. Generally, the feedback was positive, and we were able to release within a few days.

Involving multiple team members in one testing session is expensive. However, we've needed to do it only for major, risky new features where concurrency is critical, and generally one group hug is enough to provide necessary feedback.

The Place for Group Hugs

We build quality into our product with test-driven development (TDD), acceptance-test-driven development (ATDD), and constant pairing and collaboration. We have multiple suites of automated regression tests providing continual feedback in our continuous integration system. We do have automated tests for concurrent changes, but they don't cover every possibility. In addition to the extensive exploratory testing we do on each new feature, the group hugs provide a quick way to get information that we can't get in our normal process.

Consider group exploring (see Figure 12-7) if concurrency is a vital feature of your product, and your automated tests and exploratory testing by individual or paired testers can't cover every scenario. Use these sessions judiciously, and add only as much structure as you need. Sharing a document where everyone records the results is helpful, but in some cases it's too heavyweight. The same goes for preparing charters in advance.

Another option is exploring with a trio (programmer, tester, BA) aimed for fast feedback. Julian Harty calls this "Trinity Testing" (Harty, 2010). The programmer can give feedback on the charters or testing paths based on his or her knowledge of the code, the BA on the business risk. When issues arise from testing, the BA can explain any business impact while the programmer assesses coding risks and time to fix the problem.

Figure 12-7 Exploring in groups

However you choose to run your group session, be prepared to learn from each one, so you can improve your next group testing session and learn even more about the software you're testing.

RECORDING RESULTS FOR EXPLORATORY TEST SESSIONS

It is important to record your exploratory test results and coverage as well as to share your thoughts with others. Some of the reasons to record results or make notes are: it gives you an opportunity to review your results with a peer and have a meaningful conversation about your findings; it allows you to track progress and issues as Christin showed with her TBTM story; it provides the opportunity to review your own results for later testing or if you want to review charters; and last (and our least favorite reason), it demonstrates to management what you've done if problems occur.

Recording can be as simple as taking notes on paper, on a wiki page, as a mind map, in a text document, or on a session sheet. Record issues, unexpected behavior, or features that seemed to be lacking. Hold a debriefing session to go over what you discovered. You're likely to think of ideas for future sessions as you discuss your most recent one with peers.

Keep your notes brief and simple. If multiple team members are exploring individually or as a group, agree on one format for note taking so you can easily understand each other's findings. Post results in a place where your whole team can see them for reference, and use these notes to improve your testing.

Lisa's Story

When we wrote charters based on personas, we created a chore (a task) in our team's online tracking tool for each charter. This was a good way to track the testing we felt was needed, and we could easily assign ourselves charters and see at a glance who was working on which charter. We could also track which charters were complete, in progress, or not yet started. We tried putting the results of our sessions in these chores, but we didn't find it convenient to refer back to the results this way. Next, we experimented with writing up our test session results on our wiki. Here's an example:

> Explore being Paul, the project manager, in an iteration planning meeting.
>
> **Browsers:** Chrome and Firefox
>
> **Initial setup:** On Test01, used project 101 populated by the test data fixture.
>
> **Observations:**
> - Deleting stories required a reload.
> - The velocity shown for iterations in the backlog didn't change as I reprioritized stories until I reloaded.
> - Need to do more exploring in projects with custom point scales.

Spreadsheets are a simple way to record exploratory test sessions. Adam Knight uses Excel for the top-level charters and exploratory note taking because it provides flexibility to present test results in many forms: text, graphs, tables, and external links. He then has a set of small macros that provide input boxes to allow very fast input of test notes and tracking of status. He can record status but also can indicate if an issue is "off the charter" and merits the creation of another charter to follow up.

Bernice Niel Ruhland stores her threads in one Excel tab with additional columns for testing notes. It's like reading a story about the testing. At a glance she knows how many threads are done, in progress, and not started. It also allows her to review any issues quickly.

There are products available that record notes as you do exploratory testing. See the "Tools" section of the bibliography for a link to one of these. Some session-recording tools let you record your keystrokes and the pages you've visited so that you can go back and reproduce your steps if you find something worth investigating further. They even let you specify how many pages you want to keep in memory or what type you want to save.

Janet's Story

I decided to try a tool I heard about at a conference called qTrace from QASymphony. (*Note:* I am not recommending this one over any other.) It is a recording tool for exploratory testing and captures screen shots, notes, and other details. I created a charter for exploring my own website, www.janetgregory.ca:

Explore the blog page

With the search function

To discover if it returns what is expected

I set a time limit of 30 minutes, but with the focus narrowed, I immediately found two issues that I had not noticed when I first checked the search function. The screen prints allowed me to check where I had been without thinking twice. The interesting thing was that I found one issue that bothered me enough that I put in a new request (story)—to search only in blog posts rather than the whole site—and one defect—showing posts authored by Mark (strange, since my name isn't Mark, and nobody else posts) that weren't posts, as highlighted in Figure 12-8.

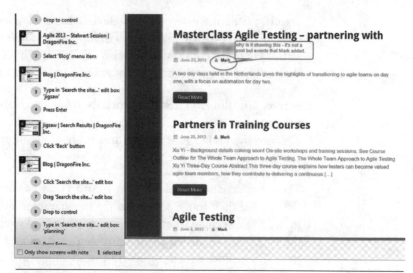

Figure 12-8   Exploratory test session using qTrace

Some recording tools record extensive additional information, such as data about the environment. This helps when you need a reproducible bug so that programmers can write a failing automated test and a fix. You may also use this information to write new user stories and new tests for features you found lacking or to tweak existing features you'd like to improve.

Whatever method you choose to record your results, remember to make them accessible to the whole team. Share the valuable knowledge you gained by exploratory testing.

WHERE EXPLORATORY TESTING FITS INTO AGILE TESTING

We think that exploratory testing is an integral part of agile testing, and it's important to see where it fits in an agile context.

Part IV, "Testing Business Value," was all about testing for business value. Another way to think of it is testing ideas and assumptions early—before we start coding. That type of testing is about building the right thing. There is another kind of testing designed to answer the question,

"Are we building it right?" We included exploratory testing in Quadrant 3 of the agile testing quadrants because we are usually exploring the workflow to see if we delivered the business value we anticipated. We challenge our assumptions to see what we did not think about earlier when building.

Consider our levels of precision from Chapter 7, "Levels of Precision for Planning"—the product release, the feature, the story, and the task— and what type of exploratory testing might be useful at each level.

- **Product release level:** This is where you would test an integrated product delivery to the integration team, or a release candidate during the end game. This would be a good time to explore dependencies between teams and high-risk workflows and perhaps do tours.
- **Features:** Once all associated stories are "done," you can explore the complete feature. At this level, good candidates for exploration are feature workflow and interaction with other applications. This might be a good place to try what Lisa calls "group hugs"—more than one person exploring on a charter.
- **Stories:** Once the story meets the expected results—initial coding has been completed and all the automated tests specified before or during coding pass—you can start exploring. Think about the development risks, boundary conditions, more detailed functionality issues, and different variations of formats or states.
- **Tasks:** Exploring at this level would happen during coding. Examples might be programmer exploration on an API, pairing on performance issues with a tester, or maybe even exploring some of the boundary conditions on strings. Consider programmer-tester pairing to create exploratory charters for the code being developed.

Agile teams benefit from continual exploring. When you're brainstorming new features, you can explore how your different personas might use them. You can explore released software to identify what features may still be missing. Focus your exploratory testing by using charters, tours, heuristics, or session- or thread-based test management. What you learn will help your team improve quality, not only in the impending release, but as the product evolves in the future. Use the resources in the bibliography for Part V to grow your team's exploratory testing skills.

Summary

Whichever techniques you use, exploratory testing is a powerful way to test new stories and features as they are incrementally delivered.

- Use exploratory testing approaches
  - In conjunction with your automation strategy
  - To give feedback quickly to stakeholders to see if you are building the right thing
  - To prepare for releases with manual regression testing
- Experiment with different methods to create your test charters.
- Experiment with new test charter ideas, such as using personas, tours, or journeys.
- Manage your test charters with SBTM or TBTM or your own approach that meet your needs.
- Practice to build your exploratory testing capabilities.
- Exploratory testing adds value in most, if not all, agile development activities.

Chapter 13

OTHER TYPES OF TESTING

In Chapter 8, "Using Models to Help Plan," we reintroduced the agile testing quadrants. In the section on testing early, we covered Quadrant 1 and 2 tests commonly used by agile teams. In Chapter 12, "Exploratory Testing," we outlined several approaches to exploratory testing. There's a seemingly endless list of different types of tests that may be appropriate for your application. For example, some domains require unique approaches, such as the specialized testing techniques needed for business intelligence and data warehousing software, which we will cover along with contexts in Part VII, "What Is Your Context?" In this chapter, we'll cover a few different types of testing other than functional testing and focus on ones we don't normally talk about in agile teams but that we think are important.

Remember that the numbering of the Quadrants doesn't indicate when different types of testing should be done. Q4 tests should be considered as soon as you start discussing a new feature or theme. For example, if there is a constraint that all pages in the application must respond in less than two seconds, make sure everyone on the team is aware of it. Capture that requirement as tests, and keep it in mind during development.

In *Discover to Deliver* (Gottesdiener and Gorman, 2012), Ellen Gottesdiener and Mary Gorman represent the quality attribute dimension in two different areas: operations and development. In Chapter 11 of *Agile*

Testing, we covered some of the basic operational attributes that need testing, such as security, reliability, availability, interoperability, and performance. That is not a complete list, but it gives you an idea of the attributes and constraints we need to consider. The Quadrants can help you brainstorm about the different kinds of testing you need to do on your particular feature or product.

SO MANY TESTING NEEDS

Our first Extreme Programming (XP)/agile teams back in the late 1990s and early 2000s were focused on finding out what our customers wanted and then delivering that functionality. We and our teammates tended to be generalizing generalists, and we sometimes neglected areas such as security, reliability, accessibility, performance, and internationalization—at our own peril. It became clear that agile teams must be diligent about all aspects of software quality, even if our business stakeholders don't mention them.

New types of testing have accompanied the proliferation of platforms, devices, and technology. Many consumer products have software that must be tested. Fitness machines have embedded software. The Tesla automobile has an API! At the same time, outside forces require more test coverage. Security threats to software systems increase all the time, so we must find better ways to test security. As hardware advances in processing speed and graphical display quality, we have to ensure that our products perform well and look good.

Your team may need additional infrastructure to accommodate some types of testing. Let's say you have a reliability requirement of no more than one failure in 1,000 transactions, or the need to do soak testing. Your team may want a second test environment to be able to drop stable code for reliability testing. You may need extra monitoring tools for watching overnight performance against minimum requirements. If you're testing an Android app, you'll need lots of devices in your test lab, and possibly some outside help.

We've heard of lists of more than 100 kinds of testing (see the bibliography in Part V, "Investigative Testing," for an example), although we find that those lists often contain some duplication. They include the usual ones you would expect to see, such as load testing or browser compatibility testing. However, they also tend to list "types" such as "agile testing," which really isn't a type but an approach. When you start thinking about all the different kinds of testing, you might start to wonder when you'll possibly have the skills, much less the time, to do it all, and it can be overwhelming to new testers. One of the problems we see is the vocabulary misalignment with so many different types. For example, when new people come into the organization and talk about integration tests, everyone else assumes they share the same definition, when perhaps to them, integration testing has a totally different meaning.

We suggest keeping your list of test types as simple as possible and creating a common understanding within your organization. You might start with the types that Wikipedia lists (Wikipedia, 2014l) and differentiate among types, levels, and methods. Bernice Niel Ruhland (Ruhland, 2014) maintains a list of testing types specific to her team, which includes an explanation of how her teams do or do not use a technique. She finds keeping a list helpful for onboarding new testers, and it provides a standard vocabulary shared by everyone in the department. Here's one example from Bernice's list of test types:

> *End-to-end testing is used to test whether the flow of an application or product is performing as designed from start to finish. It typically represents real-world use cases by walking through the steps similar to the end user. The purpose of performing end-to-end tests is to identify system dependencies and to ensure that the correct information is passed between database tables and the application's modules and feature. We typically perform end-to-end testing for custom-development projects.*

Let's look at a few different types of testing that people often neglect or struggle with on their agile teams. This is not meant to be an all-encompassing list. The goal is to make sure that we remember to do certain important types of testing that often get overlooked in the rush to deliver new features frequently. In Chapter 18, "Agile Testing in the Enterprise," we will look at how some of these crosscutting concerns affect development organizations with multiple teams.

CONCURRENCY TESTING

Web and mobile applications enhance usability by providing easy ways to make updates, such as dragging and dropping items. When multiple users are looking at the same view of data, we need to verify that when one user makes a change, the other users see that change. If two users update the same piece of data at the same time, who "wins"?

Lisa's Story

The ability for one person to see updates made by another user in real time is an important feature of our product. For our new autosave feature, where changes to an input field should persist as soon as focus moves out of the field, testing concurrent changes was a must. We recognized this as a high-risk area, since users want to feel certain their changes are persisted. We had automated regression tests for concurrent updates but wanted to explore this area in more detail because we weren't feeling confident about the feature quality.

We scheduled what our team calls a "group hug," where multiple team members test at the same time, as described in Chapter 12, "Exploratory Testing." We time-boxed this session to one hour and wrote up test charters and scenarios in advance. These charters captured normal use as well as extreme worst-case scenarios.

We typed notes on the bugs we found and other observations in a shared document. Learning about a bug that one person found often inspired me to think up another test to try.

Here's a sampling of issues we noted that would be harder to find while testing individually:

- Changing an epic label when someone else has the epic open, the user who changes sees an error and the label blanks out.
- Starting or moving a story with someone else updating the description causes overwriting and disappearing history.

One interesting discovery was that we couldn't reliably reproduce some problems, which pointed to timing issues. We marked it to explore later to see if there was an issue in the implementation or in the way we tested. It turned out to be the tip of the iceberg of a bad bug that spurred a major code design change.

The group hug confirmed our suspicions that the feature still needed a lot of work. Our team needed to do some redesign, coding changes, and more exploring before we could consider releasing the feature for beta test.

During the group hug, we realized we still had questions about the desired behavior of the autosave feature. This led to further discussions within the whole team, and within a few days, design improvements and development stories were under way. We knew that there would be more concurrency testing group hugs for this feature.

If your product risks losing updates when simultaneous updates occur or when users need to see updates by other users in real time, concurrency is an important area to think about before coding, but also to cover in your exploratory testing. Solutions for this type of requirement often involve caching updates, which can lead to both performance and transaction integrity issues. Automated regression tests for these scenarios are essential because it is difficult to test them manually; however, timing issues can be subtle and hard to find. Experiment with creative ways to test your features in the same way that customers will use them in production. Take advantage of regular events; for example, check your system's response time while the Olympics are being streamed live.

INTERNATIONALIZATION AND LOCALIZATION

With global markets come global challenges. Many organizations must support multiple languages due to changing business needs, and that creates challenges for agile teams. In traditional projects, the application is built, and then the strings that are to be translated are sent off to experts. The translators have the full context of the application, so the translations are generally correct. In agile teams, we have quick releases with the possibility of releasing to the customer every iteration or perhaps even continuously. Traditional methods do not work in that environment.

All Ÿøur βugs βeløñg tø Us

Paul Carvalho, *a test specialist from Ontario, Canada, shares his experiences with internationalization and localization testing in an agile way.*

A Roman walks into a bar, holds up two fingers, and says, "Five beers, please." *Ba-dum-cha.* This old joke relies on knowledge of a culture that is not your own. If you already know the answer to the joke, are interested in finding out, or are looking for new cool ways to bring value to your software systems, internationalization (i18n) and localization (L10n) testing may be right for you.

I'll start with a couple of definitions. i18n lays the groundwork or framework for software and systems to be used in a particular language or region. L10n testing (on a properly internationalized base product) involves checking that the system is translated correctly and looks and works as expected according to some language or culture.

In simpler terms, i18n means the system is *ready to be* translated into another specific language. It's like having a box of Legos with the right pieces to build something—like a fire truck or *Star Wars* set. Meanwhile, L10n means the system *is* translated into another language. Continuing the Lego analogy, you have now built the Lego set into the desired product for someone.

Think about the end product and users' desires. You don't expect a *Star Wars* set to satisfy a medieval castle fan. While there might be some similar pieces, you will need to reexamine the requirements and put the fundamental (i18n) pieces into the box to be successful with different audiences.

This example illustrates one of the advantages to developing internationalized systems in agile ways. An agile team focuses on delivering working software frequently and satisfying the customer through early delivery of valuable software. That is, don't try to solve all your i18n and L10n problems at once. Make different customers happy as you go.

As a team, before you start building anything, get together and come up with specific examples of how the system should look and work for people in a particular target region or country. Remember the Lego example—BEWARE OF ASSUMPTIONS. Not all languages are the same everywhere.

Take English, for example. In my travels, I have heard English spoken, spelled, and used in many different ways. English from England (EN-GB) is different from English in the United States (EN-US) is different from English in Australia (EN-AU). If you say your software supports English, I will ask, "Which one(s)?" For example, if a child asks for a *Star Wars* Lego set for his birthday, you'd better be sure you know what that means to him. There is a big difference between an Ewok village set and a *Millennium Falcon*. Guessing wrong may lead down the path to suffering.

Use an iterative approach to building localized systems. For instance, in the first iteration, you may settle on EN-US (if you work for an American company or market) in order to complete a particular feature that provides some value to your target market. When you complete that feature and decide to take on your next target region or audience, always make sure you consult with people who are local to that particular region. You are *loco* (aka crazy, aka nuts, aka . . .) if you don't use locals for localizations.

For example, let's say a U.S. company wants to localize software for its Canadian neighbors (EN-CA). A Canadian could easily tell you that there are more than just spelling differences in some of the words. Yes, the dictionary of terms for labels and outputs is an important piece. However, units of measure require more than just label changes.

Once, before a presentation on i18n and L10n, I used a web-based translation program to translate the following sentence from English to French:

Before: "We need **40,000 lbs** of fuel."

After: "Nous avons besoin de **40.000 kg** de carburant."

Eek! No! Translation requires conversions, too! Let's say it's a hot day and your EN-US weather app says it's 100°F outside. If the user switches to EN-CA, changing *only* the unit label to now say it is 100°C is so many levels of wrong. "People are dying" kind of wrong. We never want to make mistakes that threaten people's lives.

So now you need to add code to your software that takes an input value and makes the appropriate conversion before applying the appropriate unit label. This is where test-driven development allows you to safely make changes to the system to account for new and changing requirements while remembering the requirements on the base features.

Internationalization and localization need to be designed into the system. As with other important quality requirements, we iterate on the design and seek feedback frequently. To be successful, you need access to a specialist on your team, just as with security, performance, or user experience.

Some languages and regions have specific needs that you might never guess on your own, such as capitalization rules or name sorting. Even when translating into European languages that use the same base character set, you need more than just support for the extended ASCII character set.

Does the delivery team need to immerse themselves in a particular culture to be successful? I think it might be fun to bring the team closer to their target audience by getting out of the office and exploring multicultural multimedia opportunities to enrich their appreciation for other cultures and regions.

I'm convinced that Hawaiian English needs more exploration and that my employer should support a research expedition. With my luck, I'll probably get a DVD copy of the Elvis movie *Blue Hawaii*.

If your product has a global clientele, do what you can to avoid frustrating customers who use other languages and character sets. Support globalization (g11n), which includes internationalization and localization, with tests that guide development, exploratory testing, and perhaps other types of testing, such as linguistic testing. Internationalization is a constraint that developers must consider as they are coding and incorporate into every story. For example, it would include encoding, formatting, and externalizing strings across the code base. If you are working on legacy code, perhaps you have stories specifically to address some of the i18n requirements.

Localization is the translation piece, not only of the language itself, but often of nuances for specific locales. Terminology needs to be established, but perhaps all of it doesn't need to be done up front. The point when teams break features into stories might be a good time to think of the terms that should be used. Maybe the first story is for an analyst to determine what words will be used for consistency across the product. Frameworks to support localizing and translating can speed up the process, but they don't eliminate the need to verify the translations and suitability for specific cultures and regions.

In Figure 13-1, Lisa shows the terminology for the parts of a donkey harness. To Janet, it seems like a foreign language, but at least now we have common terms and can point to the same piece of harness and mean the same thing. Even writing this book, we had to compromise between EN-US and EN-CA spellings. Since our audience is global, we tried to avoid using slang and colloquialisms.

Figure 13-1   Donkey harness vocabulary

Your organizational culture may have a large impact on how you approach localization on your team. As Paul Carvalho mentions in his story, having local support for languages is ideal. However, that may not always be possible, since it is expensive to have many experts available at all times for translations. There are alternative solutions that may allow you to take advantage of fast (or faster) feedback than is usual on a phased-and-gated-style project. Perhaps you can use machine translations, which are getting better all the time. The trade-off is the need for significant post-editing to make sure you catch the errors in the automated conversions.

Another approach might be a hybrid, where agile teams create a "drop" for translators. This drop would include a whole feature, rather than specific strings to translate from each story, and would allow translators to have some context for their translations. If your release cycle is six months long, perhaps a drop of every four weeks could give you fast enough feedback to correct any mistakes before the end game, while minimizing the overhead of translations. Figure 13-2 shows this alternative. It is all about balancing speed with quality, time, and functionality.

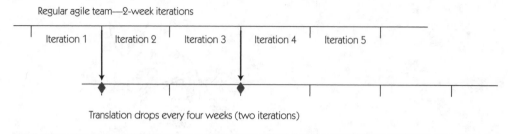

Regular agile team—2-week iterations

| Iteration 1 | Iteration 2 | Iteration 3 | Iteration 4 | Iteration 5 |

Translation drops every four weeks (two iterations)

Figure 13-2   Possible schedule for translation drops

Remember, if you are using third-party vendors, have agreed-upon time frames and expectations, and take advantage of automation in file drops for consistency in the process.

It is a different mindset to embrace rapid release cycles, and we encourage teams to think about how they can make changes to their process to get fast feedback. Perhaps, just perhaps, the local experts exist on some of your global teams.

REGRESSION TESTING CHALLENGES

First, we give a quick definition of what we mean by regression testing because it can be a contentious term. To us, regression tests are those tests that run regularly to give you confidence that changes made to the code do not affect existing functionality unexpectedly. We believe that automated checks can do this with the fastest feedback. At a minimum, these should run nightly.

Now that many teams release once a week, several times per week, or several times per day, regression testing is an even bigger challenge. Even if you automate your regression tests, they may not all run fast enough to complete in time for the next release.

Many companies faced with this problem turn to "testing in production." Seth Eliot has written and presented extensively on this subject. He defines testing in production this way (Eliot, 2012):

> *Testing in production (TiP) is a set of software testing methodologies that utilizes real users and production environments in a way that both*

leverages the diversity of production, while mitigating risks to end users. By leveraging the diversity of production we are able to exercise code paths and use cases that we were unable to achieve in our test lab, or did not anticipate in our test planning.

Lisa's team has good coverage from automated test suites running in the continuous integration system at all levels: unit, functional, and user interface (UI). They also spend lots of time doing exploratory testing, but it's hard to cover every scenario. For new major versions, they use a TiP approach. They enable the new version for a small percentage of users and monitor production logs to see if users are experiencing errors. As they identify new defects, they fix them as needed. They have a rollback plan to disable the feature if there are unacceptable results. When the new features appear to be stable, the team enables them for more users, continuing to watch logs carefully, until all users are able to use them.

As much as we automate regression tests, there may be tests that are difficult to automate in a way that provides proper feedback, and other tests that are too costly to automate. It's also a challenge to do manual regression tests for quality attributes such as look and feel when releasing so frequently. The testers on Lisa's team created wiki pages with manual regression test checklists for different areas of the product based on risk. Often, programmers use the checklists to do the manual regression testing, or at least help with it. The team regularly audits the checklists to see if any tests can be or have been automated. They keep the lists as concise as possible, focused on the high-risk areas. In Chapter 12, "Exploratory Testing," there were a couple of examples of managing regression testing with session-based test management or thread-based test management if you do not have automation. How you manage your regression suite will depend on your context, the risks within your system, and how often you release to production.

USER ACCEPTANCE TESTING

User acceptance testing (UAT) is part of Quadrant 3, business-facing tests that critique the product. We describe user acceptance testing as "making sure the actual users can do their job." UAT may be performed by product managers, but preferably it's done by the actual end users of the product. As we explained in *Agile Testing*, UAT is often done as part of a post-development testing cycle (pp. 467–68), but this does not mean it has to be left to the end game. Janet encourages companies she works with to think of ways to bring it earlier into the development cycle.

Janet's Story

I started with a team that was on three-month delivery cycles, which should have meant that they released to the customer every three months. However, the UAT testing took another six weeks, so new features weren't actually in production for almost six months. I found out that the reason for such a long UAT cycle was that the person (I'll call her Betty) doing the testing had to do it in addition to her own job. She had to "fit it in" around her regular duties, and six weeks was how long it took.

I suggested that we have Betty sit with the team at the end of each two-week iteration and play with the new features we were developing. I paired with her for a while to show her the features and then let her be. At the end of the three months when we were ready to deliver the new features, Betty asked for only three weeks (instead of the usual six) for UAT.

This was a substantial improvement, but I wanted it to be even better. We got her a workstation in the team work area, and Betty started coming in every Friday afternoon. She gained confidence in our work and what we were delivering. At the end of that release, we included one full dedicated day of UAT and were able to put the release into production within the three-month delivery cycle.

Lisa's current team develops a software-as-a-service (SaaS) product that is also used internally by the entire company. This provides a great opportunity to release new features for internal-only beta and get feedback from actual users who happen to be in the same company. Problems with real-life use are identified and fixed before the new features are made available to paying customers.

Understand your customers, your real users, and brainstorm ways to get them to use the system to make sure they can do their job and use the system appropriately. Customers are the ultimate judges of software value. End users are probably the best people to critique your product.

A/B TESTING

A/B or split testing is often used in lean startup products or in existing products that are changing their look. It is a different type of testing in that it validates a business idea, so in some ways it is a Q2 type of test. However, it is done in production by real customers, so it's really a way of critiquing the product.

The idea is to develop two distinct implementations, each representing a different hypothesis about user behavior, and put them out for production customers to use. For example, you can move UI elements around or change the steps of a UI wizard. The company monitors statistics on which customers "click through" and which leave right away. In this way, companies can base decisions on real results and can improve their applications based on continued A/B experiments. When appropriately done, A/B testing can help companies make decisions about everything from user experience (UX) design to pricing plans.

Small Changes Can Have Big Impacts

Toby Sinclair, *a tester in the UK, shares his experiences at a retail company that did extensive A/B testing.*

Whilst I worked with a large online UK retailer in 2011, they introduced the concept of A/B testing. The usability and customer experience teams wanted to have more confidence in the design decisions being made, and they saw A/B testing as a way to do this.

The initial tool used was Campaign Optimizer, as it integrated with our existing Oracle ATG e-commerce platform. It allowed the business to set up A/B tests without code deployments. This meant they could easily switch tests on and off without contacting the development teams. The tool also provides the administration facility (reporting, switching tests on/off, etc.). Some initial development and integration testing was required to get it up and running.

The first A/B tests the team implemented were very simple, for example, a 50/50 split between these two choices:

- **Existing version:** 20 items on shopping gallery page by default
- **The challenger:** 50 items on shopping gallery page by default

The winner was decided based upon a number of metrics. These included

- Pages viewed by a user
- Particular items on a page viewed by a user
- Products added to a shopping cart by a user
- Purchases made by a user

Deciding how to split your tests and how long to run them is quite an art. Some of the factors include:

- How many visits did you get to your site? You need a high count in order to have confidence in your results.
- How experimental is the challenger? You may want to send only a small number of customers to the challenger if the impact is unknown.

Generally most of our A/B tests ran for two weeks, as we found that gave us a good statistical result based upon the average customer visits. To validate the results from the A/B tests, we also compared information from our analytics partners (Coremetrics and Speed-Trap). This ensured that we had full confidence in the winning version.

We also developed the capability to run tests against specific customer segments. This made the results obtained even richer and provided further insights to the targeted content team.

Today, every day, there are tests running across the website providing rich information to the teams about how best to design the website. The capabilities of and focus on A/B testing have grown considerably over the past few years. There is now even a separate A/B test team that recruits people with both a technical and marketing background.

A/B testing is definitely not limited to agile projects, but it fits agile values well. The goal of A/B testing is to identify which changes to your website will have the greatest impact. This type of testing is all about iterating with fast feedback to select a design or achieve and maintain other quality characteristics that help the business achieve its goals. If you think your team might benefit from A/B testing, check the links in the bibliography for Part V to learn more.

USER EXPERIENCE TESTING

User experience (UX) designers have many ways to get feedback on functional website design and designs in progress. They use methods commonly found in industrial design and anthropology to test designs and design concepts before producing anything on screen or even on paper.

User Research

Drew McKinney, *a product designer on Lisa's current team, shares some of his experiences with user research and user experience testing.*

One of the projects I led was to develop a project planning and management system for Disney Animation Studios artists and technical staff. My team conducted ethnographic studies with software developers, technical directors, technology managers, and animation technologists to understand their collaborative work processes. In a process known as contextual inquiry, the designer or researcher observes the user perform day-to-day activities and discusses them with the user while taking part (Wikipedia, 2014b).

In our case, these predesign sessions revealed several problems with the artist software delivery system and technical project management. Ongoing communication issues coupled with a poorly designed software indexing system resulted in numerous headaches for both technical and artist staffs. As a result of these early predesign exercises, it was easier for our team to design an appropriate solution to Disney's software (and people) management problem.

Prototype Testing and Paper Prototypes

Design testing can be a lengthy process if done incorrectly. Testing too late in the process can reveal fundamental flaws with a new system's design, requiring costly redesigns and rewrites. To provide early feedback on product designs, UX designers use a number of prototyping methods throughout the product development process. These prototypes can range from full-color printouts to simple sketches.

The easiest way to achieve quick usability feedback is also the cheapest: paper prototypes. Paper prototypes are paper representations of interfaces. On a different project, my team designed an iPhone app for a weight-loss program. Again, we used early paper prototypes to see how users would respond to an app concept. We noticed that users were confused about the meaning of representations on a map, so we improved the graphical design to make the meaning clearer. We observed that the iPhone users were more attracted to applications that provided a fun and fresh experience, so we designed their system to accommodate that need.

Sometimes paper prototypes are not enough, and a more functional example needs to be used. In another example from Disney, our team was tasked with building a collaborative canvas interface to allow senior animators to critique remotely located artists, a process that still relied on fax machines and phone calls. This was a clear opportunity for a functional prototype: a working example that artists could use as if it were final. Rather than build a prototype, we used off-the-shelf hardware and software to accomplish this. We attached a Teradici remote workstation to a Cintiq monitor and placed a MacBook above the workspace with a FaceTime call to the other artist. While by no means a final product, this quick prototype allowed us to vet the design to understand the benefits and limitations of such a system. Two Disney animators worked together remotely to test a design prototype. Figure 13-3 is a representation of this collaboration.

Figure 13-3   UX animators collaborating remotely

User experience testing is an example of a type of testing that can fit into more than one of the agile testing quadrants. You can get feedback from users before any coding is started, using paper prototypes and other techniques such as the ones Drew describes. This is a form of Quadrant 2 testing, creating customer-facing examples and information that will guide development. You can also do usability testing after coding is complete or monitor the product already in production to learn whether the current design and functionality are adequate. Those are examples of Quadrant 3 activities, evaluating the software from a business and user perspective. Feedback from this may result in new features and stories to be done in the future.

Nordstrom Labs recorded its in-store innovation testing efforts for an iPad app that would help customers choose eyeglass frames (Nordstrom, 2011). The video shows testing activities ongoing throughout iterations that lasted minutes rather than days. Designers and testers on Lisa's team have done usability testing with both internal company users of a product and people outside the company, taking advantage of user group meet-ups. Look for ways to test with real end users rather than speculate about how they will use a particular feature.

Sit with your product's existing users and see where they struggle. Take your new design to your local coffee shop and see what people think of it. Involve current and desired customers early and often. Chapter 20, "Agile Testing for Mobile and Embedded Systems," has a bit more on user experience but focuses more on how it relates to mobile apps. Check the Part V bibliography for more links on these different types of testing.

SUMMARY

Don't repeat the mistakes of our early XP/agile teams and focus exclusively on functional testing. In this chapter, we discussed some of the types of testing that are outside the scope of what is generally known as functional tests. Many of these tests can be done with an exploratory approach.

- Use the Quadrants to think about all the different types of testing your product requires.
- Talk with your business stakeholders to learn their expectations for attributes such as stability, performance, security, usability, and other "ilities."
- Concurrency testing is key for products whose users may update the same data simultaneously. Use both automated and

exploratory tests to ensure that updates are reflected correctly and in a timely manner.

- Internationalization and localization testing requires looking at cultural differences as well as languages and character sets. Specialists in this field are needed, just as many software products require security, performance, or UX testing experts.

- Testing (monitoring) in production is one approach to finding defects that are missed by checking and exploring during development.

- Completing user acceptance testing during development, rather than after, shortens the UAT cycle needed during the prerelease end game.

- A/B testing is one way to get fast feedback from production users about aspects of the application design, using a series of experiments, each one building on what was learned from the last.

- Usability testing can be done simply and productively with paper prototypes and conversations with users to help your team refine your designs and features.

Part VI

TEST AUTOMATION

Test automation is necessary. We need to automate to manage technical debt, make time for critical testing activities such as exploratory testing, and guide development with customer-facing examples. Automated regression tests tell us quickly if we've broken existing production code. As well, our automated tests provide excellent living documentation for our application.

Test automation is hard. Some types of automation are fairly painless and can even be rewarding once you get past the "hump of pain" of learning how. Some present ongoing challenges, such as testing JavaScript and logic-heavy user interface pages and experiencing sporadic failures due to timing or automatic browser upgrades.

Agile Testing included a large section about automation. To learn more about the reasons to automate tests, barriers that get in the way of automation, and how to put together an agile test automation strategy based on the test automation pyramid and agile testing quadrants, please refer to it.

Here in Part VI, we will explore more ways that testers and agile teams can succeed over the long term in creating maintainable test automation. Automated tests can help teams achieve a sustainable pace with manageable levels of technical debt. But this works only if your tests provide quick feedback at a low-enough cost. We'll look at alternative interpretations of the test automation pyramid and how those can inspire us to do more experiments involving the whole team in solving automation problems.

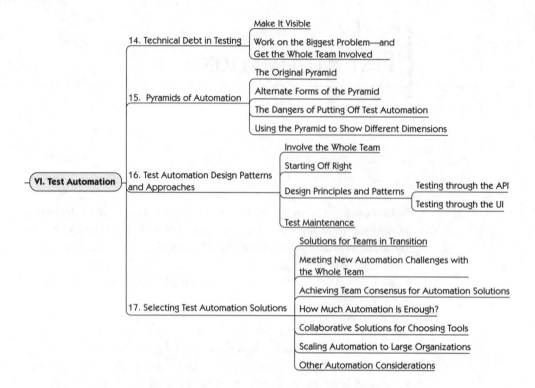

- **Chapter 14**, "Technical Debt in Testing"
- **Chapter 15**, "Pyramids of Automation"
- **Chapter 16**, "Test Automation Design Patterns and Approaches"
- **Chapter 17**, "Selecting Test Automation Solutions"

Chapter 14

TECHNICAL DEBT IN TESTING

Ward Cunningham coined the term *technical debt* (Cunningham, 2009) to represent rushing delivery of a feature or user story without ever going back to refactor the code to express your learnings. We can incur crippling technical debt in our automated test code as well as our production code. Teams often make mistakes in their initial attempts at functional test automation partly because today's frameworks and drivers make it easy to automate tests quickly. However, if we don't pay as much attention to code design principles and patterns with automated test code as we do (ideally) with production code, maintaining test scripts may become a burden. It's tricky to refactor automated test code; is a test failure a mistake in the refactoring or an actual regression bug in the software? One of the first references to technical debt in testing that we found is Markus Gärtner's blog post "Technical Debt Applied to Testing" (Gärtner, 2009).

If test automation is inadequate, or if automated tests take too much time for maintenance, there's less time for other crucial testing activities. If time is short, teams give in to temptation and skip test activities from Quadrants 3 and 4. (See Chapter 8, "Using Models to Help Plan," for more on the agile testing quadrants.) If the team feels pressure to meet a deadline, and automated tests are failing, they may rationalize that they need to fix the production code, but fixing the tests can be put off until later. When testers are consistently playing catch-up by testing code that was checked in a prior iteration, they won't have time to collaborate with the customers to elicit examples and specify business-facing tests to guide development for the current stories. This becomes a vicious cycle; no time, so we skip important testing activities, which results in more regression failures and less likelihood that we will build the right features for the customer. When testing and coding are equally valued, we can avoid this pitfall.

You can do a pretty good job of automating tests at the different levels of the test automation pyramid (see Chapter 15, "Pyramids of Automation") and still find that it wasn't enough. As a product changes, some teams find that it gets harder to update the automated regression tests accordingly. As with production code, test code might be hard to read and understand or contain unnecessary duplication. It needs the same care and feeding as production code.

Let's look at ways to manage technical debt in your testing.

MAKE IT VISIBLE

As with many impediments that agile teams face, you can start cutting your team's test technical debt down to a manageable level by first giving it visibility. For every story in the backlog that involves changing code, think about what existing automated tests might be affected. If necessary, take a quick look at the automated tests to get an idea of the possible effort needed. Make sure the estimate reflects the time needed to update the tests, and write a task card for doing so (see Figure 14-1).

Figure 14-1   Task example for addressing existing automated tests

Write stories for any large test code refactoring that you need to do, just as you would for production code.

Track how much time you spend on test maintenance, and make it visible. See where you're spending your time. Is it on debugging tests that fail, or updating tests that give false results or were otherwise poorly designed? Perhaps you can write task or story cards for each failure that has to be investigated and for maintaining or refactoring test scripts to create visibility.

Similarly, make sure estimates and tasks reflect the amount of effort that goes into manual regression testing of each release. Remember that the whole team is responsible for all testing activities, including regression testing. It is common for programmers and other team members to help with manual regression testing. We call this "sharing the pain," and it enables the team to make better decisions about how to move forward.

Reducing Defect Debt—Zero Tolerance

Augusto Evangelisti *shares how his team reduced their defects and gained more enjoyment.*

Disclaimer: This won't work for everybody; all I claim is, "It worked in my context," and you might try to use it at your own risk.

One day, a few years ago, I had a conversation with an inspirational man; he was my CTO at that time. He talked about zero tolerance of bugs and how beneficial it is to remove the annoyances of bug management from the development of software. I listened, but at that time I didn't grasp the concept completely; I had never seen or envisioned a situation where a development team could produce zero or for that matter even close to zero bugs. Since then, a few years have passed and I have worked hard on his vision. Today I can say that he was right; a delivery team can deliver value with zero known bugs. I even learned that the project team doesn't have to spend half of its time playing with a bug management tool to file, prioritize, and shift waste.

Let me give you some context around my project and current practices. We have two colocated, cross-functional agile teams, each with four developers, one tester, one business analyst, one product owner, one DevOps guy, and a team lead who functions as kanban facilitator, for a total of 18 people.

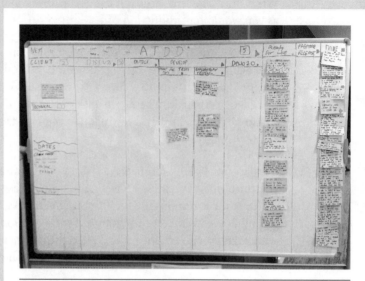

Figure 14-2   Augusto's kanban board

We use kanban to visualize our process, and we have the ability to deliver every time we complete a user story if we want. Our kanban board (see Figure 14-2) visualizes our process. In the top center, there's an "ATDD" (acceptance-test-driven development) section with column headers borrowed from Elisabeth Hendrickson's work: "Discuss," "Distill," "Develop," and "Demo."

We keep our user stories small, so that we can deliver them in less than three days. The stories are vertical slices, meaning that no integration is required between teams. Each team works on the full code base, which spans multiple applications.

We use a hybrid of ATDD and specification by example (SBE) [*authors' note*: see Chapter 11, "Getting Examples," for more on those], which I've specifically developed to fit our context. Programmers code-review every line of code before every deployment; they also practice some pair programming and test-driven development (TDD) (Hendrickson, 2008).

We automate close to 100% of our acceptance tests, using jBehave and Thucydides. See Figure 14-3 for a visual of our ATDD cycle. It's based on a model by James Shore, with changes suggested by Grigori Melnick, Brian Marick, and Elisabeth Hendrickson, and the SBE concept from Gojko Adzic. It also contains the "Red, Green, Refactor" image from *Agile in a Flash* (Ottinger and Langr, 2009c).

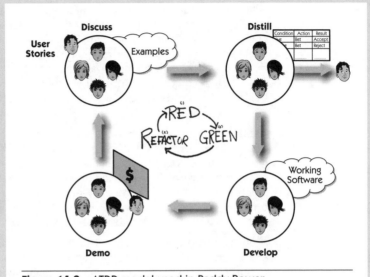

Figure 14-3   ATDD model used in Paddy Power

We have an internally developed "platform-on-demand-style" build and deployment pipeline that runs all our functional tests, as well as performance/load tests that check variations against a known baseline. Every automated test runs after every push to trunk in the pipeline.

We perform exploratory testing on a story once all the automated acceptance tests pass. Once exploratory testing is complete, we demo to our product owners, who subsequently do user acceptance testing (UAT) before accepting the story.

If a bug is found during exploratory testing or user acceptance testing, the programmer(s) who worked on that user story drops everything else he or she might be doing and fixes the bug immediately. The card will *not* progress if a valid bug is not fixed. The build must always be green. If it fails (turns red), the developer who caused the instability drops everything else and fixes the issue straightaway.

When a programmer fixes a bug, he or she writes automated tests that cover its path. You may have noticed that I've mentioned bugs. Yes, of course, we are humans and we make mistakes. This doesn't mean that we need to celebrate the mistakes and make them visible by logging them in bug-tracking tools or that we need to maintain them along with the waste stored in them, when the poor bug has the life span of an unlucky butterfly.

> When I find a bug while doing exploratory testing, I simply go to the developer and say in a friendly way, "I think there might be an issue; come to my desk and I'll show you." If the programmer needs to go home and can't fix it straightaway, no problem; I stick a red sticky note on the user story card on the physical kanban board with two words describing the bug as a reminder. That card is not going anywhere until the bug is fixed and buried. The red sticky note goes into the trash bin after the death of the bug.
>
> The development approach we follow allows us to have a good understanding of the business value we deliver because we have group discussions to derive examples for each user story. When you add a bunch of excellent developers who follow good engineering practices to that mix, you find out that the bugs you discover when exploring the software are very few. When you act upon them immediately, with no excuses, bugs don't really bother you.
>
> In our situation, logging and managing bugs would simply be waste. We all live happily with no bug Ping-Ponging between programmers and testers, no bug prioritization or triage meetings, no bug statistics, and no need for bug trends to identify product release dates. And guess what? We deliver software that has no known bugs and delights our customers.

Augusto's team has found ways to build what their customers want as well as to prevent defects from finding their way to the customer. Part of their strategy is to put a red sticky note on the story card whenever they find a bug while testing the story, providing visibility. Everyone can see at a glance when there's a bug blocking the story. Make both testing activities and defects visible in your project-tracking system, whether it's a physical board on the wall with index cards or a virtual online board. With this visibility, everyone can see if the team is taking on too much work and running out of time for testing within an iteration. Carrying testing tasks over to the next iteration is sometimes unavoidable, but it may be a red flag that the team has built up too much testing technical debt, if not overall technical debt.

Janet's Story

In one organization I worked with, we had a large set of automated regression tests, but they started failing and taking longer and longer. We investigated and found out that the technical debt in that set of tests was enormous. The tests were not only brittle and complex, but there were many that tested the same thing. That might be manageable in a waterfall process, but it becomes a burden in agile. No one had been watching or paying attention to test designs. We measured how much time was spent on maintenance and made a decision to have one person spend half days for a month to refactor to remove duplication and simplify the tests. This approach reduced the maintenance costs; not only was it easier to find and fix any problems, but it also reduced the time to run the tests and improved the quality and coverage of the tests. By making the problem visible, the team (including the product owner) was able to make a choice about how to fix it.

WORK ON THE BIGGEST PROBLEM—AND GET THE WHOLE TEAM INVOLVED

Once you have visual cues of technical debt, such as testing tasks left uncompleted at the end of the iteration, red (broken) continuous integration (CI) builds, or too much time being spent on test maintenance, take action. Test technical debt is something the whole team must manage. Remember that the whole team is responsible for all testing activities, from turning examples into automated tests that guide development to exploratory testing and regression checking.

Team retrospectives are a perfect opportunity to bring up areas of test technical debt that need to be repaid. The team can discuss contributing factors for each source of debt and use dot voting or a similar technique to identify the biggest problem that should be addressed first. Think of small experiments you could try to chip away at that problem.

For example, let's say your biggest testing problems are that the automated regression tests take too long to run, failures take a long time to pinpoint, and tests constantly get spurious false passes or failures (Janet calls these "flaky tests"). One way to speed up the builds is by adding build slaves on a virtual machine and multiple test suites in parallel. Flaky tests could be separated into a separate suite and could automatically be retried once before investigating the failure. They could be measured to see how often they fail or pass, and decisions could then be made about whether to fix or rewrite them so they could eventually be moved back into the regular regression suite. Maybe some tests are no longer worth keeping around, or they cover the same ground as lower-level automated regression tests and need to be pruned out. Perhaps some unused test data could be removed so that setting up data for the tests goes more quickly. It might even be a more complex process of reviewing tests to see if some could be pruned out or if tests require refactoring.

As your team thinks of potential ways to address test technical debt, make the potential solutions visible, just as you did the problems. Write and estimate stories for activities to start eliminating your test technical debt. Lisa's team uses a separate project to track stories and chores (tasks) for things like reducing spurious CI job failures. They hold a short meeting each week, and high-priority stories and chores are moved into the team's active backlog as needed. If several experiments fail to make the problem better, a small cross-functional group brainstorms more solutions, and individuals take responsibility for trying different ones. They revisit the issues they have chosen to work on during each retrospective until they're no longer holding the team back.

Reducing Test Technical Debt through Collaboration

> **Chris George,** *a tester in the UK, tells us this story of how a tester and a developer joined forces to do what many thought was "impossible."*

The "impossible" task was turning around a legacy test suite from a 10% failure rate (just not always the same 10%!) in 8,000 tests that took over 12 hours to run, to 100% passing in significantly less time. There had been many attempts at fixing it with varying degrees of success, but other project work would usually interrupt any progress.

These tests had developed notoriety among the delivery teams, and the estimate for fixing the test suite was in the order of several months. Unfortunately, the tests could not simply be deleted because the code they covered was used by several products, one of which was moving to a frequent release strategy, and these tests were blocking its progress.

Jeff, one of the developers, and I decided that we would take a look at the tests. We had experience in improving test suites and figured we could apply our experiences to this one. We were given two weeks to see how much we could do. Previous attempts to fix the tests involved major rewrites of the underlying test framework. The approach we wanted to take was somewhat less invasive and did not involve a rewrite.

We started by each of us taking a small section of the failing tests, analyzing and categorizing the failures, then fixing the easy ones. Most of the tests used databases and database backups, and it turned out that many of the failures were due to configuration issues. These were fairly easily fixed.

Over the course of two days, we fixed roughly 50% of the failures! Another two days, and surely we'd be finished!

As we investigated the remaining issues, we found that the tests were creating lots of databases but were not clearing up after themselves. We've both worked with SQL Server long enough to realize that the more databases you have on a server, the slower it gets. So even if a tenth of the total number of tests created one database each, this would really harm the server performance and add significant time to the test run.

If this had been left up to me, I would have put database drop commands in the test teardown. Thankfully, it was not left up to me, and in fact we paired on the problem. Jeff came up with the idea of applying the Dispose pattern to this problem, which is used to handle resource cleanup. We already created a database object when we restored a database, so we simply made this object disposable. The dispose method then called the drop command. By doing this, the author of the test does not need to remember to drop the database!

For the remainder of the week, Jeff and I applied this pattern to every test. Our rationale behind doing this was reducing the issues we knew about. Once we removed obvious causes of instability and failure, we would be left with a set of real failures to investigate.

As a break from fixing tests, we had a stab at profiling some of the long-running tests. This actually proved to be very lucrative indeed! We discovered that one of the main comparison routines for validating results used an $O(N^2)$ algorithm! (For information on O notation, see Bell, 2014.) This was fine for a result set with only a few entries, but the time it took to run this comparison increased exponentially as the result sets grew! This was bonkers, and using Jeff's expertise, we refactored the routine to be simply $O(N)$. This change alone knocked hours off the running time!

Some of the other quick wins were things like upgrading third-party libraries to the latest versions, and general "make-it-better" refactoring of the code, applying the Boy Scout rule (Kubasek, 2011) of leaving the campsite cleaner than we found it.

We fixed many more tests over the remainder of the week, some easy, some hard, and where we needed to, we paired. We used Jeff's development expertise, but we also leaned on my testing expertise to determine the usefulness of many of the tests.

> At the end of the two weeks, the number of tests had actually increased to 9,000 (after we "found" 1,000 tests that were not being run because of a configuration error), but we had successfully reduced the failing tests to one, and now the average test suite run time per platform was down to around two hours.
>
> This would not have been possible without the combined skills of Jeff and me. Having the two different perspectives and overlapping skill sets put us in a really good position to solve any issue we encountered. We also proved that an apparently impossible task was actually possible given a methodical and multipronged approach.

 Chris's story shows the value of team members in different disciplines taking responsibility for managing test technical debt. The same is true when making the decision to incur this debt. There are times when it's appropriate to cut corners in order to meet a crucial business deadline, but make these decisions consciously, and involve testers, programmers, business stakeholders, DevOps staff, analysts, and other roles as appropriate. Explain to the business customers the future costs of deferring any kind of testing, and make sure they understand there will be more work later to rectify the shortcuts taken. Document the decisions in some way, perhaps via user stories for the future or on the team wiki, so the reasons for skipping some essential testing activity aren't lost in the mists of time—or worse, forgotten altogether.

SUMMARY

Teams may decide to incur test technical debt by deferring test automation or other testing activities in order to accommodate the business, but that debt has to be managed so it doesn't slow the team down over time. Inadequate test automation, in particular, often leads to spending more time on testing activities and causes testing to fall behind coding.

In this chapter, we looked at some ways to manage test technical debt, especially as it relates to test automation.

- Make the time spent debugging test failures and maintaining automated tests visible by writing task cards for these activities or reflecting the extra time in story estimates.
- Making bugs and the resulting blocked stories visible reminds the team to fix defects quickly, focus on defect prevention, and avoid incurring technical debt in the form of defect queues.
- The whole team needs to take responsibility for managing technical debt—both code and test.
- Identify the biggest source of technical debt, and try experiments to reduce that debt.
- Have team members with different specialties work together and apply those different skill sets to reduce technical debt.

Chapter 15

PYRAMIDS OF AUTOMATION

One of the questions we hear most often is, "How do we decide what to automate?" Our preferred model is the pyramid, although other models, such as the agile testing quadrants, can help as well. In the past few years, practitioners have adapted Mike Cohn's test automation pyramid that we presented in *Agile Testing*. We've seen some useful extensions, but the basic ideas behind the model stay the same. In this chapter, we'll explore the potential benefits of the newer interpretations.

THE ORIGINAL PYRAMID

The basic principles of the test automation pyramid shown in Figure 15-1 still apply for most teams and projects, with most of the benefit based on how fast the feedback is received. The lowest level, the unit tests, gets the fastest feedback by running with every commit of new code.

We changed some wording on the pyramid to clarify its purpose. Testing business rules at the API layer gives fast feedback because the tests at that level don't go through the user interface (UI). The top layer, mostly workflow tests through the UI, tends to give the slowest feedback. The one change that we made to Mike Cohn's original pyramid was the little cloud on the top representing manual and exploratory tests that cannot be fully automated. Many teams require some manual regression tests to supplement their automated checks; they should find ways to keep this feedback timely.

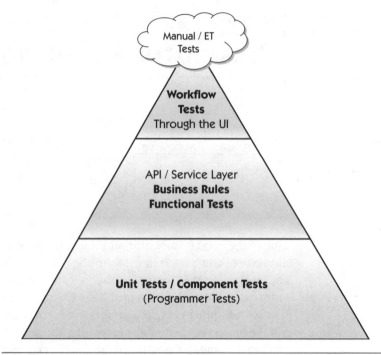

Figure 15-1   Test automation pyramid

The frameworks and tools for testing at the API/service layer and at the UI level keep improving, and they allow us to automate tests for more complex software. See more about this in Chapter 16, "Test Automation Design Patterns and Approaches."

ALTERNATE FORMS OF THE PYRAMID

Over the years, we've realized that the original pyramid doesn't fit all situations, and advances in technology have changed some of the assumptions. We've learned some good ways to modify the pyramid to fit various situations but still keep the original idea of where to automate.

Janet's Story   In one organization that I visited, the team had read *Agile Testing* and told me that the pyramid was useless to them. I couldn't understand how that could be, but I listened to why they couldn't use it. Their problem was that the programmers really didn't do very much unit-level testing, since they didn't do a lot of code, and they didn't see how they could automate at the API level. They mostly gathered data from a lot of different data feeds and then manipulated it to display to the decision makers. I understood their problem and facilitated a workshop to figure out alternatives.

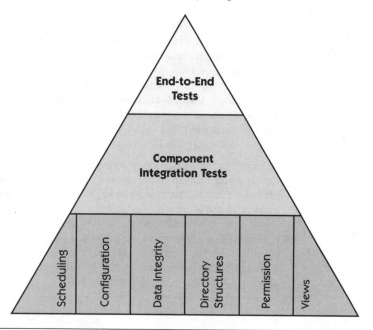

Figure 15-2   Alternative test pyramid—no unit tests

First we discussed the types of problems they were experiencing and then worked through what kinds of tests might help mitigate those problems. We then discussed when the best time to run the tests might be and who might be the best people to own them. The result is the pyramid shown in Figure 15-2. The lowest layer consists of the tests the programmers took ownership of because they wanted fast feedback. They discussed ways they could automate them and decided to experiment with several options. The middle layer comprised their component integration tests, and the slowest feedback came from their end-to-end tests.

Software products are becoming more complex, and users demand quicker response time and more intuitive interfaces. Web applications increasingly rely on JavaScript to improve the user experience, so the abstraction between business logic and the presentation layer has blurred. There are tools that allow programmers to unit test these complexities in the UI, but extensive functional UI automation may be required in these situations. Many teams can't rely on lower-level tests to guard against regressions.

Lisa's Story

The team I joined in 2003 resolved to keep our web-based financial services application's UI as thin as possible. However, as technology and user expectations evolved, we needed to provide a richer, mistake-proof user experience. More business logic on the front end required more sophisticated UI tests. Through experimentation and time spent learning, we were able to do these in a maintainable way. The top level of our test automation pyramid expanded, but the value far outweighed the costs of the additional UI tests (see Figure 15-3).

My current team's tests are a bit more hourglass shaped, for similar reasons. Our JavaScript-based UI contains highly complex business logic. When we plan and estimate front-end stories, we include time for test-driven development at the UI level as well as for adding or updating UI regression tests. This is a great illustration of why testing and coding are integral parts of software development. Although there is usually testing to do when coding is completed, test and code can't be treated as separate phases. When we talk about planning our testing, we always intend that this be part of general story, iteration, and release planning.

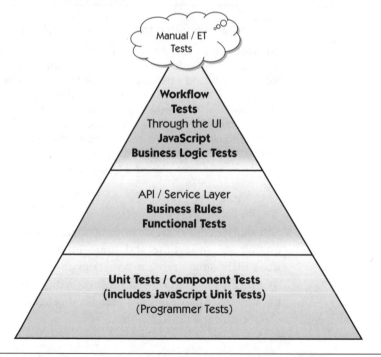

Figure 15-3   Test automation pyramid with JavaScript complexities

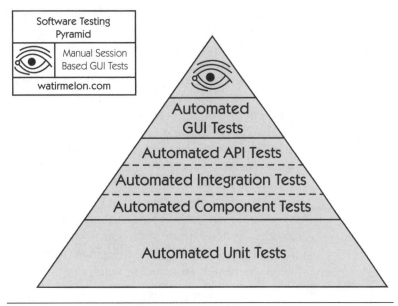

Figure 15-4   Automated test pyramid, with the Eye of Providence
Source: Scott, Alister, http://watirmelon.com/2011/06/10/yet-another-software-
testing-pyramid, 2011. Used with permission.

We've met several teams whose situation just doesn't fit the original
pyramid model. That's OK. Each team should evolve a model that fits
their needs. What's important is to remember the principles behind the
pyramid. The lower levels represent the fast feedback teams need as they
add and update code. The goal is to involve the whole team in automating enough regression tests so that the project doesn't become mired
in technical debt. Pushing tests to lower levels where they are generally
easier to write and maintain helps achieve the best ROI.

Alister Scott has created a test automation pyramid that is similar to
the original but puts a bit more emphasis on exploratory testing. In his
opinion, exploratory or session-based testing ensures confidence in the
automated tests that are being developed and run. Without it, an automated testing strategy is fundamentally flawed, which is why he includes
exploratory testing as the "Eye of Providence" in his pyramid, as shown
in Figure 15-4 (Scott, 2011b).

THE DANGERS OF PUTTING OFF TEST AUTOMATION

The test automation pyramid is a model intended to guide teams in
getting the most value from their test automation for the minimum

investment. Matt Barcomb used the pyramid as the basis for a fable about what happens when there's no whole-team effort to implement adequate test automation, especially at the lowest level.

In the Legend of the Test Automation Volcano (see Figure 15-5), a development team lives in a little oasis at the side of a test automation pyramid. The programmers lounge under the palm trees, enjoying umbrella drinks. They're too busy doing what they think they enjoy most to actually automate any regression tests for their software product. Meanwhile, sweaty testers labor in the bowels of what is not an automation pyramid but a volcano, frantically doing manual regression testing and falling further and further behind. The tests within the volcano that would normally cool it off are missing. There's no time to devote to that exploratory testing sun at the top. Technical debt accumulates in the form of red-hot lava. If the development team doesn't collaborate with testers and automate sufficient regression tests, the lava keeps building

Figure 15-5   Automated Test Volcano

and heating up until the volcano erupts, burying the unfortunate programmers in their oasis.

Though Matt turns this into a hilarious story, which in his telling includes sacrificial virgins, the message is serious. Real-life teams working under the strain of ever-growing technical debt feel real pain. In the long term, insufficient automated regression test coverage and lack of time for essential activities such as exploratory testing will slow the team down and could possibly stop it in its tracks.

Fortunately, we hear of more and more teams that are able to apply the test automation pyramid model to get control over their technical debt and shorten their feedback loops. Let's look at some success stories.

How We Flipped Our Pyramid

Here is a story from **Paul Shannon** *and* **Chris O'Dell**, *agile quality enthusiasts from the UK whose team suffered from an inverted pyramid, about how they managed to flip it to stability.*

The first incarnation of the 7digital API was a single monolithic application that started small and was tested mostly with full end-to-end tests. With the application being so small, these tests were very useful, but as the application grew, the number of end-to-end tests grew with it. A point was soon reached when a full run of the test suite would take nearly an hour, and as you can imagine, this was extremely damaging to the feedback cycle and subsequent development speed.

Developers started to employ tactics for handling this long-running suite of tests, for example, running only the tests that were obviously relevant to the area they were working in on their local machines, and then relying on the continuous integration (CI) server to run the full suite. By the time the full suite had completed, the developer had often moved on to something else, so any failures were likely to have been overlooked.

The tests themselves were also prone to unexpected failure. Due to their end-to-end nature, they were very susceptible to changes in any part of the stack, such as a database becoming momentarily unavailable or a fluctuation in the internal network. These frequent instances of instability reduced trust in the tests, causing the developers to be even less inclined to run them.

The team realized that this situation was unsustainable. These end-to-end tests had been used to cover all scenarios, including all edge cases and all possible variations. It was a habit that had started when the application was small and had continued throughout its growth.

We decided that we needed to tackle this problem directly, but it was difficult to pin down—the scope was large, and it was impossible to see what was required without diving in. We took the approach that when programmers were working in a given area, they would review the associated tests, isolate the main "user journeys" to remain as end-to-end tests, and push the edge cases down to integration and unit tests.

This significantly extended the time for each feature or bug fix to be completed, and there were times when a change to the tests was so big that it needed to be tackled on its own. In these cases, we would write up a card—a work item—for the refactoring, label it as technical debt, and prioritize it against the rest of the backlog. This was not difficult to do as our product manager was very supportive of the work. He could see the effect these poorly performing tests were having on our ability to implement new features.

We also had a small whiteboard in the team area where we recorded some refactoring ideas and goals, such as "Refactor any web forms to use an MVP pattern to allow for testing of the Presenters." This kept us focused because we were doing refactoring as part of other work.

The change was gradual and in many cases very frustrating. The state of the code base became far worse before it got better due to the transition period when different approaches were in use. The overall code base was confusing to look at, and there was a temptation to give up and start again, but we persevered. The chart in Figure 15-6 shows the huge increase in time taken to complete work items when we started to tackle the problem. You can clearly see at point A when we started this initiative as the cycle time increased. The positive effect on cycle time can be seen later at point B, when the hard work began to pay off and cycle time was reduced, showing an overall downward trend.

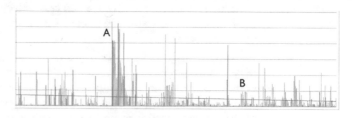

Figure 15-6   Cycle time of work item completion

The effort paid off and the end-to-end tests' run time came down from nearly an hour to under five minutes with more than quadruple the number of unit tests. Developers were able to run the unit tests on their local machines after each change, remaining confident that virtually all scenarios were covered. The full suite of tests is now run only before pushing changes back to the main branch.

Using the Pyramid to Show Different Dimensions

We call it a pyramid, but really it is a triangle. We prefer simple models and to use more than one when applicable, such as the simple pyramid and the agile testing quadrants. We find that the more complex a model is, the harder it is to understand. People have been adding dimensions to the pyramid, some with more success than others. The next story is one of those successes.

The Test Automation Pyramid—Expanded

Sharon Robson *gives the test automation pyramid some new dimensions, reflecting the various dimensions quality teams need to build into their software products.*

I interpret the agile testing pyramid as a beginning to a discussion about test strategy in an agile team. I really like the pyramid analogy because a pyramid is a self-supporting structure that cannot exist without each of its sides. Each has a different focus (or direction), but each ties into the whole unit. I go through four steps to explain the pyramid to teams.

Step 1 is a basic explanation of the pyramid (see Figure 15-1)—what each layer means and what each layer is designed to test. This aids in appropriate test design for the team members.

Step 2 is adding the next (right) side to the pyramid (see Figure 15-7), which encompasses the tools that we can use to execute these tests. Each tool is chosen for the test type and the test executor. For example, at the functional and business rules test layer, we are looking at system testing and making sure the fundamental functionality of each of the architectural elements works both individually and together. At the UI level we are looking for user acceptance testing. This means that we need to have the right type of tool for the executors of the testing at that level to use.

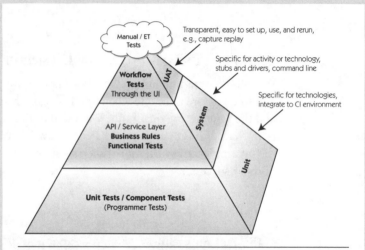

Figure 15-7   Step 2—the tools and testers

This expansion allows people to understand that there is not one tool that will do everything, and that when we are automating we need to match the tool to the tester as well as the testing. This model allows clarity about how the tool types and tool users change depending on where inside the application or architecture we are focusing.

Step 3 is to extend the pyramid to show three sides (see Figure 15-8), with the overlay of test types or system attributes. These allow us to be sure that we consider all the aspects of the solution that need to be tested.

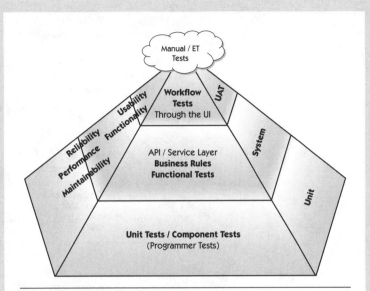

Figure 15-8   Step 3—the test types

After these three steps we can see who is going to focus on what type of testing—for example, functional versus nonfunctional—and why these tests should be run at the various levels. This then allows us to check and see if the tool selection and the tests have been designed for coverage of the system attribute we are trying to evaluate.

Once a test attribute is assigned to the test level, people in the team begin to understand how much testing may be involved, and we start to talk about data sets, reuse of data, tests and test design, as well as test design for specific attributes. We also encourage technical team members to share their knowledge of how to test the more technical (architecture and design) attributes at the higher levels. Nontechnical team members start to understand why test automation and test design are important for coverage and for building the testing resources for regression.

Visually it is pretty hard to represent that fourth side of the pyramid, so I leave the regression tests as lines running down the third side, indicating that the regression can be on any system attribute that has been considered as part of the testing (see Figure 15-9).

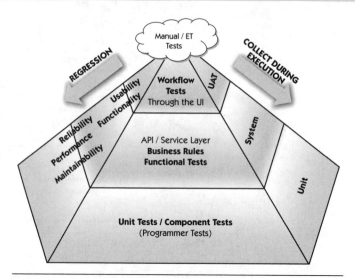

Figure 15-9   Step 4—regression tests

I use this four-step process when I am talking about automation in general, not just in the agile framework. It is very useful when considering testing done by the whole team, identifying the consistent and reusable test and data sets that will be required, and explaining the need for different types and levels of testing to prove that each of the system components, elements, and attributes hangs together in a solution that "works" in a way that we expect.

Adapt the test automation pyramid to fit the needs of your team, your technology stack, and your product. Use it to automate tests at the optimum level for fast feedback on regression failures. The pyramid model helps your team remember to push tests down to the lowest level that makes sense, maximize its return on the investment in automation, and find ways to build in a variety of quality characteristics.

SUMMARY

The original test automation pyramid is useful, but it's not perfect for every situation. We've shared some ways we and other agile testing practitioners have adapted and expanded the pyramid to represent automated test strategies in a visual model. These different models include

- The tried-and-true original test automation pyramid
- Test pyramid with no unit tests but other programmer tests instead
- Pyramid showing where JavaScript tests fit
- Alister Scott's test pyramid with the Eye of Providence representing exploratory testing
- The lessons learned in the Fable of the Automated Test Volcano from Matt Barcomb
- Sharon Robson's expanded test pyramid representing multiple quality dimensions, tools, and types of testing

Chapter 16

TEST AUTOMATION DESIGN PATTERNS AND APPROACHES

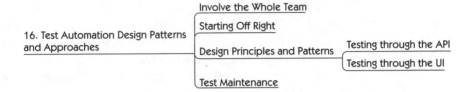

Since writing our first book, we've met more and more teams that have achieved their test automation goals. This is great news. However, it is still hard to learn how to automate tests and probably always will be. Current automation frameworks enable teams to automate tests at all levels in a syntax that business experts can understand. Yet difficulties such as sporadic test failures due to timing issues in user interface (UI) tests continue to plague us. The test automation "hump of pain," as described in *Agile Testing* (p. 266), still looms as an imposing barrier to teams that are new to test automation.

Teams that adopted agile found existing functional test automation frameworks and drivers wanting, so they created their own. Then, many of them open-sourced those tools. Today we have many sophisticated functional test tools designed for use in agile projects. Testers and programmers doing acceptance-test-driven development (ATDD)/ specification by example (SBE)/behavior-driven development (BDD) no longer have cause to envy the cool tool sets available to test-driven development (TDD) practitioners.

We need to evolve our tests and processes to take advantage of the tool changes. Our products will change, which likely means changes to existing test structures. Adam Knight (Knight, 2014) suggests asking ourselves some questions, such as, "Is our test structure extensible if we need to support new interfaces?" Over the years, and through the ability to develop and extend the test harnesses, Adam has been able to add in support for parallel execution and include iterative scaling of test execution and multiple server runs. We hear about experiences like Adam's more frequently with each year that passes. Each team must be prepared to take on similar challenges.

INVOLVE THE WHOLE TEAM

The whole-team approach to testing and quality is possibly most critical when it comes to automating tests. Automated tests are code. Not only do they protect us against regression failures, but they help us to document our production code, telling us exactly what our system does. As we've mentioned before, they deserve the same care and feeding as our production code.

When testers own test automation, they must spend large portions of time writing test scripts for stories in the current iteration, investigating test failures, and maintaining the existing automated tests so they continue to work as the production code is updated. There's often little time left for crucial activities such as exploratory testing. Programmers who aren't automating functional tests have no incentive to create testable code because they don't feel the pain of code that's not automation friendly.

When the whole team is involved in test automation, the programmers recognize how they can make their code testable. For example, they can design the code with different layers, each of which can be tested independently. For a web-based application, simply using unique identifiers for HTML elements rather than using dynamic naming makes automating UI tests easier.

It is important for the whole team to own, and see the value of, automation, so that the work can be shared where it makes the most sense. It makes sense for the people who are best at writing code to write the test code. We do know people who self-identify as testers who are also excellent coders and do a great job of designing automated tests. However, on most teams, the people with the most coding experience are the programmers, and their skills can be used for the test code. Creating tests and writing the code to make them run are two different skill sets.

Testers are good at knowing which tests to specify and which tests to change if existing functionality is being changed. Collaborating with each other to implement test automation makes sense (see the section later in this chapter on "Testing through the UI"). As we said in *Agile Testing* (pp. 300–01), team members in other roles, such as system administrators and database administrators, also contribute to good automation solutions.

STARTING OFF RIGHT

As more test automation frameworks and drivers dazzle us, it's tempting to go the, "Oooh! Shiny! And it would look good on my résumé!" route. However, as Markus Gärtner advises (Gärtner, 2012), each team must first decide what their tests should look like. This takes lots of thought and experimentation. You need to answer many questions, such as, "Who needs to be able to read the tests? Who will specify them? Who will automate them? Into what continuous integration (CI) tool will they be integrated? Who will maintain them?"

Liz Keogh (Keogh, 2013a) suggests that teams get certain capabilities in place before "heading down the tools path": an eye on the big picture, the ability to question and explore, the ability to spot and embrace uncertainty, as well as having great relationships between people. Learn how to have conversations to elicit examples of desired behavior before deciding how to encapsulate them into a particular tool. This keeps the focus on collaborating with business experts and helps the team creatively find what works best for their situation.

Create a domain-specific language (DSL) that will let your team guide development with customer-facing tests. A good place to start is by getting examples from your domain experts (see Chapter 11, "Getting Examples," for more about that). Then, and only then, look for the right tools to help you create tests that business users can read; these in turn become executable specifications. By starting with Quadrant 2 tests (business-facing tests that guide and support development), the programmers will continue to use the same language throughout their unit tests and production code. This continuity creates a common language that helps to provide living documentation—documentation that is guaranteed to be up-to-date, as long as the tests are passing. As a bonus, these tests are incorporated into test suites run by your CI process, where they also protect your end users from regression failures. See the bibliography for Part VI, "Test Automation," for resources on learning more about DSLs.

DESIGN PRINCIPLES AND PATTERNS

In *Agile Testing* we noted that principles of good code design apply to test code as well as to production code. Principles such as Don't Repeat Yourself (DRY) help avoid duplication and ensure that when something changes in the system under test (SUT), only one test component needs to be updated. The Arrange-Act-Assert pattern (Ottinger and Langr, 2009a) is commonly used in unit tests but applies to higher-level acceptance tests as well. In this pattern, you arrange the context by creating an object and setting its values, act by executing some method, and assert that the expected result was returned. The software community has

Table 16-1   Simple Rules to Live By for Automating Tests

Rule	Reason
Single purpose	Easier to debug; easier to change if business rules change
DRY (Don't Repeat Yourself)	Ability to change tests in only one place
Use a DSL (domain-specific language)	Makes communication about the tests easier
Abstract code out of the tests	Makes the tests business readable
Setup and teardown tests	Can run the tests repeatedly
Independence	Tests can run independently and do not depend on order to run consistently
Avoid database access (if possible)	Database calls slow down the tests (note that somewhere you may need to test the access)
Tests must run green—all the time	Confidence in the tests; living documentation
Apply common test standards (including naming conventions)	Enables shared code/test ownership and common understanding of tests
Separate the test (the what) from test execution (the how)	Abstracting the what from the why can allow the layers to evolve separately; you can add more examples to the human-readable specification (the test), or you can change the underlying automation without affecting the business rules

continued to evolve design principles and patterns that reduce the cost of writing and maintaining automated test scripts.

Whether you are automating at the unit, API, or UI level, look for ways to improve your test design to keep long-term maintenance costs to a minimum while getting fast and useful feedback. Simple steps such as documenting your test design patterns for your team or development organization can help ensure consistency and maintainability, as well enable others to understand the structure of the tests.

Table 16-1 shows some basic design rules we think are important to keep tests maintainable. It is by no means exhaustive, but it can give you a good start on experimenting to see what works best for your team.

Testing through the API (at the Service Level)

When you start out to automate business-facing tests that guide development, spend time with the stakeholders and the delivery team deciding how you want the tests to look. The tests should be useful and understandable to all who need to use them. Remember that these tests will provide valuable living documentation about how the system behaves, if they continue to pass when changes are made.

Figure 16-1 shows how API-level testing frameworks generally work. The diagram doesn't reflect the overhead needed to create test libraries

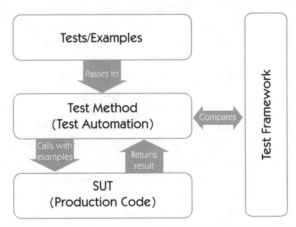

Figure 16-1 API test structure

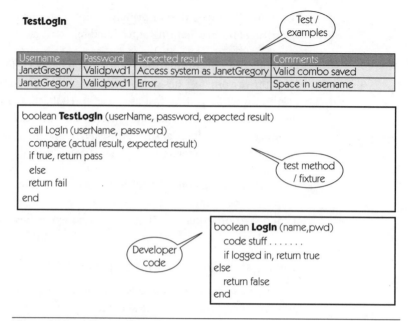

Figure 16-2   API test example

and abstractions. Rather, we want to draw attention to the magic in the middle piece—the "glue," or test method. When testers and programmers collaborate to determine what the tests should look like, amazing things happen to enhance the shared understanding of the story. Once you have that, writing the automation code is a smaller effort.

Figure 16-2 is an example of a test for a simple login. There are two tests: one for the happy path, a valid username and password; and one with an invalid username. The input data that is passed in the first test to the TestLogIn test method would be <JanetGregory, Validpwd1>. It is then passed through as input variables to the production code. The expected result <Access System as Janet Gregory> is what will be compared to the actual results coming back from the production code via the test framework. Of course, how the data is passed back and forth is something testers and coders must discuss. This collaboration on what is being passed, and how to represent it, is where the magic happens.

Chapter 11, "Getting Examples," has more on testing below the UI and discusses how to guide development with examples. There are multiple patterns that can be used to work with this structure. One example is the Ports and Adapters pattern (Cockburn, 2005) discussed in *Agile Testing* (p. 112).

Testing through the UI

In recent years, the agile community has come up with more effective patterns and practices for designing automated tests that deliver a great ROI. This is true for all levels of automation, including the regression tests that run through the application's UI.

Automating tests that exercise the application's UI continues to pose the most difficult challenges. Many teams have invested time and money to automate UI tests, only to find the long-term maintenance cost overwhelming. Over the years, better approaches have evolved. Gojko Adzic (Adzic, 2010b) recommends thinking about UI automation at three levels:

- **Business rule or functionality level:** what the test is demonstrating or exercising—for example, get free shipping within the continental United States with an order totaling a certain amount
- **UI workflow level:** what high-level activities the user has to do in the UI to exercise the functionality being tested—for example, create an order whose total amount qualifies for free shipping
- **Technical activity:** the technical steps to exercise the functionality in the test—for example, open a page, type text in input fields, click buttons

This approach can be implemented via several popular testing frameworks, using step definitions and scenarios, keywords, and, with some additions at the business level, Page Objects. Alister Scott also shares his experience with the three-level split approach, with examples of executable specifications and living documentation using Cucumber (Scott, 2011a).

Page Objects, and page resources for non-object-oriented frameworks, can be used to encapsulate all the things that are testable on each page of a UI. The Page Object (see Figure 16-3) includes all the functionality to

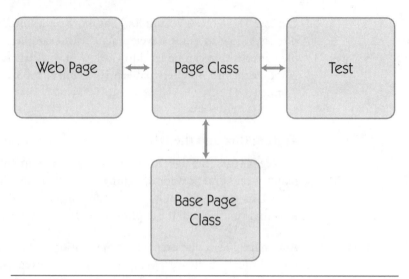

Figure 16-3 Page Object pattern

interact with the SUT via third-party test libraries such as Selenium. It is most applicable where pages and activities are well aligned. When most activities span multiple screens or pages, or where a single screen does multiple activities, the Page Object may not be a good fit, and that may lead to maintenance problems.

Jeff "Cheezy" Morgan created an open-source Page Object Ruby Gem for testing browser-based applications (see the "Tools" section of the bibliography for the link), and there are other implementations for different programming languages. It can be used in testing web applications, desktop applications, mobile applications, and even mainframes. See Chapter 20, "Agile Testing for Mobile and Embedded Systems," for Cheezy's story of how he automates testing mobile apps.

Cheezy explains how the Page Object pattern can be used with the three-layered approach (Morgan, 2014):

> *PageObject is a great pattern for building an abstraction over the system under test. You still need to provide a place where you clearly express the business rules to be verified, the workflows or paths to be taken through the application to complete the behavior, and the data needed by the*

application to complete the workflow. I look at these three additional parts of the test as very distinct. I use a BDD tool like Cucumber to express the business rules or behavior and other libraries to provide the navigation and tests. I find that this separation of concerns makes my test code much cleaner and easier to adapt as the application changes.

Your team should decide how you want your tests to look and then experiment with different patterns and approaches to see what works best.

Lisa's Story

Our team's product was a web application that originally had a thin client. The business logic was all on the server side, and we automated regression tests for it at the API level. Our UI test tool worked through the HTTP layer, so we sometimes had trouble with client-side events, but it worked well to cover the UI regression testing.

Later, our team came up with new front-end code that we knew would help reduce costly user mistakes, but our UI test tool couldn't "see" the event. We felt it was too risky to implement it without automated regression tests, so it was time to find a new UI test driver and framework.

The Page Object pattern provided an appealing way to create maintainable UI tests. We kicked off a series of "bake-offs" to identify the best approach that used the Page Object and enabled the testers and coders to collaborate closely. We used a set-based-development-style approach. First, we agreed on how we'd like our tests to look. We considered a given_then_when style, which our product owner liked. But knowing that he preferred not to look at the detailed test cases, we decided to stick with an assertion format close to that of our existing tests.

Next, two people each tried a different set of tools for a proof of concept and shared their results with the rest of the team. It took a couple of rounds and a lot of time, but the investment paid off. The whole team chose the best tool set for our needs, and we brought in an expert coach to help us get a good start. The learning curve took a few weeks, but soon we were writing new tests quickly and enjoying a short feedback loop from maintainable tests.

Some people might think that taking time to experiment with how tests look, and the best framework to create them, is too expensive. But I can tell you from experience, it's much more expensive over the long term if you're trying to make do with the wrong test format and framework. Tests will fail more frequently, and every test failure will take longer to diagnose and correct. You will spend more and more time refactoring.

Lisa's experience illustrates the value of team members with different specialties and skill sets collaborating to find the most appropriate automation solutions for their team. One of the main proponents of the Page Object on her team was the lead system administrator, who also is a programmer and a proponent of useful test automation. His story follows.

Page Objects in Practice

Tony Sweets, *an information technology architect from Colorado, USA, describes the advantages of using a Page Object pattern for automated tests through the UI. He has given us some code snippets and technical details, which we included in Appendix A, "Page Objects in Practice: Examples," for those readers who want more details. Full code for the example can be found on Tony's GitHub account (Sweets, 2013).*

Object-oriented software is a time-tested way to produce maintainable, easy-to-modify code. Design patterns are key when writing in an object-oriented way; knowing what they are and how to use them will improve your code. A design pattern can be thought of as a recipe for how to build something. One pattern the software developer and testing community has accepted is the Page Object pattern that enables you to implement your automated tests in an object-oriented manner.

Understanding the Page Object Pattern

One of the problems that Page Objects try to solve is reuse. It is better to encapsulate the piece that you would have normally cut and pasted into a single module (or object) and reuse that single object where you need it. That way, you can generally just update the single object. As long as the interface to the object stays the same, the implementation details do not matter, and your tests should continue to work.

Your goal as an automated test writer is to separate your test from how it is implemented. For example, when you need to write a login test, the high-level test should not need to change when something in the application changes. Let's say this is your high-level test script:

Step 1: Open web browser and go to SUT site.

Step 2: Verify we are at the home page and there is a login box.

Step 3: Log in as Jane Doe.

Step 4: Verify that we are at Jane Doe's landing page.

Notice how I did not say how to log in. I did not say, "Type 'jdoe' in the username box and 'password123' in the password box, then hit Submit." I simply said, "Log in as Jane Doe." The thing or object that I'm calling should have those details. What if down the road a new requirement comes down from the product owner to add a third box to the login dialog for a PIN, such that you need a username, a PIN, and a password to log in? If you had 50 tests that started with logging in, you would have to make 50 changes. But if you're using Page Objects, you have to make the change in only one place.

The idea is simple; you need a layer between your test and the implementation of the test. Your test can call methods on an object whose interface should be fairly stable. When changes happen in the system and you must account for them in your test (for example, there is a new requirement to add a CAPTCHA field on the login page, or the PIN in the preceding example), you can merely change the implementation of the login Page Object but not its interface; thus, you will not need to change your actual test.

Implementing the Page Object Pattern

The simple idea behind the Page Object pattern is to represent each page in your system as an object. This Page Object will encapsulate the elements of the page as well as any operations that can be done while viewing that page.

The first thing that a Page Object must do is verify that it is actually representing the page being displayed. This is usually done when the object is initialized. For example, a Home Page Object might verify that the words "Cool System Home Page" are in the title bar.

Operations (or methods) should return a Page Object. If, after logging in to an application, you expect to see a dashboard, your login method should return the dashboard Page Object.

There are no tests in the Page Object (other than verifying that the page has been rendered correctly) itself. Your tests are separate, and they are written like a script, but they do include these Page Objects and use them. The following script snippet shows the test script for verifying that a user can navigate to a specified page in the application under test:

```
    // Goto the List of Nissan Cars
    log.info("Clicking List of Nissan Cars");
    NissanCarListPage nissanCarListPage =
nissanPage.selectListOfCars();
    Assert.assertNotNull(nissanCarListPage);
```

> The test framework (in this case, the `Assert` class of JUnit) lets you check for expected results such as nulls, equality, and true/false. A test failure stops the script and logs information about the failure so you can debug it in the test results via the build system, command line, or a report. At the end of the test script we send a quit command to the WebDriver object, which does cleanup such as closing down the browser.

See Appendix A, "Page Objects in Practice: Examples," for Tony's examples of how to implement the Page Object pattern, with code snippets and technical details. See the Part VI bibliography for more resources, including one from Anand Ramdeo on handling common problems with the Page Object model (Ramdeo, 2013).

TEST MAINTENANCE

As we noted earlier, you need to apply good design practices to create automated test code whose value exceeds its cost of maintenance. If you're new to test automation, Dale Emery's paper on how to write maintainable automated tests is a good place to start (Emery, 2009). Remember, this is an area where both programming and testing expertise is required, so collaborate and experiment to evolve test automation that works for your team.

Many teams automate and then forget about the tests, as long as they are passing. Over time, though, you may notice that the tests take longer and longer to run. Automated tests require continual attention. You may want to watch for duplication or places for refactoring because you find a better way. You may discover gaps in your automated test coverage. By giving visibility to your automated test results, you can continually monitor and ensure that they are still doing what you expect. Today's test frameworks, whether you are testing at the service level or through the UI, can make writing automated tests fast and easy, so be aware that that isn't the end of the story. You have to maintain those tests over time, make sure they return accurate results, and keep their feedback loop short. There are many areas to think about beyond writing the initial test.

The Importance of Test Data Management

Jeff "Cheezy" Morgan *shares his story about the importance of managing test data for automation.*

There is no worse feeling than coming into work in the morning, only to see that a large number of the tests that ran overnight have failed. As you investigate the reason for the failures, you quickly discover that somebody has changed the data that your tests depend on.

This scenario is all too common. Testers spend a lot of time investigating test failures, trying to discover if they failed due to a problem with the system under test or due to some environmental issue. When tests fail because of environmental issues, the team often loses faith in the tests. When that happens, they will likely start ignoring failures. Test data is a major contributor to environmental issues.

It is extremely important that our automated tests run consistently time and time again. In order to do this we have to have a good test data management strategy. Our tests can never fail because somebody has changed the data our tests depend on or because some data we were expecting to be in the database was not there.

The only way to ensure that the data is available in the exact state you want it to be is to have your tests create the data before each test runs. Also, in order to put the system back into a known state, your tests should clean up the data at the end of execution (see Figure 16-4).

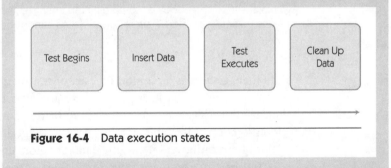

Figure 16-4 Data execution states

If your test suite has direct access to the database, this is easy. You can simply insert the data into the appropriate tables, execute your test, and then delete the data from the database.

Sometimes we do not have direct access to the database but instead must use some type of web service in order to set up the data. The pattern should remain the same. We should use the services to create the data we need, execute the test, and then remove the data we used for our test.

What should we do if the data we are using comes from another company and we have no control over it? Further, what if that data is completely volatile? In cases like this we often need to build smart surrogate services that our test suites can run against in order to have consistent data. These services should allow the tests to specify the data to be returned when they are called under certain situations. These services introduce risk for our team, as we are not running against the actual services that our application will run against when in production. In order to mitigate this risk we need to test against the real services frequently.

If you are using the system under test to set up the test data you will use, you should consider using the Default Data pattern (Morgan, 2010) with randomized data. This will allow you to specify the data that matters while leaving the remainder of the data for the framework to create.

There are a few reasons why we remove the data after each test run. The simplest reason is that if we insert some data, modify it via a test, and then during a later test run attempt to insert the same data, we are likely to get an error. This error might be because some database tables have constraints that do not allow multiple copies of the same data.

Another reason to clean up the data with each test run is that data that sits in the database for long periods of time is suspect. We are never sure if somebody or something has changed the data since it was originally inserted. As a result, this data cannot be trusted.

Data management is an important part of test maintenance and often doesn't get the respect it deserves. There are libraries to generate randomized but realistic test data, such as Ruby Faker and jdefault (see the "Tools" section of the bibliography for links). Experiment with different options for creating and managing data for automated test to use. Make sure you have a way to reproduce any issues uncovered by automated tests using randomly generated data.

Another aspect of maintainability is ease of debugging test failures. It's important to be able to drill down into test failures to quickly identify exactly what went wrong. It can be helpful for test scripts to write information to log files for more in-depth debugging when appropriate. Note that if you have kept your tests to single purpose, you may not need as much logging information, because it is simpler to find the failure.

SUMMARY

The same design principles, such as Don't Repeat Yourself (DRY), that help create robust production code also apply to test code. How we develop our tests will determine how much value we get out of them.

- Automated test code is as valuable as production code. It makes sense for the team's programmers to collaborate with testers to write that automated test code.
- In this chapter we discussed different design principles and patterns, including a three-level approach for UI automation and the Page Object pattern. Experiment with different principles and patterns to find what applies best to your tests.
- Understand how to collaborate to take advantage of tools that automate through the API/service level and beneath the UI layer.
- Data management for automated tests is critical, so spend time creating the right data strategy for your team or organization.
- Monitor the costs of maintaining automated regression tests, and take steps to keep them timely, with a positive return on investment.

Chapter 17

SELECTING TEST AUTOMATION SOLUTIONS

You have some ideas about how to conquer your test technical debt. You've used the pyramid models from Chapter 15, "Pyramids of Automation," to consider a strategy for automating tests at different levels. You've used techniques from Chapter 16, "Test Automation Design Patterns and Approaches," to figure out what your tests at one or more levels should look like. Now you need to get down to specifics. For example, your team must build an infrastructure for writing and running automated tests, which might require new hardware and software. You have to select appropriate test drivers and frameworks, and in most cases this is a long-term effort. An incremental and iterative approach lets you apply what you learn along the way to grow valuable automated tests. In this chapter we will share not only our ideas, but stories from teams that have struggled through automation adoption and how they overcame their problems.

SOLUTIONS FOR TEAMS IN TRANSITION

Choosing and implementing new test automation solutions is especially challenging for teams that are also new to agile development. Getting a coach or having team members with experience in this area doesn't guarantee an easy path to success, but it may help the team over the "hump of pain" of learning automation (*Agile Testing*, p. 266).

Implementing Automation Solutions in a Large Organization

Here's a story from **Cirilo Wortel**, *an automation test consultant in the Netherlands, about how automation solutions evolved in a large banking organization.*

Being an all-around hands-on tester, with a lot of field experience, I was anxious to start coaching the next generation of agile testers. The company I work for specializes in agile coaching and was running a full-fledged agile adoption program at one of the largest banks in the Netherlands. The transition went remarkably well; big open spaces with enormous Scrum boards marked the office spaces, and lively collaboration between most disciplines was already common practice.

Something that was not as successful as the general agile adoption was the integration of testers into the teams. Yes, there were testers in every team, and yes, they were attempting to collaborate. But most of them had little experience with agile development, and only a few had experience with test automation. Our goal was to bring automation to a higher level and get the testers more involved in the process.

I started out coaching three teams that already had started to use FitNesse in combination with Selenium. Both tools were well known to me, which was one of the reasons I was selected for the job.

The teams faced similar practical problems. Test automation was immature, test environments were unstable, and there was no version control on either tests or tools. There also was no configuration management, which resulted in many different combinations of tool and browser versions. There was no concept of test architecture and no focus on test maintainability. Figure 17-1 shows what happens if there is no collaboration when there isn't any focus.

I spent my time on practical solutions, helping out with technical problems and introducing more mature configurations and version control. I had to explain the fundamentals of test automation and teach all the required technical skills. We (the assigned coaches and I) collaborated to try to create more synergy among programmers, testers, and analysts.

Figure 17-1   Working without collaboration

The teams I had started with became quite successful, and the news spread throughout the bank. Soon people in other departments started using the same configuration. This caused the number of teams I had to support to grow rapidly.

With this expansion came new obstacles. Lots of time was lost just doing installations and configurations, and there were many technical problems to solve. Besides more on-topic issues, like having to deal with annoyances or peculiarities of FitNesse and Selenium, there were also infrastructure or software problems, which were outside the scope of my activities. The more the new approach spread, the more obstacles appeared. It was soon obvious that the settled establishment was not so open to change.

I talked to managers who were promoting test automation and agile testing and encouraged the department of "Tool Support" to allow the tools we were using to be spread more easily. Convincing the "Test Automation Center of Excellence" that they would gain positive new options also took time. Often, bureaucracy and company "standards" were used as a barrier. The company's use of commercial off-the-shelf tools was defended on the basis of their expensive licenses, although the tools served no purpose for the teams.

Many people fear change and will do anything to prevent it. The reasons they used against my proposed solutions ranged from funny to ridiculous and seldom made any sense. The company standard was simply not agile. I created the following rule set to convince my "opposition" that a change was required:

1. When working in an agile environment, automation is of **vital** importance **to keep up with the pace of the project**. Relying on only manual testing is not an option.

2. Automation must be possible within the multidisciplinary team; **no external expertise should be required** to create or maintain tests.

3. A test tool should be flexible, making it **easy to respond to change** in terms of environmental, data, and technical constraints.

4. Creating automated test cases should be relatively **simple and intuitive**.

5. Tests should be **readable and understandable** for anybody. Documenting and formatting tests in unambiguous and ubiquitous language supports this.

6. Tests should be **easily accessible and interchangeable** between team members and preferably also for other stakeholders. Anyone on the team should be capable of adding, viewing, and running tests.

7. Test execution should be **fast and reliable**, since fast feedback is the main objective.

With lots of persuasion and perseverance, not to mention teaming up with the right people, the popularity of the tool set grew, and most agile teams switched to using it in one way or another.

The tools got more popular, but the attention I could actually pay to coaching was limited. FitNesse is in many ways an excellent tool and allows users a lot of freedom. For many inexperienced testers, this can be too much freedom. With the limited time available to me, the entire endeavor got out of hand; it grew beyond my capabilities. It was time for more change!

In order to balance my activities, I had to spread knowledge in a more efficient way. To spread in-depth information, I started to organize courses. The courses would fit 10 to 15 people at a time, which was much more effective than passing information one on one.

We set up a wiki with basic knowledge on agile testing. It contained a substantial tool section, along with an installation guide, with workarounds for most common installation issues. It had a FAQ section, filled with the most common problems collected in the past period, and contained actual methods that could be used in specific complex situations.

To actively build a community, I arranged knowledge sessions, and these monthly sessions attracted a substantial audience. Testers were invited from different successful teams to present their efforts, especially ones that used very different approaches to try to broaden people's views. These sessions were extremely valuable; people started exchanging ideas, and it seemed to me that more cohesion among the teams emerged. Figure 17-2 shows how collaborating and working together can move us forward.

Figure 17-2   When we collaborate

Colleagues began to make FitNesse more appealing to a broader audience, which eventually resulted in a complete refactoring of the framework.

I collected more measures of progress. A management trainee started an experiment with two comparable teams to measure effectiveness, one using the agile approach and the other a more traditional method.

Unfortunately, just when things were finally on a roll, an organizational change meant my role was no longer funded and my assignment ended.

In retrospect, I have to conclude that the degree of success of my work was somewhat disappointing. The overall level of quality was below my personal standards, and some teams actually completely failed at automation. When considered from a broader perspective, however, the testers became more involved in test automation and in the agile process. I often heard the change had drastically increased their job satisfaction. Many teams still use the same approach and the configuration that was introduced, and it became the standard for agile projects within the bank.

What in the end is most important to me is the personal growth I experienced. A learning experience like this is invaluable.

Cirilo succeeded in helping teams within the banking organization implement a specific tool set that worked for their context. Organizational culture is difficult to overcome, but he had good strategies for helping teams succeed with automation. He set rules so that the approach would be consistent across teams. He and his colleagues refactored one of their open-source test frameworks, FitNesse, to better fit their needs. He found effective ways to measure progress, and he built a test automation community. Consider these ideas as your team implements your own test automation solutions.

MEETING NEW AUTOMATION CHALLENGES WITH THE WHOLE TEAM

If you need to fill a gap in your test automation, improve your automation ROI, or automate something that defies current solutions, get your whole team thinking of new experiments to try.

Lisa's Story

Our team was writing a new version of our API. Each time we tested a newly delivered story, we found missing requirements. There were also multiple failures, often with authorization issues and boundary conditions. We ended up rejecting the stories multiple times, which was costly.

We discussed this problem and realized that the stories were written for an audience of programmers who were familiar with old versions of the API.

However, recently hired programmers were coding the stories, and they weren't familiar with all the details of how the API should work.

We decided that the best way to express examples would be acceptance tests that would be automated as the story was coded. We needed a framework, so I paired with a developer to spike a specification by example (SBE)–style framework. In hindsight, we should have had two pairs, each trying a different approach, taking advantage of the benefits of set-based development. Still, I thought we came up with an interesting domain-specific language (DSL), related to the RSpec approach that our team was using for test-driven development (TDD).

Unfortunately, when we showed our scripts to the rest of the team, they were worried that our tests, which tested the API through the HTTP layer, had too much duplication with the functional RSpec tests written as part of the TDD process. I personally disagreed but felt I had to go with the team desires.

I still wanted to help guide coding at the acceptance or story test level, so I wrote tests in pseudo-code fashion, using a similar DSL to what we had tried for our first SBE effort. I was able to get a programmer to pair with me to automate my test cases in this modified DSL. We found three bugs in the process of automating them!

Once these were working, I specified tests in a similar fashion for a different API endpoint. The programmers used these tests as they worked on the stories, found them helpful, and made suggestions for improving them, along with additional test cases. The number of rejections for API stories went down, showing the value of using tests to illustrate requirements.

However, some of the programmers found that the learning curve for the modified DSL was extra overhead for them. Though it was more readable for testers, there was enough of a difference from their own RSpec tests that it felt like task switching. They felt it was slowing them down too much. Our team's culture was that the pair writing the code also automated tests at all levels. Switching DSLs seemed too expensive, so they wanted to use the same RSpec format for the SBE tests.

One downside to this approach was that the tests couldn't go through the HTTP layer, so some tests couldn't be automated. This approach also meant I couldn't participate in the test automation, but we needed an approach everyone was comfortable using.

I continued to specify test cases using a pseudo-code format, documenting them on the team wiki, and linked those tests to the story. The programmer pair then automated these tests using the same framework as for their unit tests. This was still a type of SBE approach, and it did provide value, although it felt clumsy to me. Also, the test cases that required going through the HTTP layer couldn't be automated, which led to holes in the automated regression test suite. We have to do more manual checks to compensate, and this constitutes testing technical debt, slowing us down.

I continued this practice for the major endpoint stories, but it felt too heavyweight for smaller stories. I switched to listing test cases in the story itself, but I found that programmers sometimes missed them, and the delivered story got rejected. In my experience, if the programmers aren't including automating the acceptance tests as part of their development effort, they will often miss those requirements.

I found that after this series of experiments, the programmers thought of more test cases on their own as they coded using TDD. Guiding development with customer-facing tests is new to the company culture, and it will take more discussions and experiments to find the right approach.

In our daily efforts to deliver value to our customers, it can be hard to take time to try something new. However, that investment is worthwhile to improve our ability to build quality and value into our software products over time.

ACHIEVING TEAM CONSENSUS FOR AUTOMATION SOLUTIONS

Getting a team, especially a large team, to agree on an automation framework or other solution can be tough. However painful it may be, when you're faced with a tough problem, the whole team needs to discuss it and come up with experiments to try to find a solution.

Lisa's Story

For eight years, my previous team had been satisfied with our user interface (UI) automation framework. Our tests kept regression failures out of production, and though they could have been better designed, they were reasonable to maintain.

But we needed some new features in our UI to help prevent users from making mistakes that caused our team to lose valuable time doing production support. The programmers decided they should use Ajax to implement these features, but our test tool wouldn't work with the client-side code. We had our own rule to never release code that wasn't supported with automated regression tests, so although the coding solution was ready, we had to defer delivery until we addressed the test automation problem.

We researched some potential automation drivers and frameworks but needed a plan of action. I got the team together for a meeting to decide what to do next. After we discussed the problem for a while, there was a long, painful silence. I was sitting there thinking, "Yeah, I tell other people how to solve automation problems, but I can't even get my own team to talk about it."

I gathered my courage and listed some of our potential options. We could hire an experienced coach to come in and tell us what UI test driver and framework to use and teach us how to use it. We could keep looking for drivers and frameworks on our own.

Finally, from behind a cube wall (see Figure 17-3), our system administrator (whom I had failed to invite to the meeting) piped up. "I think WebDriver will do what we need. I'll do a spike." We were all relieved. Finally, a plan!

Figure 17-3   Invite the right people

The spike succeeded, and we moved on to "bake-offs" to determine what framework would work best for us with WebDriver. It was all a big investment, but the most important investment was that initial, painful meeting.

Even when you think your team has good regression test coverage in place, changing customer needs and new technology may require a new approach. Whether you're taking your initial baby steps in meeting automation needs or considering a change to a previously successful approach, make sure you invite the right people to help address the problem. The whole-team approach works when there's a diversity of skills and perspectives. And when all else fails, hold your meetings within earshot of the people you forgot to invite.

What's your team's biggest problem right now? Is it related to automation? Maybe you need a way to identify performance bottlenecks or holes in security. Pull interested people together. Brainstorm ideas. Do a proof of concept. Experiment with some bake-offs. Seek outside expertise if needed. Spend time learning, and, yes, this is often extremely hard to do! Get a like-minded teammate to help, and remember the agile tester value of courage.

Yes, it's hard to step back and think of ways to chip away at a difficult problem when your customers want features X, Y, and Z out the door. Always plan your workload so that you have time to make progress in areas that are crucial to your team's long-term success, such as the right automated tests.

How Much Automation Is Enough?

In Chapter 14 of *Agile Testing*, we gave examples of testing activities that benefit from automation, as well as those that need human involvement or where automation is difficult. Over the years, we've enjoyed many new and improved test frameworks and drivers that help us use automation in more ways and with less pain. For example, we can write and manage our test code in the same integrated development environments (IDEs) and source code control systems as our production code.

As teams produce more production code and its accompanying test code, we face a new problem, especially with respect to automated regression checks. Continuous integration (CI) should provide quick feedback if any changes have introduced a regression failure. But as you add new regression tests each iteration, test suite build jobs take longer and longer. It's easy to lose that short feedback loop.

We can speed up our builds in various ways, perhaps by using virtual machines to run many test suites in parallel. Even so, we have to investigate every test failure. More tests mean more possibilities of failures that aren't a regression in the code but a problem with the test itself. More tests mean a larger test code base that requires refactoring and updating to stay current with production code.

Lisa's Story

Our team struggled with the CI being red for days on end. At least one pair was devoted 100% each day to getting the builds to green. This was a major roadblock to getting stories delivered, tested, and accepted. And real regression failures often weren't identified for hours or days. The biggest problems were with tests through the UI, which failed spuriously for various reasons. This was a constant topic of discussion at team retrospectives, but solutions were elusive.

The development manager created a shared document where team members could brainstorm ways to tackle the long-running and often-failing CI build. We were invited to share problems, concerns, questions, dilemmas, and realities, as well as potential solutions or improvements.

This was turned into a spreadsheet. For each idea, we listed benefits, disadvantages, risks, and notes about complexity. A small group of interested programmers and testers with a variety of skills met to discuss each idea. We rated each idea on benefits and complexity, using a point scale of 1 to 10. Then we subtracted the complexity score from the benefit score.

Using the results, we identified the "low-hanging fruit" and wrote stories to do these. Some were fairly simple; for example, we started rebooting the CI boxes nightly to help ensure that the builds always started with a clean environment and no stale or hung processes.

The browsers in the test environments that ran the end-to-end tests were subject to automatic browser version updates that often caused test failures. A second set of test environments was created, where the browser settings were changed to prevent automatic updates. That made it easier to know if an automatic browser update caused a test failure.

Another idea was to put together a short-running smoke test that would verify the most critical parts of the UI and take only a couple of minutes to run. The full suite of UI tests would still run, but the automated deploy to the test environment would be based on the success of the smoke test in addition to the unit and functional-level tests.

These high-benefit and relatively simple actions improved the stability of the graphical user interface (GUI) test suites. Newly finished stories are now deployed more regularly, evening out our workload and making it easier to do regular releases.

It is valuable to use automation to help verify every edge case and boundary condition during development. However, depending on the system under test (SUT) and the risks involved, it may not make sense to run every permutation of every test case in the CI. Not every test case run during coding a story may need to be added to the regression suite.

You might have a particular suite of selected integration tests that are slow to run, but it's enough to run them once a day or perhaps just before release. Depending on your situation, the same may apply to performance tests, UI tests, or any tests that may be inherently slow and can be run less often without too much risk.

Collaborative Solutions for Choosing Tools

When you are deciding what tools to choose, there are many considerations to evaluating any given one. In Chapter 14 of *Agile Testing*, we advised taking on one tool need at a time, identifying your requirements, and deciding what type of tool to choose or build that fits your needs and infrastructure. Since we wrote that, we've learned even more about good ways to choose the right test drivers and frameworks, as well as other tools, for your team. As we mentioned in Chapter 16, "Test Automation Design Patterns and Approaches," your team should first decide how you want your automated tests to look, and then find tools to support that. If you choose the tool before you know how you want to express your tests, you've automatically eliminated many of your options.

One of the most important characteristics of a test framework is whether it fosters collaboration among the different roles on a team. In Chapter 16, "Test Automation Design Patterns and Approaches," we talked about the test method that glues the tests to the production code and the criticality of collaboration between programmers and testers. It's essential to use tools that enable and enhance this collaboration. Table 17-1 shows some of the differences between what we think of as collaborative tools and those that are noncollaborative.

The one negative comment we have heard from some people is that when programmers spend time working on tests, that's time they are not spending writing production code. However, programmers who work in the way we have described have told us that it helps them write better, more testable code, with fewer defects.

Scaling Automation to Large Organizations

In large organizations, it is typical to have multiple teams working on the same product line, often five, six, or more. This has repercussions for

Table 17-1   Collaborative versus Noncollaborative Tools

Collaborative Tools	Noncollaborative Tools
Enable testers/business to define tests	Tests are usually through the UI
Test code can be in a common programming language	Programmers aren't usually willing to help
Programmers can run tests as they code	Tests are implemented after the code is written
Testers can ask programmers for help	Testers create and implement all tests
Make tests visible so team members can discuss testability before coding	

how we think about many aspects of testing the product. In this section we will concentrate on ways to scale automation for large, multiteam products.

Common test standards, including naming conventions, become even more critical when several teams work on a shared code base. Different teams may be touching different pieces of the production code and need to be comfortable changing tests and the test code behind them.

There also needs to be consistency in tool selection. If you are part of a small colocated team working on one product, selecting the tools that are best suited for your needs is relatively straightforward. When you need to consider other teams, and perhaps a support and maintenance team, there's a compelling need for common tools.

One way to accomplish this is to define classes of tools that are acceptable for different needs. For example, if you are on a team that works on Java code on product X, you may have a standard calling for Selenium for your UI tests, a choice of either Cucumber or FitNesse for your API (service)-level tests, and JUnit for your unit tests. This gives the team some autonomy but allows consistency for the maintenance team and other teams working on the same product.

Cirilo Wortel's sidebar earlier in this chapter illustrates how a common set of tools, guidelines, and community building promote successful test automation across a large organization. Let's look at another example.

Transition Challenges: Agile Test Automation

Geoff Meyer, *a test architect with Dell Inc., explains how his large development organization found a more suitable approach to test automation.*

As the Dell Enterprise Solutions Group (ESG) transitioned to agile-based development, one of our projects in particular illustrated some of the test challenges inherent in such a transition. The project team was staffed with top-notch programmers and testers, one of our top development managers, and probably one of the best and highly engaged product owners in the organization. As with most of our projects, this one also had an extensive hardware test matrix. The team recognized that test automation was a critical success factor and took steps to ensure that as features were developed, an automated regression suite was in place to guarantee working software across the broad compatibility matrix.

Unfortunately, one of the things that eventually slowed the project's ability to add features was the test automation philosophy. The test manager and test members responsible for the effort brought with them many years of experience, most of which were founded in black-box testing and UI automation on waterfall-based projects. Although the testers on the team quickly transitioned to the collaborative, Scrum-based, two-week sprint cycles, their test approach remained firmly founded in a UI-based test methodology.

As the launch date of the first release approached, the team found itself in catch-up mode to update the UI-based automation scripts to accommodate the late-breaking changes to the UI in the final sprints. As a result, the team had to undertake unexpected manual testing efforts while it simultaneously updated the automated UI tests. On the plus side, the UI-based automation test suite enabled an automated regression suite. However, because the functioning regression suite was two to three sprints behind the completion of the user stories, the project incurred a much longer manual test back end than had been originally planned.

We revisited the test automation philosophy for the project in the follow-up release. Because the application used a model-view-controller (MVC) architecture, we proposed a change in the test automation approach from UI-based to the SOAP (Simple Object Access Protocol) service level. Because of the relative stability of the SOAP interfaces versus the UI interface, we were confident that the test members of the Scrum team could develop in-sprint test automation at the service level, thus minimizing the need for additional testing on the back end of the schedule. The resistance to this change in approach was captured quite succinctly by one of the Scrum team test members: "If we do web services automation and UI automation, then we're doing double the effort."

I was unable to convince the team before the start of the next release that what was actually being proposed was a trade-off. Instead of doing UI automation within the sprint, the team would focus their in-sprint test efforts on automation at the service level and manual testing of the UI. The second release had similar results, but the problem was worsening. Because the automation backlog was growing, an increased number of testers had to be assigned to complete manual testing. Prior to this release, the ratio of programmers to testers was 3:1. During this release of the project, that ratio began to approach 1:1.

As the team prepared for the third release, I took another run at altering the team's approach to test automation. We assigned one of our most experienced service-level automation testers to dig into the application with the goal of demonstrating how service-level automation could be used to help the team keep the test automation on pace with new development. Unfortunately, after two full releases, the inattention by the team on the testability and automatability aspects below the UI had led to more business logic and error handling being built into the UI layer instead of below the services interface. After detailed analysis, the business team decided to refactor the business logic and error-handling application over the course of the next few releases to further enable a services-based test automation approach.

There were several lessons that we've taken away from this experience. First, a test strategy based predominantly on UI automation is likely to lead to unplanned time and effort to harden the product late in the cycle. Also, even when members of the Scrum teams have a shared understanding of the importance of test automation, determining the appropriate types of automation (UI or service level) within the application and the right time to employ them is equally important. Last, the recognition that the application architecture can be either an enabler or an inhibitor to a project's test automation strategy is an important lesson to apply throughout all stages of a product's life cycle.

Insufficient test automation hurts your product and its users, and the risk of regression failures escaping to production is higher. If your team has a policy to release only those features supported by automated regression tests, implementation of new features that could make the product more usable or valuable may be held up by an inability to automate tests. The product's architecture may need refactoring to support the improved ability to automate.

OTHER AUTOMATION CONSIDERATIONS

So far we've focused on functional test automation. Automation is also required for most Quadrant 4 tests, the technology-facing tests that critique the product, such as performance, load, scalability, capacity, reliability, and installability testing. Tooling is also needed for monitoring and checking memory management. Then there's all the tooling needed for CI, configuration management, version control, the deployment pipeline, and data management. Check Part VI, "Test Automation," and the "Tools" sections of the bibliography for sources that will guide you in those areas.

Automated testing is a series of checks, but we use it first to help guide development with customer-facing examples turned into tests. We need it for living documentation to show how our system behaves. We need it to quickly inform us of regression failures. We need it to keep technical debt to a manageable level and to ensure that we have enough time for all the valuable testing activities that help deliver high-quality software.

Even if your team has solid automated test suites in place, be prepared for continual challenges as your product and the technology you use evolve. Be alert for innovations that can help with tough automation problems. For example, Lisa's team recently discovered a production issue that was missed in spite of extensive unit test coverage. To find a better regression test approach for this, one of the developers experimented with generative testing. In a generative test, you define expected properties for expected outputs instead of hard-coded values, and the test runner generates randomized data for checking. It even "shrinks" the test failures to the minimal failing case automatically (Kemerling, 2014). The new tests found reproducible failures so the code could be fixed. These didn't replace the unit tests, but they provided additional confidence.

Use the whole-team approach, always work on your biggest problem, and be patient. Your automation needn't be perfect to be valuable, and you should continually make it better.

SUMMARY

There is no one right test automation solution. Be patient; involve the whole team in experiments to find good solutions for your team. Use the pyramid models described in Chapter 15, "Pyramids of Automation," to help. In this chapter, we looked at some of the most challenging steps in implementing valuable test automation. Some key points:

- Teams new to agile benefit from having an experienced practitioner who can help select solutions, find ways to measure progress, set standards across teams, and build community to share experiences.
- Involve the whole team in selecting automation solutions. It can take courage to get consensus on decisions about how to proceed. Focus on trying experiments, knowing there is no one "right" solution.
- Be judicious in what you include in automated test suites, and keep builds fast for timely feedback.
- Try to find automation frameworks that promote collaboration among testers, coders, and practitioners with other specialties on the team.
- Take time to learn together and grow the technical solutions; that is often where much of the value is created.
- Push automation to the lowest level that makes sense. Refactor code architecture if needed to allow for cost-effective test automation.

Part VII

WHAT IS YOUR CONTEXT?

Context counts. In this section we will present a set of specific challenges that may not apply to everyone. We've gathered many stories from expert practitioners working in these diverse areas to help you.

Agile development has spread to large organizations with enterprise-wide solutions. We start this part of the book by looking at the particular challenges of "scaling up" agile testing. Chapter 18 is centered on the story of how one such organization transitioned its testing to agile.

Organizations large and small find themselves increasingly spread among different locations, perhaps around the whole planet. Our next chapter is, therefore, about testing on distributed teams. We will share strategies to cope with language, cultural, and technological barriers to keep everyone engaged in testing before, during, and after coding.

Other areas that have expanded dramatically over the past few years are mobile apps and embedded systems. These applications have high risks—both for safety and for success—in a fast-changing, opinionated market. They also pose unique testing challenges. Chapter 20 will look at what you need to test and how to fit all that testing into short release cycles using a whole-team approach.

Another domain that has puzzled teams that want to embrace agile is regulated software. Many teams feel that compliance and documentation constraints are mutually exclusive with agile development. We will share some success stories in Chapter 21 that show how well agile can meet the demands of regulatory agencies. Testers have unique opportunities to contribute their domain expertise and collaboration skills to help build products that delight customers and satisfy regulators.

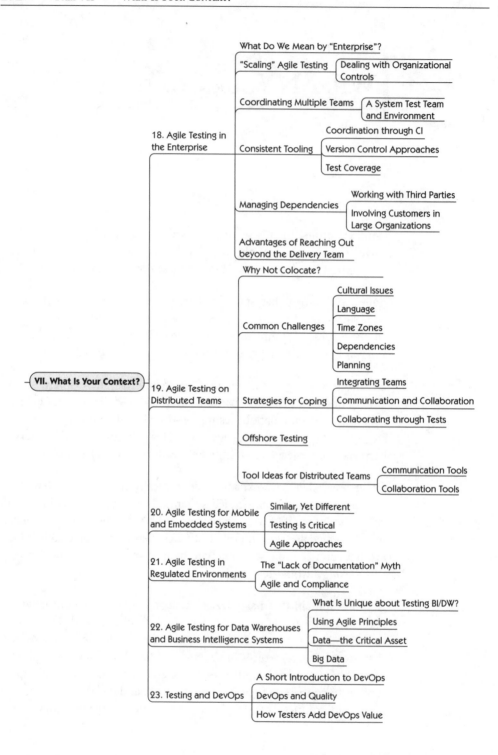

VII. What Is Your Context?

18. Agile Testing in the Enterprise
- What Do We Mean by "Enterprise"?
- "Scaling" Agile Testing
  - Dealing with Organizational Controls
- Coordinating Multiple Teams
  - A System Test Team and Environment
- Consistent Tooling
  - Coordination through CI
  - Version Control Approaches
  - Test Coverage
- Managing Dependencies
  - Working with Third Parties
  - Involving Customers in Large Organizations
- Advantages of Reaching Out beyond the Delivery Team

19. Agile Testing on Distributed Teams
- Why Not Colocate?
- Common Challenges
  - Cultural Issues
  - Language
  - Time Zones
  - Dependencies
  - Planning
- Strategies for Coping
  - Integrating Teams
  - Communication and Collaboration
  - Collaborating through Tests
- Offshore Testing
- Tool Ideas for Distributed Teams
  - Communication Tools
  - Collaboration Tools

20. Agile Testing for Mobile and Embedded Systems
- Similar, Yet Different
- Testing Is Critical
- Agile Approaches

21. Agile Testing in Regulated Environments
- The "Lack of Documentation" Myth
- Agile and Compliance

22. Agile Testing for Data Warehouses and Business Intelligence Systems
- What Is Unique about Testing BI/DW?
- Using Agile Principles
- Data—the Critical Asset
- Big Data

23. Testing and DevOps
- A Short Introduction to DevOps
- DevOps and Quality
- How Testers Add DevOps Value

Testing data warehouses and business intelligence systems in agile environments also benefits from short feedback cycles and an incremental approach. In Chapter 22, we will share ways to expose data quality issues early. We will also discuss specialized technical skills and business domain knowledge needed to verify the data used for business decisions.

The term *DevOps* gained popularity starting in 2009, but practitioners with operations and development backgrounds have collaborated with testers and other team members for many years. In our chapter on testing and DevOps, we will show how testing and DevOps work together.

- **Chapter 18**, "Agile Testing in the Enterprise"
- **Chapter 19**, "Agile Testing on Distributed Teams"
- **Chapter 20**, "Agile Testing for Mobile and Embedded Systems"
- **Chapter 21**, "Agile Testing in Regulated Environments"
- **Chapter 22**, "Agile Testing for Data Warehouses and Business Intelligence Systems"
- **Chapter 23**, "Testing and DevOps"

Chapter 18

AGILE TESTING IN THE ENTERPRISE

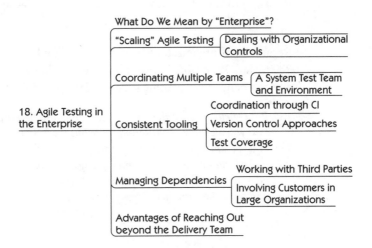

We hear a lot of talk about scaling agile. From the early days of agile, some experts have insisted that agile principles and values are only for small, colocated teams. Some practitioners believed that large enterprise organizations should not even try agile development. However, many have attempted an agile transition, and we've heard lots of success stories. The challenge is not so much scaling agile as trying to maintain the principles of agility in the context of organizations that mandate strict discipline and practices on their teams. This chapter is not meant to tell you to how to scale agile in large organizations. For that, we suggest you look in the bibliography for Part VII, "What Is Your Context?," for books on that subject. Our focus is on good approaches for agile testing in enterprise companies.

WHAT DO WE MEAN BY "ENTERPRISE"?

First, we don't mean the *Starship Enterprise*, although we often feel we are exploring strange new worlds and civilizations. We use the term *enterprise* to mean large, all-encompassing, crossing business units or geographies, the whole of your business operations. "Enterprise" applies to more than large businesses. Universities, nonprofits, and governments are examples of huge organizations that need enterprise-wide software to meet a variety of needs. These organizations may be distributed, but not necessarily. Chapter 19 is about testing in distributed teams, so in this chapter, we'll concentrate on large application systems, which usually mean large organizations.

Regardless of organization size, the focus should be on the customer. In 2009, Mark P. McDonald gave a bit of advice that we believe holds true for any company implementing agile and lean principles (McDonald, 2009):

> *Put the customer at the center of the company, because it is the one thing that you all share. That sounds trite but it's true. Look to reduce barriers or impediments to internal operations that reduce customer service or make it harder for the customer to engage all parts of the company. After all as an enterprise your economic model rests on the ability to engage and serve the customer across your entire operations.*

"SCALING" AGILE TESTING

In his keynote at Agile Testing Days 2013 (Hassa, 2013), Christian Hassa talked about scaling test-driven development (TDD) to the enterprise. His description sounded suspiciously similar to what is done in many agile teams. He recommended that teams set a desired goal, figure out the stakeholders, define a desired behavior change, determine deliverables, write a failing acceptance test, write the code to make that test pass using TDD, and so on. This sounds like the "Discuss—Distill—Develop—Demo" acceptance-test-driven development (ATDD) cycle as described by Elisabeth Hendrickson (Hendrickson, 2008).

Christian recommended that enterprises measure the impact of the deployed system and refine the deliverable accordingly. You can continually refine your strategy based on what behavior change actually happens, which elevates your testing. His conclusion was that scaling isn't about how to do more work with more people. Rather, it pays to test goals and impacts as early and as often as possible, in any size organization.

Christian applies Tom Gilb's planning language, Planguage (Gilb, 2013), for defining goals. In the process of defining goals, you select a scale: decide what to measure. Next, you choose a metric: how you will measure. Set levels by first benchmarking the current situation, setting constraints such as the minimum acceptable result, and defining the target, or desired result. Impact mapping, story mapping, and incremental and iterative delivery can all help you set goals and achieve the desired business value. Chapter 9, "Are We Building the Right Thing?," explained impact mapping and story mapping in more detail. The same techniques work in companies of all sizes, but as companies grow, more diligence is needed in setting goals and assessing impacts frequently.

Learning: Align the Target Setting across the Organization

Eveliina Vuolli, *operational development manager at Nokia (Networks Business), shares lessons she learned when trying to introduce automation in a large enterprise system.*

The whole organization needs to understand the benefit of doing test automation. For example, product management should be involved to ensure that they don't see test automation only as a "funny R&D practice." Instead, there needs to be a discussion of how test automation benefits product development; for example, automation improves the product quality in general and makes it easier to make last-minute changes in the software. In my experience, it is good to have example ROI calculations. They reinforce the message, especially when discussing test automation with the business stakeholders.

It is also good to have a common target setting for test automation throughout the whole organization. This is one way to create a common understanding of what the expected level of automation at different test levels is. When we did the target setting the first time, we used the same test automation percent coverage level as a target for all the teams. However, because the teams were in very different situations, the target number for one team was very challenging, whereas others had already achieved it. We learned that it is better to have the target setting done from the bottom up. You can still have a defined minimum level for all the teams, but above that, the exact target numbers may vary. In one target setting, the goals for different areas in unit test coverage varied between 60% and 95% and for the acceptance tests between 50% and 100% for a certain time period.

During the test automation (TA) target-setting discussions, the organization as a whole sometimes missed a common understanding of the testing-related terminology, which led to misunderstandings when we talked about TA status in different areas. We learned to start the target setting by defining the nomenclature. I have found it useful even to have an official definition for counting the test automation ratio. In principle it's a very simple formula: automated test cases/all test cases = TA ratio. With legacy software you need to agree on the formula and take old releases and their test cases into account in the calculation.

We found it essential to have a follow-up for the topic so that people realized it was important. If no one is asking about the topic after the "first rush," it loses immediacy, so we do the follow-up monthly. We have one centralized dashboard to show the status online.

We hear comments such as, "But the TA ratio actually doesn't tell much about the quality or coverage of the testing, even if it's 100%." Teams often need help to really consider how to increase the coverage of their TA cases or to optimize the run time of the automation rounds, so that they can move to the next level. Instead of just watching the number, they will also start to realize how to benefit from the test automation. One example is to have the computers do the "dummy work" so people can concentrate on more challenging testing areas or have a good safety net to enable refactoring and fast changes.

Dealing with Organizational Controls

Large organizations tend to have controls in place to ensure consistency. They develop over the years as the company grows and tries to solve specific problems. Many organizations are reluctant to change or drop these controls because that is what has worked in the past for them. One example would be enforcement of quality models such as CMMI (CMMI Institute, 2014) or internal audit requirements. Another example would be the way functional silos work together and have signed handoffs. In this chapter, we want to take you back to basics and have you think about how to apply the agile values and principles—even if you are dealing with enterprise solutions. We will talk more about regulatory restrictions in Chapter 21, "Agile Testing in Regulated Environments."

The history and culture of the organization are the most difficult to overcome. We have found that to be successful, teams often have to prove themselves and be able to articulate what benefits agile can offer. We also need to be able to articulate to management how teams can still give them confidence in their ability to deliver without the sign-offs, without the constant reporting, and without the existing measures. Management has learned over many years how to make decisions based on those reports, and teams need to be able to give them a realistic alternative to the old reporting structure. It is not enough to say, "Trust us." They need feedback loops, too.

Janet has found that using simple but visible tools such as the test matrix in Figure 7-6 in Chapter 7, "Levels of Precision for Planning," can boost the confidence level of management that testing is being considered and tracked.

The Dell Journey—Part 1

Geoff Meyer, *a test architect at Dell, shares the agile journey he has experienced at Dell. His story is similar to that of many organizations we have seen. Here's his story of Dell's initial steps toward agility. It is broken up into five parts, and we'll examine each step along the way.*

The Challenge

In most large enterprises, developing and testing software is not always a nimble process. Such was the case with Dell's Enterprise Solutions Group (ESG) in 2008. Functional silos and waterfall development processes had created an entrenched and antagonistic "development versus test" culture. This lack of cohesion was exacerbated by teams being physically located on different floors and sometimes different time zones. Moreover, the test practices that had been optimized over years of waterfall practices were based on the black-box approach, and test automation skill sets were limited to user interface (UI) automation tools.

The Context of Agile @ Dell in 2009

- The software projects encompassed Embedded Systems and Server Systems Management products.
- Functional silos had created an entrenched, antagonistic "development versus test" culture.

- Development and testing were physically located on different floors.
- The large hardware compatibility testing matrix was based on supporting three generations of servers.
- Testers conducted only black-box testing.
- Test automation skill sets were limited to UI automation tools.

The Solution

Enter Brian Plunkett and Dave Spott, two software development executives, both of whom had come to Dell with prior agile experience. It was then that our agile journey began, largely because of the full backing and support of these two agile proponents.

Dell ESG first adopted agile practices in mid-2008. We started on a small scale using a pilot project, with a single team consisting only of programmers. Within the first six months, the results of the pilot project were sufficient to demonstrate to managers across the organization (especially those in the Test organization) that this new approach to software development might just have some merit.

Because the Test team was hosted in a separate functional organization, a good amount of lobbying on the part of Dave and Brian was required to bring them into the agile fold. At first, it was a tough sell. How could we suggest such drastic changes to program management, project staffing, and consequently the testing itself? Initially, there was resistance, but once Test had experienced being an integral member of the iterative development process, the Test organization became one of the biggest proponents of and champions for agile.

As you can see from Geoff's story so far, Dell had the same problem many enterprise organizations do in adopting agile principles and practices. The testing organization resisted the idea of integrating with development. However, they were fortunate to have two executives on the management team to help sell the idea. If management has decreed that software teams "must" go agile, find someone on the management team to be a sponsor to stand behind the changes that need to be made. Recommend a pilot project first to work out the kinks in the process. Talk to the management team about what changes need to be made throughout the organization to be successful. Be willing to make compromises such as reporting defects, but have regular retrospectives with management and talk about benefits and trade-offs. Be aware that some groups have understandable fears about making fundamental changes to the development and test process.

Let's see what Dell did next.

Implementation: Bumps in the Road—Dell, Part 2

In the first full year of the agile adoption, it became evident that the traditional testing techniques of black-box testing, UI-based test automation, and the need to log all defects were not a good fit with the collaborative, time-boxed guidelines of Scrum. Within the Scrum team, the testers were developing and executing manual tests against the UI of each user story. The only automation that was being developed was test scripts against the UI. To top it off, a traditional performance indicator of the Test organization was "number of defects found"; therefore, test Scrum team members logged each and every defect. As you can imagine, the result was test tasks for a user story that did not complete within the sprint boundary, which led to carryover user stories. Moreover, test automation was unable to keep up with the subsequent changes to the UI in follow-on sprints. Testers spent more time on maintaining test cases than on developing and executing new ones. Finally, the entire Scrum team became burdened by the administrative overhead of processing defects.

And these were just at each Scrum team level. At the organization level, test automation was already recognized as a critical success factor. However, the directive to "go forth and automate" only compounded the team-level problems since different UI automation tools, such as Rational Functional Tester (RFT), Ranorex, and Telerik, were employed due to the differences in the product architectures.

As you can see from Geoff's story, not all problems are people problems. Because of the short iterations and the need for quick feedback, many underlying issues such as architecture or tooling become very visible. Large organizations tend to move more slowly because of their structure and approval processes, so changes come slowly, and with difficulty. Large organizations often have the need for additional roles such as test architect. There are many moving parts to an enterprise solution, and no one team can know it all.

Geoff Meyer continues his story with Dell and explains how they solved some of the testing issues with their agile adoption.

Agile Evolution—Dell, Part 3

I came into the Test organization in 2010 as the test architect; my objectives included evolving the agile test strategy to support large-scale projects and improving the test automation capabilities. An essential read for these challenges was *Agile Testing: A Practical Guide for Testers and Agile Teams* by Lisa Crispin and Janet Gregory. The automation pyramid and agile testing quadrants became foundations for the next step in the evolution of our Agile @ Dell test strategy.

One of the first things we did was to analyze the state of testability and automatability of our application architectures below the user interface, such as the command-line interface (CLI) or web services SOAP or RESTful layers. Next, we started training our test engineers in these new skill sets. In the case of projects where we were onboarding new hires, we hired to these skills, as well as agile experience.

We then, purposely, curtailed any UI automation from within the Scrum sprints. We also removed the requirement to log all defects and instead encouraged teams to collaborate in real time to root-cause, resolve, and verify them. Finally, we directed our Scrum testers to "automate first," at the service level, and worked with the product owner and development teams to incorporate test automation into the user story acceptance criteria.

The latter was a lofty goal, unimaginable to many in the Test organization at that time. However, over the course of the next two years, the Scrum testers became very efficient at test automation development and execution at the CLI and web services interfaces within the sprint. Test automation was able to keep pace with user story development, resulting in active automated regression and build verification suites running for each project. Figure 18-1 shows coding and testing activities within the two-week sprint cycle.

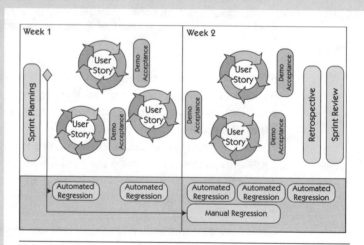

Figure 18-1 Two-week sprint life cycle example

We have noticed that in large organizations, where command-and-control hierarchies exist, it's harder for teams to self-organize and adapt than in smaller organizations with less structure. In Geoff's story, we see that a certain amount of direction was needed to get the teams to accept the new way of working. Over time, however, the new practices became the status quo.

COORDINATING MULTIPLE TEAMS

Testing in a large enterprise means thinking about many moving parts. Often, changing one component or one application has repercussions all the way through the system. More complexity is added when some teams are practicing agile, while others are working in a phased and gated traditional process. Agile transitions, which usually require big changes in company culture, are especially painful for large corporations. There are some unique challenges that teams in smaller companies do not face.

There are several possible ways you might approach multiple teams working on the same product. In Part III, "Planning—So You Don't Forget the Big Picture," we talked about levels of precision and test planning at each level for the product. We'll use some of those concepts for testing in the enterprise.

Let's use a simple example. Figure 18-2 shows a context diagram for a school system based on the assumption that the school system owns the buses. The new functionality that is needed is to automate bus scheduling so that parents are notified if there is a problem with delivery of their children. The scenario we will use as an example is "A bus breaks down, a new bus is dispatched to transport the children, and parents are notified the children will be late."

The priority features we need are

- Ability to locate buses if they have problems
- Ability to contact a substitute driver and assign a substitute bus
- Ability to notify parents with text, phone, or email
- Ability to notify school administration of issues with bus maintenance and late delivery of children

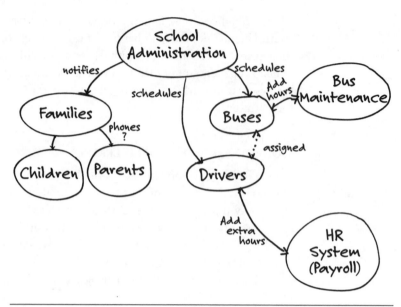

Figure 18-2 Context diagram for a school and bus system

Let's apply the concept of levels of precision to an organization with multiple applications and several teams working to deliver the product enhancement. Each team tests their features to the best of their abilities, but it would be naïve to think that there are no dependencies between the teams or that they can test everything about a story or feature within their own team. In our experience, products within an enterprise have very complex systems, which results in very complex test environments.

A System Test Team and Environment

One of the options when there are multiple teams working on the same product is to create a system test team, perhaps consisting of both programmers and testers. This team works closely with the other delivery teams. Everyone participates in a project inception or high-level planning meeting at the start of the project. Each team has its own continuous integration (CI) environment but also integrates its code into a master build for the entire product. The system test team continually tests the "potentially shippable" product delivered at the end of each iteration, or possibly more frequently. The post-development testing

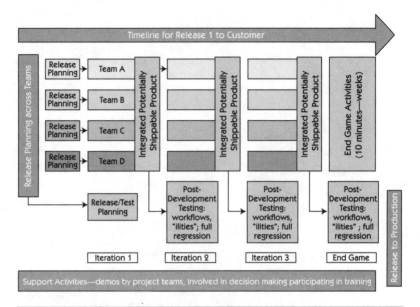

Figure 18-3 One possible solution for multiple teams

and end game activities aren't hardening or bug-fixing iterations. (See *Agile Testing*, pp. 456–57, for more on the end game.) Rather, they are an integral part of the development process, testing the entire system end to end in a production-like environment, which may not be available to each individual team. In Figure 18-3, we show four teams working on separate features, each enhancing the product as a whole.

In our school bus scheduling example, each feature would be assigned to a different team. For example, Team A might take on the feature "Locate buses that are in trouble," while Team B has "Contact driver and assign a replacement bus." Each team would figure out what stories they needed in release planning and estimate approximately how long it would take to complete their feature. However, as you can imagine, there are dependencies between teams, so they also need to consider how to test those. Once the teams understand their features, they come together, think about testing at the higher release level, bring up dependencies, and make decisions about how to test them (see Figure 18-4). Sometimes, test managers are a natural fit in large organizations, helping to coordinate the dependencies between teams.

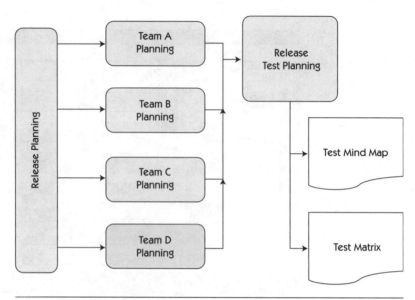

Figure 18-4   Test planning—product level

Testing activities for stories should be completed within the team as much as possible. Sometimes it is hard to complete testing, because a team may not have a complete production-like system test environment—it may be too expensive. Stories are small and granular, so a team needs to be able to get them to Story Done within the iteration.

Since features may consist of many stories, it may not be possible for an individual team to completely test a feature in their own test environment, for example, making sure that the extra hours for the substitute driver can be tested only in the full system environment that has access to the human resources (HR) system. This might be part of Feature Done, and not Story Done.

However, since the delivery team is ultimately responsible for the completion of that feature, there needs to be a way to show when a feature needs more testing and when it is completed, so communication between teams is essential. Validation that the product is shippable can be completed by a system test team that has access to a full, production-equivalent system that allows them to take advantage of economies of scale for types of testing that are difficult to justify in individual feature teams. For example, performance, load, interoperability, and browser compatibility testing may require specialized test environments. Full automated system regression testing may be part of this system test team's responsibility as well. During the end game, we would suggest that all teams participate in the activities necessary to take the release to Release Done.

There are a couple of different ways to manage a system test team. One way is to have programmers as part of the team to help identify and immediately fix issues that are found. Different organizations may choose to define different processes to deal with defects and issues. Sometimes, any defects found will go back to the originating team. However, this sometimes can be a problem; if there is no clear-cut owner, teams may defer the defect to another team, which can degenerate into a blame game. Lisa worked with a 25-team company where defects caught by the CI were brought up in a "helps-only" Scrum-of-Scrums. A ScrumMaster would speak up and say his or her team would take responsibility. As with any agile process, finding and fixing defects needs to be a short feedback loop.

Let's go back to Geoff Meyer's story of how Dell handled scaling up its agile testing.

Growing Up—Dell, Part 4

In mid-2011, we began to apply agile practices to our first large-scale projects. One project had nine Scrum teams, and the other had 15. We formed feature-based teams, with embedded testers developing in-sprint test automation for user stories (just as we had for our smaller projects).

However, we determined that this level of testing was going to be insufficient for such a large-scale effort, since no single Scrum team had visibility to the usage of the application from a customer perspective. Thus, we introduced the concept of software system test (SST), which took a more traditional black-box approach to testing, focusing on the user interface of completed features. This approach included automation of the UI test cases. Our goal was to start this testing as early as possible—in parallel to the sprints—but not so early as to hinder the development of in-progress user stories (realistically no earlier than the second or third sprint).

Another aspect of these large-scale projects that the test team needed to address was testing new features, in the form of user stories, across multiple generations of existing servers. This is where the in-sprint automation at the service level truly paid off. We empowered Scrum teams that had user stories encompassing a large compatibility matrix to limit their acceptance tests to one or more reference configurations.

We then established an "extended sprint test" team that took accepted user stories (which included automated test scripts) as input. This team then set up the physical test environments and executed the automated test scripts against these extended compatibility configurations to complete the user stories (see Figure 18-5).

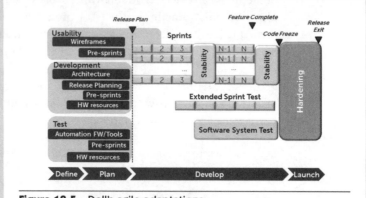

Figure 18-5   Dell's agile adaptations

During the 2012–13 stages of our agile test automation journey, we made our initial foray into Lisa and Janet's fourth quadrant of testing: nonfunctional tests. The emphasis was to apply our automation skills to those areas where manual efforts generally proved impractical. Longevity, scalability, and performance baselining were areas that had received limited coverage in the past, but we were able to build them into the agile development process and run them in parallel to our sprints. We also applied automation to time-consuming test tasks unrelated to test cases.

You can see from Geoff's story that it took time for the large development and test organizations at Dell to discover new ways of working through adaptation and experimentation. The extended sprint test team took advantage of economies of scale and worked in parallel with the Scrum teams to provide feedback as quickly as possible. Often teams need stabilization iterations while they are adapting, but over time, the need for them should decrease.

CONSISTENT TOOLING

There are several other practices that can enhance enterprise success. For example, we can take advantage of the current tools available to organizations. In Chapter 17, "Selecting Test Automation Solutions," we included a section on selecting tools for automation. However, it is common to have existing tools in place, and many organizations hesitate to change. There needs to be a compelling reason to change, so teams need to be able to articulate those benefits.

Coordination through CI

Continuous integration with automated regression testing across the teams with all teams working on the same code base ensures that most integration issues are caught as soon as the code is checked in. Achieving this may take lots of time and effort, but the payback is more than worth the trouble. Lisa worked at a company where it took a few years to get a system-wide CI running just a couple of times a week. But once they achieved this, it was a matter of months to get it running twice a day, and problems were fixed the same day by whichever teams were responsible for the regression failures.

One of the biggest problems that large organizations face is prioritizing bug fixes. Who fixes the defects found by the automated regression tests? How do we determine what the priority is? Many organizations have a production support team that is responsible for fixing customer-reported production defects, but no one cares about the internal defects found. Automated regression test failures must be fixed immediately by the team that checked in the code that caused the failed test; otherwise, the benefit of the fast feedback is lost. Teams need to decide how to handle bugs found during development or in production. As we discussed in Chapter 14, "Technical Debt in Testing," bugs that linger in a defect-tracking system add to the team's technical debt burden.

Use your CI to communicate the results of automated functional regression tests across the development organization. There are several possibilities for managing test failures. One is to have a system test team investigate failures, decide which delivery team is responsible, and assign the broken test to them. They need a good overview of features being developed so they may have the best insight into what may have broken the tests. Another option is to rotate which team looks at the regression failures. The disadvantage to this approach is that the person or team responsible for checking the results may not know what the other teams are working on and may find it hard to determine the source of the problem. The advantage is that it shares the responsibility of investigating failures and may offer a bit of cross-training. There's no one right approach, so experiment with alternatives.

Version Control Approaches

We like having all teams work on the same code base. This not only mitigates integration risks but also reduces testing risks. We know the automation test suite runs (at a minimum, nightly) on the code so we catch issues early. We do our exploratory testing on the same code base so we know how it behaves on each deploy. Each delivery team has its own test environment, but shared environments may be used as needed. If there is a production defect and we have to do an emergency fix and deploy, we have only two branches to test: production and the main development branch. Figure 18-6 shows a chart of environments Lisa's team tracked while they upgraded their Ruby and Rails versions.

Another approach, which we've seen in some large organizations, is for individual teams to work on separate branches and merge to the main trunk at the end of the iteration. Although there may be extra trouble fixing integration issues for the merge, this approach can work well, as long at the version control system handles merges correctly. One disadvantage to this process is having to decide which branch gets the production fix in emergency situations. Which team will make sure it gets tested before the merge and after the merge? Who keeps track of making sure testing is done in the production branch as well as the development branch? There is a higher risk of something slipping through the cracks when using this strategy, although it can be mitigated if the system test team has a good understanding of the risks and dependencies between teams. The risk is also reduced if the team has dependable test automation coverage and can follow up with some exploratory testing on risk areas.

Environment	Owner	Deployed by	App 1	App 2	Rails	Ruby
DEV	devs	Automated	4.1.0_124	2.1.0	3.2	2.1.1
TEST	testers	Tester pairs	4.1.0_122	2.1.0	3.2	2.1.1
AUTO	DevOps	Automated	4.1.0_124	2.1.0	3.2	2.1.1
SHARED	DevOps	Deploy pair	4.1.0_120	2.1.0	3.2	2.1.1
LOAD	DevOps	Deploy pair	4.1.0_120	2.1.0	3.2	2.1.1
STAGING	DevOps	DevOps	4.1.0_110	2.1.0	2.3	1.87-2012
PRODUCTION	Ops	Ops	4.1.0	2.1.0	2.3	1.87-2012

Figure 18-6 Make your test environments visible.

Test Coverage

One of the risks of multiple teams working on the same product is potential overlaps and gaps in testing. In an ideal world, all features would be self-contained with no dependencies on other features. However, we do not live in an ideal world, especially when it comes to large corporations. They likely have grown over the years through mergers and acquisitions. Coordination of testing between teams that may have originated in different companies, working on separate software products, can become a nightmare.

There are tools now that can help you understand what test coverage your system has. At a recent conference, Janet saw a demonstration of a product designed to help visualize where the gaps in testing might be. Understand your problems and your risks, and then see if you can develop or adopt a tool to help solve it. No tool will address all your test coverage problems.

We encourage teams to experiment, but always keeping in mind that the goal is not to buy more tools, or automate more and more tests, but to reduce risk by fast feedback. This means you want to address integration issues as early as possible and avoid finding them during the end game immediately before release.

Managing Dependencies

Teams try to break up features and stories so there are no dependencies, but that is almost impossible, especially when dealing with enterprise solutions. There are both external and internal third-party vendors, other delivery teams, or even customers that teams may depend on before they can deliver their stories and features.

Working with Third Parties

One of the bigger issues that large organizations have is working with development organizations outside the immediate team. There are both internal and external third parties, and we encourage you to think of them similarly. External vendors may include organizations such as credit card providers over which you have no control, or smaller product companies that are willing to work closely with your team. Internal third parties may include your database team or the accounting department. These internal groups can be as difficult to work with because we expect them to respond when we want them to. However, they have their own sets of priorities and may not respond as expected.

Agile practices for developing in partnership with third-party vendors are becoming well established. Techniques such as moving to an output-and-outcome-focused contract are becoming more frequent (see McDonald, 2013). Perhaps not surprisingly, while practices for integrating third parties into the programming work of a project have emerged, there is little agreement on such practices for testing of agile projects.

Janet's Story

Lately it seems that many of my clients fall into the large enterprise category. Sometimes, one of the first red flags I see is a column in their story board for blocked stories or tasks. It says to me that they are planning to have blocked stories. I would like to see that as an exception rather than a rule.

One piece of advice I give to these teams is to watch out for stories that have a hard dependency on another team or an external third party. I suggest the team take the story out of the iteration until the dependency is removed. That way, the team can focus on other stories instead of waiting for another team to deliver some code or a third party to deliver a promised deliverable.

One way to remove dependencies is to have a "Ready" column or status on your stories. For example, if your story has a dependency where you need to have a database administrator help you with some new database tables, or you need the user experience group to create a wireframe, keep the story in the backlog until you have the necessary artifact or commitment from them to work with you on your story. Contact those groups in advance so they are prepared to provide their deliverables before the story is prioritized. This is part of your story readiness planning. Work to remove these dependencies during planning. Some teams hold meetings specifically to discuss dependencies prior to their iteration planning to deal with situations such as those we described.

Lisa's Story

My last team started doing something similar when we had a lot of stories where the business folks didn't have the business rules ready. They figured we knew the domain so well that we could just make up the rules ourselves. Um, no! We pushed back. If we didn't have all the requirements, mock-ups, and business rules needed for a story by day two of the sprint, that story got taken out, and we used the time to work on our own initiatives to manage technical debt. When business stakeholders realized that not having everything to us by the start of the iteration meant a two-week delay for the story, they were more disciplined about preparing ahead.

When you're working with external third parties, automation can actually work to your advantage. Get the API description from the vendor and create test harnesses to replicate the vendor's inputs to your system, and then you can test your system behavior with automation. This allows you to test your system without actually having the third-party system in place. Yes, there will be changes along the way. However, you will be further ahead and understand what the issues are more easily since you have defined behavior. One of the biggest complaints we hear from teams is, "I can't get that information." Try asking for small pieces at a time if you really need to start developing without having the full API. You might be surprised at how opening the door and starting the conversation creates a better working relationship with the third party, whether it's another team within your corporation or an outside supplier.

Accepting new third-party applications can be scary if you don't trust their changes. Work to improve that trust, but at the same time consider how you can make your team feel more confident about accepting the latest changes. Perhaps create a test environment where you can compare what the system did before the change with how it handles critical functionality after the change. Think about sharing your tests with the vendor to try to get a common understanding of what is being delivered. The vendor may even learn to test before delivering.

Think of all your stakeholders, including your customers, the people actually using your system. If you are an external third party delivering a product, think about how you can make your customers confident in what you deliver.

Involving Customers in Large Organizations

Testing in enterprise systems requires collaborating not only within each development team but also with many outside groups. The most important of these third parties is, of course, our customer. In many corporations, development teams are far removed from their end users. Getting customers involved in the testing and developing process may require extra creativity.

User Acceptance Testing in the Enterprise

Susan Bligh, *a business analyst in Alberta, Canada, tells her story about what happened when the delivery teams didn't include their customers in their testing and how mistakes slipped through the cracks.*

One of the biggest issues we encountered when I was a business analyst working on a major company-wide software implementation was how to integrate the design across all the many functions (silos) of the program. We implemented six different functions that integrated with each other, including Finance and Accounting, Supply Chain, Asset Management, Planning and Budgeting, Capital Projects, and Human Resources.

At the beginning of the program, we were well aware that we needed to have an integrated design that spanned all of the functions. Naturally, throughout the implementation, the functional teams worked to design, test, and document their own functions with only minimal cross-functional design and testing. We performed end-to-end integrated testing during two of the four major product testing cycles, with the project team members executing the tests. These team members were very knowledgeable about the software but were not always a part of the larger business design considerations.

Near the end of the program a decision was made to forgo user acceptance testing (UAT) and instead perform a business simulation in a few key pilot areas. The business simulation was led again by the project teams, but this time the end user was involved. End user documentation and training were created separately by each functional team.

A look back to the project revealed some implementation flaws that led to design issues and inefficiencies that could have been avoided. Some of the lessons learned from the project include:

- Spend more time designing and testing the bridges between the silos than designing the silos. Design teams should be composed of business, technical, and testing team members.

  Our story: Only a couple of weeks before go-live we found out that one functional team was creating purchase orders of a certain type, only to realize that the Accounts Payable team did not support that type of purchase order. Had we gone live with that design flaw, any purchase orders of that type issued to a vendor could not have been paid. This issue could have been avoided had we spent more time collaborating on the areas of integration between the functions.

- Train the end users using the end user documentation and training programs, and allow them to perform UAT with the knowledge provided. The project team should be involved only to help document the test results (including system, training, and documentation defects). This allows the users to test not only the system design, but also the end user documentation and training programs.

  Our story: We provided some documentation for the business simulation, but the training was performed by the project team members who knew and understood the design in detail. Not all end user documentation was available. The business simulation was performed by members of the project team with the end users. Although not realized at the time, the project team was performing work-arounds to the design flaws to allow the tests to pass. Had the end users performed all the tests themselves without assistance from project team members who had been working with the system for months, the design flaws would have been found much earlier. As well, since the project team members were readily available to answer questions during the business simulation, many documentation and training defects were not found.

As you can see from Susan's story, even the highest level of diligence on the part of the delivery teams might not be enough if you don't involve all stakeholder representatives in the testing activities.

ADVANTAGES OF REACHING OUT BEYOND THE DELIVERY TEAM

We started the chapter by talking about impacts and understanding the goals of the customer. When we adapt our processes to deliver to their needs, we not only meet, exceed, or even delight our customers; we usually end up with positive team dynamics. Join us in reading the final part of Geoff Meyer's story about Dell's journey.

Results—Dell, Part 5

The Enterprise Solutions Group is ultimately responsible for delivering value through our products, and our product deliveries are oftentimes tied to partner milestones.

The adoption of agile has provided Dell ESG with an increased level of schedule predictability. Within Engineering, the day-to-day work environment for programmers and testers has been greatly enhanced. Scrum teams are highly engaged, collaborative, and friendly and receive regular satisfaction from completing working features in a regular cadence. Development team members welcome and respect the skill sets brought by the test members of the Scrum team, and Test is now a full partner in the entire software development process. The inclusion of test engineers in the early requirements process, combined with their natural inquisitiveness about how features may work or may fail, has improved the usability and functionality of our products.

Within the Test organization, agile has led us to an advanced skill set profile for our testers. The necessity of test automation in support of agile has led us to acquire and/or develop software engineering skills. The automation skill sets, in turn, have led to cycle time reductions in test execution runs and increased test matrix coverage that would have not been conceivable prior to agile and automation initiatives. All in all, it's been a very productive journey for both the business and individuals.

Geoff's organization added different roles and specialist groups, such as test architects and an extended sprint test team, to enable the large and complicated organization to take advantage of agile principles and practices. They focused on solving one problem at a time and experimented with a variety of approaches to integrate coding and testing. It sounds as if the newly cross-functional team members enjoy collaborating, and each team member contributes his or her specialized expertise. Enjoying your work while delighting your customers is a great outcome of practicing continuous improvement.

No matter what the size of the organization or how many products it supports, agile principles apply. Teams in large enterprises are subject to a more extreme level of the difficulties we find with most teams practicing agile testing. For example, it's much harder to keep an eye on the big picture and identify ripple effects across a large system made up of multiple software products than with one application. It can be harder to communicate effectively with stakeholders since more of them are involved. There are different ways of tackling large-scale testing problems, but agile principles and values help guide you to try useful experiments, get quick feedback, and make good choices. The story of how Spotify scaled agile development is a good source of ideas on how to use agile principles without getting too rigorous (Kniberg and Ivarsson, 2012).

SUMMARY

Enterprise environments magnify testing challenges for agile teams as they do for teams using any development process. You need more discipline, and more experiments to try, but still always starting with the simplest possible approach.

- Learn to work within the organizational controls, but try to find new solutions by offering suggestions. Understand the history and organizational culture so you can offer alternative solutions.
- Specification techniques such as Planguage may be useful to define goals and use consistent language when describing quality attributes.
- When large enterprises implement agile, it helps to have a champion at the executive level to help support teams in the transition.

- Fast feedback is critical in enterprise solutions when many teams and applications need to work together. Understand the big picture and the dependencies between teams to determine the best way to give and receive feedback.
- Managing dependencies is challenging in large enterprises. Make the dependencies visible to encourage thinking about them during planning.
- Consider adding additional roles such as test architects or test managers to help coordinate activities among many teams.
- Consider a system test team to take advantage of economies of scale in test environments.
- Use consistent tooling; CI and version control help multiple teams working on the same or related products coordinate.
- Reach beyond the single delivery team and the tests that they can do. Include other members of the organization, customers, and end users to make the solution complete.

Chapter 19

AGILE TESTING ON DISTRIBUTED TEAMS

Why Not Colocate?

Common Challenges
- Cultural Issues
- Language
- Time Zones
- Dependencies
- Planning

19. Agile Testing on Distributed Teams

Strategies for Coping
- Integrating Teams
- Communication and Collaboration
- Collaborating through Tests

Offshore Testing

Tool Ideas for Distributed Teams
- Communication Tools
- Collaboration Tools

Almost every book that we have read on scaling large or distributed teams recommends that feature teams exist in one location if possible. This is seen as a prerequisite to the collaboration that is so necessary in agile. However, we recognize that it is difficult, if not impossible, for some organizations to change their existing distributed structure. There may even be advantages to their distributed nature that they'd rather not give up.

We make a distinction between dispersed teams, distributed teams, and offshore testing, but we will use the term *distributed teams* to mean all three, unless we are specifically talking about dispersed or offshore.

- **Dispersed teams** may have several team members working remotely from home, although there may also be some colocated team members. They work together as one team (see Figure 19-1).

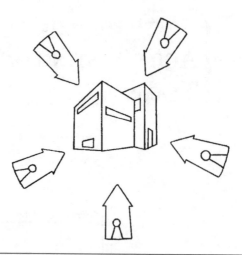

Figure 19-1   Dispersed teams representation

- **Distributed teams** are those that have sub-teams or full teams colocated in multiple locations, possibly in different time zones or different countries, all working on the same product (see Figure 19-2).

Figure 19-2   Distributed teams representation

- **Offshore testing** is when an organization chooses to subcontract its product testing to a vendor in another location, usually in another country where labor costs are lower. Near-shoring is a variation of this, where testing is outsourced to countries in a closer location. For example, a U.S. company might near-shore with a company in South America or Mexico. Near-shoring usually means there is no, or little, time zone difference.

There are other variations on these categories. A company might keep testing at its main location but offshore some development work. The recommendations in this chapter still apply.

We consider ourselves a dispersed team. Both of us work remotely but work as one team with no home base. While writing this book, we used many of the tools we suggest to you in this chapter. For example, we used Google Docs and Dropbox to share information to which we both needed real-time access, such as our release plan. We used MindMeister for our mind-mapping sessions, sometimes collaborating in real time on an idea, and other times each of us making updates to share with the other later. When we needed to connect and have real-time conversations, we used Skype or Google Hangouts. We tested our ideas and tried to get fast feedback by sharing chapters with reviewers on Google Docs, and we used a Google Group for reviewers to share ideas or to collaborate on clarifying something that might be confusing. It may not have been the ideal situation, but we made it work (Gregory, 2014).

There are many books and resources to help you make your distributed team successful. The difficulties aren't confined to testing. However, it's much more difficult to collaborate on testing activities and to share collective responsibility for quality on distributed teams. In this chapter we'll look at how testing can succeed on distributed teams.

WHY NOT COLOCATE?

There are several reasons why organizations have distributed teams. Often it is due to mergers or acquisitions as the company has grown. One of the main reasons that teams have remote team members is because they cannot find qualified candidates in their geographical area. For example, it is becoming more and more difficult to find good testers in some areas of the world. Good people help software projects succeed. Some teams have changed their norms to accept people who work from elsewhere. In these instances, the disadvantages of non-colocation are offset by the value that remote employees bring to the team.

There are advantages to distributed teams, but this next section will cover testing-related challenges that distributed teams face, and we'll offer some suggestions to help overcome those challenges.

COMMON CHALLENGES

It doesn't matter if you have globally distributed teams or individual remote team members; learning to work together from multiple physical locations is difficult. For new agile teams where testers are learning to collaborate with programmers, customers, and other team members, physical distance makes the transition more difficult.

Cultural Issues

Teams distributed around the world need to deal with cultural issues. For example, people from one country (let's call it Reservandia) may be quiet and reserved, while in another country (we'll call it Assertivana) the people speak their mind.

Take a moment to think about these two perspectives. We expect these two groups to work as one team. The programmers are in Assertivana, and the testers are in Reservandia. The programmers start to talk about how they think the software should be implemented. The testers sit back and listen; they may feel that they don't even have a chance to say a word. This may not always be the case, but we have heard this same story over and over, from both sides. The programmers from Assertivana complain that the testers never speak up, while the testers say they never have the chance to offer suggestions.

These are troublesome differences, but with some coaching on both sides, they can be overcome. First, both sides must feel safe to share their concerns or suggestions, especially Reservandia. Assertivana's programmers can learn to listen first and then give their opinions. Reservandia's testers can be prepared and perhaps introduce their ideas through email to start with, and then be prepared to speak on the subject.

Companies that choose to offshore certain development activities such as testing should be aware of the impact that decision can have on team culture, both in the main location and for the offshore team. As Jan Petter Hagberg pointed out to us (Hagberg, 2013), the team members "back home" probably didn't choose to work with an offshore team. The process of offshoring may have been traumatic for the team members still in the original location. Make sure they get help through this transition, which can take a long time.

Cultural differences can cause a comment intended as a joke by one person to be insulting to another. Slang also can get in the way of smooth communication. Take the time to learn about the team members in other locations and their culture. Experiment with ways to improve communication.

A word of caution: too often we see teams use the term *cultural issues* as an excuse not to look for a solution.

Language

Teams that span countries face language problems. English is the most commonly used language, but it is not everyone's first language, and when spoken, it is often with an accent. Even with English as a first language, the speaker's accent and speed of talking affect how others hear. Slang and colloquialisms within the same language also can create misunderstandings. Creating a common language when talking about stories and features is even more important for distributed teams.

Janet's Story

I spend a lot of time in other countries training and consulting. In one training session in Denmark, one of the participants came to me and complimented me on speaking slowly and using common words, but he said that he probably missed 5% to 10% of what I said. I was surprised because he spoke excellent English. We discussed it further, and it made me realize the impact of communication within teams.

Let's consider three teams: one in the United States, one in China, and one in France. When the folks in France speak with a French accent, and maybe struggle to find the right words, the people in the United States probably lose the typical 5% to 10% in translation. What do you think happens when the team in China is trying to understand? How much do we really come to a common understanding when we are all losing a little bit, or perhaps a lot?

Awareness is half the battle, but we can help ourselves and our teams make it better. Try things like repeating an idea, or paraphrasing, to make sure you understood, or having a spokesperson repeat the sentence or concept. People need to feel that it is safe to say they didn't understand and ask someone to repeat a comment. Give people time to mentally translate what's been said before moving on. Perhaps summarize decisions in writing on a team wiki so team members can read and have time to internalize. Think before you ask a question. "Let's take a poll to get everyone's opinion" instead of, "Anybody have any objections?" will help determine if everyone understood the question. Of course, it still might not work the way you would like, but you have a better chance. Lars Sjödahl gave us that little piece of valuable advice during his lightning talk "The Damage Done by Acts of Silence" at Agile Testing Days 2013.

In the section "Strategies for Coping" later in this chapter, we'll give some testing ideas that may help you win this battle.

Time Zones

One of the main problems that distributed teams face is time zones. When one sub-team, or the entire testing group, is 12 hours away, it probably means there is little or no verbal communication, unless someone works late into the evening. Some organizations arrange for one team to work at night to match hours with another. Others have one team member join a daily standup remotely late in the evening or early morning to try to keep some level of verbal communication.

When face-to-face communication isn't an option, teams must find a way to describe their needs so that one team does not sit idle, perhaps because they didn't know what to do next. Another example of problems faced by distributed teams is the lack of environments for testing.

Support needs to be available for all teams, all the time, if the teams use a common code base and continuous integration (CI) environment.

Janet's Story

In one organization we had teams in two different countries and practiced continuous integration so that testers living in Europe could come to work in the morning and pick up stuff to test. One of the problems we discovered was that they didn't always have people available to answer questions, so the actual feedback loop was lengthened. One of the work-arounds we put in place was nightly emails—what we had worked on, what was outstanding, what issues existed. We made them as complete as possible.

There was a seven-hour time difference, so when it was 4:00 p.m. their time, it was 9:00 a.m. our time. We tried to have people come in early (7:30 a.m.) so we had at least a couple of hours of overlap if we needed to talk in person. These days, I would probably have a Skype call every morning.

Dependencies

Be aware of the dependencies between groups. If you are waiting for a deliverable from people in a different time zone, and they don't have it ready, you may have to wait at least another 24 hours. Team members may start other tasks while they are waiting, which results in task switching among multiple commitments. Discuss potential dependencies in planning meetings, and find ways to make them visible or eliminate them. Online tracking tools can be used to show whether testers are waiting for stories to be delivered or are getting them all at once, or if too many stories are waiting for someone to accept them.

Planning

Planning sessions are especially difficult when your teams are not all in the same location. It is helpful to gather the whole team physically in one place for the release kickoff or project inception meetings. Teams that have done this have seen significant benefits in how the team works when team members are back in their respective locations. In Chapter 9, "Are We Building the Right Thing?," and Chapter 11, "Getting Examples," we talked about how testers can help by testing business value while it's still in the idea stage. Those benefits apply to distributed teams but are much more difficult to realize if the whole team is not in one place.

Experiences Working on Distributed Teams

Huib Schoots, *who works at Improve Quality Services in the Netherlands, shares what he's learned working on distributed teams.*

"Coming together is a beginning. Keeping together is progress. Working together is success." —Henry Ford

I've worked on many international projects in my career. And without exception, projects always went more smoothly when I was on-site. Collaboration improved, communication was much better, and work got finished faster. A project I did in Jakarta had the same pattern; at the start I was there for only a week every month, and later I was there full-time. The collaboration improved dramatically! Why? Because we got to know each other better and we took time to overcome our cultural differences.

When not in the same physical location, people can hide more easily and tend to isolate themselves. Communication gets more difficult and less rich. The things everyone is working on become less transparent, and to overcome this issue we use our tools in combination with more comprehensive documentation. In my experience, teams rely too much on documentation and tooling. These can actually make it harder to keep everything up-to-date, and information isn't shared as easily.

People need to run into each other to be really successful. Organizations need to make mixing as simple and obvious as possible. Get people together on a regular basis; give them time to build trust and get to know each other. Effective communication is in the details, and to recognize these you have to know your team, so spend as much time together as possible.

In my experience, the most important thing is to acknowledge that communication is the biggest risk in the project. When everybody is aware of this risk, teams have the best chance of overcoming the difficulties they will have. Teams will put in deliberate effort to make sure that communication is effective; they need to be creative to make the best of what they have.

We used Skype and Google Hangouts a lot, but there are many tools available to facilitate communication online. We used video to see each other, and this helped us to get to know people better. You at least have the feeling you know who you are talking to. We also prepared for our meetings; the team leads from each location got together (online) before the actual meeting to discuss the highlights.

By doing this we always got a good agenda for each meeting, and we invited only the people who really needed to be there. Another thing we learned from videoconferences is that those meetings take longer than normal face-to-face meetings. As well, in-depth discussion with big groups is very difficult; therefore, we avoided it. An advantage of using videoconferencing is that you can record the meeting and play it back to people who weren't able to attend.

We experimented with online agile boards, but in our situation they didn't really work out. They were handy in the communication with the other location, but they did not work in my team on location. We didn't have an overview of the stuff we were working on, so we used a whiteboard as our agile dashboard and updated the online tool daily before the meeting with the other teams.

To create team spirit we tried webcams at each location so we could see what was happening on the other side. This has an extra advantage, since you can see who is available to talk to. It worked out quite well.

Testing Considerations

Testing had to cope with communication difficulties as well, and asking questions, sharing information, and pairing became more difficult. It is harder to involve programmers in a different location to show them your findings or ask questions. Technology helps, but we still had to write down findings and use the bug tracker more often than we would normally. Pair testing became distributed, and using screen-sharing tooling via the web partially solved this problem. After we found out that pair testing was working quite well using tooling, communication improved and became more frequent.

Making It Work

To build good relations I encourage distributed teams to get together as much as possible. It helps to get to know each other, to get acquainted with culture and work ethics, but also to optimize communication. It is especially important to use face-to-face communication for retrospectives and in-depth discussions.

Distributed teams can work, but be aware of the consequences. Try several ways of communication and discuss and evaluate them often. Adapt them when they are not working. Working together is about relationships, communication, and people. When people are far away from each other but still have to work together, there are many ways, including various tools, to make that possible. Yet, no matter how well the tools are working and no matter how passionate and talented your colleagues are, distributed teams are always suboptimal.

Huib shares some good strategies to enable team members to collaborate for testing and has provided some links that we included in the bibliography for Part VII. Let's look at some more ways to make agile testing possible in distributed teams.

Strategies for Coping

Ideally, your distributed team members can regularly meet in one location to discuss the challenges that geographical distance presents. If this isn't possible, you can still find good ways to communicate and build relationships. There are plenty of tools available to enable remote pairing and group collaboration. See the "User Research" story of Disney's user experience designers collaborating remotely in Chapter 13, "Other Types of Testing."

Integrating Teams

We, along with other practitioners, recommend that team members in different locations travel as often as possible to maximize "face time" and shared experiences. This is the best way to build the trust needed to work together productively. We recommend trying to cluster self-sufficient teams around features if you can, to reduce the dependency problem and help the team feel more cohesive. Make sure all team members have access to business stakeholders so they can get questions answered quickly. Having experienced coaches, team leads, or subject matter experts in each location helps the cohesiveness of the teams.

Team members in the various geographical locations should agree on the same definition of "done." We have seen teams in one location think that Story Done meant coded and tested completely, while the other team, on which they depended, thought it referred only to completed code, ready for integration testing. This caused issues and a great deal of antagonistic feelings between teams.

Extra time and discipline are needed to help everyone understand responsibilities and accountabilities. You may spend extra time identifying how people interact, how decisions are made, and how the work is split between teams. Try keeping the tasks and stories small enough that they can be completed in a timely manner for the other teams to work with.

Lack of trust is one of the greatest obstacles that distributed teams face. They can't get together for team-building exercises, drinks, or a meal. They have no easy way to establish the relationships necessary for building trust. In lieu of face-to-face contact, take the time to learn about the other remote teams, their cultures, and their work area. Find some way to have social interaction online. Create a wiki page where people can post pictures and share some personal information. Set up a space for personal blogs so team members can tell personal or professional stories. Have a team chat channel devoted to social exchanges and sharing jokes. Play online video games together.

Lisa's Story

My current team is separated by only two time zones. Even so, we need a lot of discipline to maintain good communication. Programmers pair for all production code, and we also often pair between roles, such as a tester with a designer, or a designer with a programmer. Every team member diligently keeps an eye on the team chat channel in case someone can answer a question or just wants to share a funny picture. Sometimes on Friday afternoons, team members play a collaborative video game or watch fun video clips together.

But what's probably most important is that every couple of months, the entire team gathers in one place for a week. During this week we have social activities together and an in-person team retrospective. In between those times, individuals travel to other locations to work. The travel is expensive, but the increased level of trust and ability to communicate enables us do better work, more efficiently. With few testers on the team compared to the number of programmers, creating an atmosphere of comfort and trust is especially helpful.

Communication and Collaboration

When teams span the globe, they need to find ways of communicating that span language, time zones, culture, and communication styles. The whole team needs to be aware of all tasks that are being worked on, including testing activities. Collaboration tools must work equally for all team members. In colocated teams, team members can have spur-of-the-moment conversations. Distributed teams do not have this luxury. They need to create structured conversations and find a way to share information with all team members in all locations.

Figure 19-3   Take advantage of technologies—create a virtual you.

When most of the team is in one location but some team members are working from another location, perhaps from home, it is critical that those team members have some face time with the rest of the team. Lisa has been on dispersed teams, sometimes as one of the remote team members, and has experienced the positive effects of face-to-face communication—even if it is virtual. Lisa felt part of the team when she was included in the conversations. One of her teams created a "Virtual Lisa," using a telepresence device, much like the one in Figure 19-3. They rolled her into iteration-planning meetings, daily standups, and to whoever was her pair for the day. Virtual Lisa consisted of a laptop on a rolling cart, with a good-quality microphone that could pick up even casual conversations in the room, and a webcam that could be controlled remotely. This made Lisa feel truly part of the team in every way because she could participate in conversations and not worry that she missed something.

Agreeing on a telecommuting policy helps promote the kind of culture and discipline needed for teams with remote members to work effectively. Chris McMahon outlined an example policy in his "Telecommuting Policy" blog post (McMahon, 2009). Transparency and visibility may be even more important on distributed teams than on colocated teams. Think about what information you want to share and what is the best way to share it. How can you convey essential information at a glance? Can you make a simple test matrix to show testing progress for a release and put it on the landing page of the project wiki? Lisa's previous team took a picture of their task board every day and put it on the wiki so the remote team members could see the current status of the physical story board.

In his "Visualizing Quality" Agile Testing Days 2013 Keynote (Evans, 2013), David Evans recommended showing each team member's picture (Figure 19-4) along with their stories and tasks on the kanban system or

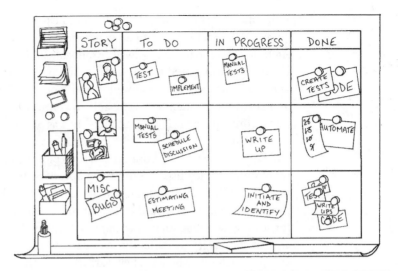

Figure 19-4   Get to know your distributed team members.

story board. This is particularly helpful for distributed teams. It helps everyone visualize who is anchoring each story or task, and it also shows when someone doesn't currently have work to do. We've met teams that include a photo or avatar of the person anchoring each story on their online project-tracking tool. They reported that it helped with communication and helped prevent stories from falling into black holes. Lisa's previous team did this with their physical task board and had some fun with the pictures. Since photos of the task board were posted to the wiki every day, remote team members got to join in the fun.

Collaborating through Tests

Examples and tests are powerful ways to communicate, but teams often fail to take advantage of them. Tests can be written in a domain-specific language (DSL) that crosses language barriers. Ideally, team members can collaborate at the same time, but that isn't always possible. If testers are in one country and programmers in another, perhaps the testers can write tests, which the programmers can review prior to discussions about the story. By starting early when there's a big time zone difference, team members can be prepared and use the tests to spark discussions. Product owners should be part of these discussions, too, vetting the examples and the tests and continuing the conversations until the whole team has a shared understanding of the story.

If the time zone difference allows, try remote pairing to keep the feedback cycle short. Janet listened to an experience report on remote pairing at Agile 2013 by Johannes Brodwell (Brodwell, 2013) which described testing that was offshored to Sri Lanka, while the rest of the delivery team and the customers were in Sweden and Norway. Time zones were not an issue, so team members were able to connect remotely and collaborate through pairing. They used tools such as Skype to be face-to-face as much as possible. Screen- and file-sharing tools such as GoToMeeting and Dropbox eased collaboration. To keep paired programming moving more quickly, they used a Ping-Pong approach to test-driven development (TDD): one programmer writes a test, and the other programmer writes the code; then they switch roles. This approach could work for testing activities such as specifying tests or debugging test failures. One of the biggest benefits this company found was that the pairs got to know each other better. They learned each other's idioms and preferences, and their mutual respect grew. Their process provided real-time training for new team members. Domain knowledge was passed on quickly, as was business understanding.

OFFSHORE TESTING

Some organizations believe that offshore testing is cheaper, because the perceived cost per person-unit of testing is lower. However, the overhead in extra layers of communication and the miscommunication that happens between people whose first language is not the same might outweigh the cost savings in labor. Often offshore testing means "throwing code over the wall" for testing and is not really about getting fast feedback.

Janet's Story

I was recently talking to a globally distributed organization (Company A) that was trying to move to agile. The company's multiple applications were very tightly coupled, yet owned by multiple vendors as well as the company's own internal agile development teams that supported the front end. One of the vendors was using a flow-based system to develop its application, but because it was delivered to many different clients, the timing did not always match Company A's needs. The other vendors were using traditional phased and gated methods for development. An internal test team handled the integration testing, but user acceptance testing (UAT) was outsourced to another vendor whose testers worked both on-site and offshore to keep costs lower for the client.

They faced many issues, including how to get features delivered when multiple applications and vendors were involved, and they had to rely on requirements and specification documents. Company A wanted to take advantage of "following the sun"—that is, having work constantly in progress by a team in at least one time zone. Extra effort was needed to make sure that the handover from one group to the next was seamless. For example, they created a position in the North America office to work with the offshore testing team to act as a liaison between the teams. They also had a person on call so that there was support for the offshore team if the test environment became unavailable.

I tell this story to show the difficulties some teams face when an organization does not understand the cultural and structural changes necessary to enable the teams to take advantage of agile. This organization has a difficult time ahead to align all these groups and vendors to deliver in small chunks but is determined to make it work.

One way to make offshore testing work with an agile approach might be to involve a system integration team from the beginning and give the full workflows to the teams so that there is consistency in delivery. Perhaps specific flows could be developed in priority order, using the "steel threads" approach described in *Agile Testing* (p. 144), working on thin end-to-end slices incrementally. This allows the flows to be tested earlier to reduce the risk. This may prevent, or at least mitigate, the problem where one team delivers its part of the system but breaks all other applications associated with the capability.

Developing multiple applications concurrently increases the likelihood of integration problems. In Chapter 18, "Agile Testing in the Enterprise," we mentioned the idea of a system integration team. Complex distributed organizations may warrant having such a team that continually tests the overall system, including all the enterprise applications. In Janet's example, perhaps a virtual team made up of members from both the integration and the UAT teams would ensure that everyone understands what is being delivered on an iterative basis.

Many companies that offer testing as a service have started to offer agile testing. If these organizations find ways to provide fast feedback, they may have some success. If your company provides this type of service, work with the product teams to determine the best place for testers to add value. Perhaps you can embed testers in the client's product teams.

Often the testing service companies offer UAT or system integration testing. They can add value if they build good communication channels between the product team and the outsourced test team. For example, increments of features could be passed for testing while coding is still in progress, rather than waiting until the whole release is ready to test. Figure 19-5 shows one possible way to deliver to a system integration test team at the end of every iteration, and then to perform UAT when a feature is completed. This requires that all product teams work together to produce testable features for frequent delivery.

Testing-as-a-service organizations working with agile teams need a different relationship with agile development teams than with teams that use phased and gated development. They need new ways to specify contracts and must work harder to interact with the client development teams. See the links in the bibliography for Part VII, "What Is Your Context?," for options you can explore for agile contracts.

If your agile team is using offshore or near-shore test teams, it's a good idea to have at least a few testers colocated with the development team to represent the offshore testing team. They can attend the planning

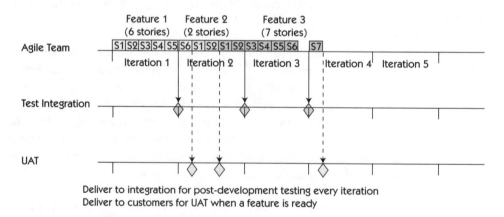

Deliver to integration for post-development testing every iteration
Deliver to customers for UAT when a feature is ready

Figure 19-5   Testing as a service for integration testing and UAT

meetings and daily standups, pair with programmers, and keep the offshore team in the loop. Recognize that while an offshore scenario may have perceived benefits for the business, it requires a lot more work and discipline to maintain sufficient communication and collaboration.

Working as an Offshore Testing Team

Parimala Hariprasad, *who blogs at www.curioustester.com, discusses challenges and solutions she's found working on offshore testing teams.*

I have served many teams that handle testing remotely. Some of these are startups scattered all over the world with limited resources and infrastructure. These small startups often collaborate with other developers, designers, and infrastructure providers to implement their business ideas. This means that my team is often acting as an offshore test team for multiple groups at once.

Introduction and Project Context

When any testing project starts, we get introductions in emails. We send a peppy five-liner about each tester on our team in the email with a funny picture. This sets an informal environment to start off. The email is then followed by audio calls for daily standups. Demos are usually done using Skype, Google Hangouts, WebEx, or other video-conferencing tools; we have explored a good mix of open-source and paid tools. In my experience, showing up face-to-face has worked best for my team because when someone speaks, putting a face to that voice gives a personal edge. Face-to-face doesn't necessarily mean flying your team to the main location. It could be facilitated by sharing pictures of each other, video calls, fun videos of a typical day at work, and so forth.

We get into the project context, explore the product under test, get additional information, ask questions, and start to work on the test strategy. I state early during initial conversations that work progress will be slow for the first couple of days as we are learning and exploring. We also share our deliverables with stakeholders 24/7 using tools like Dropbox and Google Docs so they can see who is working on a particular task at any point in time and what changes have been made since the previous day. This provides great visibility to our stakeholders at main locations.

Working Protocol and Ownership

We reiterate the working protocol that was agreed upon during the negotiation stages of the project (oh, yeah, our team does that). We talk openly about work timing in same/different time zones, testers who can provide backup (shadow testers), service-level agreements (SLAs) for critical issues, and so forth. We set common rules that go in as requests for collaboration, daily meeting times, test reporting format and processes, infrastructure availability, and necessary approvals to get started with work from day one. With some clients, we share samples of our previous work (masking confidential information) to help them get a better understanding of what value we bring to the table as a remote test team.

In distributed teams, the biggest challenge is lack of ownership between teams in remote and main locations. When things go wrong, some team members resort to blame games. In addition to skills, attitude plays a key role in how people take ownership of their work. Many teams I worked with had a mindset where everyone felt responsible for the team's success or failure. They constantly huddled to collaborate with all the teams with a common end goal in mind. They had a vision for the product they were testing. They didn't see testing as an isolated process, but as a key enabler in helping build great products.

Fun and Family

One of our team members hadn't seen one of the cofounders of a startup, although she interacted with him on a daily basis. A new idea was born. We shot funny pictures and video of our team at our cubicles and shared them with team members at the main location. They responded with a big smile and reciprocated this action—talk about a butterfly effect! We also sent flowers and gifts to our clients and their team members on special occasions. If we learned about their travel plans to our location, we hosted them at our expense, took them out for dinner, and discussed work over food. This has helped us to build strong bonds with our teams in main locations.

The latest videoconferencing technology also gives us the luxury of interacting with people in an informal setup where it's face-to-face—well, almost! Not many organizations can afford traveling to client locations. Low-cost videoconferencing tools can reduce travel costs. In some cases, some of my teams were airlifted to main locations after the clients saw the value we added to their work. This was a result of the credibility we built with them while working remotely.

Visibility and Feedback

Trust and credibility play a major role in defining how work gets done between the main location and the offshore testing teams. In the team on which I worked, I provided great visibility into our day-to-day work, which included daily status reports, daily standups, weekly calls, separate emails for critical issues, having backup for testers going on leave or long breaks, and so forth. We didn't need a camera fitted to our desk to do that. We were very transparent. Seeking feedback during project retrospectives and responding to feedback are other key actions that will build trust and credibility.

In the next sidebar, "Will the Real Manager Please Stand Up?," Parimala shares a few more challenges that are more conflict-based: working with managers who have different goals, or managers who only know how to say yes. She explains how she worked with her team to solve some of the conflicts.

Will the Real Manager Please Stand Up?

In one distributed team I worked for, my testing team reported to a line manager who handled operations like procuring systems, approving leave requests, doing performance appraisals, and determining compensation at the remote location. Technically, my team reported to a technical manager who sat in the main location with his team there. Many decisions used to be pushed onto our team with hardly any discussion or information. Many times, we had to blindly do what they asked us to do. We were not supposed to say no. We were not supposed to ask questions. At least, that's what our line manager told us. The way we dealt with it was by building credibility about my team's contribution to the project. Over a period of time, team dynamics between us changed for the better. Sometimes, you may need to work harder to create a healthy working culture between teams.

In some projects, it is common that the line manager and the main location manager have a different understanding of what's important. In such cases, the teams suffer because they don't know whom to listen to and whom to please. If you keep the line manager happy, the other manager is going to shout from the rooftop about poor deliverables. If you keep the other manager happy, your performance appraisals are going to be affected—this is how the testers are threatened at times. This leads many testers to try to please both of them as much as possible by keeping both of them in the dark. Such office politics end up hurting team morale and eventually disintegrating the team.

An extreme case is when offshore testing teams end up saying yes to every demand that comes from the main location whether it is reasonable or not. I have personally worked on a couple of projects where offshore testing teams overcommitted without keeping delivery challenges in mind. This in turn brings stress due to unrealistic expectations.

Handling Conflicts of Interest (When Gods Go Crazy)

Any team's true strength and character are revealed when conflicts arise. Sometimes, conversations around conflicts go on forever. The following methods have helped the teams I work with immensely:

- **Switch the media**: If a topic is bounced back and forth more than three times in an email, it's time to pick up the phone or call for a meeting.
- **24-hour rule:** It's OK to write a heated email; just wait until you calm down before you send it, perhaps 24 hours.
- **Face-to-face rule:** Initiating difficult conversations is one of the most challenging things to do in a conflict-filled environment. A wrong start can have devastating consequences. I coach my team to initiate difficult conversations with empathy, face-to-face (on video or in person). We start with stating the problem and the context in which it occurs, explain what attempts we have made to resolve the problem, and maintain a positive resolve. In cases where it is already known that two individuals have conflicts, we bring in a common colleague/positive influence to take charge and help resolve the conflict.

In my experience, skills, language barriers, and time zones have been small challenges. Passion, attitude, courage, and excellence are more difficult to learn yet necessary for working in harmony in a distributed setup.

Parimala brings up issues that teams may not anticipate, such as conflicting messages from managers in different locations and a lack of a feeling of ownership by teams in different locations. You can't anticipate every problem, but having some guidelines such as Parimala's rules about switching media when the current communication style isn't working, or having difficult conversations face-to-face, will help you deal with issues as they occur.

Tool Ideas for Distributed Teams

Throughout this chapter, we've mentioned tools that may help you solve a particular problem. Here's a summary of what we think might help you. If you think a particular tool will work in your team's process, experiment with it for an iteration or two. The tool should fit the process, not the other way around, so don't retrofit your process to fit the tool. These need to be simple techniques, such as starting an impromptu "Three Amigos" conversation to discuss requirements for a story or pairing for exploratory testing. If the learning curve is too steep or the practices are too complicated, they won't be adopted long-term.

Communication Tools

Use **email** for broadcasting information that is one-way, such as follow-ups on individual conversations. Since emails can easily be misinterpreted or misunderstood, try reviewing emails on sensitive topics with someone else before pushing the Send button.

Use physical or virtual task/story/kanban **boards** to track progress and make testing activities visible. Try the simplest solutions first. If it's enough to post a photo of the kanban board on the wiki twice a day, do it. If an online tracking tool is more appropriate, try more than one to see which fits best. Some tracking tools aren't designed to accommodate testing tasks, but you can usually find a creative solution.

Collaboration Tools

Phone, Voice-over-Internet Protocol (VoIP), and **videoconference** tools enable two or more people to collaborate and share ideas. Experiment to see which tools work best for you since each one seems to have its own problems. Use something as simple as Skype, Google Hangouts, or Zoom to have a three-way conversation can prevent many misunderstandings, such as how a feature should behave or what browser versions are supported.

Be aware of language issues, and remember to speak clearly and slowly if participants on the call don't share a common first language. Use headsets when appropriate to keep your hands free to type, make notes, or look up information, but if you're in a group meeting, pay attention to the conversation instead of multitasking. Use **video** if bandwidth permits; it allows people to connect on a much more personal basis. This means that all team members need good-quality webcams and microphones. Think about the story of Lisa's virtual telepresence device in the section on strategies.

Lisa's Story

When I joined my current team, they had been using Skype voice-only for daily standups. We started using the video feature of Skype. This helped everyone feel more connected, and the visual communication added value. However, each day, at least one participant's call would get dropped, or the audio would echo or start "roboting," meaning that voices sounded like a mechanical robot talking.

We decided to try Google Hangouts for standups and meetings. At first this was a big improvement. But after a few months, it started to exhibit similar problems to what we'd experienced with Skype.

Our next experiment for standups and meetings was Zoom. So far, this has been the most reliable solution, though sessions can freeze up and audio can echo.

Our programmers pair all day, and since we're distributed, this means that there are always a few remote pairs. They also use Skype, Google Hangouts, or Zoom for pairing. These tools usually work better when there are only two participants, but they do seem to go through cycles of problems when upgraded to new versions. We also sometimes experience bandwidth issues. We get help from our IT department, discuss the issues in our retrospectives, and continue to experiment with videoconference tools.

For some situations, **text chat** is good enough. Two or more people can easily share ideas, especially if they type fast! We have written much of this book via Google Talk, asking quick questions when we are writing. Text chat allows you more time to think about what to say. It also lets you ping someone who might be in the middle of something now but can get back to you in a few minutes. It works well for questions that are not urgent. If the discussion gets more complicated, you can jump on videoconference.

As mentioned earlier, a team **group chat** is an effective way for a distributed team to communicate in an unintrusive way. Group chat software can be set up with alert sounds, so that if someone types a name, that person will know to check the chat. This allows the team to be heads-down on work but still seek and give help as needed.

Wikis are widely used in many companies, while others use other collaboration tools such as SharePoint. These are good ways to record decisions and share information across multiple locations, but be sure they are kept well organized and easily searchable.

Mind mapping is a powerful collaboration tool for many testing-related activities such as test planning, brainstorming test scenarios, and tracking results. There are many mind-mapping products available that support real-time collaboration. Experiment with different offerings to see which works best with your team's infrastructure.

To pair test or code remotely, you need **desktop sharing** so that each person can see and control the screen as desired. You can use screen sharing built into your operating system, or try a variety of solutions such as a virtual private network (VPN), Skype, and Office Communicator. Obviously, make sure that whatever you use is secure.

As we noted in *Agile Testing* (pp. 82–83), **defect-tracking systems** (DTSs) are not a good communication tool, and debate in the agile community continues as to whether bugs should be logged or simply fixed and documented with an automated test. Experiment with different approaches to find what works best for your team. Revisit your defect-handling process periodically to see if what you're doing still fits.

Short feedback loops are the heartbeat of an agile team. We need reliable infrastructure to support that quick feedback. CI, developer sandboxes, test servers, databases, shared drives, virtual machines, test labs, and other infrastructure are critical to any team but, like everything else, even more of a challenge for distributed teams. A green CI ensures that the team halfway around the world can be productive as soon as they get to work. Hardware and software needed by team members in various locations must be reliable. Remote team members need the capability to solve their own infrastructure issues or have help available at all times.

Don't forget to include your system administrators and DevOps practitioners when teams from different locations gather together or hold team-building activities in their own locations. Make sure people in these roles in various locations stay connected with each other. They can collaborate to **build the infrastructure** that best supports the distributed teams (Hagberg, 2013).

If your team is distributed, you may have a stronger need to test your infrastructure. Teams are now testing their infrastructure and environments with automated regression tests, just as they test their production code. See Chapter 23, "Testing and DevOps," for more on infrastructure testing.

Use your team **retrospectives** to identify impediments to collaboration and communication in your distributed team. Try different brainstorming techniques such as impact mapping and mind mapping to set goals for improvement and think of different solutions you could try. We recommend trying two possible approaches side by side for easier comparison.

SUMMARY

Today's technology provides good ways for distributed team members to collaborate and communicate. However, your distributed team will need extra discipline and creativity to keep everyone engaged in testing before, during, and after coding. In this chapter, we discussed many ways distributed teams can succeed at building quality into their software and preventing defects.

- When talking about distributed teams, we include dispersed teams with remote members, teams with sub-teams in multiple locations, and offshore teams. All these situations can get in the way of whole-team responsibility for quality and testing activities.
- Be aware of language and cultural barriers. Help teams in different locations feel safe and free to ask questions. Give them time to make sure they understand what's been said.

- Get everyone together in person often. When that's not possible, use video meetings, and try some fun activities to help the team members build their comfort and trust levels.
- If possible, have managers, customers or their representatives, coaches, and leaders in different disciplines available at each location.
- Tests written in a shared DSL help ensure that all development and customer team members have a common understanding of how features should behave.
- Experiment with the communication and collaboration tools discussed in this chapter and seek out more if needed to find the ones that work best for your team.
- Make use of CI and other infrastructure to keep code integrated and up-to-date, and feedback loops short.

Chapter 20

AGILE TESTING FOR MOBILE AND EMBEDDED SYSTEMS

20. Agile Testing for Mobile and Embedded System	Similar, Yet Different
	Testing Is Critical
	Agile Approaches

Humans have been embedding software in devices and machines for decades. Early on, this was the province of rocket science. The Apollo Guidance Computer, developed for the Apollo space program, is one of the earliest examples (Wikipedia, 2014c). The use of embedded software spread as microprocessors and microcontrollers became less expensive and more widely available.

What do we mean when we use terms like *mobile app* and *embedded software*? We like the definition Jon Hagar uses (Hagar, 2014):

> *Mobile software can be found in smartphones, automobiles, and other devices that move. Typically, mobile systems have Wi-Fi and/or cellular network connections, are powered by batteries, have large numbers of hardware platforms, have various resource constraints such as screen size, limited user inputs, and smaller amounts of memory, storage space, and CPU speed than a laptop or desktop computer.*

> *An embedded device is an electronic device that contains software, yet the users may not fully appreciate that they are using software due to unique hardware and a limited user interface. Examples of embedded software devices include braking systems in cars, control systems in airplanes, medical devices such as pacemakers, and "smart" light switches. Mobile and embedded software programming introduces unique programming and testing challenges compared to IT systems.*

Proprietary embedded devices such as heart monitors and health and fitness equipment have similar testing challenges. Many of these embedded software products and proprietary devices are in regulated industries such as health care and aerospace. We will focus on agile testing in regulated environments in Chapter 21, "Agile Testing in Regulated Environments."

Agility is especially important in a fast-changing market such as mobile apps, and agile development is a natural fit for teams in that space. With the explosion in the number and types of mobile devices, from smartphones to "wearable" computers, more agile teams are faced with the challenge of developing embedded and mobile apps.

In Chapter 12 of *Agile Testing*, we described an example of testing a system that used embedded software. We've gathered more examples here to illustrate how agile testing values, principles, and practices help teams that deliver embedded and mobile products, with more focus on mobile.

SIMILAR, YET DIFFERENT

Agile testing values, principles, and practices apply to mobile and embedded software just as they do to any other types of software applications. Short feedback loops, collaborating with the customer, the simplest thing that could possibly work, test-driven development (TDD), guiding development with tests, and a whole-team commitment to quality all apply to testing software that runs on mobile devices or as part of a larger software solution.

There are definitely differences, though. As Jonathan Kohl notes (Kohl, 2013), we are unlikely to pick up our monitors or laptops and shake them. We're not going to rub our hands all over their screens, although that is changing. For example, Janet just purchased a new laptop with Windows 8.1 and used the touchscreen to scroll while editing. Certainly we'll use our laptops at the local coffee shop, but we're less likely to use them while riding the subway or hiking in the mountains. We don't switch continually from portrait to landscape orientation on laptops, but we do these things all the time with our mobile devices, which are full of sensors, cameras, and other bells and whistles. Then there are all the other components that allow mobile devices to work, such as cell phone towers, GPS satellites, and batteries.

The number and variety of the different mobile devices add yet another level of complexity to mobile app testing. Even the service provider can make a difference. Trying to test every permutation of platform and device approaches the impossible.

There are tools to help. We can take advantage of analytics software to see what users are doing when the software fails. If many users bail out of a mobile app on a certain view, we'll know about it, and we can try to figure out what usability issue might have caused it. It's about getting fast feedback, only this time it is from the users themselves.

The Ministry of Testing created a mind map of mobile testing ideas that you can see online (Sherry, 2013). Use it to generate your own ideas and to create your own mind map specific to your app. Figure 20-1 shows the data node of the mind map as an example.

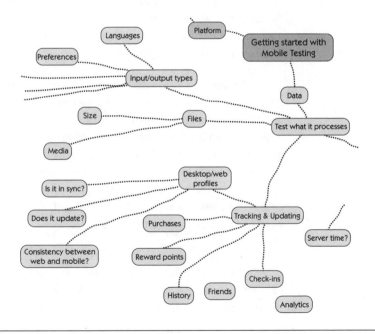

Figure 20-1   Ministry of Testing mind map for mobile apps

Embedded software products are more likely to be confined to one device and environment. The elliptical machine at your fitness center gets a lot of use, but it stays in one place, and its software executes in predefined ways. However, more and more consumer products, even automobiles, offer APIs that allow users to customize their own applications. As we use more software throughout our daily lives, building the right product for all customers gets more challenging.

TESTING IS CRITICAL

Testing has the potential to add even more value in embedded and mobile product development than in other software products. As Julian Harty has pointed out (Harty, 2014), if you release a new mobile app and get negative reviews right away, your app may never recover. If users aren't delighted by your product, it may have a one-star rating within a matter of minutes, which could be the end of your app before it's begun. It's difficult to fix problems fast enough to reverse the first impression. Your customer has many more choices that are easily available in the App Store. Just to get your product off the ground, you must be confident about all of its quality attributes. Validated learning techniques such as A/B testing, which we talked about in Chapter 13, "Other Types of Testing," may be an appropriate type of testing to use.

Some dimensions of quality may be more important in some than in other types of software products. For example, the ability to download an app via your mobile provider or to display the user interface (UI) on a small screen is important to verify when testing a smartphone, but not as critical on a tablet. The personal nature of mobile apps adds dimensions not seen in web-based or desktop software products. Julian Harty notes that since mobile apps may want access to your location, your contact list, your calendar, and other highly personal information, users need to feel they can trust the product.

Testers, programmers, and user experience (UX) designers can work together to ensure that end users feel safe and find the app valuable and easy enough to use. Peter Morville (Morville, 2004) describes different facets to consider for user experience as shown in Figure 20-2.

Testing mobile apps is, of course, different from verifying high-risk applications such as computers that guide space capsules and rockets

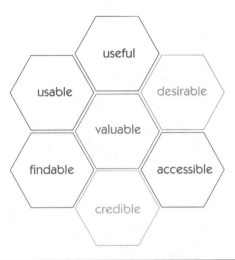

Figure 20-2   The user experience honeycomb by Semantic Studios

that use embedded software. Embedded software is also developed for safety-critical products such as medical devices, where testing outcomes may be a matter of life or death. In this context, it's more obvious that testing must be an integral part of software development. Teams must verify quality attributes such as reliability, stability, and tolerance of certain hardware changes.

AGILE APPROACHES

These products derive the same benefits from agile practices such as TDD, pair programming, continuous integration (CI), a whole-team approach to quality, and guiding development with customer-facing examples as in acceptance-test-driven development (ATDD)/specification by example (SBE)/behavior-driven development (BDD).

Lisa's Story

I jumped at the chance to help with testing our team's iOS app. I was an extremely late adopter of smartphones and tablets myself, and I couldn't even intuit the correct gestures for standard touchscreen functionality. Luckily, the iOS developers quickly got me up to speed with testing basics for physical devices, Xcode, and Crashlytics. They practice TDD and pair programming to develop our iOS code, which is supported by CI.

Testing a mobile app as a newbie is one way to find bugs and usability issues. I found that my general testing experience applies to iOS testing as well. As with any software product, we're trying to deliver the most valuable features for our users and our business. We also have to satisfy the App Store, which is a major stakeholder. Also, the mobile app supports our software-as-a-service (SaaS) web product, so it is helpful that I'm familiar with how it should work.

However, as I started learning more from conference sessions, articles, and books by mobile testing leaders such as Julian Harty, Karen N. Johnson, and Jonathan Kohl, I realized there's another huge level of complexity to mobile testing. I have to learn new skills and new ways to think to be more effective.

As I learn more, I'll be able to contribute more to our team, which has already started improving the design and architecture of our mobile app code. They're also learning new ways to automate more functional and regression testing.

We asked agile testing practitioners who are experienced in mobile app and embedded software development to share their insights into doing agile testing in these domains. We hope their stories will inspire experiments for you to try with your mobile or embedded teams.

Lessons Learned with Agile in Mobile and Embedded Domains

Jon Hagar, *the author of* Software Test Attacks to Break Mobile and Embedded Devices (Hagar, 2013), *tells about mobile and embedded teams using agile testing principles and practices.*

Once upon a time, embedded systems were typically created using phased and gated development methods, so agile practices were seen as a big change. This is a bit of a misconception. There were early and successful adopters of agile in the embedded domain. The Atlas rocket embedded software team (Waters, 2004) adopted some agile principles and practices over time. For example, they used CI with smaller, more frequent software builds; focused more on developer-level testing with automation (not quite TDD but close); allowed the system to unfold over time versus following rigid plans and specifications; ran automated tests with an exploratory focus; and had direct user/customer involvement.

I've heard people say that agile is for software only, not for hardware-focused projects (as embedded and some mobile devices tend to be). Success stories provide the counterpoint to this generalization. For example, Wikispeed (Wikispeed, 2014) is largely a hardware project following agile ideals. Wikispeed uses Extreme Manufacturing, which involves agile design, Scrum, kanban flow optimizations, Extreme Programming practices, and other agile approaches to rapidly turn ideas such as comfortable commuter cars into products customers can use.

Parallel hardware and software development efforts mean gaps in functionality and integration issues are likely to happen. Agile test concepts with CI and fast feedback help this by providing information to developers. For example, in embedded systems, typically the hardware is being developed at the same time the software is being created. It is a constant "chicken and egg" problem. The hardware defines how aspects of the software are to be built, and the software needs to be in place to assess many of the features that the hardware provides. In the CI of embedded systems, it is common to build a little hardware, integrate with some software, change the hardware in a final design, and then at the end have a more complete definition needed to finish the software. CI makes this parallel evolution efficient.

It is also common in the embedded domain to have last-minute software changes to accommodate hardware problems. I hear statements such as, "Well, the hardware is fixed, and it is easier to change the software," which may be true, but it comes at the risk of last-minute bugs introduced into the software.

A similar situation exists in the mobile app world where the app may need to work with many different OS versions and/or hardware platforms. Here, the CI problem arises across these different configurations and leads to concerns about combinatorial testing and "will it work" for enough of the market to be a success.

Based on stories such as these, here are a few of the lessons I've learned in implementing agile in mobile and embedded domains:

- Many teams, especially those that develop mobile apps, believe that time to market overrides the need to do testing. However, if you look at online reviews and ratings, you will see that having many bugs lowers ratings, and thus the likelihood of an app being successful.
- Late changes in hardware impact the product even more strongly than changes in software, so testing must be very agile

to accommodate them. When hardware and software are developed in parallel, CI is especially important. Testers should expect last-minute changes in the software in order to solve hardware problems. Both automated and exploratory testing is needed. Look for patterns of errors in the code. Include attack testing to prevent bugs from escaping into production.

- Start testing as early as possible. Use test doubles such as mock objects and test stubs for components that aren't yet delivered. Simulators can also help give testing a head start.

- Test automation can be more difficult in mobile and embedded domains. Although they're changing, many older test tools do not work for mobile and embedded devices because of the unique hardware interaction. Because of this, testers in agile teams may need many more technical skills on top of basic test knowledge. For example, understanding hardware design concepts, code, and development tools may be needed for successful testing.

Do you recognize your team in any of Jon's lessons learned? Consider these hard-earned lessons to help your own team build quality into your mobile or embedded software product. The practices and techniques Jon describes aren't new; they may just be needed at different times and in different ways than for testing web applications or other products. You can adapt familiar patterns and strategies for effective mobile and embedded testing, as we'll learn in the next story.

Strategies for Test Automation in Mobile Testing

Jeff "Cheezy" Morgan, *author of* Cucumber and Cheese *(Morgan, 2013), explains how he tests as he develops mobile apps and accommodates short release cycles.*

I approach mobile testing in nearly the same way I approach testing a web application. I create my Screen Objects (Page Objects) for each screen in the application, define the data sets I will be using, build out my different navigation routes, and then construct the tests to leverage these artifacts. Although the structure of the code is nearly identical, there are a few things about testing mobile applications that are completely unique.

When testing web applications, you have to test against the various target browsers and versions of those browsers. You have the same thing with mobile applications, but it is more complicated. You have to concern yourself with different devices as well as different versions of those devices. In addition, you have to test your application on different versions of the operating system on all of those different devices. The matrix of targeted platforms can get quite large very quickly.

To make things even more complicated, there are different types of mobile applications. There are native applications, web applications, and applications called hybrids, which are a combination of the two. The tools or coding libraries you use to automate the tests might have to change depending on the type of application.

Finally, there are two major categories of tests that need to be performed on mobile applications: testing the behavior, and testing the appearance. The appearance is divided even further depending on the type of application. If it is a native application, you are really testing the layout of the controls that constitute the screen. If it is a web application, you are testing the responsive design of the web pages as displayed on the screen. I always build automation to test the behavior but rarely to test the appearance. I find that automating the visual aspects of the application takes a long time, and the tests tend to be brittle, causing a lot of false test failures. With all of this complexity, it might seem like an overwhelming task to figure out how to adequately test your application. Here's what I do.

The first thing to do is clearly understand your target devices. It is not difficult to get mobile usage reports on the Internet. (See the bibliography for Part VII, "What Is Your Context?," for links to examples of these.) I use these lists to create my own list of devices we plan to target. Don't forget that you need to make it a combination of devices and operating systems. In some cases the same device will appear more than once but with different versions of the operating system.

With that list ready, I acquire one or two of the top four devices. I connect one of each device directly to my build server so all of my automation runs continuously against the devices every time a developer checks code into the source code management system. If I have only one of each device, I also create an emulator for those devices on the build server and configure the build to first check for a device and run the tests on the emulator if it does not exist. I perform visual verification and exploratory testing against any device that is not connected to the build server.

The final thing I do is create several emulators to perform testing on devices that I do not have. I place these emulators on the build server and create a build that runs nightly and runs the automation against each of these emulators. In addition, I create three emulators on the tester's computer that represent the large-, medium-, and small-screen resolutions of the targeted devices. These emulators on the tester's machine are used for visual verification of the application.

Cheezy combines automated tests and humans to verify the behavior and appearance of mobile apps. If you don't already have the type of infrastructure he describes, such as build servers and emulators, your team can address this together, perhaps with help from DevOps (see Chapter 23, "Testing and DevOps," for more on testing infrastructure).

In our experience, leveraging automation to make exploratory testing more effective is a winning strategy. The following story illustrates some aspects of this.

Automation-Assisted Mobile Exploratory Testing

Jon Hagar *explains how exploratory testing of mobile and embedded software can benefit from automation.*

Many practitioners think of exploratory testing as something that should be done manually by a thinking tester who plans, designs, executes, and then learns about the product interactively in real time. Automation can support exploratory testing of mobile and embedded systems without restricting the tester's freedom to explore different avenues. For example, automation is helpful in creating test inputs, especially for combinatorial testing, database population, and supporting test techniques such as boundary value analysis and equivalence classes.

Data capture and playback tools can assist in providing some repeatability during an exploratory test session. After testing, automation can help with analyzing test results. Automated test scripts can help with reviewing large log files or scanning for particular patterns, incorrect outputs, or negative trends. Bug reports and other test information can be generated automatically, providing good ways of visualizing the data. This information can be used for further analysis and manual exploration.

Above all, we need thinking testers, but test automation can help in certain contexts. The following examples illustrate situations where automation was invaluable for the exploratory testing effort.

My first story concerns an embedded medical system. Here the software under test could pose a risk to human life, so risk-based test planning with supporting tool analysis was needed throughout the project's development cycles. Testing focused on high-risk items first. The testers were also worried about tester bias, so they included the use of combinatorial test tools to provide mathematically sound input cases. The test inputs and outputs for the software-device under test were processed at a 10-millisecond rate. Consequently, a large real-time test simulation automation environment was needed to provide inputs every 10ms and record over 1MB of test data outputs generated during each test sequence. The large amounts of data generated and recorded also needed computer processing tools to locate possible bugs, look for trends, and visualize the test data results. Finally, the results were reported in online tools such that developers and user/customer stakeholders could review and analyze test results quickly and at their convenience. Each of these areas of automation required its own development effort to create the tools, but these added efforts were offset by better testing and a higher-quality embedded product.

My second example concerns a mobile app game under first-time development. Here, the developers wanted the ability to quickly repeat the actions the tester had done to find a problem. The testers used a capture-playback tool running on both a simulator and the actual mobile phone devices to capture the exploratory session. If a bug was found during the iteration, the captured session was electronically sent to the programmers, so they could replay it to support their debugging efforts. If no bugs were found, the capture script was kept only until the end of the next iteration, since changes were rapid and scripts would be out-of-date quickly. However, sometimes a script might be reused if changes to it were insignificant. Also, the testers used an online gaming checklist tool (see the bibliography for Part VII for suggested links) to help testers remember what to look for and test during an exploratory test session. This feedback with rapid semiautomated test execution produced the information that allowed a fun and functioning game to be produced. After the product was fielded, new releases used more advanced forms of test data generation and test case reporting to continuously improve the game. The initial time to market was quick with a very short final test phase, and later the product was continuously tested to improve it for players.

See Chapter 12, "Exploratory Testing," for more ways to use automation to facilitate exploring. Get hardware and software team members together to look for automation opportunities. For example, use automation to record hardware and OS conditions on timing, temperature, or voltage while the tester invokes a series of user steps of software functionality.

Learning Agile Testing for Mobile Software

JeanAnn Harrison, *a software tester from the Boston area in the United States, explains how working closely with programmers helped her get up to speed quickly.*

My first introduction to mobile software testing, which was on the Los Angeles Police Department's traffic ticket device, also gave me exposure to applying an agile methodology to a software project. Prior to this project, I had no formal agile training or mentoring. That first experience with testing mobile software was an immense learning experience.

Oh, sure, there were requirements to start, but most of our requirements were written while we were "feeling out" the software design. I realized how closely I needed to work with the developer, to be able to learn the intent of the design. At the same time, we were testing to see if the design made sense in terms of the overall set of requirements from the customer. We discussed scenarios such as the police officers needing to be able to store all their data from a day's work on the device, and then upload that data once their shift was done. Timing and performance became critical to how the mobile software requirements unfolded.

Decisions on usage turned into design discussions based on exploratory testing. Quickly, I realized that with each sprint I needed to set some goals prior to testing. Planning what kinds of tests needed to be done within the scope of the project and schedule made my testing task much easier.

The experience turned out to be a relatively short project, but this is where I was first exposed to time-boxed iterations even though we didn't give our process a name. I basically taught myself what would work based on how I interacted with the builds and the programmer. We did what worked for us, the project, and our users.

Taking on a new domain and development process is easier when you collaborate with other delivery team members. Mobile software testers have to go beyond the software to understand how the OS and hardware conditions affect software behavior. Continual collaboration among programmers, testers, UX designers, system administrators, and other specialists is vital for products to succeed in today's ultracompetitive market.

SUMMARY

Agile testing values, principles, and practices apply to mobile and embedded software development, but these domains present unique challenges. Extra attention has to be given to testing embedded software and proprietary mobile devices that operate in life-critical situations.

- Mobile devices and other devices with embedded software get used in ways that traditional computers don't, and these differences present unique challenges for testing.
- Device size and resource constraints require different approaches to test design.
- Testing may add even more value on mobile and embedded systems due to potentially high risks from both marketing and safety perspectives.
- Agile approaches work well for testing mobile apps and embedded software because of the fast feedback cycle, but there are unique obstacles such as limits to beta releases and slow store approval processes for iOS devices.
- Some automation may be needed for effective exploratory testing of software in mobile and other devices. Teams should collaborate to see what tooling can help.
- Experiment together to find testing approaches that are appropriate to the product, device, and delivery time frames.

Chapter 21

AGILE TESTING IN REGULATED ENVIRONMENTS

Since the dawn of Extreme Programming, we've been told by some experts that agile development isn't appropriate for safety-critical, highly regulated software, such as medical device and space flight software. Apparently a lot of teams didn't get that memo. As you saw in Chapter 20, "Agile Testing for Mobile and Embedded Systems," we've heard many success stories about teams in regulated domains such as aerospace and medical devices that have embraced agile values and principles. Many businesses must comply with financial regulations such as Sarbanes-Oxley (SOX). These companies have adapted agile development to fit their needs, and they've found how they can reduce risk with agile practices.

THE "LACK OF DOCUMENTATION" MYTH

Some articles explaining why agile is not appropriate for regulated domains cite lack of documentation. We continue to hear this fundamental misunderstanding even as the term *agile development* is well into its second decade. As we've mentioned earlier, agile development is about delivering value frequently, at a sustainable pace. There's no inherent reason that software developed using agile values, principles, and practices would have inadequate documentation.

When we use an example-guided approach to software development, we turn examples into tests, and we can automate many of those tests. As David Evans and Gojko Adzic have noted (Adzic, 2011), the automated tests become living documentation. The beauty of documenting code by way of automated tests is that since you have to keep regression tests passing, you are always keeping your documentation up-to-date. We gave an example of this in *Agile Testing* (p. 402). Accurate documentation is critical in domains where people's lives, security, or money is at stake.

Agile and Compliance

Regulatory agencies impose rules, and everyone governed by those rules must prove that they are complying with them. We must test to make sure that our software that tests compliance produces accurate results.

Lisa's Story

In my eight-plus years working on a team that developed a financial services application, I got lots of experience with verifying that our software complied with federal regulations—or that it helped our customers comply with those regulations.

Our customers used our software to manage employees' 401(k) retirement plans. Each year, they had to prove that they operated within IRS rules. For example, executives couldn't take advantage to pad their own accounts with tax-free savings. The rules were extremely complicated and often counterintuitive, but I enjoy learning challenging business domains.

Our product owner gave us many examples of sample inputs and expected outputs. Turning those into tests that guided coding ensured our success. We fearlessly delivered highly complex software that reliably automated compliance testing for our customers, so they weren't at risk for incurring fines.

Our competitors couldn't believe we were able to do this. But we had the tests to prove it!

Later, we were faced with "Bernie Madoff rules," regulations to help prevent brokers from scamming investors. These involved things like disclosing record-keeping fees and preventing plan advisers from changing investors' personal information. The software to comply with these rules didn't generate revenue, but failure to comply could mean significant fines for our company and our customers. For each regulatory requirement, we worked with the business stakeholders to find the simplest software solution, minimizing cost but ensuring compliance and security.

Audits and regulatory submissions impose accountability and other requirements needed to get a stamp of approval. Many of those

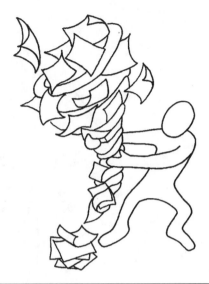

Figure 21-1   Wrestling with documentation

regulations say, "show evidence that" or something similar; unfortunately many organizations often interpret this to mean, "give me more documentation," and they spend their time, not testing, but documenting (see Figure 21-1).

Janet's Story

A while ago, I was at a company that wanted to start doing more agile development and still needed to be SOX compliant. I looked at the company's standards and saw that they were anything but agile. The test strategy document had layer upon layer of required documentation, and the people who were tasked with writing it weren't even sure who was reading it, or why it was needed.

The agile teams were struggling to figure out what was absolutely necessary to fulfill their compliance but not get overwhelmed in documentation that had little meaning and did not satisfy their needs.

There are many companies that are able to comply with regulatory rules without excessive documentation (see Figure 21-2). Generally, as long as the company documents what it does, does what it documents, and

Figure 21-2 Simplify your documentation.

can produce evidence that it is doing what it says it is doing, regulators will be fine with that. It is worth your while to read the regulations and then take a pragmatic approach to meeting them. For example, taking photos of the story board on a regular basis and having those available for review may be a perfectly legitimate way to document what has happened for compliance purposes.

Make your auditors (they are stakeholders) part of the solution, and define their needs as stories or tasks so the deliverables are built into the solution. Consider tasks that need to be completed to comply with regulations when your team creates a definition of "done" for the next release. Teams need discipline to follow their process consistently and produce the required artifacts. Testing activities contribute much to ensure compliance. As mentioned earlier in this chapter, automated tests are a great way to create consistent test results and living documentation. Compliance is part of Release Done, and therefore part of the product, not an exam to pass at the end.

Janet gets asked one question fairly often: "Are there any domains that shouldn't attempt to use agile methods, like regulatory?"

Is Agile Possible in a Regulated Environment?

Griffin Jones, *an agile tester who provides consulting on regulatory compliance, gets asked this question anytime someone moving to agile realizes he is an expert in testing in regulatory environments. Here's how Griffin answers.*

For me the question is personal. One of my roles is to represent the organization to external authorities that may be unfamiliar with agile. I usually start with an acknowledgment that we are regulated, what that means to the organization, and how we have implemented compliance in the context of an agile software development and testing process. Getting the team's thinking clear on the topic is critical.

First, the team has to recognize that it is simultaneously creating two things: the product *and* the regulatory documentation.

Second, the behaviors, tasks, and artifacts of the project have to address both the product needs and the regulatory needs at the same time. They are part of the same flow of actions. You can't complete one and then try to bolt the other on top. They have to be different faces of the same coin.

Third, be context sensitive and create reasonable flexibility in processes to allow quick interactive learning. The control of processes and procedures needs to be "*Auftragstaktik*," or mission-focused. Try to minimize the amount of additional work to create the artifacts to tell and substantiate the project's regulatory story.

Fourth, if you are honestly doing good competent engineering work, how can you naturally capture evidence to support the regulatory story, without breaking the flow of the work and creating inefficiency and ineffectiveness?

For me, it is about taking responsibility and preparing the project to survive the review and criticism of an external authority. Throughout each workday I ask three questions:

- Would the stakeholders be happy if they saw and heard what we are doing right now?
- Is it important that the project be able to share this information with stakeholders in the future?
- What would be the most effective and efficient way for me to memorialize this so that I can access and share it in the future, without breaking the flow?

By focusing on these key points and questions, the project is able to do regulatory-compliant agile software development. The specific project "hows" become just context-specific details.

What a great message—make your regulatory requirements part of your work, constantly thinking about how to make them as simple and effective as possible.

Testing in regulated environments is an opportunity to grow our T-shaped skills by collaborating with programmers and other team members, as you will see in the next story.

Collaborating to Test Medical Device Apps

In Chapter 20, "Agile Testing for Mobile and Embedded Software," **JeanAnn Harrison** *recounted her first experience both testing mobile software and working in an agile environment. She subsequently joined a team that develops medical devices and again found benefits in collaborating with the whole team, especially when it came to meeting regulatory needs.*

I was hired by a medical device company to help bolster the current testing team, provide support to that team, and do some mentoring in the software development life cycle. The medical device domain was a brand-new experience, but my experience with testing mobile device software came in handy.

As I started out checking tests previously written by an outsourced group, it became clear the tests were only functional tests, with little regard for performance, stress, boundary condition, and usability tests. Hardware and operating system conditions were not considered in the requirements, which meant we lacked the minimum test coverage for a medical device. Not only were our users our customers, but they were patients wearing a monitor to provide heart data to their physician.

The difference between our medical device's software and a tablet or phone application was how many smaller applications were needed for an end-to-end system to reach its conclusion. It was a highly complex testing project that helped prepare me for single mobile app testing projects, and it shone a light on understanding how hardware conditions and operating systems integrate with the mobile app. Considering tests beyond the functional user interface (UI) is vital to planning any mobile testing project.

I needed to learn more about how the files were created, processed, and then transmitted, as well as the high-level code design. I needed to learn the architecture of the entire system to better understand how each application interacted with another application. The interdependencies were very complex, making test cases more complex. In order to provide solid test coverage, I needed to spend time with the development team and ask a lot of questions, sit in code reviews, and review log files to better understand where those interdependencies existed.

By spending time with the development team, I found our shared sense of humor helped us bond. My development team became comfortable working with me and were willing to show me what they wanted me to learn from them. We all recognized how valuable my observations could be to their design. One of the biggest problems with mobile software development is the lack of requirements. You don't know what you don't know. Benchmarks in particular tend to be extraordinarily vague. Exploratory testing can help by providing information for developers to more accurately design. Testers can use the opportunity to further learn the architecture when they are directly involved in the design process.

For example, while performing stress testing, I recognized I could, in a short period of time, see how the device's software would react to the added load, and I uncovered a major long-standing bug. Working together, the programmer and I discovered that the bug occurred more often than we would have thought possible. The bug had to be addressed immediately, so the programmer and I paired to solve the issue. In the end, I learned not only more about the software design, but also how to be more accurate in my testing. In mobile testing, working directly with the development team helps the tester to be educated in the architecture, which leads to a wider range of test coverage beyond functional and UI testing.

With medical devices such as the mobile heart monitor, the delivery team is required to provide documentation that could be traced to the requirements directly. Many people feel this traceability means matching up a specific requirement directly to a specific test case. However, not all requirements were written or submitted to be tested directly. Instead, the team designed use cases to prove to the auditor that the device and software worked as expected. These use cases provided a trace to design documents where I could develop more use case tests. The process was less intrusive for the programmer, and the testers submitted the necessary test documentation to satisfy the regulatory stakeholders.

Testing a mobile medical device has its challenges, especially when the device is a proprietary one. However, all mobile testers need to work closely with their development team to learn as much as they can about the architecture. Timing, various hardware conditions, the firmware dependencies, and the sequence of how the code is executed are all critical components when designing test cases. Working with the development team as a whole made our agile software project on the mobile heart monitor a fairly successful one.

JeanAnn's team found a lightweight solution for traceability of requirements that was acceptable to their regulatory auditors. There's a perception that regulated always means heavyweight, but in our experience, auditors are usually open to simple alternatives to meet their information requirements. Experiment and collaborate to find an optimal solution.

SUMMARY

Many aspects of agile development, such as short feedback loops and automated regression tests to provide living documentation, make agile practices suitable, even advantageous, in regulated environments. Bringing the subject matter experts together with testers and other development team members allows us to guide coding and mitigate risk with a wide range of examples. Regulated environments provide unique opportunities for testers who enjoy mastering business rules and helping the team deliver the right thing. Some of the aspects of agile approaches to testing in regulatory environments we covered in this chapter are:

- Contrary to popular belief, agile does not mean no documentation. Teams that use examples to guide development turn those into automated tests that provide living documentation that can help meet regulatory requirements.
- Complying with auditors' requirements for information doesn't necessarily mean producing old-school, heavyweight documents. Work with auditors to find lightweight ways to comply that fit with your team's needs.
- Government regulations add quality characteristics that need to be verified, even if they don't directly add business value. Avoiding fines and ensuring customer security are critical to the business.
- Tester-programmer collaboration can be essential for testing high-risk, regulated software products. Understanding the system design, hardware considerations, and timing issues helps in preventing defects or finding them early.

Chapter 22

AGILE TESTING FOR DATA WAREHOUSES AND BUSINESS INTELLIGENCE SYSTEMS

A data warehouse (DW) is an integrated environment that contains operational as well as decision support data. It also stores data that is created within the data warehousing environment such as aggregates, summaries, and calculations. It is an effective way of managing the decision support function in an organization by treating data like a strategic asset that can be used for competitive advantage. A good system provides easy access to relevant data, allowing modeling as well as retrospective and predictive analysis to better inform business decisions—hence the idea of business intelligence (BI). Modeling the enterprise for a data warehouse is a huge effort, and in traditional data warehouse development approaches that require the full data model to be defined first, it takes years for the business to see any benefit.

With agile methods, using fast feedback cycles, the business people can prioritize what information they want to see first. They generally have little or no idea of what they want until they see it, so again, the fast feedback cycle is beneficial to them. The idea of working incrementally means that data quality issues are exposed early, preventing massive issues later on.

WHAT IS UNIQUE ABOUT TESTING BI/DW?

Under the BI umbrella, you use the system as a consumer of the data—more of an end user type of role. For DW, you get down into the technical delivery and need to understand the architectural solution. Figure 22-1 is an example diagram of a BI/DW solution.

One huge challenge is finding testers with the necessary skills: technical knowledge to verify the data movement from source to target, technical knowledge of databases, testing skills in data integrity to ensure that the data is consistent, security testing knowledge, and analytical skills to understand what the data represents. Is it even reasonable to think these skills can be found in one person? It begins to sound like that "whole-team approach" again, doesn't it? The whole team needs to encompass even more disciplines. It is important that application development consider the data warehouse, because data quality issues can hamper testing and completion of stories.

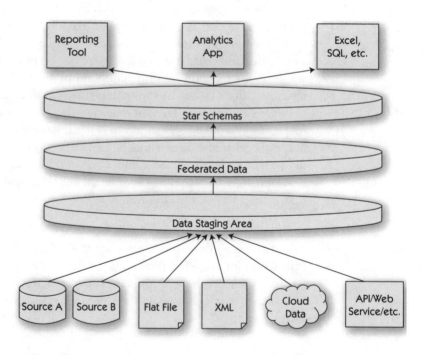

Figure 22-1   Example of a data warehouse setup (supplied by Mike Heinrich)

Teams implement agile practices differently with business intelligence and data warehouse features from the way they do in a regular web application. For example, there may be nothing visible to demo via a user interface for a long time. The value is in the data, which may be best demonstrated early using command-line tools. Data warehousing is based on a batch model, where the functionality is about moving high volumes of data in batches, rather than processing transactions continuously, so continuous integration (CI) is not as meaningful. This means that the regression tests might not be run as part of a daily build, but rather as part of the daily operational load processes. However, if automated tests with related test data are created for each story, many of the tests can be run in a CI environment.

Traditionally, DW/BI teams have used large volumes of data to test code. It often could take many hours or days to load all that data and see the test results. Agile teams are finding ways to either reduce the volume of data needed to adequately test stories or leverage new technologies that significantly speed up extract, transform, and load (ETL) processes to allow testing on large volumes of data. Our contributor stories in this chapter will show you some of the ways people have adapted.

Unit tests for DW/BI look different from application unit tests. A typical unit test might ensure that row counts and totals match from source to target, and these types of ETL tests can be automated. However, the transformation step changes the way data is represented. For example, data types may be converted, calculations applied, or daily values aggregated into monthly totals. These types of transformations represent some of the risks in data management that often make it harder to unit test.

To test DW/BI, an excellent understanding of data boundary values, ranges, and type transformations is essential. It's easy to fall into a trap of having many automated tests running that are so simplistic they don't add any value. Simple tests might be generated or copied easily since inputs are generally through a command-line interface. The difficulty is in understanding the different decision rules and paths that the data can take and executing those. Problems in data manipulation and transformation often occur at the boundaries between types. Understanding the nature of data types within database systems and the decision rules that are applied to the data as it is processed is needed for creating valid and informative tests.

Table 22-1   Simple Checklist for Automation

Test #	Description	Risk	Objective
1	Verify no records are lost	High	Records are transferred completely
2	Verify no fields are lost	High	Records are transferred completely
3	Verify source and target totals match	High	Records are transferred completely
4	Verify no data size errors	Medium	Records are processed correctly
5	Verify no data type errors	Low	Records are processed correctly
6	Verify data format changes are performed correctly	Low	Records are processed correctly

Collaborating with the programmers and product owners enables testers to target tests effectively. A combination of communication and exploration can help to identify the right tests to automate to reduce the risks of ineffective tests.

Automation is necessary, but it has a different appearance from what we discussed in Part VI, "Test Automation." Often it is in the form of simple scripts that compare fields. A simple checklist may help identify some of the issues and highlight what can be automated for testing data warehouse applications. A colleague of Janet's started with a simple checklist, similar to Table 22-1.

You may have to apply formatting or masking of data in order to perform a consistent check, storing the original state of the data at each stage of the test to help track where any problems have occurred. In addition, capturing all of the logs and traces from the process will help in diagnosing any problems later.

Try using an automated process to execute tests, creating and injecting data, and then examine the results and use exploratory testing to investigate further. Adam Knight's teams use the automated harnesses to run their exploratory tests, since it is easier to manipulate data that way. Note that due to the large amounts of data involved, you may need to monitor activity in production to ensure that edge conditions are handled correctly.

Using Agile Principles

Trying different test approaches iteratively helps teams discover good ways to demonstrate data quality and the value it can add to the business. Basic agile principles such as simplicity, fast feedback, and breaking things into small chunks can be applied to BI/DW systems.

Learning to Test BI

Mike Heinrich *shares his experiences in learning to test in a data warehouse project. Trial and error ruled for the first little while, but it didn't take long for him to get into the rhythm.*

During the process of building our data warehouse and business intelligence environment, we learned very quickly that the business was not interested in the intermediate steps required to stage and transform the data through multiple databases. The statement, "But I can do this in Excel much faster" was a common refrain. With that in mind, it became very evident that we needed to show the business its usable, modeled information early and often. Of course, to stage all the data, federate it, and transform it into something the business could evaluate via traditional ETL processes is expensive, time-consuming, and change averse.

This led us to find ways to abstract the logical data models and to consider what the business cared about, rather than concentrating on the storage medium. Using our reporting tools to do rudimentary data federation and transformation shortened the feedback loop and allowed the business people to use a tool they were familiar with to refine their data requirements. By giving our business something tangible to explore, we reduced the number of data quality issues and even helped refine from where data should actually be sourced.

As the data requirements became better understood, the development team was able to determine whether ETL and data persistence were required or if the existing solution was satisfactory. My role as tester throughout all of this became less about verifying the functionality of ETL scripts and more about brokering the communication between the business and the development team around data quality and performance expectations.

As we moved into user acceptance testing (UAT), the iterative approach was once again necessary as we learned that the concept of a "rubber-stamp UAT," where the testing team had already discovered and communicated all the issues, would be completely unsuccessful and guarantee we would never get to production. UAT became an intensive process for which we needed even more frequent communication between the business and the delivery team as they finally worked through their completed, overall model. Accepting that what we had called UAT was really just the final "dev and test" iteration of the product was perhaps the biggest mental hurdle we had to overcome.

The concept of model-driven development, or populating a loosely defined (and changing) logical model to allow the business to understand the data earlier, was not necessarily a popular approach. However, the shortened feedback loops allowed a project that had cost millions and languished in development for years to finally deliver valuable insight into customers and costs to support the profitability of the organization.

Mike used many agile principles in learning how to test his first BI/DW project. By understanding what the customer found valuable, the team was able to adapt its approach to meet those needs. Fast feedback loops gave the team the confidence to experiment to see what worked best. Janet was fortunate enough to talk with Mike during the project, and one of the many problems they had was bad data. The team suffered with an age-old problem—GIGO (garbage in, garbage out). With the fast feedback cycles, they were able to start cleaning up the data as they were developing, rather than having to wait until everything was built.

To ensure smooth iterative development, identify your test environment requirements at the start of each activity so that you are not blocked waiting for hardware and environments where you can execute your tests.

DATA—THE CRITICAL ASSET

Data warehouses are generally governed by strict rules. One example is that the data may not be volatile—it must never be overwritten or deleted. Once database transactions are committed, the data is static, read-only, and retained only for future reporting. This may involve huge amounts of unique data with a limited-value life cycle, which is why we hear so much these days about Big Data. Testing with so much data becomes an issue of its own, and we will cover that later in this chapter.

Another issue is privacy and security. It's not always possible to use production data for testing. Most countries have a privacy regulation protecting personal details. This means that production data needs to be "scrubbed" or "depersonalized." The database administrator on Lisa's previous team created a procedure using keys with a mathematical computation that replaced sensitive information such as IDs within the system. If needed, the IDs could be decrypted to identify the values in production. If a unidirectional approach is acceptable, you can simply use randomly generated numbers. Some database products have built-in procedures that can be used. Make sure that the substituted values meet the same constraints to which production data is subjected.

In business intelligence, the data is the most important asset. Since business decisions are based on that data and how it is represented, the way we handle the data for testing is critical.

Solving the Bad Test Data Problem

Lynn Winterboer, *an agile trainer and consultant for BI/DW solutions, tells how her team solved one problem they faced when testing without appropriate test data.*

All who work in the data warehousing and business intelligence industry understand how data quality can impact BI results. This is true for testing as well as production loads and can be particularly painful when the business rules being applied in the ETL are complex and overlapping. A BI team can save itself many headaches by starting out with a clean set of specific test records for unit and regression testing for the main scenarios of the project.

For example, I worked with one company that had grown over 20 years, largely by acquisition. When companies were acquired, their order data was integrated into the enterprise resource planning (ERP) system by people unfamiliar with data management. They were only concerned about getting the data to somehow fit in the target operational system so that the combined businesses could continue to operate. Unfortunately, this caused many data anomalies in the ERP system.

On a revenue allocation project that required order data from this ERP system, our DW/BI team worked to implement complicated business rules. To test the ETLs that applied these rules, we used random samples of production data. We repeatedly experienced trouble due to the quality of our test data. Problems looked like this:

1. Code and test Product A.
2. Code and test Product B.
3. Regression test Product A with the same record we used to test it the first time, but this time, the test fails.
4. Working with the business lead on the project, we eventually figured out that the record we had used for Product A had an anomaly in it that caused a false negative on the regression test when the rules for Product B were also in the ETL. On a clean record for Product A, the test would have passed.

Because of these issues, we struggled just to code and successfully test our happy path scenarios, much less the corner cases. The team was frustrated.

The business lead decided to focus her time on creating a small, accurate set of test data that could be used to confirm that we had all our coding logic correct for the main scenarios in new orders. She identified 16 clean orders that we could use to test and regression test the ETL as each scenario was added, and then manually calculate the appropriate revenue allocation results for each.

This allowed our team to refocus on the most important deliverables. We could trust that when a test failed, it was due to a real code issue within a specific scenario related to the record that failed the test, and not bad test data. This saved lots of wasted time. Our business lead now had time to research the data anomalies and decide whether to fix them in the source, provide business rules to address them, or determine whether they should be included in the initial load. She was also able to clarify data input standards on the source system going forward, so we could avoid this problem with the next inevitable acquisition or data integration.

Can you spot some of the agile practices that Lynn used in her story? Guiding development with examples is the first one we noticed. It's not the normal format we think about, but the practice is the same. Provide real examples, and then code to make the tests pass. The second practice that stood out for us was the business lead creating the test data based on the most important scenarios. They used small experiments with fast feedback to evolve their testing and coding approach.

Managing Data for Tests

In this next story, **Jeff "Cheezy" Morgan** *shares a pattern that he found useful when he was trying to automate and populate test data.*

A few years ago I was working with a team that was developing a data warehousing application using ETL. The source was a very large database with about 140 tables, and the target was a large star schema database (Wikipedia, 2014n).

When I first arrived, the testers were testing the application by running about 500,000 records through the system each night. When they came to work the next morning, they ran queries against the source to find records that matched the condition they wished to test. Once they found an appropriate record, they looked for the same record in the target and interrogated the data to make sure the business rule was triggered and that it correctly modified the data. Needless to say, this process was extremely laborious and error-prone.

Right away I wanted to automate the process, but in order to begin the automation I needed a way to set up the data in the source. It was very intimidating to think about having each test insert data into so many tables. The complexity was going to be enormous, so I began looking for a way to simplify the test data management.

I soon discovered that each business rule performing the ETL process looked at only a small subset of the overall data passing through it to determine if it should trigger the rule or not. I realized that for each test, I could simply populate the tables with default values. Then for each specific test, I could replace only the few values that changed the outcome of a specific test with the values I wanted for that test. This dramatically simplified everything. It took me four days to create a framework that provided this ability. After that, each tester was able to supply specific values for a small subset of data needed to verify a particular test case and let the test use the default values for everything else. Figure 22-2 shows this setup.

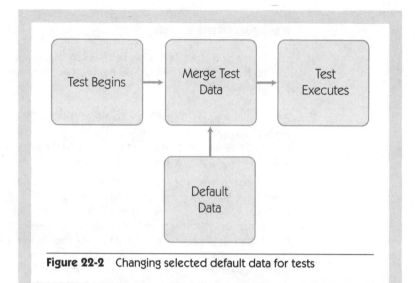

Figure 22-2   Changing selected default data for tests

The next project I worked on was a web application. I soon discovered that the same pattern applied. A lot of data was needed for each test workflow, but the amount of data that actually changed the outcome of the tests was a small subset. By specifying only the subset of data and allowing a framework to populate the remainder, I was able to simplify the tests.

The final discovery that I made was when I started executing the tests in parallel in order to get them to finish within a shorter amount of time. When you do this, you lose control over the order in which your tests run. If two tests running at the same time are trying to use the same data, it is likely that each will modify the data the other needs, and one or both of the tests will fail. To avoid this type of failure, you can use automation to randomize the data used by the tests so that each test has its own unique input values, and multiple tests can safely be run concurrently.

Data management can be painful. Writing scripts to iteratively create data sets may be preferable to extracting and scrubbing vast quantities of data from a production database. One approach is to iteratively build a data generator. Start with records that test the simplest rules, and then add support for different rules as you identify them. For example, null values, orphan records, and high-cardinality records may provide useful tests for the integrity of the data transformations and reporting. Building a generator rather than manually creating records allows your team to scale your data once you are happy with your functional coverage.

BIG DATA

Big Data is a challenge for many organizations. The concepts of volume, velocity, and variety are really what define Big Data, and traditional data warehouse approaches may not scale sufficiently for testing. When performance and data volume are high-priority considerations, agile teams need creative testing solutions.

Testing Performance and Scale in Agile

In testing a product that operates on a Big Data scale, **Adam Knight** *addresses one of the biggest challenges for testing agile projects: ensuring that the software meets the performance and scale requirements within the short time-boxed iterations available for testing.*

One of the biggest challenges when testing a data warehouse or data processing system is ensuring that the system can meet the performance and scalability demands that are placed on it. Performance and scale are important quality characteristics of any application development. However, they are a particular priority for systems that manage large quantities of data.

This presents something of a challenge to agile teams. When working in small teams, testing sufficiently against performance targets within the short sprint iterations can appear to be a daunting task. In production environments, it can take many days or weeks to accumulate the volume of data that constitutes the operating capacity of Big Data systems. We rarely have the luxury of these timescales within agile sprints.

Scale at Speed

In the past, a brute-force approach to testing at scale may have been an option as part of a nonfunctional phase of a staged testing project. In an agile context, we need to be creative when testing these important characteristics at the required scale and at the speed needed for agile development. Over the years of tackling exactly these types of problems, my team has come up with a number of approaches to help us:

- **Scaling layers:** In order to process large data volumes in parallel, large data systems typically incorporate scalability layers of metadata within them. These often take the form of metadata indexes or databases. If we can understand and control these layers, we can quickly generate installations that exhibit the same characteristics as production systems in terms of the metadata processing but require a fraction of the time and space to generate. Working with the programmers to understand the metadata structures of the application and how to manipulate these is an excellent approach to help in testing the scalability of the various system components in isolation.

- **Backup and restore:** By making use of our own backup and restore mechanisms, we can quickly generate environments in which we can test, whilst also creating extra confidence in our disaster recovery capabilities.

- **Static installations:** One effective approach is to maintain a number of environments that are populated with data at production scale against which we can schedule checks of key performance targets. In the simplest approach, we maintain a static system where we exercise new versions of our querying engines. In more advanced testing we maintain a rolling test in order to continuously cycle data in and out of a fully populated system. In this way we test the performance of the features at realistic scale without having to build the data up from scratch for every run of the tests.

Automating for Scale

As well as approaches to managing the software and data, there are a number of techniques within our automation harnesses that specifically help us target testing scalability and performance targets:

- **Iteration:** If we design our test packs carefully, our automation harnesses support the ability to run these iteratively. This allows us to scale up to large volumes of data loads and track the performance of other system operations. We can use iterative automation in exploratory testing to allow us to examine characteristics with increasing activity, or as part of ongoing testing such as running iterative tests against static installations as mentioned previously.

- **Parallelization:** Most data processing systems support parallel processing across multiple CPU cores or machines in order to manage the volumes of data that are involved. It seems inevitable that our test automation must then also run in parallel if we are to exercise the application realistically. The ability to execute tests in parallel allows testers to drive realistic mixed workloads that deterministically exercise the multiple processes that we would expect to see when running a clustered application. It is sensible both to parallelize activity within a single test run and to parallelize automated test runs on different machines. This allows different workloads and types of tests to be run on different environments, optimizing the information that we obtain within an iteration. Smaller nightly test runs for the most important tests, combined with large-scale weekend testing across dozens of servers, allow us to develop quickly and with confidence. We also are able to maintain large-scale test suites that provide confidence in larger-scale characteristics.

- **Monitoring:** In addition to the outputs required to furnish checks, we capture information on the executing software and its environment whilst tests are executing. As we run tests iteratively and in parallel, we use the information gathered to graph system characteristics and model system behavior to identify potential scalability problems.

When working in an agile manner, it is easy to overlook testing of performance and system scalability. However, these are essential quality characteristics of data storage and analysis applications. By adopting a philosophy of making performance integral to our testing and using some creative ideas in both exploring and checking approaches, we can achieve a surprising amount of confidence in these characteristics, even within short iterations.

Big Data is a new and growing challenge for many teams and requires a diligent and multifaceted approach such as the one Adam describes. Performance testing in data warehousing is required to establish whether the application or system is capable of handling the ingestion of data and query workload. If, for example, the hardware or database software is not capable of processing the workload, attempts at performance tuning will not help. If the hardware and database can accommodate the scale of work, though, the team can take steps to tune the performance, measuring results and rerunning to evaluate results. Testing can help identify key scenarios, but having testers work in tandem with the programmers in an iterative manner pays off in ensuring data quality.

Summary

Testing in a data warehouse or business intelligence system is a good example of a context that stretches the bounds of agile for a development team. In this chapter we shared ideas that we hope will help struggling teams.

- Consider the specialized skills your team will need to test a data warehouse or business intelligence system and fill gaps with training or bringing in people with those in-depth skills.
- In-depth technical skills, along with broad business domain knowledge, are needed to succeed with testing BI and DW systems.
- Agile principles and values such as testing early and using fast feedback apply to software that builds data to help with business decisions.
- To meet the challenge of verifying performance and scalability when dealing with huge amounts of data, look for creative ways to use metadata, parallelize automated test processing, and work in layers.
- Monitor system data in test and production to evaluate scalability and check for system response to edge cases.
- Remember privacy and security concerns when testing DW and BI systems.
- Data integrity is critical to business intelligence. If the data is bad, the decisions based on that data will be bad. Make sure the test data reflects real data.
- Keep in mind that scaling and performance need to be addressed from the beginning. Build your test strategy to scale with Big Data.

Chapter 23

TESTING AND DEVOPS

We've worked for many years with team members who do activities that are now called DevOps. As Jez Humble says, team members engaged in DevOps build "a platform that allows developers to self-service environments for testing and production (and deployments to those environments)" (Humble, 2012). They provide tools that enable delivery teams to build, test, deploy, and run their systems. In our experience, everyone on agile teams is doing DevOps activities, but one or more team members contribute in-depth specialized skills. Giving the skill set a label has called attention to its importance in building quality into software. DevOps is an integral component of successful agile testing.

A SHORT INTRODUCTION TO DEVOPS

The term *DevOps* was first popularized by the DevOps Days conference in Belgium in 2009. Since then there have been some excellent publications devoted to DevOps and how it fits into agile development. *Continuous Delivery* (Humble and Farley, 2010) and *DevOps for Developers* (Hüttermann, 2012) are two good guides to DevOps.

DevOps includes practices and patterns that improve collaboration among different roles in delivery teams, streamlining the process of delivering high-quality software. These practices and patterns help teams write testable, maintainable code, package the product, deploy it, and support the deployed code.

One area of focus for DevOps is shortening cycle times. Some businesses are able to take this to an extreme, delivering new code to production

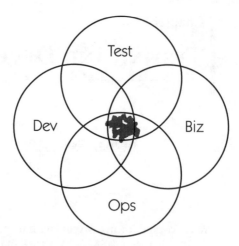

Figure 23-1   Intersection of development, testing, operations, and the business: the whole-team approach!

many times per day. Delivery team members find reliable, repeatable ways to get from an idea to delivered business value, with a cycle time that's not only short, but safe. This helps prevent defects and build in quality.

DevOps activities are designed to improve the maintainability and speed of automated tests and deployment. Examples include maintaining test environments, providing fast feedback from continuous integration (CI), and ensuring reliable and frequent—perhaps even continuous— deployment. Many teams now test their infrastructure continually to guard against spurious intermittent regression test failures due to server, deployment, or configuration failures. Business stakeholders are also involved, helping to hire the right people, obtain the necessary hardware and software, and gather information to guide future development. Figure 23-1 illustrates that DevOps is the intersection of programming, testing, operations, and the business. It is another way to look at the whole-team approach to agile testing.

DevOps and Quality

Agile team members' skills often include scripting, system administration, coding, configuring CI, tooling, and collaboration and communication skills that enable them to perform DevOps activities. These activities are instrumental in agile testing and continually building quality into our products.

Janet's Story

Years ago, before the idea of continuous integration existed (at least in my world), I worked with a person I consider to be one of the first DevOps practitioners. Darcy's role included implementation of our product at client sites, first-level support for clients, keeping our servers running, as well as being our technical tester, setting up our test environments, and keeping them running. He was able to bring what he knew from the world of clients into our testing, including recovery testing. I did not realize the value he brought to the development of our product until I worked in an organization where that crossover role did not exist.

In another organization, we had an infrastructure test team. They worked with the programmers and the teams that supported the hardware and communications. They worked with each of the agile teams to help them understand the impacts of changes to the infrastructure on the new features.

People with specialized operations and system administration skills help the team improve quality on many different fronts. They can help set up appropriate development, test, and staging environments, optimize the CI, and refine the deployment processes for these environments. They can also help find or build and implement automation frameworks and other tools that suit the team's needs. In our experience, they're terrific at diagnosing problems and have many useful tools at their disposal. They can help with the infrastructure to support automated tests, such as generating test data.

Figure 23-2 illustrates the idea that DevOps crosses into all four of the agile testing quadrants. It helps guide development with many different types of testing activities, provides tools and environments for evaluating the product, and builds the technology that enables testing of diverse quality attributes such as performance, reliability, and security.

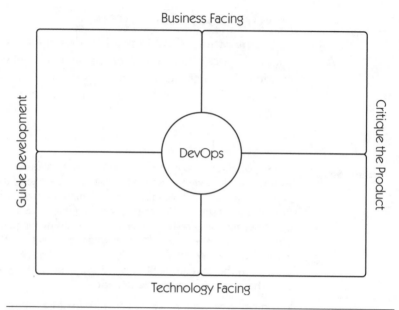

Figure 23-2   Test activities intersect at DevOps.

Lisa's Story

Back in the mainframe days when I worked as a programmer/analyst, I collaborated closely with the machine room operators. Together, we learned ways to solve and prevent problems with processing batch jobs.

In the early 1990s I was fortunate to learn UNIX system administration skills from experts on my team. I learned the importance of repeatable release processes and ways to verify the packaged product. In the 2000s, my teammates with in-depth system administration skills helped find better test automation frameworks and ways to configure CI jobs for quicker test feedback. They showed me how to use monitoring and log files to help with debugging and exploring.

My current team is the first I've worked with that uses the term *DevOps*. We have a backlog of DevOps user stories to improve all aspects of our infrastructure, including our test environments, CI, and deployment process. Interested team members join a weekly DevOps meeting to prioritize work, and these activities are planned along with product features. Programmers work with the company that hosts our production site and maintains our search engine software. We do our own production deploys and can respond quickly to operational problems. We experiment with ways to continually improve our delivery process.

Some companies maintain separate operations or IT departments. The members of these silos often have to support multiple teams, juggling development needs with production maintenance. They may lose touch with the development teams and their needs.

Lisa once facilitated a workshop for a large company where participants from teams working on different product areas identified issues that were impeding various aspects of their testing. Testers complained that the other parts of the system had incompatibilities with theirs, and they had no idea how to overcome these. One of the workshop participants was from the operations department. Once he saw the obstacles that were listed, he said, "I had no idea you were struggling with this. My team can take care of these problems. From now on, contact me directly!" Sometimes solving a thorny testing problem just takes getting people from different departments in the same room.

Seeing the Whole: Add Infrastructure to the Testing Scope, DevOps Style

Michael Hüttermann, *author of* DevOps for Developers (Hüttermann, 2012), *shares a success story he had with a whole-team approach to supporting infrastructure and testing through DevOps.*

In a bigger project with about 100 developers, we had to cope with aggressive time-to-market targets, protecting competitive advantages, a lot of technical complexity, as well as high demands on availability and capacity. These were the main drivers to implement the DevOps approach. This approach included applying "the infrastructure as code" paradigm, which starts with putting Puppet manifests to version control, in our case Git. [*Authors' note:* See the "Tools" section of the bibliography for links to all tools mentioned in this chapter.]

An end-to-end, department-spanning delivery pipeline was in place, starting with stage 0, the developer workspace, and closing with higher test machines, a production mirror, and production. From the version control system, baselines were created continuously. Those baselines contained different configuration units that made up a release, including business code, unit tests, integration tests, and infrastructure information. Building on top of these baselines, we created release candidates continuously. Cherry-picked release candidates were promoted to be released to production. Those releases were both fit for purpose (by containing the functional scope) and fit for use (by conforming to the nonfunctional requirements).

After we applied DevOps concepts, the processes and tools of both development and operations were aligned with each other. Each used the same approaches to provision machines, including installation and configuration of infrastructure, middleware, and the business application. Development and operations continually collaborated to ensure maximum knowledge and open information exchange. We had slack time to learn and experiment, and we built mutual respect. We used kanban to manage the flow and reviewed the design early in the process. This enabled early and frequent learning, and "failing fast."

By applying DevOps practices, service-level requirements and service capabilities could be defined and checked early in the process. Developer machines and test machines were production-like, thus they delivered fast and meaningful feedback of installation and configuration, as well as nonfunctional requirements such as security and monitoring.

As part of the continuous delivery platform, Puppet was used together with Vagrant and Jenkins to set up and remove virtual machines for reproducible testing of the provisioning process itself, as well as the defined result on the target machine.

In order to find errors early and often, we started with checking for more basic failure categories. As part of a continuous build, the infrastructure code in the form of Puppet manifests was validated early in the process. When syntactical errors in the manifests were found immediately, the process was aborted and no binaries were produced for further usage. Finding this category of errors is easy to achieve by just applying a `puppet parser validate` as part of a dedicated build step in the continuous build.

After the actual configuration of the target test environment with Puppet, another downstream stage was added to check the correct provisioning. We introduced test manifests that were applied by `puppet apply-noop` to check for Puppet compilation errors, and then checked the resulting log of events. A basic automated smoke test compared actual and desired results.

When the delivery pipeline was mature enough, we added code-style verifications. We found it helpful to agree on a shared format for all our artifacts. Many checks on business code were done with SonarQube, but we also checked style guide compliance of infrastructure code with `puppet-lint`.

Applying DevOps practices taught us that it was crucial to foster the spirit of the "one team" that consists of members of development, coders, testers, business, and operations, along with network, systems, and database engineers. All involved experts became developers of the solution.

The combined team shared business goals such as reducing cycle time. Shared processes, such as using the same provisioning concept for all machines, and shared tools, such as Puppet, also aligned the combined team. Many production incidents are caused by changes to the IT infrastructure or by unplanned work, such as firefighting production incidents due to broken processes or badly tested solutions. Puppet allowed us to define executable specifications of target infrastructure behavior, making the infrastructure testable. This made automation reliable, which shortened feedback cycles. The documentation about the machines is always up-to-date, facilitating conversations between developers and operations staff.

It was elementary to distinguish between accountability and responsibility. Colleagues of the "one team" of devs and ops were collectively responsible, but only one person from the development department was accountable for development machines and one person from the operations department was accountable for operations machines. Other colleagues who were neither responsible nor accountable were consulted or informed, early and often.

Overall it was a great success to emphasize the entire flow of work from start (inception) to end (operation), to extend agile development testing practices to operations, and to intensively include operations staff starting with the early phases of software development.

To achieve the reliable test automation and shortened feedback cycles that Michael's team enjoyed, you need to understand your build pipeline. Know what tests run in which environment. The concept of build pipelines works well for talking about test environments. Building good test environments has been an obstacle to many of the testers and teams with which Janet has worked. In Chapter 5, "Technical Awareness," Figure 5-2 was an example of a very simple build pipeline. Generally speaking, there is an automated push to the development environment if the CI tests all pass. However, one of the practices that we recommend is to use a pull system for the test environment. This gives testers control over their test execution. In our opinion, there is nothing worse than to be halfway through an exploratory test cycle, only to have the build

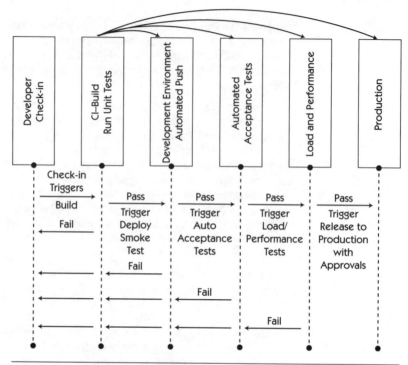

Figure 23-3   Automated build pipeline

you were testing overwritten. That often means starting the testing over from scratch.

Figure 23-3 is a diagram of an automated build pipeline. If you compare it to the simple build pipeline in Figure 5-2, you'll see that the test and the staging environments in this example are not part of the automation. Those are two environments where you would perform exploratory testing.

In Chapter 18, "Agile Testing in the Enterprise," we presented Dell's testing strategy for its enterprise solution. This next story gives more details on the infrastructure needed.

Automated Build Verification Testing

Kareem Fazal, *a software engineer at Dell, talks more about their complex build verification and how they adapted it after their first attempts.*

The Hardware Test-Matrix Challenge

One of the challenges faced in virtually all of our software test environments at Dell Enterprise Solutions Group (ESG) is the extensive hardware compatibility matrix that our software is expected to support. This is most evident in our Server Systems Management firmware and software projects supporting our twelfth-generation servers. When we first applied agile practices to our 12G servers, we established a CI and automated build verification test (aBVT) environment. This CI and aBVT environment supported a project with 15 Scrum teams distributed across India and the United States. Since new code was checked in several times an hour, there was a constant demand for frequent, "known-good" builds. The automated build and tests needed to finish within 90 minutes, running against multiple physical unit-under-test (UUT) environments that were configured with specific network interface card (NIC) and RAID combinations.

The procedures that we initially used for aBVT were not very flexible. It was difficult to add test suites that did not follow a predefined interface format to the existing suite. Also, since test cases were bound to servers, if a specific configuration was required that wasn't already in place, a server had to be taken offline and reconfigured. This meant that we had to be very careful about what tests were run and how much time a test scenario took in order to balance resource use with testing requirements. Under these conditions, it was easier to simply reduce the number of tests run and limit each test run to only those test cases that matched the hardware configuration that was in place. To make matters worse, this was a single-threaded environment, so although there were multiple incoming build requests every hour, they were bottlenecked behind the single, in-progress build verification test run.

The Solution

In preparation for the next update release, the CI and aBVT team took steps to address the limitations of the test environment. The build team envisioned a solution that provided

- Scrum teams with "ease of use" in developing and submitting test cases to achieve maximum hardware coverage
- Build teams with "efficient use of hardware resources" without requiring manual intervention between test runs
- Scrum teams with the "flexibility" to prioritize test cases on specific configurations

In response, our team developed the generic resource manager (GRM). The GRM achieved the flexibility and ease of use we were seeking by having all configurations defined by a simple set of stand-alone XML files. The name space was defined in a way that did not place arbitrary limitations on what information could be defined, while remaining basically simple and easy to understand. The manner in which the configuration was used allowed for good scalability as well. The tester could define as much or as little information for each testing scenario as was required with very little superfluous effort.

The GRM achieved efficient use of server resources by making sure that they were used in parallel as much as possible, and it allocated resources based on the test requirements. If a test takes longer than expected or ends with an error, the GRM adapts to the conditions at hand. Resource requirements that are defined for a particular test can be as broad or as narrow as required without having an effect on other tests in the test run.

The GRM can be used for small-test setups, but it can also scale and support complex scenarios with many types of resources and thousands of tests in the mix. This is accomplished with a robust, easy-to-understand configuration methodology using a standard XML file format.

Results

With the deployment of the GRM into the aBVT environment, the teams were able to maximize test matrix coverage for each run of a test suite. Because test cases for a particular run did not always require, or consume, all available configurations, additional aBVT runs were initiated in parallel, to make maximum use of available configurations. The GRM provided the build team with the flexibility to scale up and add configurations and test cases without disabling any in-progress test runs, easing maintenance concerns.

As you can see from Kareem's story about his experiences, there is no "one size fits all." Dell ESG custom-built a flexible solution that worked for teams around the globe. Look at your own environments, and strive to simplify the build and deploy and test cycle so that it is consistent and maintainable.

How Testers Add DevOps Value

One area of DevOps where testers can contribute their specialized skills is in helping to test the infrastructure. They can help identify places where infrastructure might break simply by asking questions like, "How do we test what happens if the network goes down?" Testers may not know all the answers, but they are good at asking questions.

Janet worked with a company whose infrastructure testing group worked closely with the individual feature teams, but on a more formal basis. They created an agreement with the teams that looked something like this.

The "Levels of Service" that infrastructure testers are prepared to provide are:

- *No involvement: If testing is required, it will be planned, executed, and monitored by a representative from a team appropriate to the activity (e.g., DBA, Network, Infrastructure).*
- *Guidance: Infrastructure testers will provide guidance to assist with planning an appropriate test. The test will be executed by a representative from a team appropriate to the activity (e.g., DBA, Network, Infrastructure). Testers may review test results and assist with risk assessment for a release/acceptance decision.*
- *Planning: Infrastructure testers will prepare a risk-based test plan that defines the testing approach and scope, lists tests to be conducted and acceptance criteria, and identifies risks associated with the project. This plan will be turned over to a representative from a team appropriate to the activity (e.g., DBA, Network, Infrastructure) for execution. Infrastructure testers may review test progress and results and assist with risk assessment for a release/acceptance decision.*
- *Infrastructure testing: Testers will prepare a risk-based test plan that defines the testing approach and scope, lists tests to be conducted and acceptance criteria, and identifies risks associated with the project. Infrastructure testers will execute the tests, providing feedback to*

the project team on execution status. Issues will be recorded, tracked, actioned, and escalated using the standard defect-tracking system. Infrastructure testers will present test results and risk assessment for a release/acceptance decision.

Those definitions are more formal than we'd normally use in agile teams. However, it shows how testing specialists can contribute in different situations, helping to manage risk and provide feedback about the infrastructure, including the test and production environments. Earlier in the chapter we learned how Michael Hüttermann's teams tested their infrastructure using open-source tools such as Puppet, Vagrant, and Jenkins. We'll look at more examples.

Testing Infrastructure

Stephan Kämper, *a tester from Germany, explains more details about how he tests infrastructure.*

In my context, the infrastructure is the extra hardware and software that you need to execute tests. It typically includes a CI system, including jobs the system executes; build tools like make, rake, or Maven; and the machines on which the CI runs. Whether or not the (wireless) network or firewall should also be considered part of your testing infrastructure depends on your own context.

In my current team (as of late 2013), we run automated checks against every single commit to the source control system, create new software artifacts (deployable build items) regularly, and run stand-alone integration tests against these artifacts on newly built virtual machines. These artifacts are put through a system integration test and finally brought onto the production system via the CI system.

The whole workflow, from a single commit to production, is orchestrated and supported by the CI system. Since we wrote the code to do all this, it seemed like a very good idea to also test it. The ability to go live with changes depends on that code.

What Part of the Infrastructure to Test

I do not suggest that you test your CI system as such, and neither do I recommend that you test your build system. However, I do think the code you write and feed to these systems should indeed be tested.

As an example, let's assume you're using Jenkins as the CI system and rake as the build tool. We use the Jenkins Job DSL/Plugin, which allows us to write Jenkins jobs as code, in contrast to the usual way of setting them up via the graphical user interface. That way we can have our Jenkins code under version control.

Since rake tasks are Ruby code, the tasks delegate the work to Ruby classes, modules, or methods, which in turn can be developed and tested like any other code. The same is certainly possible for other combinations of build systems and programming languages.

One Caveat

Some Jenkins jobs actually change the "world"—that is, they deploy software to production systems. This is hard to test in a laboratory environment since the whole point of a production system is, well, leaving the safety of a test environment.

But even in this case, you can parameterize the Jenkins jobs so that you can deploy to a test or staging system and production using the same script. That way, deploying to a test system is in fact the test for deploying to production. Note that even when this works nicely, the deployment to production may still be broken, since you might deploy to the wrong server.

Stephan emphasizes the value of testing automated deployments. Other types of infrastructure testing that testers might perform are often part of Quadrant 4 tests, including connectivity, reliability, failover, or backup and restores.

Teams are often called upon to test in production, monitoring site activity or performance. Pairing to monitor production log files has advantages similar to those of pair programming and testing. It is easy to concentrate on one thing and completely miss another, so a second pair of eyes is invaluable.

We've talked about what DevOps does for testing and quality and how testers can help with DevOps activities. In the final part of this section, we'll cover the intersection of both.

Automated Provisioning of Configuration Base States

Ben Frempong, *a storage test engineer, continues the Dell story, describing how they automated configuration base states to make the setup for testing much easier.*

In mid-2012, our Storage Test team was faced with budget and staffing challenges. We had to devise a sustainable solution to a reality that faces most test organizations at one time or another: how to do more with fewer resources while continuously improving the quality of products we deliver to our customers. The solution required us to reinvent and implement sustainable and innovative automation strategies in our testing process to achieve three key goals:

1. Maximize the utilization of our hardware resources.
2. Improve the efficiency of our test execution staff.
3. Capture automation metrics.

The first task was to establish some standards for our automation initiatives. We chose Python as our standard scripting language and selected a centralized, internally developed automation framework for remote script deployment. Next, we focused on two teams that had similar needs: one local and the other remote. After analyzing their daily tasks, we organized their testing activities into the following workflow sequence:

1. Configure base hardware.
2. Install OS.
3. Install updates (firmware/BIOS/OS device drivers).
4. Install solution/product peripherals.
5. Install and configure solution/product-specific packages.
6. Run a suite of manual and automated test cases.
7. Perform exploratory testing.
8. Tear down and reprovision the system for another configuration.

I observed that the first three steps, the base state of provisioning workflows, was often a manual, time-consuming, and repetitive sequence of tasks with the same operating system, on the same hardware or platform families. There were sometimes minor configuration changes such as add-in storage peripherals, but these changes did not impact the base state of any configuration. Additionally, the base state configurations often had to be redeployed to validate software build releases or bug fixes during a program's test cycles. An automated process could be used to create disk images, files containing the contents and structure of a disk volume or data storage device, with the necessary base configurations. These images could be used to automatically reprovision each configuration's base state.

Existing imaging solutions at that time worked very well in large-deployment environments but not so well in test environments, where one is continuously reprovisioning the same hardware. Also, they took up to 90 minutes or more, depending on the operating system, to capture an image. It might take several hours to restore non-Windows images such as Linux OS. This explained why testers preferred the manual method. We tried to automate existing off-the-shelf imaging solutions, but no single solution supported automated image capture and restores for all three required system environments that we needed to support: Windows, Linux, and ESXi5. Considering the matrix of hardware that needed to be validated, we would have to either purchase more hardware and assign more configurations per tester, or add more testers. Due to our budget challenges, neither solution was an option.

Instead, we prioritized automating the provisioning workflows with some innovative ideas by developing our own fully automated imaging/redeployment solution. First, we repackaged the kernel for the open-source imaging tool Clonezilla to work with our automation framework. Next, we wrote fully automated imaging and redeployment scripts for Windows, Linux, and ESXi5 images. These scripts automatically capture and redeploy base-state images in 10 to 15 minutes or less.

The results have been positive. One of the project teams had typically required up to three testers per test iteration to cover 12 to 18 configurations. After implementing the automated imaging and restore tasks, the team lead was able to single-handedly execute the test iteration himself without additional resources. He even had more time for exploratory testing because the test execution framework allowed him to launch a sequence of automated tasks, which could run overnight or during lunch.

With our new approach to workflow test automation, we are now able to do more with fewer resources, while giving our skilled staff more time for exploratory testing. This allows us to continue to deliver quality products. We are also able to reduce expenditure and maximize the utilization of our hardware resources. Last, from a process perspective, we are able to use the information about our automation capabilities in our test planning, test strategy, and business decisions.

Testers, programmers, and operations experts can collaborate on the CI process to make build jobs more robust, test results more reliable, and deploys to various environments timely and sane. If the whole team understands their operating environments, they may save many hours spent investigating test failures. For example, DevOps may be able to help create checks for connectivity or configuration before deploying, which eliminates wasted time rejecting builds. Alternatively, testers and programmers can analyze test suites to identify duplicate tests, tests that don't add value, and ways to improve reliability. They can also look for gaps in regression test automation and work to fill them.

DevOps practices help our teams efficiently build regression test code and deploy it as needed to environments that support effective exploratory testing. Skilled DevOps practitioners help us implement tools to support testing all necessary quality attributes such as security, performance, and reliability. These abilities are essential for cross-functional teams to deliver high-quality software that provides business value frequently, at a sustainable pace.

SUMMARY

DevOps is a perfect example of the whole-team approach to quality at work. It brings together generalizing specialists with different T-shaped skills to help ensure several aspects of quality. Even when development and operations are separate departments, they can work together to achieve shared goals. Here are some points about DevOps that we covered in this chapter:

- DevOps is a blend of development, testing, and operations engaged in practices that streamline the delivery process, provide timely feedback to improve cycle time and software quality, and facilitate collaboration among all roles on the team.
- Team members with operations and system administration skills collaborate with other team members to build a CI and deployment infrastructure that supports short cycle times.
- Development teams, including testers, can help implement a test-guided approach to building that infrastructure and ensure that the infrastructure continues to operate effectively.

- DevOps practitioners help build and implement test automation drivers, libraries and frameworks, and test data generation tools.
- Understand your team's build pipeline and test environments to take advantage of where you can use automation to supplement your exploratory test efforts.
- Each organization needs to experiment with different hardware configurations to find ones that provide flexibility, consistency, and maintainability.
- Testers can contribute to infrastructure testing by asking good questions and helping with a risk-based approach as well as by actively engaging in testing configuration and deployment.
- Automating the provisioning of configuration base states lets teams do more with fewer resources, using sustainable automation strategies that provide useful metrics and enable more exploratory testing time.
- DevOps can help the team find ways to overcome impediments such as fragile or slow automated tests.

Part VIII

AGILE TESTING IN PRACTICE

We wrap up *More Agile Testing* with recommendations we feel will do the most to help you and your team build quality into your software products. One crucial practice is making testing activities transparent and providing information that's accessible and easy to understand. Visibility makes impediments immediately obvious, promotes discussion and collaboration, and provides guideposts along the way, as we strive to continually improve our process and our software. In this part we and our contributors share ways to make testing activities highly visible.

Finally, we share practices that build confidence in delivering software products that give value to our customers and our business. Using examples to guide development, exploratory testing, feature testing, continual learning, context sensitivity, and keeping it real while testing help teams gain courage and continually improve. The Pillars of Testing, explained by David Evans, give us the base from which to grow our confidence in releasing software changes.

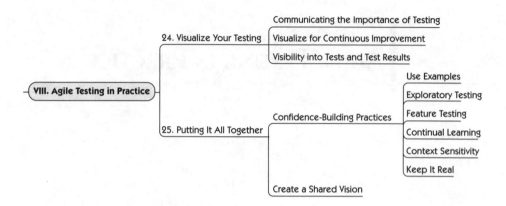

- **Chapter 24,** "Visualize Your Testing"
- **Chapter 25,** "Putting It All Together"

Chapter 24

VISUALIZE YOUR TESTING

One reason agile development works so well is that it makes the development process transparent. Walk into any agile team's work area, and you'll likely see some big visible charts. You can tell at a glance what the team is working on, what impediments may be in its way, how much work has been completed, and whether or not the regression tests are currently passing. We devoted a section of *Agile Testing* (pp. 354–66) to preparing for visibility. Here, we'll explore more ways to increase the visibility of testing in an agile team.

COMMUNICATING THE IMPORTANCE OF TESTING

Agile teams represent work that is planned, in progress, and completed in visual ways, with sticky notes or cards in rows and columns on a wall, or an online project-tracking tool that simulates a physical board. Anyone who looks at the board should be able to understand at a glance what testing activities are planned, which are in progress, and what stories have been tested and accepted.

Making testing tasks highly visible encourages team members to take on uncompleted tasks, even those that fall outside their area of specialty. Impediments can also be clearly represented, so that they are addressed in a timely manner. These boards should be designed to help the team focus on completing one story at a time, or at least a small set of stories. They help teams remember to complete testing activities for a story before rushing to start the next story.

Kanban and Testing

> **Steve Rogalsky,** *an agilist at Protegra, explains how kanban boards provide one way to make testing activities highly visible.*

Some Background

I'll start by saying that my first agile experiences were Scrum-like. Once I started to understand agile, I quickly gravitated to flow-based systems like kanban. It took me a while to get comfortable with kanban's work-in-progress (WIP) limits. For the first several projects, we ignored WIP limits and instead paid attention to the board—our goal was balance instead of limits. Once we got tired of trying to keep the board in balance ourselves, we switched to WIP limits.

Note that we pair our kanban flow-based approach with a few events that happen every two weeks—demos, planning/design meetings, and retrospectives. Also, we don't currently have trained testers on our team. Our business analysts and programmers share the testing load. We do have customers who do a final acceptance test, but they are trained as business experts and only recently have started testing due to this project. They are learning fast and help us a lot!

Our Board

Our initial boards were pretty basic. "Ready," "WIP," and "Done" columns were soon replaced by "Ready," "Analysis," "Development," "Testing," and "Done" columns. After getting exposure to the "Get Kanban" game, we added a "Ready for Next Status" column.

Our board has gone through a few iterations since then, but Figure 24-1 shows what we are currently using.

Figure 24-1   Steve's kanban board

The "Analysis & Design" column includes sub-columns of "WIP" and "Ready for Dev." The goal of this "WIP" column is to write test cases (examples) with our customers to make sure we understand what they expect from this story. The definition of "Ready for Dev" is test cases (examples) written down and reviewed by the customer with at least one failing test. (Of course, at the start, all of them are likely to be failing tests.)

The "Development" column includes sub-columns of "WIP," "Ready for Smoke Test," "Smoke Test," and "Ready for QA." "Ready for Smoke Test" indicates that the story is deployed to our test environment, it has been code reviewed, and the developer thinks that all tests pass. We define smoke test to mean that an analyst, programmer, or tester has tested the feature and believes that all the test cases pass. A story qualifies for "Ready for QA" when all its smoke tests pass.

The sub-columns of the "QA" column are "WIP" and "Ready for Final Approval." Here's where our customer makes a final pass. At this point we would be very surprised if they find a defect or missed test case. If they do find something, we try to fix it immediately and add any missing tests if necessary. The definition of "Ready for Final Approval" is that the customer believes all test cases pass, and the story is complete. The final approval rests with our main customer. She's pretty busy so she doesn't test everything, but she wants to have a final look before moving any story to the "Complete" column.

How do we define "complete"? The customer is happy, and it's ready to deploy!

How It Relates to Testing and Testers

We've seen several benefits from using a flow-based system. It provides powerful visualization. Everyone, including testers, can see what is coming up and prepare for it. Since our definitions in most of the kanban columns include the phrases "passing tests" or "failing tests," it communicates the importance of testing to the whole team and supports a whole-team approach to quality.

The "Ready for" columns offer a lot of freedom from task assignment. We all pull our own work rather than having work assigned by a manager. With almost no exceptions, once we move a card to "Complete," it doesn't come back. When the board becomes unbalanced, it supports building cross-functional skills. If testers are low on work, they help programmers where they can, or more often they help analysts facilitate and gather the test cases and examples. When programmers or analysts are low on work, they generally look to help with testing first. This creates more understanding on the team about the role and importance of testing. Their experience as testers has nudged both programmers and analysts to pay greater attention to the test cases.

Although we aren't doing any significant pairing yet, we keep seeing small instances of pairing—including development-customer pairing during QA. We hope that trend continues.

On the whole, we love this approach. It gives us a lot of pride and confidence. We get the feeling that Deming smiles down on us every time a story moves to "Complete."

Steve notes that the visualization that the team's board provides is a key benefit. However, Mike Talks reminded us about a potential downside of kanban boards. They allow you flexibility, but if you add too many states to cover all eventualities, you end up draining all the simplicity out of what started as an elegant solution. Constantly review your workflow and ask a question Liz Keogh suggests (Keogh, 2014b): "Is this a useful representation of reality?" If it seems as if tasks are leaping over multiple states, it may be a red flag to indicate that those states may not be relevant.

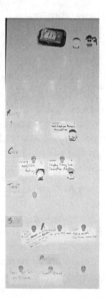

Figure 24-2 A vertical kanban-style board makes use of the only available wall space.

Use your creativity and experiment with different ways to keep testing activities front and center. Lisa worked on a team where the only wall space was on a column in the middle of the room, and two of the five members were remote. The team put a kanban-style board in a vertical format on the column (see Figure 24-2) and posted photos of it each time a card moved in the team wiki. Lisa, who worked remotely, kept her own copy of it on a cupboard door in her home office. She could see at a glance what to work on next.

A simple story board, such as the example in Figure 24-3 with only four columns—"To Do" (or "Ready"), "In Progress," "To Review," and "Done"—is an effective way to visualize testing progress. All tasks, including coding and testing tasks, move along the board. When the team puts in WIP limits at the story level, say only two in-progress stories at a time, team members must help others to complete at least one story before they start the next. When color coding is used to differentiate the testing activities, it is easy to see when they are piled up, either

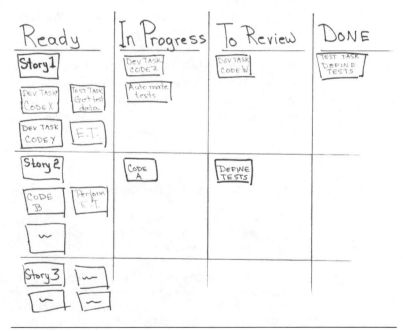

Figure 24-3 Simple story board

"In Progress" or "To Review." This visibility reminds team members to help out on tasks to get each story finished. Perhaps a programmer can help review tests or pair for exploratory testing.

Dispersed and distributed teams may prefer to use an online board to track testing progress along with other development activities, but we encourage those teams to find a way to keep it in front of everyone as much as possible. Some distributed teams use oversize monitors or projectors to keep their online project-tracking board and continuous integration (CI) dashboard on view in each team area.

We provided more story board examples in Chapter 15 of *Agile Testing*, and an online search of "agile big visible charts" or "agile story boards" will provide more examples to fuel your imagination.

VISUALIZE FOR CONTINUOUS IMPROVEMENT

One of the Ten Principles for Agile Testers we described in *Agile Testing* is to practice continuous improvement. We should always be looking for ways to do a better job. Use big visible charts to show goals for improvement, experiments in progress, and results of completed experiments.

In our experience, if your team has an obstacle in its way, it helps to make it visible. When it's "in your face," you remember to do something about it. When you identify areas for improvement in your retrospectives, set SMART goals (specific, measurable, achievable, relevant, timeboxed) or find some way to make the problem more visible. This sets the stage for continuous improvement.

Using Kanban to Continually Improve

Mary Walshe, *a tester at Paddy Power in Ireland, shares her team's experiences with using a kanban system to visualize areas of improvement.*

We have been using kanban in our department for well over a year now and have made huge improvements in our process. We use it to visualize areas that we could improve, to tune our process, and to see where we can experiment. It's a tool that the whole team owns and that we use for continuous improvement. If we notice that the board has not changed in a while, we know that we may be slacking on our experiments.

One of our most recent improvement goals was to try to reduce our cycle times by three days. Our kanban board, and its WIP limits, helped us identify an area of possible improvement. We saw there was a bottleneck in our "Awaiting UAT" column, and conversations began around the duplication of effort in this area.

Multiple user stories delivering business value were spending over three days in acceptance. All that business value could have been getting to our customer three days earlier!

The acceptance bottleneck impacted product owners, developers, business analysts, operations staff, testers—in short, everyone! Product owners spent more time preparing, executing tests, and documenting the activity. Customers had to wait longer for business value to be delivered. Long cycle times meant a longer feedback cycle. Development slowed down. Repeating tests already done during exploratory testing slowed things down.

Our product owners suggested that we try to "pimp the demo," in other words, focus on satisfying product owners with the demo of newly completed work. We did some research and decided to try introducing Demo 2.0. A hypothesis story for this might read something like what is shown in Figure 24-4.

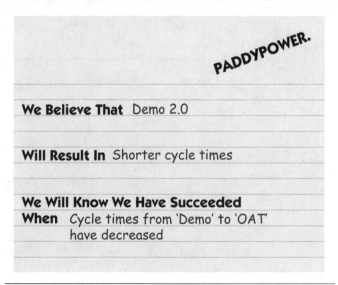

PADDYPOWER.

We Believe That Demo 2.0

Will Result In Shorter cycle times

We Will Know We Have Succeeded When Cycle times from 'Demo' to 'OAT' have decreased

Figure 24-4   Shorter cycle time hypothesis

A few members of the team took it upon themselves to work with our product owners and ensure that Demo 2.0 would satisfy their needs. They wrote a demo script and sent it along with the acceptance test report in the invitation to the demo, which was scheduled in advance with the product owner. During the demo, we walked through the acceptance tests for each feature and executed the demo script. We allowed time for product owners to ask questions and do extra tests as needed.

So that's it. Seems pretty simple, right? As of this writing, it's been nearly a month since the first Demo 2.0. Looking back at our hypothesis story, we have indeed succeeded by decreasing cycle times from demo to operational acceptance testing (OAT).

Let's look at the metrics. In Figure 24-5, we can see that the average cycle time (the lower line) from demo to OAT in September was three days.

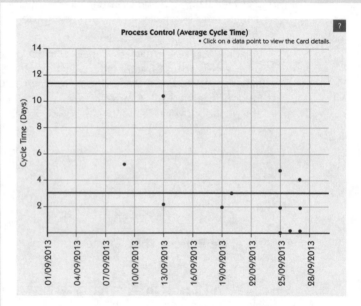

Figure 24-5 Average cycle times from demo to OAT before Demo 2.0

Figure 24-6 shows the cycle times from demo to OAT starting on October 1, the day of the first Demo 2.0. We can see that the average cycle time from demo to OAT in this month has come down to under one day. (*Note:* The scale on the *y* axis was adjusted to provide a better visualization of the differences.)

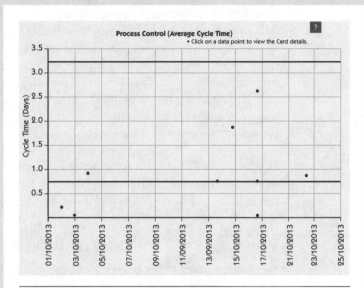

Figure 24-6   Average cycle times from demo to OAT after Demo 2.0

We can see the decreased time via metrics from taking the cycle times from demo to OAT from the previous month of September and comparing them to the current month of October where we introduced Demo 2.0. So, have we succeeded? Yes, we knocked two entire days off our cycle time with this one initiative!

Critics might wonder if the longer demo added to the cycle times from starting a story to accepting it, counteracting the saving of two days, but the metrics show that the demo hasn't increased cycle times. In fact, the time taken in the demo lane has decreased in the last month. This may be due to the fact that reducing waste is in the forefront of the team's mind.

The whole team put a lot of effort into getting this off the ground, including the initial organization of what the new demo would look like, putting it into action, getting feedback, and improving it along the way. All in all, I think Demo 2.0 has been a great success. In the future, we might look at whether we even need the acceptance phase.

Steve's and Mary's stories have much in common. The message isn't that everyone should use a kanban system. Rather, it's essential that a team be able to visualize its testing work and quality level and make this information transparent for the business. You can try any type of story or task board or online tracking system to see if that gives you the visibility you need. It might involve a big monitor displaying live CI results in your team room or something as simple as a whiteboard drawing, spreadsheet, checklist, or wiki page. The main criterion is making it front and center for the whole team and all stakeholders. This transparency helps teams easily identify the biggest problem to work on next. They can brainstorm experiments to chip away at that problem and continually improve their testing efforts.

Don't wait until the end of the iteration to start demonstrating small increments of completed work to your stakeholders. Frequent collaboration helps you stay on track and avoid wasting time.

VISIBILITY INTO TESTS AND TEST RESULTS

We've often heard development teams complain, "We don't know what the testers are doing!" To us, this translates into, "We have no confidence in what is being tested." There are many ways to show what is being tested.

We talked about using testing mind maps to brainstorm with the team in Chapter 7, "Levels of Precision for Planning." Figure 24-7 shows a mind map Lisa and another tester created on a rolling whiteboard to visualize a new batch account fee collection process, which would be integrated into an existing transaction processing system. As they created the mind map, they thought of questions to ask the product owner and programmer. The team used the mind map over several iterations as they worked on the new features. Whenever questions came up, team members would gather in front of the mind map to discuss them. As testing was completed for each mind map node, they checked it off on the whiteboard, making progress visible.

Teams can expand initial acceptance tests to give the whole team visibility into testing. Making them accessible to everyone fosters

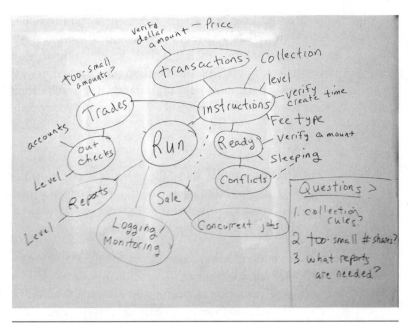

Figure 24-7   A testing mind map

collaboration and encourages developer and customer team members to comment and suggest new ideas.

In Chapter 7, "Levels of Precision for Planning," Figure 7-6 showed an example of a test matrix. This is a simple way to make high-level testing visible to stakeholders outside the team. It also gives a different perspective on testing to help stay away from the problem of getting caught up in stories and forgetting the big picture.

Testing is about providing information as quickly as possible. Think about how you can make the information learned from testing visible. How can you communicate it? How will people in other roles hear and see it? As we discussed in *Agile Testing* (pp. 357–66), visible test results are one of the most important ways we can measure progress.

This information takes many forms. Continuous integration provides a critical snapshot of the current status of your builds and perhaps your automated test runs. Results from exploratory testing sessions can be consolidated in a shared document, a team wiki, or a simple test dashboard. Tests and results can be noted on the story or featured in an online tracking tool. Bug fixes can be captured as automated tests, and defects not fixed immediately can be tracked in as simple and visible a way as possible. Most importantly, test results should be discussed at team standups. Use the feedback to guide your next steps.

SUMMARY

The transparency that agile provides is one of its biggest benefits to an organization. Testing is about providing information, and when we make that information easy to see, everyone can talk about it. It's not enough "just" to be visible—it needs to be useful.

- Look at ways to make various aspects of testing more visible on your story, task, or kanban-style board. If your process has a definition of "ready" and a story isn't on the board until it meets that definition, it's easy to see when a new story is ready for the testing tasks to be addressed.
- Experiment with different styles of physical story boards and, if necessary, online tracking tools to see what provides the most visibility into testing progress for your team.
- Demonstrate new work to customers early and often to make progress visible, get quick feedback, and reduce story cycle times.
- If your team encounters obstacles to successfully completing testing activities, find a way to make those obstacles visible. It can be as simple as a bright red blocker card on a story board.
- Consider techniques such as mind maps that help teams visualize their work and progress. Visual representation helps teams stay grounded in reality.
- Testing generates information about quality and risk. Use a variety of ways to make test results and current status visible to everyone.

Chapter 25

PUTTING IT ALL TOGETHER

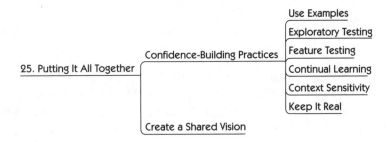

Agile Testing wrapped up with seven key success factors for testing in agile projects. In fact, we feel they are critical for success in any project, whether you call it agile or not. They are:

1. Use the whole-team approach to quality.

2. Adopt an agile testing mindset.

3. Automate regression tests.

4. Provide and obtain feedback.

5. Build a foundation of core agile practices.

6. Collaborate with customers.

7. Look at the big picture.

We and our contributors have shared in this book what we've learned since *Agile Testing* was written, addressing challenges that are becoming more common for teams. The original success factors apply to large enterprise environments, globally distributed teams, testing in different contexts such as mobile and embedded software, data warehouses, and continuously deployed products. However, we have more and better tools and techniques available to help with ongoing challenges.

CONFIDENCE-BUILDING PRACTICES

While we don't believe there are any "best practices," we do believe there are core testing practices that benefit most agile teams. These practices give teams confidence to deliver quality products that delight their customers. With that confidence comes the courage to try new things and continually improve.

Use Examples

Learn to guide development with examples, using acceptance-test-driven development (ATDD), specification by example (SBE) or behavior-driven development (BDD). Make your examples as concrete as possible using visual means where possible (see Figure 25-1).

Among the core development practices we recommend are test-driven development (TDD) and continuous integration (CI). These go a long way toward building quality into the software and learning from fast feedback. However, by themselves they are not enough. When delivering a new feature is complicated, guiding development with business-facing

Figure 25-1   Use real examples.

examples helps prevent stories from being rejected multiple times. When proposed features have high uncertainty or are so complex that it's hard to even come up with examples of desired behavior, you may need some short cycles of spikes and learning before you can distill the information into concrete examples.

We can help our business experts identify the most valuable software features to implement by combining testing and business analysis (BA) mindsets. Agile techniques such as story mapping and impact mapping help the business and development teams focus the team's effort on the right goals. BA techniques such as the 7 Product Dimensions described in Chapter 9, "Are We Building the Right Thing?," further our efforts to create valuable products. Although we don't want to waste time with big up-front analysis of ever-evolving requirements, there are good, quick ways we can flesh out story details before we start coding a particular feature or story.

This information can be turned into tests that guide development, many of which can be automated and form part of the regression suites. It helps ensure that we deliver useful value and helps us build in short feedback loops to learn more as we develop and deliver incrementally. We still have more testing to do once we think coding is finished, but we've minimized the chances of rejection without a huge up-front cost. Part IV, "Testing Business Value," described techniques to help extract desired behaviors and misbehaviors from customers and learn to guide development with examples.

If CI is the heartbeat of an agile team, guiding development with examples is the heart monitor that shows we are on the right track.

Exploratory Testing

Although some early agile teams had testers who did some exploratory testing, the value exploratory testers contribute through their ability to see beyond the story functionality has become more visible in recent years. Testing for business value (testing early) is about preventing defects—exploring ideas if you like. We, however, refer to exploratory testing as testing the software—if you can't prevent defects, find them as early as you can (see Figure 25-2).

Figure 25-2   Explore.

Chapter 12, "Exploratory Testing," discussed several exploratory testing techniques. We encourage you to use the links provided in the bibliography for Part V to experiment to discover what works best for your situation. If some members of your team aren't familiar with exploratory testing, hold a workshop or testing dojo to let them learn and practice techniques.

Some exploratory techniques are ideal for collaborating with other disciplines on the team. Involve your user experience (UX) designers to create user personas. Get testers, programmers, and analysts together to create and prioritize testing charters. Share information learned in exploratory sessions with the developer and customer teams, making the information visible and actionable. Experiment with different approaches, and see what adds the most value for your team.

Feature Testing

Incremental and iterative development is a cornerstone of agile. Slicing stories into a tiny, consistent size helps teams make predictable progress, but in these small components of stories, we may lose the bigger picture. Looking at the big picture is a key success factor. We need techniques

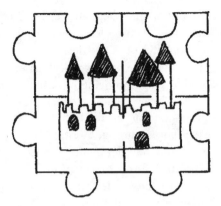

Figure 25-3 Remember the big picture.

to test at the feature level once the building blocks are complete (see Figure 25-3).

Janet often compares feature testing to assembling a jigsaw puzzle. You don't necessarily have to piece together the entire puzzle to derive value from it. She focuses on the parts of the picture that are the most meaningful to her: faces of people in the picture, beautiful sections of scenery (Gregory, 2011).

When we test software features, we must identify the areas of most value to the end users, the parts that "have to work," and focus our testing there. These may not be in the actual functionality; performance, security, or convenience may be what the customer values most.

As your team discusses your next big feature set, think about the different types of testing explained in Chapter 13, "Other Types of Testing," as well as different models such as the agile testing quadrants. Write stories with testing activities that focus on aspects of the feature that users value most. Consider the quality attributes and constraints that affect testing during team conversations.

Continual Learning

Taking time to experiment, using short feedback cycles to evaluate what works and what doesn't, having a sense of personal safety that failure will not be punished—these are all critical components of an environment that nurtures learning (see Figure 25-4). As a team survives its initial transition to agile development and continues over the years, new problems and challenges will arise. To succeed over the long haul, we need to keep improving. We can't do that if we don't learn.

This applies to all disciplines on an agile team, of course. But in our experience, testers and testing are often forgotten in the rush to implement agile development. Testers often don't get any special training. They may also get trapped in a mini-waterfall situation, where stories aren't delivered to test until the last day of the iteration, so that testing is always playing catch-up.

When we're focused on delivering new features, it's hard to step back and take time for learning. Yet if we don't devote time to learning, we may not be able to keep our customers happy.

If you're in a management or lead position, you have a chance to nurture a learning culture. Regardless of your role, try to get your team to discuss areas of testing where the team lacks expertise, and think of ways each team member can grow his or her "T-shaped skills" (as described in Chapter 3, "Roles and Competencies") to cover the missing capabilities.

Figure 25-4 Learning

Context Sensitivity

Be aware that you may need to apply agile principles differently depending on your context. This is one of the main areas we explored in this book, although we're sure we didn't touch on all the different situations out there; new challenges come up every day. Understand your context (see Figure 25-5), and strive to apply agile principles and practices to your environment. (*Note:* We use the word *context* per its *Merriam-Webster* definition as "the situation in which something happens: the group of conditions that exist where and when something happens. We're not discussing "context-driven testing" (Kaner, 2012), though you may want to learn about that, too.)

For example, if you work in a large corporation, you may have to adapt testing around existing organizational controls. You may need additional roles to help coordinate testing activities and manage dependencies across the organization, or maybe even have additional teams for activities such as system-wide testing encompassing multiple applications. More support from the executive level can help effect cultural changes to switch testing mindsets from bug detection to bug prevention.

Figure 25-5 Know your context.

Some software teams must satisfy regulatory requirements for specific documentation. If teams think about the simplest way to provide the necessary evidence required by auditors, they may be able to reduce both the amount of documentation and the time spent on it to a minimum. It may seem counterintuitive at first, but agile testing values and practices work well in this context to comply with regulations and reduce risk for the product.

Distributed teams require innovative approaches to enable adequate collaboration and communication in their context. It's hard for a distributed team to bond if team members never have a chance to meet in person or talk directly to each other. If your team is geographically dispersed, look for creative ways to build trust and enable collaboration so that you can benefit from a whole-team approach to testing. Using tests to help define the specifications is one way to get a better shared understanding of what to build.

Mobile and embedded software teams face extra testing challenges because of the number of platforms and devices supported and many other variables, such as how and where the devices will be used. These teams can improve software quality through collaborating across roles, leveraging automation, and using fast feedback loops.

Business intelligence and data warehouse teams are tasked with making sure business experts have high-quality data for planning and making business decisions. It can be difficult to figure out how to build these systems incrementally and iteratively. Specialized technical skills and business domain expertise may be needed to succeed with agile testing in this context.

New specialized skill sets that focus on testing and quality from an operational point of view have been brought into delivery teams. The whole team engages in DevOps activities to streamline delivery, shorten feedback cycles, improve automated test effectiveness, and ensure that CI, test, and deployment infrastructures support short cycle times. Our software product is more than just the application under test, and DevOps helps expand our testing to encompass all facets of the product and the value it provides to customers. Whatever your team's context, DevOps can help you continually improve software quality.

Keep It Real

At some point we all aspire to have superpowers, and our managers often seem to think we possess them! But as Bob Martin reminds us in *Clean Coder* (Martin, 2011), the best way to be a team player is to inform management what we can realistically accomplish and help them prioritize the highest-value work.

Even if your team doesn't use a flow-based process, the concept of limiting work in progress (WIP) is essential. Each of us has only so much bandwidth. If the testers on the team can test only a maximum of two user stories at any time, it doesn't make sense for the programmers to keep cranking out stories. If the programmers stop new development and help with testing, the team can move forward much more easily. Make testing part of each story and each feature.

Don't succumb to the desire to make customers happy by saying, "We'll try" when you know it's impossible. It takes courage to say no! Experiment with ways to make the testing WIP limit visible. Rather than shrug and say, "We have a testing bottleneck," figure out ways to remove the constraint, such as having the whole team help with testing activities to keep work items moving through at a steady pace. Help your team take a reality check when needed (see Figure 25-6).

Figure 25-6   Reality check

CREATE A SHARED VISION

Your own team, its environment, its constraints, and its shared vision are unique. There's no magical set of agile testing practices that guarantees success. However, agile values and principles guide us. Trying small experiments and building in short feedback loops help us stay on track and make course corrections along the way.

We've described some core testing practices that, in our experience, are valuable for most teams. We find it helpful to take a step back and remember the purpose of testing.

Pillars of Testing

David Evans, an agile quality coach from the UK, reminds us about the purpose of testing and sums it up beautifully with his "Pillars of Testing."

Testing does not produce quality; it produces information about quality. At a high level, the outcome we want from testing is confidence in our decisions to release software changes. Better testing produces greater confidence in those decisions. Therefore, the valuable product of effective testing is Confidence.

In my "Pillars of Testing" model (see Figure 25-7), I map out the connections and dependencies of a number of factors that are critical to raising this confidence. I represent the model as a "temple," with a ceiling, four pillars, foundations, and bedrock.

At the top of our model, Confidence rests upon Courage and Safety. Courage without Safety leads to foolhardiness; Safety without Courage leads to stasis and inaction.

The four pillars that push up our level of confidence in testing are

- **Stronger Test Evidence:** How well do our stakeholders understand what has been tested and when?
- **Better Test Design:** How appropriate, meaningful, and effective are the test cases we use?
- **Higher Test Coverage:** How much of the system is tested compared to our models of risk?

- **Faster Test Feedback:** How quickly do we identify problems and their remedial actions?

Each pillar represents qualities that exist on a scale—they all exist to some extent, but they can always be improved and raised higher. The more of these qualities we have, the more Confidence we create. We must also be conscious of balance and avoid overinvesting in any one pillar to the detriment of others.

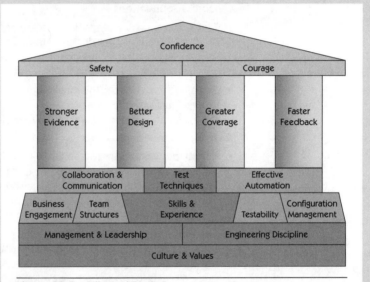

Figure 25-7   Pillars of Testing

Supporting the Pillars are the Foundations, representing three key areas: Team Foundations, Capability Foundations, and Technical Foundations. Each area includes several interconnected building blocks:

- **Team Foundations**
  - **Collaboration and Communication:** This represents the extent to which a team is able to get the most out of a variety of perspectives and skills, both within and beyond the team, and to find the most effective and informative communication modes among all stakeholders.

- **Business Engagement:** Effective collaboration depends upon meaningful and productive engagement between technical teams and the business people they support.

- **Team Structures:** Collaboration also depends on ensuring that the most appropriate team structures are in place to support effective teamwork, connecting the people with the right skills and empowering them to work as self-organizing, cross-functional feature teams.

- **Capability Foundations**

  - **Test Techniques:** Applying appropriate and effective test techniques, both in the design of formal test cases and in the dynamic exploration of the product, will contribute to Better Test Design and Greater Coverage.

  - **Skills and Experience:** The effectiveness of those test techniques (and other foundations) is heavily dependent upon the skills and experience within the team.

- **Technical Foundations**

  - **Effective Automation:** The ability to quickly and efficiently automate the majority of defined tests is critical to supporting the pillars of Faster Feedback and Greater Coverage. This in turn is dependent upon the testability of the architecture and strong configuration management.

  - **Configuration Management:** The discipline of managing versions of tests and other code, the controlled configuration of test environments and data, and the identification of all relevant artifacts in the software development and test process.

  - **Testability:** The extent to which the architecture of the system under test is designed to support automated testing. The characteristics of a testable system align with good architectural goals, such as loose coupling, dependency injection, strict separation of concerns, a well-defined domain model, and ubiquitous use of domain language.

The Foundation areas are all built upon the Organizational Bedrock, representing the leadership style and culture of the organization:

- **Management and Leadership:** The ability to hire and inspire great people, to remove or overcome organizational constraints and impediments that hinder them from doing their best work, to see and exploit the opportunities for people to excel, and to motivate individuals to achieve what is best for the team.

- **Engineering Discipline:** The guidance and support given to ensure that technical teams have the right tools and technical environment at their disposal, are empowered to make the most of them, and are given the education and personal development to ensure that their skills are always current and appropriate.
- **Culture and Values:** Ultimately, the whole environment and structure for success are built upon the culture and values of the organization.

Testing forms a big part of any team's ability to deliver business value frequently at a sustainable pace. We know we can't test quality in; we have to build it in from the start. When we begin software development with testing, we're more likely to build the right value for our customer, and when we complete the development and delivery with testing, we help ensure that we have built that value right.

SUMMARY

We encourage people to remember the seven key success factors for agile testing: use the whole-team approach, maintain an agile testing mindset, automate regression tests, focus on feedback, use core practices, collaborate, and keep the big picture in mind. In the spirit of continual learning, we encourage teams to experiment with the confidence-building practices we discussed in this book:

- Driving development with examples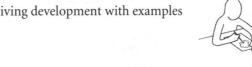

- Exploratory testing

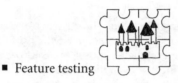

- Feature testing

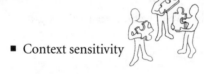

- Continual learning

- Context sensitivity

- Keeping it real

Strive to achieve confidence by applying the Pillars of Testing. It's the best thing we can do for our customers.

Appendix A

PAGE OBJECTS IN PRACTICE: EXAMPLES

In Chapter 16, "Test Automation Design Patterns and Approaches," Tony Sweets explained the concepts behind using the Page Object pattern for designing automated tests. Here are code snippets and technical details so that you can try this out yourself.

AN EXAMPLE WITH SELENIUM 2—WEBDRIVER

The following piece of code is a Page Object for the Wikipedia home page. It is written in Java using Selenium 2 (WebDriver). This particular Page Object has two public methods (or actions) it can perform. We can either click the privacy link, or we can search Wikipedia using the term "Nissan Motor Company." These two methods (plus the initializer method, which is known as the constructor) make up this Page Object's public interface. This is the interface you want to keep as stable as possible, and it is what your test script will use to navigate the site and to perform tests.

If you think you lack the programming skills required to implement this object, the programmers on the team could write the code for the testers and leave the test scripts for the team members who are actually specifying the tests.

One thing you should notice about this code is that we encapsulated the elements of the page and made them private. This helps to avoid brittle tests, as you don't have direct access to them, and they are what is most likely to change as time goes by. The only way to access them is through the public interface, which is intentionally vague. When your test script calls `searchForNissan()`, it has no idea how the Page Object will perform that piece of work, nor should it. Since we are hiding the implementation details away from the actual test, we can thus change the implementation without changing the test.

For example, let's say Wikipedia made a system update and searching for "Nissan Motor Company" no longer returns the real Nissan page. Instead it returns a blocker page, with an image of founder Jimmy Wales on it asking for a donation, and that page has a link to the real Nissan page. Without changing your test, you could modify the `NissanPage` Page Object to click the link below the donation request before returning the `NissanPage` object back to the test.

```
// This is the Home Page Class which when created (when
// the test is run) becomes a Page Object
public class HomePage {
    // This is a logging utility. Used to log to a file
    // and/or the screen
    private static final Logger log = LoggerFactory.
getLogger(HomePage.class);

    // This is the Object that acts as a web browser when
    // using Html Unit
    // or the thing that "drives" a real web browser like
    // Firefox
    private WebDriver webDriver;

    // These are elements (Links, Input Boxes, etc.) on
    // this page that I need to use
    private WebElement privacyPolicyLink;
    private WebElement searchBox;
    private WebElement submitButton;

    // Constructor of this Page Object
    public HomePage(WebDriver webDriver) {
        log.info("Page   = {}", webDriver.getTitle());
        log.info("URL    = {}", webDriver.getCurrentUrl());
        this.webDriver = webDriver;

        // Test that the page we are on is actually
        // the Wikipedia home page.
        // We know that we are on the home page if
        // the title matches the single
        // word "Wikipedia" and nothing else
        if (!webDriver.getTitle().equals("Wikipedia")) {
            throw new IllegalStateException("Requested
HomePage: current page - " +     webDriver.getTitle());
        }
```

```
        //Initialize WebElements
        privacyPolicyLink =
webDriver.findElement(By.partialLinkText("Privacy Policy"));
        searchBox = webDriver.findElement(By.
id("searchInput"));
        submitButton = webDriver.findElement(By.
name("go"));
    }

    public PrivacyPolicyPage clickPrivacyPolicyLink() {
        privacyPolicyLink.click();

        return new PrivacyPolicyPage(webDriver);
    }

    public NissanPage searchForNissan() {
        searchBox.sendKeys("Nissan Motor Company");
        submitButton.submit();

        return new NissanPage(webDriver);
    }
}
```

Let's look at a test script (I use that term loosely, as this is a real Java program/test). This is Java code and it's implemented as a JUnit. Using the JUnit framework allows us to take advantage of all of the test-friendly add-ons and ecosystem for free. For example, the JUnit output will be displayable by continuous build systems, by default, with no extra work needed. You can also run this with a simple Maven command just like any other test.

I consider this a script, because it is a top-down design. It's not really object oriented, but it uses Page Objects that you have created to represent your system under test. You need to create a WebDriver object that is part of Selenium 2, initialize it with the web browser it is going to control (HtmlUnit in this case), and point it to a URL. Then you simply hand it off to your Page Object that represents that specific URL, HomePage in this case. I'm also logging along the way because if your test breaks, you will want to know what step it was on so that you can manually investigate what happened.

```
@Test
public void testWikipedia() {
    WebDriver webDriver = new HtmlUnitDriver();

    log.info("Requesting HomePage");
    webDriver.get("http://www.wikipedia.org");
    HomePage homePage = new HomePage(webDriver);
    Assert.assertNotNull(homePage);
```

```
    log.info("Requesting Privacy Policy");
    PrivacyPolicyPage privacyPolicyPage = homePage.
clickPrivacyPolicyLink();
    Assert.assertNotNull(privacyPolicyPage);

    // If I go back I should be at the home page again
    log.info("Hitting the Back button");
    webDriver.navigate().back();
    HomePage homePageAfterBack = new
HomePage(webDriver);
    Assert.assertNotNull(homePageAfterBack);

    // Search for Nissan
    log.info("Looking up Nissan Motor Company");
    NissanPage nissanPage = homePageAfterBack.
searchForNissan();
    Assert.assertNotNull(nissanPage);

    // Go to the list of Nissan cars
    log.info("Clicking List of Nissan Cars");
    NissanCarListPage nissanCarListPage = nissanPage.
selectListOfCars();
    Assert.assertNotNull(nissanCarListPage);

    // Finally go to the Nissan Skyline GT-R Page
    log.info("Clicking Skyline GT-R");
    NissanSkylinePage nissanSkylinePage =
nissanCarListPage.selectNissanSkyline();
    Assert.assertNotNull(nissanSkylinePage);

    webDriver.quit();

}
```

JUnit uses the Assert class to check aspects of your code. You can check for nulls, equality, and true/false, among others. If the assertion fails, the script stops at that point, and it is logged as test failure automatically. This can show up in your build system, on the command line, or in a report. At the very end of the test script we send a quit command to the WebDriver object, which cleans up any resources being used. This is specifically useful when using a real browser like Internet Explorer or Firefox.

USING THE PageFactory CLASS

What we have seen already is just plain Page Objects implemented with Selenium 2. We could go a step further with Selenium 2 and use the built-in PageFactory helper class that it provides. This is an implementation of a widely used design pattern known as the Factory pattern.

The PageFactory helps you out by giving simple-to-read annotations for locating web page elements. Annotations are a relatively new feature to Java, and they always start with the ampersand (@). The PageFactory does the creation of the Page Object for you and initializes the elements based on the annotations you wrote to locate the item. Here is the HomePage object again with the PageFactory implementation:

```java
public class HomePage {
    private static final Logger log = LoggerFactory.
getLogger(HomePage.class);
    private WebDriver webDriver;

    @FindBy(how = How.PARTIAL_LINK_TEXT, using = "Privacy
Policy")
    private WebElement privacyPolicyLink;
    @FindBy(how = How.ID, using = "searchInput")
    private WebElement searchBox;
    @FindBy(how = How.NAME, using = "go")
    private WebElement submitButton;

    public HomePage(WebDriver webDriver) {
        log.info("Page  = {}", webDriver.getTitle());
        log.info("URL   = {}", webDriver.getCurrentUrl());
        this.webDriver = webDriver;
        if (!webDriver.getTitle().equals("Wikipedia")) {
            throw new IllegalStateException("Requested
HomePage: current page - " + webDriver.getTitle());
        }

    }


    public PrivacyPolicyPage clickPrivacyPolicyLink() {
        privacyPolicyLink.click();
        return PageFactory.initElements(webDriver,
PrivacyPolicyPage.class);
    }

    public NissanPage searchForNissan() {
        searchBox.sendKeys("Nissan Motor Company");
        submitButton.submit();
        return PageFactory.initElements(webDriver,
NissanPage.class);
    }
}
```

Notice that not much has changed, but it is enough that you probably do not want to mix the two styles, as your test scripts are slightly different as well. Your test script never actually creates a Page Object on its own anymore. It delegates to the factory. You are not buying much with this change; however, it is slightly cleaner to look at, and the annotations make it easier for you to write and manage the Page Object.

The test script has to change as well. When we created the Page Object ourselves it looked like this:

```
log.info("Requesting HomePage");
webDriver.get("http://www.wikipedia.org");
HomePage homePage = new HomePage(webDriver);
Assert.assertNotNull(homePage);
```

Now with the PageFactory creating the object, it looks like this (changes are highlighted):

```
log.info("Requesting HomePage");
webDriver.get("http://www.wikipedia.org");
HomePage homePage = PageFactory.
initElements(webDriver, HomePage.class);
Assert.assertNotNull(homePage);
```

The full code for this example is located on my GitHub account (Sweets, 2013). The README file has all the information needed to run this code on your local box.

If you are on a Mac with the developer tools installed, you should be able to run these commands to download and run this suite of tests:

```
> cd /tmp
> git clone https://github.com/tsweets/page-objects.git
> cd page-objects/
> mvn clean test
```

This will work on any platform given you have Java, Git, and Maven installed. The temp directory is system specific, however, with /tmp being part of the Mac and other UNIX/Linux-based boxes. This will run three versions of the same test. It will run a brittle version, the Page Object version, and the page factory version.

Appendix B

PROVOCATION STARTERS

Carol Vaage used a list of questions to get her grade 1 students to start thinking about the world and how they interacted with it. These are questions that can be used to think about your product, and how you may use them to elicit examples or uncover assumptions. See the bibliography for Part II, "Learning for Better Testing," for the link.

I wonder . . .

Could you show me . . .

Let's figure out how that could be . . .

So, in other words, if you . . . then . . . ?

What would happen next?

But why would that be?

So, now our question is . . .

Did you notice?

What have you discovered . . . ?

I know you can figure this out—go work with your team and see what ideas might work.

This (person/group) has run into a problem. What can we think of to help them solve it?

Why do you think that happened?

Describe what you see.

What does that look like to you?

How does that happen?

Why did it work that way?

How can you tell?

How is this different?

What do you think will happen?

How can you find out?

Give it a try and let me know how it turns out.

Can you show me the evidence?

What is your theory?

GLOSSARY

Acceptance test Acceptance tests are tests that define the business value each story (or feature) must deliver and help define the scope of the story (or feature). They may verify functional requirements or non-functional requirements such as performance or reliability. Although they are used to help guide development, they are done at a higher level than the unit-level tests used for code design in test-driven development. This is a broad term that may include both business-facing and technology-facing tests.

Acceptance-test-driven development (ATDD) Teams doing ATDD specify executable acceptance tests using examples elicited from conversations with customers. Each example is discussed and, if possible, specified in an executable format. Programmers use the tests as guidance to develop the feature. Once code is written to make a test pass, it may be kept as an automated regression test, documenting feature behavior.

Application life cycle management (ALM) ALM refers to managing an application product's life cycle by people in multiple disciplines working through the diverse activities involved in product delivery. Agile ALM encompasses activities such as continuous integration and delivery, collaborating with customers to describe examples that guide development, coding, testing, and managing releases.

Behavior-driven development (BDD) Examples of desired behavior from conversations with stakeholders are turned into executable tests in a given_when_then format. Programmers automate the tests and then write the code to make each test pass. BDD can be used at the unit level for test-driven design and can be used for business-facing tests that encompass multiple components and layers of the application and verify business-facing quality.

Build-measure-learn (BML) Build-measure-learn is a term from lean startup in which a team turns an idea into a deliverable product, measures customer response, and learns whether the idea should be pursued as is, changed in some way, or abandoned.

Build pipeline When code is checked into the source code control system, the commit kicks off a build pipeline. For more mature teams, this means running a quick suite of unit-level regression tests to provide fast feedback, followed by a number of test suites at the API and user interface levels to detect regression failures. Build pipelines may be configured to automatically deploy build artifacts to test, staging, and production environments.

Continuous integration (CI) In teams using the practice of continuous integration, team members check in code changes frequently throughout the day. Each check-in triggers an automated build process in which automated regression tests provide fast feedback to verify whether the code changes have introduced regression failures. These builds produce artifacts that may be automatically or manually deployed to different environments such as test, staging, and production.

Customer team Customer teams include all stakeholders outside of the software delivery team, such as product owners, product managers, business experts, subject matter experts, and end users.

Cycle time In the generic sense, it is the time from when something starts to when it finishes. Specifically, we mean the elapsed time from when a story is started to when it is accepted by the product owner or stakeholders. It often also means the time from when a story first exists to the time it is delivered to the end users.

Delivery team, development team The delivery or development team delivers the software that meets business goals and provides value to customers. Everyone involved in delivering software is a developer, including programmers, testers, business analysts, database experts, system administrators, technical writers, architects, user experience design experts, and operations staff.

DevOps   DevOps, a term that combines development and operations, refers to practices and patterns that improve collaboration among different roles in delivery teams, streamlining the process of delivering high-quality software. These practices and patterns help teams write testable, maintainable code, package the product, deploy it, and support the deployed code.

End game   The end game is the time before release when the delivery team applies the finishing touches to the product. Not a bug-fixing or "hardening" period, it is an opportunity to work with groups outside of development to help move the software into production. Examples of end game activities include additional testing of database migrations and installation.

Enterprise solutions   Software used to satisfy the needs of an organization rather than individual users, mostly found in large organizations. The software is intended to solve an enterprise-wide problem, rather than a departmental problem. Enterprise-level software aims to improve the enterprise's productivity and efficiency by providing business logic support functionality (Wikipedia, 2014d).

Exploratory testing (ET)   Exploratory testing combines test design with test execution and focuses on learning about the application under test. Please see Chapter 12, "Exploratory Testing," for a detailed guide.

Extract, transform, and load (ETL)   Extract, transform, and load refers to a process in database usage, especially for data warehouses, that extracts data from outside sources, transforms it to fit operational needs, and loads it into a target database (Wikipedia, 2014e).

Federated data   Data federation technology is software that provides an organization with the ability to aggregate data from disparate sources in a virtual database so it can be used for business intelligence or other analysis (Search Data Management, 2010).

Heuristics   Heuristics refers to experience-based techniques for problem solving, learning, and discovery that give a solution that is not guaranteed to be optimal. When an exhaustive search is impractical, heuristic methods are used to speed up the process of finding a satisfactory solution via mental shortcuts to ease the cognitive load of making a decision. Examples of this method include using a rule of thumb, an educated guess, an intuitive judgment, stereotyping, or common sense (Wikipedia, 2014g).

Infrastructure as a service (IaaS)   Infrastructure as a service is a provision model in which an organization outsources the equipment used to support operations, including storage, hardware, servers, and networking components. The service provider owns the equipment and is responsible for housing, running, and maintaining it. The client typically pays on a per-use basis (SearchCloudComputing, 2010a).

Kanban   The term *kanban* is Japanese and has the literal meaning of "card" or "signboard." In the Toyota Production System, it designates a system used for "just in time" inventory control (Agile Alliance, 2012). In agile software development, the "kanban method" is characterized by limits on work in progress, the idea of "pulling" work instead of having it assigned by managers, and a self-directed team that manages its own sustainable workload. Kanban boards are used to visualize projects and help enforce work in progress (WIP) limits (Hiranabe, 2008).

Legacy system   A legacy system is one that is not supported by automated regression tests. Introducing changes in legacy code, or refactoring it, might be risky because there are no tests to catch unintended changes in system behavior.

Minimum viable product (MVP)   The term *minimum viable product* was coined by Frank Robinson and popularized by Eric Ries for software products (Wikipedia, 2014i). A minimum viable product has just enough core features to allow the product to be deployed to a small subset of potential customers. These users form part of the "build-measure-learn" or "validated learning" feedback loop, guiding further development and decision making. An MVP is also used to represent the least amount of change that can be delivered to the customer that adds business value.

Operational acceptance testing (OAT) OAT is used to conduct operational readiness (prerelease) of a product, service, or system as part of a quality management system. OAT is a common type of nonfunctional software testing, used mainly in software support and software maintenance projects.

Platform as a service (PaaS) An outgrowth of software as a service, PaaS is a service delivery model that allows the customer to rent virtualized servers and associated services for running existing applications or developing and testing new ones (SearchCloudComputing, 2010).

Product release A software product release may consist of a brand-new product or new features for an existing product. In agile development, a feature may consist of one or more completed user stories.

Refactoring Refactoring is changing code, without changing its functionality, to make it more maintainable, easier to read, easier to test, and easier to extend.

Regression test A regression test verifies that the behavior of the system under test hasn't changed. Regression tests are usually written as unit tests to drive coding, or acceptance tests to define desired system behavior. Once the tests pass, they become part of a regression test suite, to guard against unintended changes being introduced. Regression tests should be automated to ensure continual feedback.

Release candidate A release candidate is a version or build of a product that can potentially be released to production. The release candidate may undergo further testing or be augmented with documentation or other materials.

Return on investment (ROI) Return on investment, a term borrowed from the world of financial investments, is a measure of the efficiency of an investment. ROI can be calculated in different ways, but it's basically the difference between the gain from an investment and the cost of that investment, divided by the cost of that investment. In testing, ROI is the benefit gained from a testing activity, such as automating a test, weighed against the cost of producing and maintaining that test.

Set-based development   As applied to software development, in set-based development, two development pairs or teams independently devise a problem solution or feature. Stakeholders, whether the business or other development team members, evaluate the results and choose the one they prefer.

Software as a service (SaaS)   In the software-as-a-service model, applications are hosted by a vendor or service provider. Instead of installing the software on their own hardware, as they would with "software as a product," the clients access the software on the provider's servers via a network, usually the Internet (SearchCloudComputing, 2010c).

Source code control system   Also referred to as version control, revision control, or source code management, source code control systems allow multiple team members to work on the same code base, documents, or other types of files without stepping on one another's updates. Common features include merging changes to the same file, reverting changes, comparing versions, viewing a history of changes, and retrieving specific versions. Today, hosting services for distributed code repositories such as GitHub, which uses Git as its revision control system, are popular (Wikipedia, 2014j).

Specification by example (SBE)   Specification by example uses process patterns that help software delivery teams collaborate with customer teams to define the scope of work to achieve business goals. SBE illustrates specifications with concrete examples, refines the specifications from key examples, and then automates them to validate the specifications frequently during development. The validated executable specifications are kept as living documentation (Adzic, 2011).

Technical debt   Ward Cunningham first introduced this metaphor, applying the concept of financial debt to software. When software teams cut some corners and sacrifice quality in order to help the business take advantage of an opportunity, they incur debt in the form of software that's not well designed, not protected by automated regression tests, or lacking in other quality characteristics. If the team doesn't take time to "repay" the debt by refactoring the code or adding automated regression tests, it becomes harder to deliver new features, and the "compounded" debt slows the team down.

Test-driven development (TDD) In test-driven development, the programmer writes and automates a small unit test, which initially fails, before writing the minimum amount of code that will make the test pass. The code is refactored as needed to meet acceptable standards. The production code is made to work one test at a time. TDD, also known as test-driven design, is more of a code design practice than a testing activity and helps build robust, easily maintainable code.

Unit test A unit test verifies the behavior of a tiny part of the overall system, such as a single branch of a single function. It may be as small as a single object or method that is a consequence of one or more design decisions. In an agile context, automated unit tests guide coding at a low level. A unit test is typically less than a dozen lines of code. Some practitioners prefer other terms such as *microtest* (Hill, 2009) or *xunit testing* (Fowler, 2014).

REFERENCES

Adzic, Gojko, *Bridging the Communication Gap: Specification by Example and Agile Acceptance Testing*, Neuri Limited, 2009.

————, "How Google Does Test Engineering," http://gojko.net/2010/10/15/how-google-does-test-engineering/, 2010a.

————, "How to Implement UI Testing without Shooting Yourself in the Foot," http://gojko.net/2010/04/13/how-to-implement-ui-testing-without-shooting-yourself-in-the-foot-2/, 2010b.

————, *Specification by Example: How Successful Teams Deliver the Right Software*, Manning, 2011.

————, *Impact Mapping: Making a Big Impact with Software Products and Projects*, Provoking Thoughts Ltd., 2012.

————, "The February Revolution," http://gojko.net/2013/02/13/the-february-revolution, 2013.

Adzic, Gojko, Declan Whelan, et al., "Specification by Example" diagram, https://docs.google.com/drawings/d/1cbfKq-KazcbMVCnRfih6zMSDBdt f90KviV7l2oxGyWM/edit?hl=en, Agile Alliance aa-ftt workshop, 2010.

Agile Alliance, "Kanban Board," http://guide.agilealliance.org/guide/kanban.html, 2012.

Andrea, Jennitta, "Acceptance Test-Driven Development: Not as Optional as You Think," www.stickyminds.com/article/acceptance-test-driven-development-not-optional-you-think, StickyMinds, Iterations newsletter, 2010.

Appelo, Jurgen, *Management 3.0: Leading Agile Developers, Developing Agile Leaders,* Addison-Wesley, 2011.

———, "Feedback Wrap," www.management30.com/workout/feedback-wrap/, 2013.

Ariely, Dan, "Are We in Control of Our Own Decisions?" www.ted.com/talks/dan_ariely_asks_are_we_in_control_of_our_own_decisions, 2008.

Bach, Jon, "Session-Based Test Management," www.satisfice.com/articles/sbtm.pdf, *Software Testing and Quality Engineering* magazine, now *Better Software* magazine, 2000.

Beck, Kent, *Test-Driven Development: By Example,* Addison-Wesley, 2002.

Bell, Rob, "A Beginner's Guide to Big O Notation," http://rob-bell.net/2009/06/a-beginners-guide-to-big-o-notation/, 2009.

Brodwell, Johannes, "Remote Pair Programming," www.slideshare.net/jhannes/2013-0807-agile-2013-remote-pair-programming, August 2013.

CMMI Institute, Carnegie Mellon, "Solutions," http://cmmiinstitute.com/cmmi-solutions/, 2014.

Cockburn, Alistair, "Characterizing People as Non-Linear, First-Order Components in Software Development," http://alistair.cockburn.us/Characterizing+people+as+non-linear%2c+first-order+components+in+software+development, 1999.

———, "Hexagonal Architecture: The Pattern: Ports and Adapters," http://alistair.cockburn.us/Hexagonal+architecture, 2005.

Crispin, Lisa, and Janet Gregory, *Agile Testing: A Practical Guide for Testers and Agile Teams,* Addison-Wesley, 2009.

Cunningham, Ward, "Debt Metaphor," www.youtube.com/watch?v=pqeJFYwnkjE, 2009.

De Bono, Edward, *Thinking for Action,* DK Publishing, 1998.

Derby, Esther, Johanna Rothman, and Gerald M. Weinberg, "Problem-Solving Leadership Course," www.estherderby.com/problem-solving-leadership-psl, 2014.

Dinwiddie, George, "A Lingua Franca between the Three (or More) Amigos," http://blog.gdinwiddie.com/2010/02/25/a-lingua-franca-between-the-three-or-more-amigos/, 2010.

Eliot, Seth, "A to Z Testing in Production: TiP Methodologies, Techniques and Examples at STPCon 2012," www.setheliot.com/blog/a-to-z-testing-in-production-tip-methodologies-techniques-and-examples-at-stpcon-2012, 2012.

Emery, Dale, "Writing Maintanable Automated Acceptance Tests," dhemery.com/pdf/writing_maintainable_automated_acceptance_tests.pdf, 2009.

Evans, David, "Visualising Quality," http://prezi.com/yych7sndetph/visualising-quality-atd, 2013.

Fowler, Martin, "UnitTest," http://martinfowler.com/bliki/UnitTest.html, 2014.

Freeman, Steve, and Nat Pryce, *Growing Object-Oriented Software, Guided by Tests*, Addison-Wesley, 2009.

Gärtner, Markus, "Technical Debt Applied to Testing," www.shino.de/2009/01/08/technical-debt-applied-to-testing/, 2009.

———, "Pomodoro Testing," www.shino.de/tag/pomodoro-testing, 2011.

———, *ATDD by Example: A Practical Guide to Acceptance Test-Driven Development*, Addison-Wesley, 2012.

———, personal communication, 2014.

Gawande, Atul, "Slow Ideas," *The New Yorker*, July 29, 2013.

Gilb, Tom, and Kai Gilb, "Planguage," www.gilb.com/definitionPlanguage&structure=Glossary&page_ref_id=476, 2013.

Gottesdiener, Ellen, *Requirements by Collaboration: Workshops for Defining Needs*, Addison-Wesley, 2002.

———, *The Software Requirements Memory Jogger: A Pocket Guide to Help Software and Business Teams Develop and Manage Requirements*, Goal QPC Inc., 2005.

Gottesdiener, Ellen, and Mary Gorman, *Discover to Deliver: Agile Product Planning and Analysis,* 2012.

Gregory, Janet, "About Learning 2," http://janetgregory.ca/about-learning-2/, 2010.

————, "Jigsaw Puzzles and Small Chunks," http://janetgregory.ca/jigsaw-puzzles-small-chunks/, 2011.

————, "Distributed Teams—My Experience," http://janetgregory.ca/distributed-teams-my-experience/, 2014.

Guest, David, "The Hunt Is On for the Renaissance Man of Computing," *The Independent* (London), 1991.

Hagar, Jon, *Software Test Attacks to Break Mobile and Embedded Devices,* Chapman and Hall/CRC, 2013.

————, personal communication, 2014.

Hagberg, Jan Petter, personal communication, 2013.

Haines, Corey, et al., Coderetreat Community Network, http://coderetreat.org/.

Harty, Julian, "Trinity Testing," http://julianharty-softwaretesting.blogspot.ca/2010/05/trinity-testing.html, 2010.

————, *Testing and Test Automation for Mobile Phone Applications,* Chapman and Hall/CRC, 2014.

Hassa, Christian, "Story Maps in Practice," www.slideshare.net/chassa/2013-0509story-mapsagilemeetupbp, 2013.

Hendrickson, Elisabeth, "Testing: Not a Phase, but a Way of Life," http://testobsessed.com/2006/11/testing-not-a-phase-but-a-way-of-life/, 2006.

————, "Driving Development with Tests: ATDD and TDD," http://testobsessed.com/wp-content/uploads/2011/04/atddexample.pdf, 2008.

————, "The Agile Acid Test," http://testobsessed.com/2010/12/the-agile-acid-test/, 2010.

————, "Test Heuristics Cheat Sheet," http://testobsessed.com/wp-content/uploads/2011/04/testheuristicscheatsheetv1.pdf, 2011.

————, "The Thinking Tester: Evolved," www.slideshare.net/ehendrickson/the-thinking-tester-evolved, 2012.

————, *Explore It! Reduce Risk and Increase Confidence with Exploratory Testing*, Pragmatic Programmer, 2013.

Heusser, Matthew, *How to Reduce the Cost of Software Testing*, Taylor & Francis, 2011.

Hill, Michael, "They're Called Microtests," http://anarchycreek.com/2009/05/20/theyre-called-microtests/, 2009.

Hiranabe, Kenji, "Kanban Applied to Software Development: From Agile to Lean," www.infoq.com/articles/hiranabe-lean-agile-kanban, InfoQ, 2008.

Humble, Jez, "There's No Such Thing as a 'DevOps Team,'" http://continuousdelivery.com/2012/10/theres-no-such-thing-as-a-devops-team/, 2012.

Humble, Jez, and David Farley, *Continuous Delivery: Reliable Software Releases through Build, Test and Deployment Automation*, Addison-Wesley, 2010.

Hunt, Andy, *Pragmatic Thinking and Learning*, Pragmatic Bookshelf, 2008.

Hussman, David, "Agile Journeys," www.slideshare.net/agileee/agile-journeys-by-david-hussman-2029404, 2009.

————, "Cutting an Agile Groove: A Free Educational Video Series for Newbies and Practitioners," http://pragprog.com/screencasts/v-dhcag/cutting-an-agile-groove, Pragmatic Bookshelf, 2011.

————, "Story Maps, Slices, Customer Journeys, and Other Product Design Tools," http://agilepalooza.com/austin2013/slidedecks/Story-Maps-Slices-Customer-Journeys.pdf, 2013.

Hüttermann, Michaël, *Agile ALM: Lightweight Tools and Agile Strategies*, Manning Publications, 2011a.

————, "Agile ALM and Collaborative Development," http://huettermann.net/perform/AgileALM-AgileRecord-Huettermann.pdf, Agile Record, 2011b.

————, *DevOps for Developers: Integrate Development and Operations, the Agile Way*, Apress, 2012.

Kahneman, Daniel, *Thinking, Fast and Slow*, Farrar, Straus and Giroux, 2011.

Kaner, Cem, "What Is Context-Driven Testing?" http://kaner.com/?p=49, 2012.

Karten, Naomi, "Are You Listening?" www.agileconnection.com/article/are-you-listening, Agile Connection, 2009.

Kemerling, Ashton, "Generative Testing," www.pivotaltracker.com/community/tracker-blog/generative-testing, Pivotal, 2014.

Keogh, Liz, Yahoo Agile Testing group post, August 2010.

————, "Behaviour-Driven Development," www.slideshare.net/lunivore/behavior-driven-development-11754474, 2012a.

————, "The Deliberate Discovery Workshop," http://lizkeogh.com/2012/09/21/the-deliberate-discovery-workshop/, 2012b.

————, "BDD before the Tools," http://lizkeogh.com/2013/10/24/bdd-before-the-tools/, 2013a.

————, "Embracing Uncertainty," including links to posts on Cynefin, Deliberate Discovery, and Real Options, http://lizkeogh.com/embracing-uncertainty/, 2013b.

————, "Discrete vs. Continuous Capabilities," http://lizkeogh.com/2014/02/10/discrete-vs-continuous-capabilities/, 2014a.

Keogh, Liz, personal communication, 2014b.

Kniberg, Henrik, and Spotify Labs, "Spotify Culture," http://labs.spotify.com/2014/03/27/spotify-engineering-culture-part-1/, 2013.

Kniberg, Henrik, and Anders Ivarsson, "Scaling Agile @ Spotify: With Tribes, Squads, Chapters & Guilds," http://ucvox.files.wordpress.com/2012/11/113617905-scaling-agile-spotify-11.pdf, 2012.

Knight, Adam P., "The Thread of an Idea: Adopting a Thread-Based Approach to Exploratory Testing," www.a-sisyphean-task.com/2011/11/thread-based-approach-to-exploratory.html, 2011.

———, "Fractal Exploratory Testing," www.a-sisyphean-task.com/2013/01/fractal-exploratory-testing.html, 2013.

———, personal communication, 2014.

Kohl, Jonathan, *Tap into Mobile Testing*, LeanPub, 2013.

Kubasek, Stanley, "The Boy Scout Rule," http://pragmaticcraftsman.com/2011/03/the-boy-scout-rule/, The Pragmatic Craftsman, 2011.

Lambert, Rob, "T-Shaped Testers and Their Role in a Team," http://thesocialtester.co.uk/t-shaped-testers-and-their-role-in-a-team/, 2012.

Levison, Mark, "The Beginner's Mind—An Approach to Listening," www.infoq.com/news/2008/08/beginners_mind, InfoQ, 2008.

Lyndsay, James, "Adventures in Session-Based Testing," www.workroom-productions.com/papers/AiSBTv1.2.pdf, 2003.

———, "Why Exploration Has a Place in Any Strategy," www.workroom-productions.com/papers/Exploration%20and%20Strategy.pdf, 2006.

———, "Testing in an Agile Environment," www.workroom-productions.com/papers/Testing%20in%20an%20agile%20environment.pdf, 2007.

———, personal communication, 2014.

Manns, Mary Lynn, and Linda Rising, *Fearless Change: Patterns for Introducing New Ideas*, Addison-Wesley, 2005.

Marick, Brian, "Agile Testing Directions: Test and Examples," www.exampler.com/old-blog/2003/08/22/#agile-testing-project-2, 2003.

———, *Everyday Scripting with Ruby: For Teams, Testers and You*, Pragmatic Bookshelf, 2007.

Martin, Robert C., *Clean Code: A Handbook of Software Craftsmanship*, Prentice Hall, 2009.

———, *The Clean Coder: A Code of Conduct for Professional Programmers*, Prentice Hall, 2011.

Matts, Chris, and Gojko Adzic, "Feature Injection: Three Steps to Success," www.infoq.com/articles/feature-injection-success, InfoQ, 2011.

Matts, Chris, and Olav Maassen, "'Real Options' Underlie Agile Practices," www.infoq.com/articles/real-options-enhance-agility, InfoQ, 2007.

McDonald, Kent J., "Create a Vendor Contract While Keeping Agile," www .techwell.com/2013/05/create-vendor-contract-while-keeping-agile, Techwell, 2013.

McDonald, Mark, "Is Your Company an Enterprise? The Answer Matters," http://blogs.gartner.com/mark_mcdonald/2009/06/15/is-your-company-an-enterprise-the-answer-matters/, Gartner Blog Network, 2009.

McMahon, Chris, "Telecommuting Policy," http://chrismcmahonsblog .blogspot.com/2009/12/telecommuting-policy.html, 2009.

Morgan, Jeff "Cheezy," "UI Tests—Default Data," www.cheezyworld.com/ 2010/11/21/ui-tests-default-dat, 2010.

———, *Cucumber and Cheese: A Testers Workshop*, LeanPub, 2013.

———, personal communication, 2014.

Morville, Peter, "User Experience Design," http://semanticstudios.com/ publications/semantics/000029.php, 2004.

Nordstrom, "Nordstrom Innovation Lab: Sunglass iPad App Case Study," www.youtube.com/watch?v=szr0ezLyQHY, 2011.

North, Dan, "Introducing BDD," http://dannorth.net/introducing-bdd/, *Better Software* magazine, 2006.

Ottinger, Tim, and Jeff Langr, "Arrange-Act-Assert," http://agileinaflash .blogspot.com/2009/03/arrange-act-assert.html, 2009a.

———, *Agile in a Flash: Speed Learning Agile Software*, Pragmatic Bookshelf, 2011.

————, "FURPS" model, http://agileinaflash.blogspot.ca/2009/04/furps.html, 2009b.

————, "Red-Green-Refactor," http://agileinaflash.blogspot.co.uk/2009/02/red-green-refactor.html, 2009c.

Patton, Jeff, "It's All in How You Slice It: Design Your Project in Working Layers to Avoid Half-Baked Incremental Releases," www.agileproductdesign.com/writing/how_you_slice_it.pdf, *Better Software* magazine, 2005.

————, "Pragmatic Personas," www.stickyminds.com/article/pragmatic-personas, StickyMinds/Techwell, 2010.

————, *User Story Mapping: Building Better Products Using Agile Software Design,* O'Reilly Media, 2014.

Rainsberger, J. B., "The Next Decade of Agile Software Development," www.slideshare.net/jbrains/the-next-decade-of-agile-software-development, 2013.

Ramdeo, Anand, "Test Automation—How to Handle Common Components with Page Object Model?," www.testinggeek.com/test-automation-how-to-handle-common-components-with-page-object-model, 2013.

Rasmussen, Jonathan, *The Agile Samurai: How Agile Masters Deliver Great Software,* Pragmatic Bookshelf, 2010.

Ries, Eric, "Case Study: SlideShare Goes Freemium," www.startuplessonslearned.com/2010/08/case-study-slideshare-goes-freemium.html, 2010.

Rising, Linda, "The Power of Retrospectives," www.stickyminds.com/presentation/power-retrospectives-0, SQE, 2009.

Rogalsky, Steve, "Thoughts on Beyond Deadlines by Jabe Bloom," http://winnipegagilist.blogspot.ca/2013/03/thoughts-on-beyond-deadlines-by-jabe.html, 2012.

Rothman, Johanna, "Agile Is Not for Everyone," www.jrothman.com/blog/mpd/2012/12/agile-is-not-for-everyone.html, 2012a.

————, *Hiring Geeks That Fit,* Pragmatic Bookshelf, 2012b.

Ruhland, Bernice Niel, "Developing Your Leadership Skills through a Journal Club," http://thetestersedge.com/2013/12/28/developing-your-leadership-skills-through-a-journal-club/, 2013a.

———, personal communication, 2013b.

———, personal communication, 2014.

Satir Global Network, http://satirglobal.org/.

Scott, Alister, "Specification by Example: A Love Story," http://watirmelon .files.wordpress.com/2011/05/specificationbyexamplealovestory1.pdf, 2011a.

———, "Yet Another Software Testing Pyramid," http://watirmelon .com/2011/06/10/yet-another-software-testing-pyramid/, 2011b.

SearchCloudComputing, "Infrastructure as a Service," http:// searchcloudcomputing.techtarget.com/definition/Infrastructure-as-a-Service-IaaS, 2010a.

———, "Platform as a Service," http://searchcloudcomputing.techtarget .com/definition/Platform-as-a-Service-PaaS, 2010b.

———, "Software as a Service," http://searchcloudcomputing.techtarget .com/definition/Software-as-a-Service, 2010c.

Search Data Management, "Data Federation Technology," http:// searchdatamanagement.techtarget.com/definition/data-federation-technology, 2010.

Sherry, Rosie, Ministry of Testing's mobile testing mind map, www.flickr .com/photos/softwaretestingclub/7159412943/sizes/o/in/photostream/, Ministry of Testing, 2013.

Sweets, Tony, "Page Object Example," https://github.com/tsweets/ page-objects, 2013.

Talks, Mike, *The Software Minefield*, LeanPub, 2012.

Traynor, Des, "An Interview with Andy Budd," http://insideintercom.io/ an-interview-with-andy-budd/, Intercom, 2011.

Tung, Portia, "Power of Play," www.slideshare.net/portiatung/the-powerofplay36, 2011.

Waters, John K., "An Agile Approach to Rocket Science," http://adtmag.com/articles/2004/10/06/an-agile-approach-to-rocket-science.aspx, *Application Development Trends* magazine, October 16, 2004.

Whittaker, James, "ACC Explained," http://code.google.com/p/test-analytics/wiki/AccExplained, 2011.

———, "Exploratory Testing Tours," http://msdn.microsoft.com/en-us/library/jj620911.aspx#bkmk_tours, Microsoft, 2012.

Whittaker, James A., Jason Arbon, and Jeff Carollo, *How Google Tests Software,* Addison-Wesley, 2012.

Wikipedia, "5 Whys," http://en.wikipedia.org/wiki/5_Whys, 2014a.

———, "Contextual Inquiry," http://en.wikipedia.org/wiki/Contextual_inquiry, 2014b.

———, "Embedded System: History," http://en.wikipedia.org/wiki/Embedded_system#History, 2014c.

———, "Enterprise Software," http://en.wikipedia.org/wiki/Enterprise_software, 2014d.

———, "Extract, Transform, Load," https://en.wikipedia.org/wiki/Extract,_transform,_load, 2014e.

———, "FURPS," http://en.wikipedia.org/wiki/FURPS, 2014f.

———, "Heuristics," http://en.wikipedia.org/wiki/Heuristics, 2014g.

———, "Ishikawa Diagram," http://en.wikipedia.org/wiki/Ishikawa_diagram, 2014h.

———, "Minimum Viable Product," http://en.wikipedia.org/wiki/Minimum_viable_product, 2014i.

———, "Revision Control," http://en.wikipedia.org/wiki/Revision_control, 2014j.

————, "Socratic Questioning," http://en.wikipedia.org/wiki/Socratic_questioning, 2014k.

————, "Software Testing," http://en.wikipedia.org/wiki/Software_testing, 2014l.

————, "SOLID: Object-Oriented Design," http://en.wikipedia.org/wiki/SOLID, 2014m.

————, "Star Schema," http://en.wikipedia.org/wiki/Star_schema, 2014n.

Wikispeed, website, http://wikispeed.org/, 2014.

Wynne, Matt, and Aslak Hellesøy, *The Cucumber Book: Behaviour-Driven Development for Testers and Developers*, Pragmatic Programmers, 2012.

Bibliography

Part I: Introduction

Books

Appelo, Jurgen, *Management 3.0: Leading Agile Developers, Developing Agile Leaders,* Addison-Wesley, 2011.

Beck, Kent, *Test-Driven Development: By Example*, Addison-Wesley, 2002.

Benson, Jim, and Tonianne DeMaria Berry, *Personal Kanban: Mapping Work | Navigating Life*, CreateSpace Independent Publishing Platform, 2011.

Maassen, Olav, Chris Matts, and Chris Geary, *Commitment*, Hathaway te Brake Publications, 2013.

Manns, Mary Lynn, and Linda Rising, *Fearless Change: Patterns for Introducing New Ideas*, Addison-Wesley, 2005.

Martin, Robert C., *Clean Coder: A Code of Conduct for Professional Programmers*, Prentice Hall, 2011.

Poppendieck, Mary, and Tom Poppendieck, *Implementing Lean Software Development: From Concept to Cash*, Addison-Wesley, 2006.

————, *The Lean Mindset: Ask the Right Questions*, Addison-Wesley, 2013.

Rasmussen, Jonathan, *The Agile Samurai: How Agile Masters Deliver Great Software*, Pragmatic Bookshelf, 2010.

Reinertsen, Donald G., *The Principles of Product Development Flow: Second Generation Lean Product Development*, Celeritas Publishing, 2012.

WEBSITES, BLOGS, ARTICLES, SLIDE DECKS

Adzic, Gojko, "The February Revolution," http://gojko.net/2013/02/13/the-february-revolution, 2013.

Benson, Jim, "Time to Completion," www.personalkanban.com/pk/uncategorized/time-to-completion/#sthash.WdeVZ5i7.dpbs, 2011.

Benson, Jim, and Jeremy Lightsmith, "Lean Coffee," http://leancoffee.org, 2013.

Derby, Esther, website, http://estherderby.com.

Dinwiddie, George, "A Lingua Franca between the Three (or More) Amigos," http://blog.gdinwiddie.com/2010/02/25/a-lingua-franca-between-the-three-or-more-amigos/, 2010.

Gawande, Atul, "Slow Ideas," *The New Yorker*, July 29, 2013.

Hendrickson, Elisabeth, "Testing: Not a Phase, but a Way of Life," http://testobsessed.com/2006/11/testing-not-a-phase-but-a-way-of-life/, 2006.

Keogh, Liz, "Embracing Uncertainty," including links to posts on Cynefin, Deliberate Discovery, and Real Options, http://lizkeogh.com/embracing-uncertainty/, 2013.

Kniberg, Henrik, "Agile Product Ownership in a Nutshell," www.youtube.com/watch?v=502ILHjX9EE, 2012.

Kniberg, Henrik, and Anders Ivarsson, "Scaling Agile @ Spotify: With Tribes, Squads, Chapters & Guilds," http://ucvox.files.wordpress.com/2012/11/113617905-scaling-agile-spotify-11.pdf, 2012.

Kniberg, Henrik, and Spotify Labs, "Spotify Culture," http://labs.spotify.com/2014/03/27/spotify-engineering-culture-part-1/, 2013.

Matts, Chris, and Olav Maassen, "'Real Options' Underlie Agile Practices," www.infoq.com/articles/real-options-enhance-agility, InfoQ, 2007.

Rogalsky, Steve, "Thoughts on Beyond Deadlines by Jabe Bloom," http://winnipegagilist.blogspot.ca/2013/03/thoughts-on-beyond-deadlines-by-jabe.html, 2012.

———, "A Guide to Lean Coffee," www.slideshare.net/SteveRogalsky/a-guide-to-lean-coffee, 2013.

Rothman, Johanna, "Agile Is Not for Everyone," www.jrothman.com/blog/mpd/2012/12/agile-is-not-for-everyone.html, 2012.

———, "Trust, Agile Program Management, & Being Effective," www.jrothman.com/blog/mpd/2013/08/trust-agile-program-management-being-effective.html, 2013.

Scotland, Karl, "Introducing Kanban, Flow, and Cadence," http://agile.dzone.com/news/introducing-kanban-flow-and, Dzone, Inc., 2009.

West, Dave, "Analyst Watch: Water-Scrum-Fall Is the Reality of Agile," www.sdtimes.com/content/article.aspx?ArticleID=36195&page=1, *SD Times*, 2011.

———, "Water-Scrum-Fall Is the Reality of Agile for Most Organizations Today," www.forrester.com/WaterScrumFall+Is+The+Reality+Of+Agile+For+Most+Organizations+Today/fulltext/-/E-RES60109?docid=60109, Forrester Research, 2011.

Wikipedia, "Cynefin," http://en.wikipedia.org/wiki/Cynefin, 2014.

Zheglov, Alexei, "The Elusive 20% Time," http://connected-knowledge.com/2012/05/10/the-elusive-20-time/, 2013.

PART II: LEARNING FOR BETTER TESTING

BOOKS

Adkins, Lyssa, *Coaching Agile Teams: A Companion for ScrumMasters, Agile Coaches, and Project Managers in Transition*, Addison-Wesley, 2010.

Adzic, Gojko, *Specification by Example: How Successful Teams Deliver the Right Software*, Manning, 2011.

Appelo, Jurgen, *Management 3.0: Leading Agile Developers, Developing Agile Leaders*, Addison-Wesley, 2010.

Copeland, Lee, *A Practitioner's Guide to Software Test Design*, Artech House, 2004.

Davies, Rachel, and Liz Sedley, *Agile Coaching*, Pragmatic Bookshelf, 2009.

De Bono, Edward, *Thinking for Action*, DK Publishing, 1998.

Derby, Esther, Don Gray, Johanna Rothman, and Gerald M. Weinberg, *Readings for Problem-Solving Leadership,* LeanPub, 2013, https://leanpub.com/pslreader.

Gärtner, Markus, *ATDD by Example: A Practical Guide to Acceptance Test-Driven Development*, Addison-Wesley, 2012.

Gottesdiener, Ellen, *Requirements by Collaboration: Workshops for Defining Needs*, Addison-Wesley, 2002.

Hunt, Andy, *Pragmatic Thinking and Learning*, Pragmatic Bookshelf, 2008.

Kahneman, Daniel, *Thinking, Fast and Slow*, Farrar, Straus and Giroux, 2011.

Kaner, Cem, Sowmya Padmanabhan, and Douglas Hoffman, *The Domain Testing Workbook*, Context Driven Press, 2013.

Larman, Craig, and Bas Vodde, *Scaling Lean & Agile Development: Thinking and Organizational Tools for Large-Scale Scrum*, Addison-Wesley, 2009.

Martin, Robert C., *Agile Software Development: Principles, Patterns, and Practices*, Prentice Hall, 2002.

———, *Clean Code: A Handbook of Software Craftsmanship*, Prentice Hall, 2009.

———, *The Clean Coder: A Code of Conduct for Professional Programmers*, Prentice Hall, 2011.

Morgan, Jeff "Cheezy," *Cucumber and Cheese: A Testers Workshop*, LeanPub, 2013.

Ottinger, Tim, and Jeff Langr, *Agile in a Flash: Speed Learning Agile Software*, Pragmatic Bookshelf, 2011.

Patterson, Kerry, et al., *Crucial Conversations: Tools for Talking When the Stakes Are High, 2nd Edition,* McGraw-Hill, 2001.

Rothman, Johanna, *Hiring Geeks That Fit*, Pragmatic Bookshelf, 2012.

Satir, Virginia, *The Satir Model: Family Therapy and Beyond*, Science and Behavior Books, 1991.

Seashore, Charles N., Edith Whitfield Seashore, and Gerald M. Weinberg, *What Did You Say? The Art of Giving and Receiving Feedback*, Bingham House Books, 1997.

Sullivan, Wendy, and Julie Rees, *Clean Language: Revealing Metaphors and Opening Minds*, Crown House Publishing, 2008.

Tabaka, Jean, *Collaboration Explained: Facilitation Skills for Software Project Leaders*, Addison-Wesley, 2006.

BLOG POSTS AND ONLINE ARTICLES

Appelo, Jurgen, "Feedback Wrap," www.management30.com/workout/feedback-wrap/, 2013.

Ariely, Dan, "Are We in Control of Our Own Decisions?," www.ted.com/talks/dan_ariely_asks_are_we_in_control_of_our_own_decisions, 2008.

Bolton, Michael, "User Acceptance Testing," www.developsense.com/presentations/User%20Acceptance%20Testing%20-%20STAR%20East%20 2006.pdf.

———, "Critical Thinking for Testers," www.developsense.com/presentations/2012-11-EuroSTAR-CriticalThinkingForTesters.pdf, 2012.

Cockburn, Alistair, "Characterizing People as Non-Linear, First-Order Components in Software Development," http://alistair.cockburn.us/Characterizing+people+as+non-linear%2c+first-order+components+in+software+development, 1999.

———, "Hexagonal Architecture: The Pattern: Ports and Adapters," http://alistair.cockburn.us/Hexagonal+architecture, 2005.

Crispin, Lisa, "Applying the Dreyfus Model of Skill Acquisition," http://lisacrispin.com/2012/06/25/applying-the-dreyfus-model-of-skill-acquisition-to-the-whole-team-approach/, 2012.

Gregory, Janet, "About Learning 2," http://janetgregory.ca/about-learning-2/, 2010.

Guest, David, "The Hunt Is On for the Renaissance Man of Computing," *The Independent* (London), 1991.

Hendrickson, Elisabeth, "The Agile Acid Test," http://testobsessed.com/2010/12/the-agile-acid-test/, 2010.

Karten, Naomi, "Are You Listening?," www.agileconnection.com/article/are-you-listening, Agile Connection, 2009.

Keogh, Liz, "The Deliberate Discovery Workshop," http://lizkeogh.com/2012/09/21/the-deliberate-discovery-workshop/, 2012.

Knight, Adam P., "T-Shaped Tester, Square Shaped Team," http://thesocialtester.co.uk/t-shaped-tester-square-shaped-team/, 2013.

Lambert, Rob, "T-Shaped Testers and Their Role in a Team," http://thesocialtester.co.uk/t-shaped-testers-and-their-role-in-a-team/, 2012.

Levison, Mark, "The Beginner's Mind—An Approach to Listening," www.infoq.com/news/2008/08/beginners_mind, InfoQ, 2008.

McKee, Lynn, "Inspiration and Motivation through Learning," www.qualityperspectives.ca/blog/802, 2010.

McMillan, Darren, "Mind Mapping 101," www.bettertesting.co.uk/content/?p=956, Better Testing, 2011.

Myers & Briggs Foundation, "MBTI Basics," www.myersbriggs.org/my-mbti-personality-type/mbti-basics.

Ruhland, Bernice Niel, "Developing Your Leadership Skills through a Journal Club," http://thetestersedge.com/2013/12/28/developing-your-leadership-skills-through-a-journal-club/, 2013.

Tatham, Elizabeth, "Roles in Open Source Projects," http://oss-watch.ac.uk/resources/rolesinopensource, OSS Watch, 2010, updated 2013.

Toastmasters International, www.toastmasters.org/.

Tung, Portia, "Power of Play," www.slideshare.net/portiatung/the-powerofplay36, 2011.

Vaage, Carol, "Play and Learning for Children," www.k-3learningpages.net/professional%20development.htm.

Wedig, Steve, "A Software Developer's Reading List," http://stevewedig.com/2014/02/03/software-developers-reading-list/, 2014.

Wikipedia, "5 Whys," http://en.wikipedia.org/wiki/5_Whys, 2014.

————, "Ishikawa Diagram," http://en.wikipedia.org/wiki/Ishikawa_diagram, 2014.

————, "Socratic Questioning," http://en.wikipedia.org/wiki/Socratic_questioning, 2014.

Courses, Conferences, Online Communities, Podcasts

Agile Coach Camp, http://agilecoachcamp.org/.

Balamurugadas, Ajay, et al., "Weekend Testing," http://weekendtesting.com/.

Crispin, Lisa, and Janet Gregory, moderators, Agile Testing Mailing List, http://tech.groups.yahoo.com/group/agile-testing/.

Derby, Esther, Don Gray, Johanna Rothman, and Gerald M. Weinberg, "Readings for Problem-Solving Leadership," https://leanpub.com/pslreader, LeanPub, 2013.

Derby, Esther, Johanna Rothman, and Gerald M. Weinberg, "Problem-Solving Leadership Course," www.estherderby.com/problem-solving-leadership-psl, 2014.

Filipin, Zeljko, WATIR podcasts, http://watirpodcast.com/.

Gärtner, Markus, "Testing Dojos," www.testingdojo.org.

Haines, Corey, et al., Coderetreat, http://coderetreat.org/.

Kaner, Fiedler and Associates, "Test Design: A Survey of Black Box Testing Techniques," www.testingeducation.org/BBST/testdesign/, 2014.

Khoo, Trish, and Bruce McLeod, "TestCast," www.testcast.net.

Larsen, Michael, TWiST podcasts, www.mkltesthead.com/p/podcasts.html.

Play4Agile, http://play4agile.wordpress.com/.

Satir Global Network, http://satirglobal.org/.

Sherry, Rosie, et al., Software Testing Club online community, www
.softwaretestingclub.com/.

Software Test Professionals Association, podcasts, www.softwaretestpro
.com/List/Podcasts.

Starter League, beginner-focused software school, www.starterleague.com/.

Weirich, Jim, and Joe O'Brien, Neo Ruby Koans, http://rubykoans.com/.

PART III: PLANNING—SO YOU DON'T FORGET THE BIG PICTURE

BOOKS

Freeman, Steve, and Nat Pryce, *Growing Object-Oriented Software, Guided by Tests*, Addison-Wesley, 2009.

Galen, Robert, *Software Endgames: Eliminating Defects, Controlling Change, and the Countdown to On-Time Delivery*, Dorset House, 2005.

Gottesdiener, Ellen, and Mary Gorman, *Discover to Deliver: Agile Product Planning and Analysis*, 2012.

Hendrickson, Elisabeth, *Explore It! Reduce Risk and Increase Confidence with Exploratory Testing*, Pragmatic Programmer, 2013.

Hüttermann, Michael, *Agile ALM: Lightweight Tools and Agile Strategies*, Manning Publications, 2011.

Whittaker, James A., Jason Arbon, and Jeff Carollo, *How Google Tests Software*, Addison-Wesley, 2012.

ARTICLES, BLOG POSTS, SLIDE DECKS

Adzic, Gojko, "How Google Does Test Engineering," http://gojko.net/2010/10/15/how-google-does-test-engineering/, 2010.

———, "The February Revolution," http://gojko.net/2013/02/13/the-february-revolution/, 2013.

———, "Let's Break the Agile Testing Quadrants," http://gojko.net/2013/10/21/lets-break-the-agile-testing-quadrants/, 2013.

Crispin, Lisa, "Using the Agile Testing Quadrants," http://lisacrispin.com/2011/11/08/using-the-agile-testing-quadrants/, 2011.

Gärtner, Markus, "The Testing Quadrants: We Got It Wrong!," www.shino.de/2012/07/30/the-testing-quadrants-we-got-it-wrong/, 2012.

Hendrickson, Elisabeth, "Testing Heuristics Cheat Sheet," http://testobsessed.com/wp-content/uploads/2011/04/testheuristicscheatsheetv1.pdf, 2011.

———, "The Thinking Tester: Evolved," www.slideshare.net/ehendrickson/the-thinking-tester-evolved, 2012.

Hütterman, Michael, "Agile ALM and Collaborative Development," http://huettermann.net/perform/AgileALM-AgileRecord-Huettermann.pdf, Agile Record, 2011.

Keogh, Liz, "Discrete vs. Continuous Capabilities," http://lizkeogh.com/2014/02/10/discrete-vs-continuous-capabilities/, 2014.

Marick, Brian, "Agile Testing Directions: Test and Examples," www.exampler.com/old-blog/2003/08/22/#agile-testing-project-2, 2003.

Nisbet, Duncan, "Dissecting the Testing Quadrants: Wrap Up," www.duncannisbet.co.uk/dissecting-the-testing-quadrants-wrap-up, 2014.

Ottinger, Tim, and Jeff Langr, "FURPS" model, http://agileinaflash.blogspot.ca/2009/04/furps.html, 2009.

Rising, Linda, "The Power of Retrospectives," www.stickyminds.com/presentation/power-retrospectives-0, SQE, 2009.

Whittaker, James, "ACC Explained," http://code.google.com/p/test-analytics/wiki/AccExplained, 2011.

Wikipedia, "FURPS," http://en.wikipedia.org/wiki/FURPS, 2014.

PART IV: TESTING BUSINESS VALUE

BOOKS

Adzic, Gojko, *Bridging the Communication Gap: Specification by Example and Agile Acceptance Testing*, Neuri Limited, 2009.

————, *Specification by Example: How Successful Teams Deliver the Right Software*, Manning, 2011.

————, *Impact Mapping: Making a Big Impact with Software Products and Projects*, Provoking Thoughts, 2012.

————, *50 Quick Ideas to Improve Your User Stories*, LeanPub, 2014.

Chelimksy, David, et al., *The RSpec Book: Behaviour-Driven Development with RSpec, Cucumber, and Friends*, Pragmatic Bookshelf, 2010.

Fowler, Martin, *Domain-Specific Languages*, Addison-Wesley, 2011.

Gärtner, Markus, *ATDD by Example: A Practical Guide to Acceptance Test-Driven Development*, Addison-Wesley, 2012.

Gottesdiener, Ellen, *The Software Requirements Memory Jogger: A Pocket Guide to Help Software and Business Teams Develop and Manage Requirements*, Goal QPC Inc., 2005.

Gottesdiener, Ellen, and Mary Gorman, *Discover to Deliver: Agile Product Planning and Analysis*, 2012.

Heusser, Matthew, *How to Reduce the Cost of Software Testing*, Taylor & Francis, 2011.

Morgan, Jeff "Cheezy," *Cucumber and Cheese: A Testers Workshop*, LeanPub, 2013.

Patton, Jeff, *User Story Mapping: Building Better Products Using Agile Software Design*, O'Reilly Media, 2014.

Ries, Eric, *The Lean Startup: How Today's Entrepreneurs Use Continuous Innovation to Create Radically Successful Businesses*, Crown Business, 2011.

Ulwick, Antony, *What Customers Want: Using Outcome-Driven Innovation to Create Breakthrough Products and Services*, McGraw-Hill, 2005.

Vance, Stephen, *Quality Code: Software Testing Principles, Practices and Patterns*, Addison-Wesley, 2013.

Wynne, Matt, and Aslak Hellesøy, *The Cucumber Book: Behaviour-Driven Development for Testers and Developers*, Pragmatic Programmers, 2012.

ARTICLES, BLOG POSTS, SLIDE DECKS, AND WEBSITES

Adzic, Gojko, "How Google Does Test Engineering," http://gojko.net/2010/10/15/how-google-does-test-engineering/, 2010.

————, "The February Revolution," http://gojko.net/2013/02/13/the-february-revolution/, 2013.

————, "Impact Mapping," www.impactmapping.org, 2012.

Adzic, Gojko, Declan Whelan, et al., "Specification by Example" diagram, https://docs.google.com/drawings/d/1cbfKq-KazcbMVCnRfih6zMSDBdt f90KviV7l2oxGyWM/edit?hl=en, Agile Alliance aa-ftt workshop, 2010.

Andrea, Jennitta, "Acceptance Test-Driven Development: Not as Optional as You Think," www.stickyminds.com/article/acceptance-test-driven-development-not-optional-you-think, StickyMinds, Iterations newsletter, 2010.

Gat, Israel, and Jim Highsmith, *Cutter IT Journal* issue on "Technical Debt," www.cutter.com/offers/technicaldebt.html, Cutter Consortium, 2009.

Hassa, Christian, "Story Maps in Practice," www.slideshare.net/chassa/2013-0509story-mapsagilemeetupbp, 2013.

Hendrickson, Elisabeth, "Driving Development with Tests: ATDD and TDD," http://testobsessed.com/wp-content/uploads/2011/04/atddexample.pdf, 2008.

Hussman, David, "Cutting an Agile Groove: A Free Educational Video Series for Newbies and Practitioners," http://pragprog.com/screencasts/v-dhcag/cutting-an-agile-groove, Pragmatic Bookshelf, 2011.

————, "Story Maps, Slices, Customer Journeys, and Other Product Design Tools," http://agilepalooza.com/austin2013/slidedecks/Story-Maps-Slices-Customer-Journeys.pdf, 2013.

Keogh, Liz, "Behaviour-Driven Development," www.slideshare.net/ lunivore/behavior-driven-development-11754474, 2012.

Matts, Chris, and Gojko Adzic, "Feature Injection: Three Steps to Success," www.infoq.com/articles/feature-injection-success, InfoQ, 2011.

Morgan, Jeff "Cheezy," "UI Tests—Default Data," www.cheezyworld.com/ 2010/11/21/ui-tests-default-dat, 2010.

———, Page Object gem, https://github.com/cheezy/page-object, 2014.

North, Dan, "Introducing BDD," http://dannorth.net/introducing-bdd/, Better Software, 2006.

Patton, Jeff, "It's All in How You Slice It: Design Your Project in Working Layers to Avoid Half-Baked Incremental Releases," www .agileproductdesign.com/writing/how_you_slice_it.pdf, *Better Software* magazine, 2005.

———, "The New User Story Backlog Is a Story Map," www .agileproductdesign.com/blog/the_new_backlog.html, 2008.

———, "Pragmatic Personas," www.stickyminds.com/article/ pragmatic-personas, StickyMinds/Techwell, 2010.

Rainsberger, J. B., "The Next Decade of Agile Software Development," www.slideshare.net/jbrains/the-next-decade-of-agile-software- development, 2013.

Ries, Eric, "Case Study: SlideShare Goes Freemium," www .startuplessonslearned.com/2010/08/case-study-slideshare- goes-freemium.html, 2010.

PART V: INVESTIGATIVE TESTING

BOOKS

Hendrickson, Elisabeth, *Explore It! Reduce Risk and Increase Confidence with Exploratory Testing*, Pragmatic Programmer, 2013.

Kaner, Cem, Sowmya Padmanabhan, and Douglas Hoffman, *The Domain Testing Workbook*, Context Driven Press, 2013.

Krug, Steve, *Rocket Surgery Made Easy: The Do-It-Yourself Guide to Finding and Fixing Usability Problems*, New Riders, 2009.

———, *Don't Make Me Think, Revisited: A Common Sense Approach to Web Usability, 3rd Edition*, New Riders, 2014.

Talks, Mike, *The Software Minefield*, LeanPub, 2012.

Whittaker, James, *Exploratory Software Testing: Tips, Tricks, Tours and Techniques to Guide Test Design*, Addison-Wesley, 2009.

Articles, Blog Posts, Slide Decks, and Websites

Bach, Jon, "Session-Based Test Management," www.satisfice.com/articles/sbtm.pdf, *Software Testing and Quality Engineering* magazine, now *Better Software* magazine, 2000.

———, "Testing in Session: How to Measure Exploratory Testing," www.sasqag.org/pastmeetings/ExploratoryTesting_SessionBasedTest Management.pdf, Quardev Laboratories, 2004.

Bolton, Michael, "Blog: Of Testing Tours and Dashboards," www.developsense.com/blog/2009/04/of-testing-tours-and-dashboards/, 2009.

Eliot, Seth, "A to Z Testing in Production: TiP Methodologies, Techniques and Examples at STPCon 2012," www.setheliot.com/blog/a-to-z-testing-in-production-tip-methodologies-techniques-and-examples-at-stpcon-2012, 2012.

———, "Do It in Production," http://blogs.msdn.com/b/seliot/archive/2013/05/01/do-it-in-production-testbash-video-now-available.aspx, 2013.

Francino, Yvette, "Six Tours for Exploratory Testing the Business District of Your Application," http://searchsoftwarequality.techtarget.com/tip/Six-tours-for-exploratory-testing-the-business-district-of-your-application, Search Software Quality, 2009.

Gärtner, Markus, "Pomodoro Testing," www.shino.de/tag/pomodoro-testing, 2011.

Gilb, Tom, and Kai Gilb, "Planguage," www.gilb.com/definitionPlanguage&structure=Glossary&page_ref_id=476, 2013.

————, "Requirements: The Foundation for Successful Project Management," www.gilb.com/Requirements, 2013.

Harty, Julian, "Trinity Testing," http://julianharty-softwaretesting.blogspot.ca/2010/05/trinity-testing.html, 2010.

Hendrickson, Elisabeth, "The Two Sides of Software Testing: Checking and Exploring," www.agileconnection.com/article/two-sides-software-testing-checking-and-exploring?page=0%2C1, Agile Connection, 2009.

————, "Testing Heuristics Cheat Sheet," http://testobsessed.com/wp-content/uploads/2011/04/testheuristicscheatsheetv1.pdf, 2011.

Hussman, David, "Agile Journeys," www.slideshare.net/agileee/agile-journeys-by-david-hussman-2029404, 2009.

————, "Cutting an Agile Groove: A Free Educational Video Series for Newbies and Practitioners," http://pragprog.com/screencasts/v-dhcag/cutting-an-agile-groove, Pragmatic Bookshelf, 2011.

————, "Story Maps, Slices, Customer Journeys, and Other Product Design Tools," http://agilepalooza.com/austin2013/slidedecks/Story-Maps-Slices-Customer-Journeys.pdf, 2013.

Jamie (no last name provided), "Behind the Scenes: Highrise Marketing Site A/B Testing Part 1," http://signalvnoise.com/posts/2977-behind-the-scenes-highrise-marketing-site-ab-testing-part-1, 2011.

Kaner, Cem, "Testing Tours: Research for Best Practices?," http://kaner.com/?p=96, 2011.

Kaner, Fiedler & Associates, "Test Design: A Survey of Black Box Testing Techniques," www.testingeducation.org/BBST/testdesign, 2014.

Kelly, Michael D., "Touring Heuristic," http://michaeldkelly.com/blog/2005/9/20/touring-heuristic.html, 2005.

Knight, Adam P., "The Thread of an Idea: Adopting a Thread-Based Approach to Exploratory Testing," www.a-sisyphean-task.com/2011/11/thread-based-approach-to-exploratory.html, 2011.

————, "Fractal Exploratory Testing," www.a-sisyphean-task.com/2013/01/fractal-exploratory-testing.html, 2013.

Kohavi, Ron, Thomas Crook, and Roger Longbotham, "Online Experimentation at Microsoft," www.exp-platform.com/Documents/ExP_DMCaseStudies.pdf, 2009.

Lambert, Rob, "Managing Exploratory Testing," http://thesocialtester .co.uk/managing-exploratory-testing/, 2013.

Lorang, Noah, "Behind the Scenes: A/B Testing Part 2: How We Test," http://signalvnoise.com/posts/2983-behind-the-scenes-ab-testing-part-2-how-we-test, 2011.

Lyndsay, James, "Adventures in Session-Based Testing," www .workroom-productions.com/papers/AiSBTv1.2.pdf, 2003.

———, "Why Exploration Has a Place in Any Strategy," www .workroom-productions.com/papers/Exploration%20and%20Strategy .pdf, 2006.

———, "Testing in an Agile Environment," www.workroom-productions .com/papers/Testing%20in%20an%20agile%20environment.pdf, 2007.

———, "Tools for Exploratory Testing," http://workroomprds.blogspot .ca/2008/06/tools-for-exploratory-testing.html, 2008.

Margolis, Michael, "Get Better Data from User Studies: 16 Interviewing Tips," www.designstaff.org/articles/get-better-data-from-user-studies-interviewing-tips-2012-03-07.html, 2012.

McKinney, Andrew, usability testing and user research blog posts and articles, http://andrewmckinney.com.

———, "Remote Artist Collaboration," http://andrewmckinney.com/projects/artist-collaboration-disney/, 2013.

McMillan, Darren, accessibility testing blog posts, www.bettertesting.co.uk/content/?s=accessibility, 2012.

Miller, Evan, "How Not to Run an A/B Test," www.evanmiller.org/how-not-to-run-an-ab-test.html, 2010.

Morville, Peter, "User Experience Design," http://semanticstudios.com/publications/semantics/000029.php, 2004.

Nguyen, Buu, "Exploratory Testing with qTrace 2.0," www.qasymphony
.com/exploratory-testing-with-qtrace-2-0.html, 2012.

Nordstrom, "Nordstrom Innovation Lab: Sunglass iPad App Case Study,"
www.youtube.com/watch?v=szr0ezLyQHY, 2011.

Patton, Jeff, "Pragmatic Personas," www.stickyminds.com/article/
pragmatic-personas, StickyMinds/Techwell, 2010.

Ries, Eric, "Getting Started with Split Testing," www.startuplessonslearned
.com/2008/12/getting-started-with-split-testing.html, 2008.

———, "The One-Line Split Test, or How to A/B All the Time," www
.startuplessonslearned.com/2008/09/one-line-split-test-or-how-to-ab-all
.html, 2008.

Shaulis, Carl, "A/B Testing Experience Report," http://kungfutesting
.blogspot.com/2014/03/ab-testing-experience-report.html, 2014.

Software Testing Software, "All Types of Software Testing," www
.softwaretestingsoftware.com/all-types-of-software-testing/, Software Testing Software, 2012.

Traynor, Des, "An Interview with Andy Budd," http://insideintercom.io/
an-interview-with-andy-budd/, Intercom, 2011.

Whittaker, James, "ACC Explained," http://code.google.com/p/
test-analytics/wiki/AccExplained, 2011.

———, "Exploratory Testing Tours," http://msdn.microsoft.com/en-us/
library/jj620911.aspx#bkmk_tours, Microsoft, 2012.

Wikipedia, "Contextual Inquiry," http://en.wikipedia.org/wiki/
Contextual_inquiry, 2014.

———, "Software Testing," http://en.wikipedia.org/wiki/Software_testing,
2014.

PART VI: TEST AUTOMATION

BOOKS

Adzic, Gojko, *Specification by Example: How Successful Teams Deliver the Right Software*, Manning, 2011.

Chelimksy, David, et al., *The RSpec Book: Behaviour-Driven Development with RSpec, Cucumber, and Friends*, Pragmatic Bookshelf, 2010.

Gärtner, Markus, *ATDD by Example: A Practical Guide to Acceptance Test-Driven Development*, Addison-Wesley, 2012.

Marick, Brian, *Everyday Scripting with Ruby: For Teams, Testers and You*, Pragmatic Bookshelf, 2007.

Morgan, Jeff "Cheezy," *Cucumber and Cheese: A Testers Workshop*, LeanPub, 2013.

Vance, Stephen, *Quality Code: Software Testing Principles, Practices and Patterns*, Addison-Wesley, 2013.

Wynne, Matt, and Aslak Hellesøy, *The Cucumber Book: Behaviour-Driven Development for Testers and Developers*, Pragmatic Programmers, 2012.

ARTICLES, BLOG POSTS, COURSES, VIDEOS, CODE EXAMPLES

Adzic, Gojko, "How to Implement UI Testing without Shooting Yourself in the Foot," http://gojko.net/2010/04/13/how-to-implement-ui-testing-without-shooting-yourself-in-the-foot-2/, 2010.

Bell, Rob, "A Beginner's Guide to Big O Notation," http://rob-bell.net/2009/06/a-beginners-guide-to-big-o-notation/, 2009.

Cunningham, Ward, "Debt Metaphor," www.youtube.com/watch?v=pqeJFYwnkjE, 2009.

Emery, Dale, "Writing Maintanable Automated Acceptance Tests," dhemery.com/pdf/writing_maintainable_automated_acceptance_tests.pdf, 2009.

Gärtner, Markus, "Technical Debt Applied to Testing," www.shino.de/2009/01/08/technical-debt-applied-to-testing/, 2009.

Goucher, Adam, "Scripting for Test Engineers," http://adam.goucher .ca/?page_id=305, 2007.

———, "Page Objects in Python," http://pragprog.com/magazines/ 2010-08/page-objects-in-python, Pragmatic Bookshelf, 2010.

Kemerling, Ashton, "Generative Testing," www.pivotaltracker.com/ community/tracker-blog/generative-testing, Pivotal, 2014.

Keogh, Liz, "BDD before the Tools," http://lizkeogh.com/2013/10/24/ bdd-before-the-tools/, 2013.

Kubasek, Stanley, Boy Scout rule pattern, http://pragmaticcraftsman.com/ 2011/03/the-boy-scout-rule/, 2011.

Marcano, Antony, "A Bit of UCD for BDD & ATDD: Goals → Tasks → Actions," http://antonymarcano.com/blog/2011/03/goals-tasks-action/, 2011.

Mendenhall, Connor, "Check Your Work," http://blog.8thlight.com/ connor-mendenhall/2013/10/31/check-your-work.html, 8th Light, 2013.

Morgan, Jeff "Cheezy," "UI Tests—Default Data," www.cheezyworld.com/ 2010/11/21/ui-tests-default-dat, 2010.

Ottinger, Tim, and Jeff Langr, "Arrange-Act-Assert," http://agileinaflash .blogspot.com/2009/03/arrange-act-assert.html, 2009.

———, "Red-Green-Refactor," http://agileinaflash.blogspot.co.uk/2009/02/ red-green-refactor.html, 2009.

Ramdeo, Anand, "A Software Tester's Journey from Manual to Political," www.testinggeek.com/a-software-tester-s-journey-from-manual-to-political, 2012.

———, "One Step at a Time," www.youtube.com/watch?v=dFPgzH_XP1I, 2012.

———, "Test Automation—How to Handle Common Components with Page Object Model?," www.testinggeek.com/test-automation-how-to-handle-common-components-with-page-object-model, 2013.

Scott, Alister, "Specification by Example: A Love Story," http://watirmelon .files.wordpress.com/2011/05/specificationbyexamplealovestory1.pdf, 2011.

———, "Yet Another Software Testing Pyramid," http://watirmelon.com/2011/06/10/yet-another-software-testing-pyramid/, 2011.

Sweets, Tony, "Page Object Example," https://github.com/tsweets/page-objects, 2013.

Wikipedia, "Dispose Pattern," http://en.wikipedia.org/wiki/Dispose_pattern, 2013.

———, "SOLID: Object-Oriented Design," http://en.wikipedia.org/wiki/SOLID, 2014.

PART VII: WHAT IS YOUR CONTEXT?

BOOKS

Gruverm, Gary, Mike Young, and Pat Fulghum, *A Practical Approach to Large-Scale Agile Development: How HP Transformed LaserJet FutureSmart Firmware*, Addison-Wesley, 2012.

Hagar, Jon, *Software Test Attacks to Break Mobile and Embedded Devices*, Chapman and Hall/CRC, 2013.

Harty, Julian, *Testing and Test Automation for Mobile Phone Applications*, Chapman and Hall/CRC, 2014.

Hubbard, Douglas W., *How to Measure Anything: Finding the Value of Intangibles in Business*, Wiley, 2010.

Humble, Jez, and David Farley, *Continuous Delivery: Reliable Software Releases through Build, Test and Deployment Automation*, Addison-Wesley, 2010.

Hüttermann, Michael, *DevOps for Developers: Integrate Development and Operations, the Agile Way*, Apress, 2012.

Kohl, Jonathan, *Tap into Mobile Testing*, LeanPub, 2013.

Larman, Craig, and Bas Vodde, *Scaling Lean & Agile: Thinking and Organizational Tools for Large-Scale Scrum*, Addison-Wesley, 2009.

————, *Practices for Scaling Lean & Agile Development: Large, Multisite, and Offshore Product Development with Large-Scale Scrum*, Addison-Wesley, 2010.

Larsen, Diana, and Ainsley Nies, *Liftoff: Launching Agile Teams & Projects*, Onyx Neon Press, 2011.

Articles, Blog Posts, Slide Decks, Websites

Brodwell, Johannes, "Remote Pair Programming," www.slideshare.net/jhannes/2013-0807-agile-2013-remote-pair-programming, August 2013.

Chaney, Clareice, Clyneice Chaney, and XBOSoft, "Best Way to Contract an Outsourced Agile Test Team Webinar," www.slideshare.net/xbosoft/best-way-to-contract-an-outsourced-agile-w-bnr-0718v3, 2013.

CMMI Institute, "Solutions," http://cmmiinstitute.com/cmmi-solutions/, Carnegie Mellon, 2014.

CNET, mobile usage report example, http://news.cnet.com/8301-1023_3-57605422-93/ie-usage-resurges-in-september-new-stats-report/, October 2013.

Cockburn, Alistair, "The Cornerstone of Agile: Why It Works, Why It Hurts," www.slideshare.net/itweekend/the-cornerstone-of-agile-why-it-works-why-it-hurts, 2012.

Crispin, Lisa, "Success Factors for Distributed Teams," http://searchsoftwarequality.techtarget.com/tip/Success-factors-for-distributed-teams, Search Software Quality, 2010.

de Kok, Dirk, "How to Apply Lean Startup to Mobile," http://blog.mobtest.com/2012/11/how-to-apply-lean-startup-to-mobile/, 2012.

Evans, David, "Visualising Quality," http://prezi.com/yych7sndetph/visualising-quality-atd, 2013.

Gregory, Janet, "Distributed Teams—My Experience," http://janetgregory.ca/distributed-teams-my-experience/, 2014.

Hagar, Jon, "Breaking Mobile and Embedded Software," http://breakingembeddedsoftware.com/.

Hagar, Jon, and Mark Dornseif, "Agile Evolution of Launch Vehicle Space Software Systems," AIAA Space 2004 Conference, September 2004, http://arc.aiaa.org/doi/abs/10.2514/6.2004-5802.

Hagar, Jon, and Randall Smith, "Producing Embedded Flight Software with Agile Commercial and Government Practices," IEEE Software Technology Conference 2003, May 2003, https://sw.thecsiac.com/techs/abstract/347299.

Humble, Jez, "There's No Such Thing as a 'DevOps Team,'" http://continuousdelivery.com/2012/10/theres-no-such-thing-as-a-devops-team/, 2012.

Hummel, Geoff, "Does Agile Software Development Mix Well with FDA Regulations?," www.thetestking.com/2013/09/does-agile-software-development-mix-well-with-fda-regulations/, 2013.

Kelly, Allan, "Agile Contracts," www.infoq.com/articles/agile-contracts, InfoQ, 2011.

Knight, Adam P., "Testing Big Data in an Agile Environment," www.ministryoftesting.com/2013/06/testing-big-data-in-an-agile-environment/, Ministry of Testing, 2013.

Kohl, Jonathan, "Test Mobile Applications with I SLICED UP FUN!," www.kohl.ca/articles/ISLICEDUPFUN.pdf, 2010.

Lehrer, Jonah, "Technology Alone Is Not Enough," www.newyorker.com/online/blogs/newsdesk/2011/10/steve-jobs-pixar.html, *The New Yorker*, October 7, 2011.

McDonald, Kent J., "Create a Vendor Contract While Keeping Agile," www.techwell.com/2013/05/create-vendor-contract-while-keeping-agile, Techwell, 2013.

McDonald, Mark, "Is Your Company an Enterprise? The Answer Matters," http://blogs.gartner.com/mark_mcdonald/2009/06/15/is-your-company-an-enterprise-the-answer-matters/, Gartner Blog Network, 2009.

McMahon, Chris, "Telecommuting Policy," http://chrismcmahonsblog.blogspot.com/2009/12/telecommuting-policy.html, 2009.

Mobiletech, mobile usage report example, http://mobiletechglobal.com/mobile-statistics-january-2013/, 2013.

Morville, Peter, "User Experience Design," http://semanticstudios.com/publications/semantics/000029.php, 2004.

Ramdeo, Anand, "Test Automation—How to Handle Common Components with the Page Object Model?," www.testinggeek.com/test-automation-how-to-handle-common-components-with-page-object-model, 2013.

Sanchez, Carlos, presentations on DevOps and infrastructure testing, www.slideshare.net/carlossg/presentations, 2013.

Shah, Shahid, "Writing Safety-Critical Software Using an Agile Risk-Based Approach," www.healthcareguy.com/2013/06/14/writing-safety-critical-software-using-an-agile-risk-based-approach-should-be-the-norm-in-modern-medical-device-development/, 2013.

Sherry, Rosie, Ministry of Testing's mobile testing mind map, www.flickr.com/photos/softwaretestingclub/7159412943/sizes/o/in/photostream/, Ministry of Testing, 2013.

Siener, Graham, "Inception: Knowing What to Build and Where You Should Start," http://pivotallabs.com/agile-inception_knowing-what-to-build-and-where-to-start/, 2013.

Sweets, Tony, "Virtual Hudson Continuous Build Environments: Out with the Old," www.stickyminds.com/article/virtual-hudson-continuous-build-environments-out-old, StickyMinds, 2011.

TforTesting (no other name given), "Test Cases for Games Apps/Checklists for Games Apps," http://tfortesting.wordpress.com/2012/10/04/test-cases-for-games-apps-checklist-for-games-apps/, 2012.

Trimble, Jay, and Chris Webster, "Agile Development Methods for Space Operations," http://ntrs.nasa.gov/archive/nasa/casi.ntrs.nasa.gov/20120013429_2012013093.pdf, 2012.

Waters, John K., "An Agile Approach to Rocket Science," http://adtmag.com/articles/2004/10/06/an-agile-approach-to-rocket-science.aspx, *Application Development Trends Magazine*, October 16, 2004.

Webster, C., "Delivering Software into NASA's Mission Control Center Using Agile Development Techniques," http://ieeexplore.ieee.org/xpl/login.jsp?tp=&arnumber=6187329&icp=false&url=http%3A%2F%2Fieeexplore.ieee.org%2Fapplication%2Fmdl%2Fmdlconfirmation.jsp%3Farnumber%3D6187329%26icp%3Dfalse, *IEEE Software*, 2012.

Wikipedia, "Disk Imaging," http://en.wikipedia.org/wiki/Disk_imaging, 2014.

———, "Embedded System: History," http://en.wikipedia.org/wiki/Embedded_system#History, 2014.

———, "Enterprise Software," http://en.wikipedia.org/wiki/Enterprise_software, 2014.

———, "Operational Acceptance Testing," http://en.wikipedia.org/wiki/Operational_acceptance_testing, 2014.

———, "Star Schema," http://en.wikipedia.org/wiki/Star_schema, 2014.

———, "Starship Enterprise," http://en.wikipedia.org/wiki/Starship_Enterprise, Wikipedia, 2014.

Wikispeed website, http://wikispeed.org/, 2014.

PART VIII: AGILE TESTING IN PRACTICE

Gregory, Janet, "Jigsaw Puzzles and Small Chunks," http://janetgregory.ca/jigsaw-puzzles-small-chunks/, 2009.

Kaner, Cem, "What Is Context-Driven Testing?," http://kaner.com/?p=49, 2012.

TOOLS (IN ORDER BY TOOL NAME)

Note: These links are valid at the time of writing, but there is no guarantee that the tool named or the link is still in use.

Clonezilla: Open Source, Clonezilla, http://sourceforge.net/projects/clonezilla/, SourceForge.

Fit: Open Source, originally created by Ward Cunningham, Fit: Framework for Integrated Test, http://fit.c2.com/, c2.com.

FitNesse: Open Source, http://fitnesse.org/.

Get Kanban: GetKanban.com, "Get Kanban" board game, http://getkanban.com/BoardGame.html, GetKanban.com.

Git: Open Source, Git, http://git-scm.com.

Jdefault: Sweets, Tony, "jdefault: Java Default Data Library," https://github .com/tsweets/jdefault, GitHub, 2013.

Jenkins CI: Open Source, Jenkins CI, http://jenkins-ci.org/.

Jenkins Job DSL/Plugin: Open Source, Jenkins Job DSL/Plugin, https:// github.com/jenkinsci/job-dsl-plugin, GitHub.

Page Object gem: Morgan, Jeff "Cheezy," Page Object gem, https://github .com/cheezy/page-object, 2014.

Puppet: Open Source, Puppet, http://puppetlabs.com/, Puppet Labs.

Puppet-Lint: Open Source, Puppet-Lint gem, http://puppet-lint.com, Rodjek.

Rake: Weirich, Jim, rake, https://github.com/jimweirich/rake, GitHub.

Rapid Reporter: Gershon, Shmuel, "Rapid Reporter, Exploratory Notetaking," http://testing.gershon.info/reporter/.

SonarQube: Open Source, SonarQube, http://sonarqube.org, Sonar Source.

Vagrant: Open Source, Vagrant, www.vagrantup.com, HashiCorp.

INDEX